P9-CEE-150

THE AGE OF
FLYING SAUCERS

THE AGE OF
FLYING SAUCERS

NOTES ON THE HISTORY OF
UNIDENTIFIED FLYING OBJECTS

PARIS FLAMMONDE

ISBN-13: 978-1542408301
ISBN-10: 154240830X

PRINTING HISTORY
Hawthorn edition published 1971
Saucerian Press edition published 1981
New Saucerian Press edition published 2017

©2017 New Saucerian, LLC

To
MOTHER and FATHER

EXPLANATORY FOREWORD

The original purpose of this book was to finally provide both the public and future scholars of the Age of Flying Saucers with a comprehensive, perhaps even definitive, history of the quarter of a century during which rose and fell the most curious sociopsychological phenomenon since the recession of witchcraft. I had been a student, and later a scholar, of this extraordinary period's development since my early adolescence, i.e., since the inception of the modern era during World War II, and had subsequently interviewed virtually all of its major figures from the hardest-headed scientific skeptics to the most fantasizing contactees and researched the entire range of reports even to the most incidental accounts. My library on the main and related subjects had numbered in the hundreds of volumes, my periodicals in the thousands of issues, and the items in my clipping files in the tens of thousands. I had the background, the familiarity, and an incredible wealth of material from which to draw. I only needed the organization and ability to coordinate an effective, lucid presentation.

It was to become, however, immeasurably more complicated than that. The first manuscript consisted of more than a quarter of a million words. After a considerable time this version was reduced by nearly 50 percent, but for very practical reasons the publishing opinion was that such a length would demand a retail price beyond the reach of many of the book's most likely readers, and so more thousands of words had to be sacrificed, and more. . . .

I believe that what remains is still the most comprehensive description of the Age of Flying Saucers yet to appear, and I believe that unlike many excellent works in this area it provides a sufficiently broad evolutionary picture of the era to permit a reader of it alone to have a reasonably sophisticated idea of what the epoch was all about. Yet it is with great regret that I have had to severely condense countless reports and stories, draw but brief vignettes of many essential personalities, and, in general, forfeit details and analyses in order to cover—sometimes only lightly—the entire period. Even more do I regret that many important subordinate figures had to be mentioned only in passing or, in a few cases, not at all, and I am particularly unhappy with having had to delete nearly all of the material relating to the secondary (in hierarchical, not necessarily historical, terms) cultures that derived from, or were partial progenitors of, the Age of Flying Saucers (the total Richard Shaver complex being a prime example of such a loss). I would equally like to have had the space to examine countless social, psychological, political, and economic repercussions of the Age of Flying Saucers. So many things present in the original manuscript have had to be forsaken so that as comprehensive a book as possible might be published at a price within the budget of the general reader—whether novice, enthusiast, or scholar.

I would like, however, to call special attention to the subtitle of this work, *Notes on a Projected History of Unidentified Flying Objects,* for that is precisely what it is. Although, within the framework of the foregoing remarks, I feel confident that to date this is the only work in this field which can be regarded as an actual history of the modern era—the one book presenting a broadly inclusive sketch of the entire sociopsychological phenomenon—I wish to assure the reader that the much vaster endeavor, two or three times the length of this, has not been abandoned, even though it may be four or five years before such a work is finally published.

Let me conclude by saying to those who will feel that I have given more attention to *this* report or *that* personality that my purpose has always been to attempt to distribute the emphasis in terms of two overriding considerations—the tremendous limitations of space and the importance of any specific subject or matter within the context of the entire modern history of flying saucers and unidentified flying objects. It was also because of these restrictions that I ultimately decided to devote the entire available wordage to the modern era and discard nearly fifty thousand words of "prehistory," an omission of which I am especially conscious.

In the final analysis I hope that the essence of my original intent has successfully been retained and that the reader will find *The Age of Fly-*

ing Saucers a new type of book on the subject that transfixed a large portion of the population for more than two decades, a book different in that upon the completion of it one feels he, or she, has seen unreeled —from beginning to end—a clear and understandable panorama of the most remarkable event(s) of the twentieth, if not the last, century.

P. F.

New York City

ACKNOWLEDGMENTS

The author wishes to express his appreciation to investigators of, and writers on, the subject of Unidentified Flying Objects and Flying Saucers for their assistance, especially James W. Moseley, who made available his complete back-issue file of *Saucer News*; Gray Barker, a frequent source of information, contacts, and photographs; Timothy Green Beckley, without whose help the Appendix on periodicals would have appeared in a far less complete form; Carlos Clarens, whose contributions to the Appendix on motion pictures was invaluable; and Col. L. J. Churchville, public-information officer for the United States Air Force, to whom similar credit must be accorded with regard to Appendixes I and II.

Recognition must also be given to Ray Palmer, Daniel W. Fry, Truman Bethurum, Coral and Jim Lorenzen, of the Aerial Phenomena Research Organization, as well as the National Investigations Committee on Aerial Phenomena, the Amalgamated Flying Saucer Clubs of America, and others for aid in gathering information and photographs.

I would also like to mention that conversations with Stewart Robb, Ivan Sanderson, John Keel, Dominic Lucchesi, Jack Robinson, Jackie Gleason, John Godwin, and countless others over the years on the subject of this book have endlessly opened new avenues of speculation. An acknowledgment is also made of the importance of conversations with the late Frank Edwards on these matters, and a nod of appreciation toward John G. Fuller for his excellent books and permission to quote a few passages from them.

The author wishes to mention two English publications that responded to inquiries promptly and courteously—*Flying Saucer Review* and *BUFORA Journal* (British U.F.O. Research Organization).

Particular appreciation is expressed to Sam Vandivert for his permission to use various rare photographs found in this book and to Augie Roberts for his assistance on pictures as well.

A long-delayed mention of gratitude is added here for the perpetual skepticism and frequent helpful suggestions of the master of SF (as opposed to FS), Lester del Rey, and his UFO (unpredictable female opposite) and deeply missed wife, Evelyn.

Penultimately, the author's indebtedness to John Nebel is registered, for without the many years of his friendship, the countless accesses to the heart of *The Age of Flying Saucers*, gained through him, and his many constructive suggestions, an altogether different book would have emerged. Also, a full measure of recognition is noted for the numerous occasions when my questions were answered and problems solved by Anne Pacurar.

Lastly, my appreciation is expressed to the individual without whose perpetual help and endless patience *The Age of Flying Saucers* would have remained merely midnight reminiscences, my beautiful wife, Marcia.

P. F.

CONTENTS

xiii

APPENDIXES

Illustrations appear after pages 96 and 150.

More worlds unearthed beneath your world, more stars
Behind your stars, more gods above your god.

—LOKER RALEY,
Salute to the New-Born

"You missed the point of the whole damned thing."

—JOHN VINCENT COSTELLO,
The Abingdon Square

PART I
THE GOLDEN AGE

Chapter 1

THREADS OF LEGEND, LOOM OF TIME

The Age of Flying Saucers, like most periods of religious fervor, arose into a prevailing climate of credulity from a broad, general need. With the fall of the towering father-image of Roosevelt, the devastating inauguration of the nuclear era, the end of World War II, the nightmare trials at Nuremberg, the new and bloody conflict in Korea—the time for something from *another* world was ripe. When it seemed that it had come, countless numbers welcomed it. Before the age had fixed its form, however, it shattered, shards scattering off in all directions.

Although a series of chronological, if rather arbitrary, subdivisions of the period may be suggested, the essential fragmentation came not from its tendency to phase, but from the attempts of all acolytes to become disciples, and all disciples to become messiahs. And if no two believers agreed, most skeptics were even more uncertain of the nature of their own agnosticism. Only one point seems to have attracted common support, which was that the aerial activity known as Flying Saucers was a long-standing phenomenon, dating far back in history, even to prehistory. Saucerites assert that interplanetary craft have been visiting the earth since before Solon's lost continent, Atlantis, sank from sight beneath a raging sea; the infidels take the position that since the sightings are, for the most part, of natural occurrences, it is obvious that such observations might have been made thousands of years ago. Yet despite the consensus as to the antiquity of whatever the heavenly stimuli are, when one considers the entire Flying Saucer–Unidentified Flying Object sociopsychological phenomenon, it is interesting how weak both positions are in terms of their broader connotations.

UFOs exist! Beyond conjecture, beyond argument, beyond a shadow of a doubt, Unidentified Flying Objects are real. There is no question but that you will agree by the time you have finished this book. Further, you will finally understand what it is you have come to agree with.

The "question" of Flying Saucers, or UFOs, poses a mystery; their discussion poses a problem; neither has been successfully solved. Before one can tackle the enigma of space, one is confronted by the difficulties

3

of language, specifically of jargon. A word or term readily understood by the long-time investigator or disciple of ufology or saucerology is likely to be completely misinterpreted by the general reader. In some instances such ambiguity has created confusion in the reports of serious analysts. The outstanding, even classic, example of this lies in the failure of many writers to distinguish between Flying Saucers and Unidentified Flying Objects.

Near midnight on July 19, 1952, radar equipment at the Washington National Airport picked up eight objects. They were immediately recognized as not being aircraft, as they varied their speeds from about one hundred miles per hour to a phenomenal seven thousand miles per hour. Simultaneously, visual observations were being made by a number of air crews and tower personnel. Suddenly, the unknowns vanished.

That is a UFO, or Unidentified Flying Object, report.

On sunny, clear November 20 of the same year George Adamski and a small group of friends were driving in the magnificent desert near Parker, Arizona, when an immense silver cigar-shaped vessel appeared and hovered overhead. Moving away from the party, some distance along the road Adamski encountered a scout ship of the type commonly pictured in response to the words "Flying Saucer." Beside it stood a lovely long-haired blond chap whom the wandering Adamski regarded as "unusually beautiful." Since both men were of a superior order, a few clever gestures served as an adequate language, and Adamski established that the visitor was a Venusian. After this brief exchange Orthon (whom he proved to be) spun off.

That is a Flying Saucer report.

As is immediately evident, the two have some fundamental differences; therefore it is difficult to understand why, except out of ignorance, the reportorial interchange of the two expressions has been so widely tolerated. As one pursues the subject further, the suspicion grows that the mass wish for the phenomenon to prove "true" may have been too great —so great, in fact, that despite the nearly universal ridicule, almost no one really wanted to rule out any of the possible visitors from other, and probably better, worlds. Whatever the reason for the lexical negligence, the distinction is essential to a clear picture and comprehension of the dual subject.

"Flying Saucers," deriving (although the characterization was not new) from a description of "nine disks" sighted over Mount Rainier, Washington, by pilot Kenneth Arnold on June 24, 1947, originally referred to any aerial phenomena defying recognition. Soon it included the sightings of an additional order of observers who reported not merely celestial *somethings,* but actual—presumably interplanetary—spaceships.

Inevitably, there followed the curious breed who came to be known as contactees, from their claims of direct physical encounters with alien spacecraft and with their occupants—travelers from other planets. At this point Captain Edward J. Ruppelt, director of the U.S. Air Force unit assigned to investigate the growing phenomenon, coined the phrase "Unidentified Flying Objects," sometimes called UFOs, or "you-foes," to distinguish what appeared to be rational sighting reports from ones sounding like excerpts from fairy tales and nightmares. Soon it became the general practice among the informed to refer to sightings purporting to describe spaceships, apparently intelligently operated and probably of extraterrestrial origin, as "Flying Saucers" and to any celestial phenomena whose nature was unknown and unresolved as "Unidentified Flying Objects."

Ignoring this distinction, countless authors insist that "UFOs are real!" They are absolutely right. No one, including the often—and justifiably—assailed U.S. Air Force, has ever contested the point. The Air Force has, in fact, a regulation, #200-2, which specifically defines the official usage of "UFOs" as "any aerial phenomena . . . which are unknown." Certainly there are UFOs, but that is not the question (and we aren't going to get very satisfactory answers if we don't ask the right questions); the problem is: Are there such things as interplanetary or interstellar (as some scientists who support the general thesis contend) spacecraft, presumably intelligently controlled?

It is fashionable (and regarded as considerably less eccentric) today to speak of UFOs, but what everyone really wants to find out about is Flying Saucers. Do *they* exist? The answer: Nobody knows.

Myth, legend, religion, astrology, astronomy, art, literature, social patterns, and psychological attitudes all made significant contributions to the sky-landscape into which Flying Saucers would descend and through which saucer people would conduct their remarkable adventures. A realization of the importance of this setting is essential to the most superficial understanding of the period.

The reverse side of the coin of a subject's adaptation to an environment is the suitability of the environment for the subject, and of these two faces of existence, the latter is always minted first. That is, although a foreign element—physical or psychological—may be introduced, or introduce itself, into an alien atmosphere and effect certain secondary adaptations, the environment must be initially adequate to sustain the organism or idea. Earlier intimations of a subsequent alien element may venture as atavistic scouts, precursors of the more important successor, into the atmosphere in question before it is climatically acceptable, but even in those instances the same generality applies—the surroundings must be at least minimally beneficent, sufficiently so for the primary aspect to survive. In terms of the modern Age of Flying Saucers, many such precursors—physical, psychological, sociological, etc., in nature—are historically evident, but at no time did they all combine to create that specific milieu essential for the age's inception. At countless times in uncountable places, however, "submilieus" capable of supporting one or more of these antecedents have occurred.

What were some of the contributing elements that, seen in retrospect, are recognizable in their similarity to some aspect of the modern Age of Flying Saucers? What were the surroundings in which they found it possible to survive? What in these surroundings provided the necessary atmosphere? The fundamentals needed for a suitable climate might be one, some, many, or all of the following: physical, psychological, and/or spiritual fear; reproductive apprehension; practical, emotional, or anticipated needs; childish, romantic, or intellectual fantasy—all of them on either the personal or collective levels. The environment had to provide the kind of reality from which suitable symbols might be drawn, the creation of a symbolism acceptable to a reasonably large portion of the immediate population, and the sociopsychological conditions in which the budding symbology might flourish and become influential to the degree of achieving at least a tentative reality in the minds of its users.

In most instances the evolution had to lead to a ritual, not necessarily organized in the more sophisticated sense—it might consist mainly of the jargon, a token of identification, or merely a recognition of the existence of a subsocial collective—and, of considerable importance, especially to those movements that were to survive any length of time, an oral or written literature. Obviously, the esoteric individuals who consigned some of their tradition, real or otherwise, to manuscript had a much greater chance of seeing it survive the erosion of doubt, indifference, persecution, and the headsman's ax or inquisitor's fire than those who counted on generational descent of the tradition via the whispers of the anointed to the acolytes. Generally, it was helpful if there was a conscious opposition to the symbolists and their dogma. If sufficiently concerted, this opposition frequently developed in the adherents into a functional—as differentiated from, but not necessarily to the exclusion of, a psychical—fanaticism.

Finally (of course, not really finally at all, since countless other, and for the most part subtler, components contributed to the total machinery of past saucer-related phenomena), the symbols—elemental, created, clerical—had to be consonant with the dominant reality of the time and place. That is, whereas the major theme and its counterpoints did not need to appear probable, or even possible—truly, such prosaism was to be carefully eschewed—it was essential that they remain within the realm of reasonably effortless fantasizing.

A Neanderthaler might well convince a fellow troglodyte of the existence of a demon in the water at the river's bend, but he would have little success persuading his companion of the terrors beyond the great falls. His friend knew perfectly well that not only were there no terrors beyond the wall of water—there was no world, no anything. The Greek singer might enchant his audience with stories of gods cavorting on a local mountaintop, but they went deaf if he told tales of adventures beyond the Pillars of Hercules. Everyone knew that beyond those perilous straits all of man's knowledge ceased. *Malleus Maleficarum* (Hammer of Witches), an influential fifteenth-century manual of demonology, might explain the nature of witchcraft, reveal the diverse orders of demoniacs, and advise on the jurisprudence directing their disposition—through the Church everyone knew that such dark things existed—but it would have been hard pressed, for all of its canonical authority, to have convinced anyone that flameless light could be sustained in a globe of glass.

Therefore, whereas Lucian, in a purely literary fancy, might jest of sailing up to the abode of gods; whereas Oriental tales might romanticize about aerial abductors; whereas monks might wonder if great meteors were indications of God's hand firing clay elsewhere in the universe; whereas Swift, Cyrano, Swedenborg, Steiner, Verne, Wells, Burroughs, et al. played with concepts of other-planetarians, and Lowell, Pickering, and similarly disposed astronomers began to wonder about Martian life in almost serious terms—still, the most advanced scholar knew perfectly well that interplanetary travel was ridiculous, even if man were to become convinced, by whatever means, that life did exist somewhere beyond the earth. Newton had opened vast horizons, but there would never exist engineering to translate such grand theories into tickets to the moon. Even the birdmanship of the Wright brothers was mere bravado, a mechanical amusement. Edison saw it clearly: "At best airships would only be toys."

All of which is to say that the Age of Flying Saucers, in the sociopsychological sense, could not have happened in the periods preceding the twentieth century. Not even the great sighting complex of 1897 found a climate sufficiently accommodating to inaugurate it, although it did initiate the tremor on the edge of the ocean of imagination which was eventually to become the tidal wave of modern saucerology.

Throughout history many of the elements necessary for a Flying Saucer–type period were present. Fear was one, but religion had recognized its value early and had developed the interminable cryptographic and ritualistic nostrums with which the populations were pacified—temporarily, of course, since the immortal symbol of all successful religions is the Golden Goose. Receptivity was a second element. It was virtually constant, as demonstrated by the countless cults and, most of all, by several centuries of witchcraft. Litany and literature, need and desire, hate and cowardice, imagination and intelligence, conviction and charlatanry—all of the proper ingredients for the Age of Flying Saucers had come and stayed or gone; that is, save four. The twentieth century moved through two wars, depressions, cultural explosions and dislocations, exposure to and absorption by the worlds of communications and commerce, the annihilation of the elite, and the cataclysm of egalitarianism, finally shaking down all of the "indestructible" traditions upon which fifty centuries of mankind had been raised and preserved.

The Age of Flying Saucers became possible when, at last, the world truly changed, and four new conditions began to dominate it. Although one might endeavor to relegate each to a suitable category, it is not the conditions with which we are concerned—it is the human attitude toward them. In fact, the changes in the world, the changes that created the atmosphere of invitation to the modern Age of Flying Saucers, were not in themselves the climate of which we speak, any more than the mountains and rivers are the essential ecological considerations. It was the response of life to these quite probably inevitable developments which created the necessary conditions into (or from) which Flying Saucers might come. All four of these contributing factors can easily be said to be the grand progeny of the Industrial Revolution, but two are from the direct line.

First, the most obvious and simplest to understand in this context was modern mechanics, culminating in space-age engineering. Its importance to saucerology on the most fundamental level was that it brought transportation among the planets within the realm of reasonably effortless fantasizing. It made the realization of such imaginings possible, giving them at least tentative reality to any caught up in their symbolistic possibilities.

The second condition was world-wrapping egalitarianism. Of course, the levelling process had been under way for a long time, but two things had forestalled it at most turns, and so it had been confined to particular pockets. One thwarting element was the Church—any church, all churches. Nothing is so unrelentingly antidemocratic as a successful church, for as its class consciousness diminishes, so is its substructure eroded away and its followers disenchanted. Devotees of religion seek submission and inferiority even more than they aspire to the delight of social and spiritual elevation. The other barrier against the oozing incursion of an internationally pervasive and persuasive egalitarianism was the crudity and clumsiness of communication. Whether one is enchanted by distance and knows that all who live beyond the Arabian Sea are princes, or is a practicing xenophobe and sees clearly, in his ego's eye, the southlanders grubbing on all fours, distance squared by ignorance can never equal the democratic impulse.

Although printing merely helped the "superior" to pass their "superiority," i.e., usually education, along to those whom they selected (the mails were equally implements of the ensconced), the introduction to the world of radio was an entirely different matter. The ultimate abrasion to the aristocracy—hereditary, commercial, political—was communication, and no mind could have imagined how the regionalism of the United States would be webbed together by the networks, where it had once been tessellated into a thousand city-states. Initially, the effect was very noticeable only in this country and, perhaps, England and part of the Continent, but below the long waving back and forth the shortwave wireless was weaving an international community.

Then the glass face of television blazed forth and proved that a picture was worth a million things half-heard. Television was to become the ultimate communicating device—and, by extension, the final and most unchallengeable champion of general egalitarianism. Quality fell before quantity, art before amusement, skill before facility, beauty before banality, the creative before the common, the singular before the simple; that is to say, the world began to see the artist and the politician, the famous and the fortunate, as very much like itself, neither really better, nor brighter, nor at all superior. And the populations of most countries of the earth were seeing clearly. The mundane had assumed command not only at the top—it had frequently done that—but also from top to bottom. Deep in the heart and mind of the average man, however, the doubt began, the dissatisfaction. Man was not meant to be deprived of heroes, but the titans were nearly gone. There weren't even any really evil geniuses left. The guy next door was running the world. And if his more dramatic predecessors had done poorly, he was running it right out of time into anticipated oblivion.

Four conditions, I have said, came to dominate the world: first, the acceptability of the concept of interplanetary engineering; second, the rise and oppression of the ordinary, the hopelessly ineffectual commonplace; then, nearly in concert, the Bomb! The Bomb was not merely an aspect of the modern mechanical age, because it was not merely *more*. It was *more* to the point of being *different*. TNT was more than dynamite, but it could not do anything five or ten times as much dynamite couldn't do. The Bomb introduced an entirely new level of consideration—annihilation. The Bomb projected into the pattern of nature the possibility of the end of Man, even the end of the earth. It prophesied the possibility of an eight-planet solar system and left nowhere to escape to, nowhere to hide.

For the first time in the conscious history of the human race "doom" was not an undesirable destiny, an imminent death, or even the most ominous expectation of the soul. It was being faced with the direct—and, for a while, apparently immediate—threat of literally roasting to death as an insignificant ingredient in an enormous feast prepared for the messianic scion of the oldest of all gods, the Sun, dying as one of a million tidbits on the grill of his fission. This was the third element: awareness of the ultimate futility—the end of the human race. In the face of the universal mechanization of society and the decline and disappearance of heroes and idols of any kind, even before the confrontation with the possible death of earth, one reservoir of hope remained, one final retreat from ordinariness and oblivion.

God. And then God died. Needless to say, that is meant in its broadest sense. Susceptibility to sacramental panaceas failed before the decline of the Divinity. Religion no longer worked, no longer served a purpose: that is, it no longer served a god. Even the selfless gods have always related to their believers on a symbiotic basis. When religion no longer served Man, it no longer served God; when it no longer served God, God no longer served it. To paraphrase an old American Indian wisdom, a religion without a god is only half a religion, a god without a religion is no god at all. Religion failed, and God (always of limited spiritual influence, but frequently of considerable emotional comfort) died. Now there was not only nowhere to hide but also nothing to turn to. This was the final abandonment.

The world was prepared, shaped by four conditions: the mechanical accessibility of other worlds; the destruction of the heroic image, the perpetual father-in-oneself, the dream of what might have been, given other conditions or another time; the foreboding of oblivion and the erasure of the flesh and soul forever; the ultimate, irresistible vulnerability, the last shield gone—Man, alone. The human race was ready—preconditioned, conditioned, and attuned; all of the elements necessary for the optimum environment were at hand.

Science had to exceed itself and bring forth a race of super-beings, establish there were places left to pioneer or in which to be pampered (there were still princes in Arabia, after all). God had many faces, many messengers sent from His many mansions. All was not lost. The world was ready—no, the world was anxious—for an armada of messiahs. The world was waiting for the advent of the Age of Flying Saucers.

Chapter 2
THE CHRISTENING

Modern ufology began with Kenneth Arnold on the afternoon of June 24, 1947. It is not that the Arnold sighting stands out as the most interesting in the history of UFOs—in that respect it is surpassed by many—but it was the first observation to catch the imagination of the press and public; it started the new age of aerial fascination and gave it its name.

The Coming of the Saucers,[1] subtitled *A Documentary Report of Sky Objects That Have Mystified the World,* is a full exposition of the entire incident, as well as of a rather complicated and seemingly conspiratorial series of events that followed.

Captain Edward J. Ruppelt states in his book[2] that "Arnold's own account of his sighting as published in *The Coming of the Saucers* does not jibe with what the official files say he told the Air Force in 1947." However, this is the version Arnold offers.

Shortly after noon, on June 24, Arnold was discussing a C-46 Marine transport, believed down in nearby mountains, with Herb Critzer, chief pilot for the Central Air Service in Chehalis, Washington. Arnold decided to look around during his proposed flight to Yakima, Washington, hoping to discover it and collect the $5,000 reward which had been offered.

Piloting a "specially designed mountain airplane," he took off at about 2:00 P.M., and headed directly for the "high plateau of Mount Rainier," a point varying from nine to ten thousand feet elevation.

As he was searching, he maneuvered his ship into a 180-degree turn "over Mineral, Washington, at approximately 9,200 feet altitude." Suddenly, a "tremendously bright flash" flooded his plane. Surprised and curious, Arnold spent the ensuing half minute scanning the adjacent skies, but spotted nothing. Then, again without warning, the flash recurred. He identified the source as being far to the left—and north of his position. There he observed "a formation of very bright objects coming from the vicinity of Mount Baker, flying very close to the mountain tops and traveling at tremendous speed."

The shape of the nine mysterious objects was not discernible "as they were still at a distance of over a hundred miles," but Arnold could see the formation "was going to pass directly in front" of him, "flying at approximately 170 degrees," in a reverse-echelon pattern.

His immediate evaluation was that they were jets. They appeared to have no tails, but he decided some highly effective camouflage was obscuring the tail assembly from his view. Notwithstanding the confusion about their design, the author notes that he "observed the objects' outlines plainly as they flipped and flashed along against the snow [of the mountainsides] and against the sky."

The unknowns were passing at almost right angles to Kenneth Arnold and his plane and, having Mount Rainier and Mount Adams as fixed points, he decided to try and determine their speed. As they held to their overall course, the objects "fluttered and sailed," flashing blue-white in the sun, and "swerved in and out of the high mountain peaks of the Cascade Mountains[3] between Mount Rainier and Mount Adams. Although "they didn't fly like any aircraft I had ever seen," they flew in "a definite formation," with the lead ship higher than the last, and, while functioning in unison, they moved "erratically"; or, in the now historic phrase, they looked "like a saucer would if you skipped it across the water."

Establishing their distance from his plane as about twenty-three miles, he began his attempt to determine their velocity. Basing a second calculation on a plateau between Mount Rainier and Mount Adams, Arnold concluded that the entire formation "formed a chain in the neighborhood of five miles long." Timing the echelon's north-to-south flight between the two points at around "one minute and forty-two seconds," he deduced that the craft were "traveling in excess of a thousand miles an hour."

And then they were gone.

Landing in Yakima, at about 4:00 P.M., he recounted his experience, but was not taken very seriously. Returning to his plane, he took off for Pendleton, Oregon, where he fell to speculating with friends about the maximum speeds achieved, up to that time, by the military's secret aircraft. The consensus was not more than seven hundred miles an hour. The conversation stimulated Arnold to return to his calculations. The first results of these more refined evaluations indicated the unknowns were hurtling across the heavens at more than 1,700 miles an hour. The data were minimized by measuring the flight path as from the *base* of Mount Rainier to the *base* of Mount Adams—which overcompensation naturally shortened the distance traveled considerably, actually to 39.8 miles. However, even this modification still produced a speed rate of "over thirteen hundred and fifty miles per hour."

Finally, deciding the fluttering of the craft would have been too much for the human body to sustain, Arnold settled for the conclusion that the objects must have been remotely controlled guided missiles from a military base.

The later drastic revision of this solution to his sighting is, of course, Flying-Saucer history.

The time was right, the myth was ripe—the Age began.

Within hours, things of every size and shape were being sighted in the skies across the United States. Flecks overhead no more improbable than wild duck winging home were accorded news space vastly greater than the most fascinating foo-fighter[4] report of a few years earlier. And Arnold was caught up in the general carnival and secondary consternation.

The commanding officer of the Army proving grounds at White Sands, New Mexico, Lt. Col. Harold R. Turner, dismissed the entire Cascade Mountains incident as a flight of jets.[5] Officials at Wright-Patterson Field, home of the Air Technical Intelligence Center, which was responsible for keeping track of all foreign aircraft and guided missiles, asked for a comprehensive report on the aerial encounter and Arnold complied. Three weeks after the episode he was contacted by Ray Palmer, Midwestern publisher of offbeat and science-fiction magazines, who played, and still plays, a unique role in the broader scope of this analysis.

The letter from Mr. Palmer requested an exposition of his experiences, and Arnold accommodated him with a carbon copy of the report he had forwarded to Wright-Patterson Field.

Shortly thereafter, Palmer contacted Arnold again and asked if he would be interested in investigating the story of two Tacoma, Washington, men who claimed they had seen a saucer flight. At the same time, Arnold was visited by two Air Force Intelligence men—Lt. Frank M. Brown and Capt. William Davidson—who expressed considerable interest in Arnold's sighting and, before departing, instructed him to contact them should similar information come to his attention.

On July 29, 1947, having accepted Palmer's offer, Arnold flew to Tacoma, Washington, to pursue inquiries regarding the mystery there. During the trip, above Union, Oregon, a score of brass-toned unknowns hurtled past his plane no more than four hundred yards away. Soon they were out of sight.

Arnold arrived in Tacoma and passed along the following story.

Harold Dahl, accompanied by his fifteen-year-old son and a dog, was cruising the shore of Maury Island in his coastal boat on the afternoon of June 21—three days before the original Mount Rainier sighting. Suddenly, at a point about two thousand feet overhead, the group spotted six doughnut-designed craft, one stationary and apparently in some difficulty, the other five circling it. Dahl remembered them as being approximately twenty-five feet in diameter, of some brushed metal, with port-holes around the exterior surface of the circular tube.

Pulling into the shore, the group disembarked, watching and taking several photographs.

The craft, which seemed to be suffering from a malfunction, de-scended to an altitude of no more than five hundred feet, while its com-panions remained suspended above it. Eventually a sister craft drifted down and alongside, creating a contact between the surface of the ships. Instantly there was heard a muted explosion and the seemingly disabled vehicle flushed forth a shower of mercury-colored metallic confetti. This snow of feather-weight aerial jetsam was followed by a hail of heavier, darker material, which plummeted into the sea, causing it to steam.

The obvious danger of the latter barrage caused Dahl, his son, and the crew, to seek shelter. Unfortunately, the confused dog was struck by one of the missiles, killed, and buried at sea. The boy was burned and treated by a physician later.

Apparently the explosion either aided the floundering saucer, or indi-cated its recovery, for soon the flight rose, disappearing at an incalcula-ble altitude.

Several pieces of the cooled debris were recovered and saved.

On the following day, Dahl claimed an unknown man visited him, de-tailing the previous day's outing and warning Dahl that he and his entire family would be in great jeopardy should he discuss the matter with any-one.

The episode of the rain of rocks, or whatever it was, had caused con-siderable damage to the vessel operated by Dahl, and his superior in the coastal company, Fred L. Crisman, took a skeptical view of the matter—at least, in the beginning.

After Arnold heard Dahl's tale, the seaman suggested they drive to the house of "his secretary," where he had left a few of the undefined frag-ments. In Arnold's various versions of the affair, he generally gives a rather detailed description of the house, the secretary, and the visit. To his observation that the touted pieces of debris appeared to be nothing more than lava rock, Dahl countered that he had no knowledge of metals but that the beaches near the island were now rife with whatever the stuff was.

The next morning found Dahl pounding on Arnold's hotel door, ac-companied by Crisman, who asserted that he had gone out the day after his employee's adventure and encountered a similar experience—saucers and all.

Arnold was beginning to feel a bit twisted around by now, and so he decided to engage the assistance of his friend, Capt. E. J. Smith, of United Airlines, a long-time professional pilot who had had a sighting of his own.

Upon his arrival, Captain Smith was favored with a recounting of the two narratives. Following several discussions, the two pilots tentatively concluded that involvement with Dahl and Crisman might be risky, that both were hoaxers, or that the Soviet Union and espionage might be part of the explanation for the curious state of affairs in Tacoma.

Finally, it was decided that Arnold should heed the earlier instructions of the Air Force Intelligence men Brown and Davidson—to call them should anything odd arise. But the visit of Davidson and Brown resulted in an increase of the confusion—at least in the minds of Arnold and Smith. The sum total of the inquiry consisted of interviews with the two Tacoma men and the two amateur detectives, a collecting of some of the strange fragments, and erratic fluctuation of interest in the subject from intense to indifferent. Very early on the morning of August 1, the officers commandeered a B-25, heading back to Hamilton Field.

The plane exploded and crashed around 1:30 A.M. Both men were killed.

Shortly after the deaths of Davidson and Brown, Arnold recalls, he and Smith were questioned by another Air Force Intelligence officer. This Major Sander, who seems to have behaved just about as queerly as his late predecessors, concluded his investigation by spiriting away all of the remaining bits of "saucer debris."

Arnold's departure from Tacoma was preceded by one interesting incident. Desiring a final exchange with Harold Dahl, and remembering that he had said that he would be at his secretary's place that day, Smith and Arnold decided to drive out to the house. Arriving there, they discovered that the bright, well-kept little cottage the ufologist had previously seen was now cobwebbed and abandoned. It reflected having been deserted for several months—yet Arnold's earlier visit had occurred only three days before.

Additionally, Kenneth Arnold claims—or, at least, claimed five years afterward—that he was never again able to locate any trace of Harold Dahl.

Captain Ruppelt, who in his *The Report on Unidentified Flying Objects*[6] called Arnold "Simpson" and the other participants by equally pseudonymous names, points out a number of what officialdom regarded as insupportable discrepancies in the various "reports."

The Air Force conclusion on the Maury Island sighting was that Arnold and Smith had been deceived by a complete fabrication contrived by the elusive Tacoma salvage men. According to Ruppelt, there was serious thought of prosecuting the pair, but the idea was subsequently discarded and the entire matter written off as a hoax.

However, the story remained alive through even more dramaturgic versions, like that of Harold T. Wilkins (not to be confused with the noted astronomer), who asserted that the *Saturday Evening Post* once deleted from remarks of Arnold's it was publishing his contention that he had "been visited by unseen entities" whom he "believed to be pilots of these weird disks. They were invisible. . . ." [7]

In July of 1958, Eldon K. Everett, identifying himself as a saucer investigator operating during the years of 1948 and 1954, offered a curious commentary on the Maury Island business.

Mr. Everett told of residing in a small farming community in the state of Washington in 1947, during the time of the Puget Sound sighting. He reports that he discovered that the "crash" area on the island (presumably where the strange materials were disgorged) was isolated by a barbed-wire fence and patrolling guards. Had the incident, in fact, been a hoax, he asked, why the precautions (he claims to have encountered)?

In replying to Everett and in subsequent expositions, Ray Palmer was particularly irked by Captain Ruppelt's suggestion that he had been the instigator of the hoax, if hoax it was. Palmer pointed out that if, as was argued, one of the two primary participants had said the strange material had come from a Flying Saucer because that was what Palmer had wanted him to say, why did Ruppelt also allege that the same individual had mailed Palmer the material "as a joke"—presumably on his own initiative.

Palmer even suggested that Everett's article on the Maury Island sighting might itself be a hoax. However, in commenting on it, several points were immediately conceded by Palmer: that the Maury Island incident was true, that the late Brown and Davidson had discovered whatever the truth was and had been ordered to leave and forget the entire matter, that the boat shown Arnold and Captain Smith was *not* a harbor-patrol boat, but a semiderelict fishing craft, and that the damage to it had been faked. The two investigators had never even seen the *real* boat, Palmer argued.

Yes, proclaimed the Chicago editor, there was indeed a hoax in the Maury Island incident—and it was Fred Crisman's hoax. Several years earlier, explained Palmer, Crisman had reported an encounter with Shavian Deros in a Burmese cavern, resulting in his having "a hole the size of a dime burned in [his] arm by a ray. . . ." Palmer concluded that this incident and the Maury Island mystery were inextricably intertwined, and that the latter conclusively demonstrated that Flying Saucers do not come from outer space.

In 1962 one Frank Patton suggested that Arnold and Captain Smith had been hypnotized during their Tacoma adventure. The well-known saucerologist Brinsley Le Poer Trench wrote, in 1963, that the affair was no hoax. His argument was based mainly upon other observations of "doughnut-shaped" phenomena. His most interesting bit of evidence was the sighting on May 15, 1955, over Union Square in New York City. Warren Siegmond was taking snapshots of Miss Jeannine Bouillier when they sighted an enormous, fiery, circular object above them. They photographed the phenomenon, and the pictures appear to indicate a "doughnut-shaped" unknown.

A score of years after the Maury Island affair, which culminated in the death of two men and an unfathomable confusion, the incident is still talked about. But it was Arnold and his experience that triggered the staccato of sightings that popped up like ack-ack fire across the American skies. Of course, there had been many and various sightings before, as is well known, but this was the initial stage of the popular participation in—or should one say expression of—such aerial activity. Previously, the recording of such excitements tended to be limited to individuals or small groups (with the primary exception of the 1897 complex[8]), but now the modern Age of Flying Saucers started like a sudden spacial freshet that would soon build into a flood, and the reports raced in the wake of Arnold's adventure with the nine silver disks.

A railway engineer from Cedar Rapids recounted seeing a string of ten fluttering, glowing discs, sailing at a great height, on June 23,[9] and a prospector claimed to have sighted a half dozen unknowns above the Cascade Mountains in Oregon, on the following day.[10]

Naval rocket experts at the White Sands, New Mexico, testing grounds admitted the observation of a silver disk on June 29, and there was an aerial exhibition on July 4. One report said that a group including police in Portland, Oregon, had had a multiple sighting; in Oregon, several motorers saw four unknowns; in Seattle, a Coast Guard yeoman made one of the earliest photographs of an unidentified aerial object in modern ufology. Although described in the outstanding research work *UFO Evidence* as the "first known photograph of a U.F.O.,"[11] it was, of course, preceded by half a century by the Rogers Park photograph of 1897.

The most interesting and historically important sighting of that date was made by Capt. E. J. Smith, who later aided Arnold in the Tacoma investigation, and his crew. Flying a DC-3 from Boise, Idaho, to Portland, Oregon, they noted two distinct groups of flat, circular unknowns silhouetted against the sunset. The sighting continued for about ten minutes, over a distance of approximately forty-five miles, and varied formation frequently during that period. In the second flight, three objects flew together, with another to one side.[12]

On the ninth of July, the Aviation Editor of the Statesman Newspaper, Inc., David N. Johnson, a member of the 190th Fighter Squadron, Idaho Air National Guard, recorded seeing a round, black object engaged in fifteen seconds of intricate maneuvers. His observations were confirmed by several sources on the ground.[13]

It was during this month that the Air Force began quietly investigating some of these strange reports.[14]

Dr. Clyde Tombaugh, discoverer of the planet Pluto, accompanied by his wife and two daughters, was driving along a New Mexico highway on the sunny afternoon of July 16, 1947, when the group noticed a "curious shiny object, almost immobile" among some fairly high clouds. The astronomer later described the object as being of a stabile elliptical shape, somewhat luminous, and seemingly oscillating. The unknown shot upward so abruptly, Tombaugh was convinced that he had seen "a flying thing absolutely new." [15]

"By the end of July," said Captain Ruppelt later, "the UFO security lid was down tight. The few members of the press who did inquire about what the Air Force was doing got the same treatment that you would get today [1956] if you inquired about the number of thermonuclear weapons stockpiled in the U. S. atomic arsenal. . . ." [16]

On August 9, Aubrey V. Brook, vacationing in Rock Garden, California, repeatedly shot at a flight of some score of white airborne objects which, he asserted, were designed after the fashion of Valentine hearts. His attack on the flight was not very effective, probably due to the fact that they were, he estimated, several thousand feet above him.

The record of air-to-air sightings was substantially enhanced during the month of August by the incident over Bethel, Alabama. Two pilots flying out of that community reported seeing a great black object, which they described as "bigger than a C-54." The unknown was seen in the bright evening sky, at about twelve hundred feet altitude. As the thing crossed their path, they tried to follow it, but even at their maximum speed they were swiftly outdistanced and soon lost it.

The thirteenth of the same month brought forth a claim by a Twin Falls, Idaho, farmer and his two pre-teen-age boys that an object some seven yards wide and three yards thick, adorned with side jets, had skimmed over their land.

On September 23, 1947, the first official Air Technical Intelligence Center—one of the top Air Force intelligence units—evaluation went to the Commanding General of the Army Air Forces in response to his verbal request for a preliminary study of the spate of inexplicable aerial activity. It said, among other things, "the reported phenomena were real" and urged that a full, permanent study project be set up at ATIC to investigate and analyze sightings.[17]

Three weeks later, on October 14, Maj. Charles E. Yeager piloted the first human supersonic flight in the X-1 rocket-powered aircraft.

The Age of Flying Saucers was underway as 1947 dissolved into history. The Air Force's Project Sign, set up to evaluate reports on aerial unknowns, had, in Ruppelt's words, become "a routine operation." All of the material gathered regarding the Germans' aeronautical research during World War II was being carefully sifted, the likelihood of Russia having constructed craft to match the incredible descriptions received was weighed, the possibility of humans or materials supporting the tremendous stresses concomitant with the speeds and maneuvers reported was considered. The conclusions were that neither the Germans nor the Russians could possibly have constructed such airships, and that even had such craft been designed and built, no human and no material known could have withstood the demands of their flights.

Man had lived through the first year—really half year—of the Age of Flying Saucers. Countless theories were advanced to explain where the amazing sky-things were coming from; most suggested they were outer-spacial. However, the variations in the propositions were basically regarding distance and direction. The new age might have broken, but the range of most men's imaginations was still only three-dimensional—which left them ill equipped to seek solutions to the unknowns, let alone the Unknown.

Chapter 3

THE WONDERS OF OUR DISCONTENT

The Age of Flying Saucers evolved from the inceptive to the secondary stage with the Air Technical Intelligence Center's letter to the Commanding General of the Army Air Force on September 23, 1947. It requested the establishment of a priority project with a code name and a superior security classification. "ATIC's request was granted," wrote Captain Ruppelt, "and Project Sign, the forerunner of Project Grudge and Project Blue Book, was launched." [1] The evaluative group was given a 2-A priority, the second highest the Air Force could accord.

Ufology recorded its first modern tragedy on January 7, 1948. The Louisville *Courier* headlined the incident succinctly: "F-51 and Capt. Mantell Destroyed Chasing Flying Saucer."

At 1:15 P.M., the control tower at Godman Air Force Base, near Louisville, Kentucky, was contacted by the Kentucky State Highway Patrol inquiring about a curious aircraft reported by inhabitants of Maysville, a village about eighteen miles to the east. Having no information, Godman called Wright-Patterson Air Force Base, but the men at the base had nothing to contribute.

The police called in with new reports less than half an hour later. Owensboro and Irvington, to the west, were giving accounts of a craft, "circular, about 250 to 300 feet in diameter," traveling in a general Louisville direction "at a pretty good clip." [2]

Godman's Flight Service still found no record of any such aerial operation. Since the unknown had passed north of the base, they scanned that area in case it should return.

Their attention was rewarded when an assistant called the chief tower officer's attention to an object in the sky. They agreed that they were not observing any conventional craft, nor a weather balloon, [3] and summoned the operations and intelligence officers to the tower. The four men monitored the UFO through 6 x 50 binoculars until the base commander, Col. Guy F. Hix, arrived to supervise the observation. Although these officers, as well as others, continued to watch the unknown, none was able to identify it.

Four F-51's appeared in the south sky at two thirty, on their way from Marietta Air Force Base, in Georgia, to Standiford Field, near Louisville. The flight was commanded by Capt. Thomas F. Mantell, Jr. Requesting an investigation of the UFO, the tower was told that one ship was low on fuel and had to proceed to its destination, but that Mantell and two wing men would attempt an identification.

The pilots had not yet isolated the object, but, following directions radioed from the tower, they climbed in a southerly direction. During the ascent the flight leader pulled beyond his companions and at ten thousand feet was almost out of sight. Calling in at 2:45 P.M., Mantell reported: "I see something above and ahead of me, and I'm still climbing." [4]

"What the hell are we looking for?" asked one wing man moments later.

There is some confusion as to what was actually said after that. Enthusiastic UFO debunker Dr. Donald H. Menzel quotes the next Mantell report as follows:

"It appears to be a metallic object, and it is of tremendous size. I'm going to 20,000 feet." [5]

"I've sighted the thing. It looks metallic—and it's tremendous in size . . . now it's starting to climb . . ." is the way Maj. Donald E. Keyhoe, avid supporter of the UFO thesis, relates it. His conclusion of the message reads:

"It's still above me, making my speed or better. I'm going up to 20,000 feet. If I'm no closer, I'll abandon chase." [6]

Captain Mantell's wing men searched up to fifteen thousand feet, although they, like the flight leader, were without oxygen facilities. Subsequently they landed, refueled, and canvassed the area again. At about four o'clock that afternoon the word came in. Mantell had crashed.

The United States Air Force said the pilot had perished while chasing the planet Venus.

"About a year later," wrote Ruppelt, "the Air Force released its official report on the incident. To use a trite term, it was a masterpiece in the art of 'weasel wording.' It said that the UFO might have been Venus, or it could have been a balloon. Maybe two balloons." [7]

Dismissing the official Venus nonsense, as had Dr. J. Allen Hynek, the service's astronomical authority, Ruppelt finally and dubiously decided that "it *could* [his italics] have been a balloon." [8]

Skeptic Menzel opts for the balloon explanation, although he is about equally ready to accept a "mock sun" (a solar effect of sunlight filtering through ice crystals) thesis. [9]

Notwithstanding the popularity of the balloon theory, even among serious ufologists,[10] such solutions are rather unsatisfactory when one considers that Mantell pursued the UFO "for at least fifteen to twenty minutes." [11] Nor is the mystery clarified by the persistent (to this day) rumors that no fragment of the pilot's body was ever found among the remnants of the crashed plane.[12]

Captain Ruppelt regarded the inauguration of Project Sign as having taken place on September 23, 1947. However, ufologically speaking, the inception of this program is of sufficient historical importance for us to note that the important work *The UFO Evidence* lists the official date of establishment as January 22, 1948.[13] Keyhoe also dates the initiation of Project Sign after Mantell's death.[14] The Air Force says February 11.

Shortly thereafter, on April 5, scientists at White Sands, New Mexico, reported a "disc-shaped UFO, one fifth the size of the moon," executing a series of fantastic figures against the sky,[15] and Maj. Edwin Jerome told of sighting a 9,000-mile-an-hour UFO over Labrador during a flight seven and a half weeks later.[16]

However, it was not until July 24 that the annals of ufology could boast another truly major mystification. The episode in question was briefly overtured when a rocketlike craft, featuring two rows of portholes on either side, was announced as having flown above The Hague, in the Netherlands.

Three days later . . .

Capt. Clarence S. Chiles and copilot John B. Whitted took off from Houston, Texas, in their Eastern Air Lines DC-3 on a scheduled flight to Atlanta, Georgia. The ship passed a point some twenty miles southwest of Montgomery, Alabama, at about 2:45 A.M. Suddenly, plummeting directly toward them, they saw a brilliant object. The thought of a jet aircraft flashed into Chiles's mind but was instantly discarded as the pilot realized that the unknown was approaching too swiftly, even for so powerful a propulsion.

Barely avoiding collision, Chiles banked to the left in time to see the object hurtle by, about seven hundred feet off his right wing. As the ship shook from air turbulence, copilot Whitted glanced over his shoulder and saw the UFO in a sharp ascent.

Chiles and Whitted, saying they saw the unknown clearly, described it as a cigar-shaped body about one hundred feet long, with a double row of brightly illuminated windows. The bottom of the fuselage appeared as a "deep blue glow," and it was exuding a "50-foot trail of orange-red flame" exhaust.[17] They estimated the UFO's speed between 500 and 700 miles an hour.

A single passenger observed a "strange, eerie streak of light, very intense," but conceded the UFO was gone before he had adjusted his vision to the night sky.

Robbins Air Force Base, at Macon, Georgia, reported a high-speed, glowing object overhead shortly after the earlier incident. That would have been the progressed position of the previous unknown in relationship to its near collision with the DC-3.

Dr. Donald Menzel cites the April 30, 1949, report of Dr. J. Allen Hynek's identification of the UFO as a meteor and denies Ruppelt's description of air turbulence.[18] Further, he contends, contrary to the former Air Force saucer specialist's record, Lieutenant Whitted put the object ten times as far from the DC-3 as had Chiles, i.e., about a mile and a half away. Concluding his evaluation, Menzel records that "the evidence is overwhelming that the UFO *was* [his italics] a fireball." [19]

Before the summer of 1948 was over, the Air Technical Intelligence Center decided that it was time to draw an initial conclusion regarding the UFO phenomenon and an "Estimate of the Situation" was prepared, stamped "Top Secret," and sent to the office of the Commanding General. The summation was that UFOs were interplanetary! [20]

A full understanding of the situation requires that one be aware that a number of pre-Arnold sightings were contained in that official evaluation, including one by four F-47 pilots who saw a "flying silver wing," and English radar records of "ghost ships." [21]

The third of the more remarkable sightings—or, as in the two earlier instances, more properly *encounters*—of 1948 occurred around 8:30 P.M., on the evening of October 1. Second Lt. George F. Gorman, a North Dakota Air National Guard, was piloting an F-51 into Fargo, following a cross-country flight. Contacting the control tower for landing directions, he was informed of the presence of a Piper Cub nearby. He soon spotted it below him.

Suddenly, what appeared to be a taillight flashed past his right wing, and he inquired of the tower whether another craft was in the vicinity. The reply came that nothing was in the area other than the Piper Cub. However, Gorman could still see the light, and he decided to investigate it. Wheeling his F-51 around, he closed the distance to about half a mile, from which point he estimated the sharply outlined, but blinking light to be from six to eight inches in breadth. Apparently responding to an increase of energy, the light banked sharply left, plummeted past the tower, and zoomed up again with Gorman on its tail. The "dogfight" continued, with the pilot attempting to close the distance between himself and the light, but without success. However, on two occasions, the unknown set to a collision course, with the apparent intention of ramming Gorman and his plane. In each instance, Gorman dived to safety with only a few yards' grace. Finally, without warning, the light hurtled upward and disappeared in the high sky. Several other persons supported, at least in part, the pilot's description of the encounter, including the Piper Cub pilot, Dr. A. D. Cannon, and his passenger, Einar Neilson.

Among other curious aspects of this report was Ruppelt's notation that Gorman's plane was more radioactive than similar craft which had not been recently flown. Gorman himself told Air Force investigators, "I had the distinct impression that its maneuvers were controlled by thought or reason." [22]

Ruppelt's conclusion was that "Gorman fought a lighted balloon" and that an Air Weather Service report "proved it." However, even the redoubtable sceptic Donald Menzel concedes that it was "an answer that was not entirely satisfactory," preferring the somewhat more fascinating conclusion of "balloon plus planetary mirage." [23] If it is true that the UFO "climbed toward [the] plane against a strong wind and disappeared from view at thirty thousand feet altitude, still rising," [24] it is difficult to accept the astronomer's somewhat complex explanation. Besides, according to Keyhoe, the Weather Bureau records at Fargo indicated that while a balloon had been released, theodolite tracking showed it coursing away from the UFO area. [25]

Two weeks later, on the other side of the earth, an F-61 "Black Widow" night fighter patrolling over Japan registered an unknown on radar. The object was at about 5,500 feet, traveling two hundred miles per hour. On a half dozen occasions the interceptor attempted to approach the UFO, only to have it accelerate to an approximated 1,200 miles an hour, completely outdistancing the plane. After each maneuver the object slowed down again. The pilot and crew of the F-61 were able, during one of the nearest passes, to identify the UFO as being a twenty-to-thirty-foot object shaped "like a rifle bullet." [26]

Washington, D.C., just missed an interesting incident, on November 18, when an Air Force craft, out of Andrews AFB, pursued an oval unknown. Two pilots, Lt. Henry G. Combs and Lt. Kenwood W. Jackson, engaged in a ten minute dogfight with the UFO which at times flew in excess of six hundred miles an hour. [27]

Project Sign collected several hundred sightings before 1948 came to an end. One hundred and sixty-seven were classified as "good reports," and thirty-five or forty as "unknown." However, the initial excitement had begun to recede—or was being receded. The Air Force was still confining its efforts to evaluative ones, ignoring the investigative, and there seemed no likelihood that it had any intention of inaugurating an aggressive inquiry into UFOs. At about nine thirty on the evening of December

5, Captain Goede, piloting an Air Force C-47 at eighteen thousand feet, ten miles east of Albuquerque, New Mexico, observed a great green ball of fire hurtling across the sky before him. He and his crew watched as it rose from the slopes of the Sandia Mountains, then leveled off and disappeared. The experience had been even more startling than the sighting of a similar object by the same crew less than half an hour earlier, in the sky near Las Vegas, New Mexico.

Immediately afterward, the command pilot of a Pioneer Airlines Flight 63 reported that, while passing through the same vicinity, an emerald fireball had flashed toward him. As in previous encounters with unknowns at close range, the captain banked sharply out of the path of the burning globe as it fluctuated from green to red to green. Finally the UFO dived downward and vanished.

The intelligence personnel at Kirtland Air Force Base, at Albuquerque, continued to receive green-fireball reports and soon sought the assistance of Dr. Lincoln La Paz, of the Institute of Meteorics at the University of New Mexico. Ruppelt recorded that the international authority on meteors told him "that he seriously doubted the green fireballs were meteorites." [28] Dr. Menzel also concedes that La Paz "concluded that the objects were not meteors but must be 'something unusual' because they differed from 'normal' meteors in their color, trajectory, velocity, size, brilliance, and apparent lack of fragments," which would seem a goodly number of points upon which a recognized authority might construct a knowledgable theory. However, in a rather presumptuous and arrogant manner, Menzel suggested that Dr. La Paz's deductions were "perhaps unconsciously influenced by the general hysteria of the past year." [29]

Five years later, *Nexus* (later the *Saucer News*) carried an article of considerable interest on the subject. It asserted that Dr. J. Allen Hynek, Air Force astronomical adviser then affiliated with the MacNillin Observatory, Columbus, Ohio, had stated in an official UFO report that he believed the green fireballs to be the result of some undisclosed research activity carried on by some branch of the United States Government. Supporting sources for Hynek's purported position were indicated, among them being "The First Night-Firing of a V-2 Rocket in the United States," an article by Dr. Fritz Zwicky, published in the *Journal of the Astronomical Society of the Pacific* (Volume 59, February, 1947). According to *Nexus*, Zwicky's piece tells of the initial stages of government-sponsored experimentation, the objective of which was to create *artificial meteors* or fireballs. It is stated that Zwicky identifies Dr. La Paz as one of the scientists involved in the White Sands research, which, if true, might well explain why the Albuquerque astronomer declined to classify the green fireballs as meteors.[30]

A conference was called in February, 1949, to ascertain a course of action regarding the volant viridescence in the night skies of New Mexico. Dr. Edward Teller, who achieved much notoriety via the hydrogen bomb, Dr. Joseph Kaplan, internationally regarded authority on the upper atmosphere, Dr. La Paz, and others were summoned to offer their counsel. Notwithstanding La Paz's arguments against the meteor theory —and it appears as if he may have known something they didn't—the group concluded that the phenomena were natural. Nonetheless, they did suggest that a study be established by the Air Force's Cambridge Research Laboratory to look further into this area of ufology, the purpose being to attempt to photograph the fireballs, and to determine their speed, altitude, size, and other characteristics more fully than had been done.

Project Twinkle was set up to accomplish that end.

Still, if the entire pattern and investigation of fireballs had been odd, other, even less publicized, matters were more so. Elsewhere, at an unidentified Army installation, a series of most unusual sightings were being recorded. Night after night, sometimes several times a night, V-formations of lights were seen passing overhead. Almost everyone on post observed the flights, individually or in groups, and on one occasion the entire garrison watched the UFOs soar directly above the post parade ground. Moving "faster than a jet," they pulsed from bluish-white to orange and back again, in two cycles. Two weeks of at least one-a-night sightings followed, but the Air Force expressed no interest in the remarkable aerial phenomena.

The commanding officer of the post, with an unusual initiative for the services, made a creative decision to institute a series of observation teams to monitor the UFOs. Each group was to be composed of a metric man to ascertain the elevation and azimuth of the lights, a timer, a recorder to take down each bit of data, and a radio man to maintain constant communication with the other teams and the command point. Effective interplay among the various groups offered a distinct possibility for a clearer and more accurate evaluation of fireballs.

Desiring maximum effectiveness, the post commander contacted the Air Force so that the project might be coordinated with the efforts of the sister service. Everything was prepared.

The Air Force then proceeded to kill the plan.

Its position was simple. There were no UFOs except fireballs. Fireballs were meteors. Project Twinkle would prove it—later. Anything else would be a waste of time.

Project Twinkle was created at the end of the summer. Unfortunately, to quote Captain Ruppelt:

"Project Twinkle was a bust." [31]

With the coming of the Korean War, it also became extinct.

It was no longer fashionable, in the Air Force, to be open-minded regarding UFOs. Conservatism had once again reasserted itself, and the cautious majority was swiftly aligning itself with the skeptics. On February 11, 1949, Project Sign was renamed Project Grudge, and if the revised designation was suggestive, Ruppelt stated flatly that standard intelligence procedures—*unbiased evaluation* (his italics) of data—were abandoned. In his words:

It doesn't take a great deal of study of the old UFO files to see that the standard intelligence procedures were no longer being used by Project Grudge. Everything was being evaluated on the premise that UFO's couldn't exist. No matter what you see or hear, don't believe it. [32]

The former director of UFO investigation and evaluation for the Air Force left no doubt as to his opinion of the new operation:

To one who is intimately familiar with UFO history it is clear that Project Grudge had a two-phase program of UFO annihilation. The first phase consisted of explaining every UFO report. The second phase was to tell the public how the Air Force had solved all the sightings. This, Project Grudge reasoned, would put an end to the UFO reports. [33]

However, UFO reports increased, and so did public interest. On June 5, Walter Winchell wrote:

The *New York World-Telegram* has confirmed this reporter's exclusive report of several weeks before—which newspapermen have denied—about the flying saucers. Said the front page in the *World-Telegram:* "Air Force people are convinced the flying disk is real. The clincher came when the Air Force got a picture recently of three disks flying in formation over Stephensville, Newfoundland. They outdistanced our fastest ships. . . ." [34]

The noted astronomer Clyde Tombaugh had another sighting on August 20. While sitting in the garden of his Las Cruces, New Mexico, home, conversing with his wife and her mother, he observed an elliptical formation of a half dozen rectangular unknowns traversing the sky. [35]

Meanwhile, Project Grudge became increasingly moribund, paying little attention to the dozen good reports it was receiving each month and nonfunctioning on the principle that *it* was all over.

"Unidentified Flying Objects—Project Grudge; Technical Report No. 102-AC-49/15-100" was issued on December 27, 1949. With it came the announcement that Project Grudge was to be dissolved.

The Air Force's attempt at a final summation of the UFO mystery noted that Dr. J. Allen Hynek and his staff had studied 237 of the most interesting UFO sightings for many months, concluding that 32 percent were astronomical phenomena. The Air Force Air Weather Service and the Air Force Cambridge Laboratory examined the selected reports and dismissed 12 percent of the 237 as balloons. Another third were designated hoaxes, insufficient evidence, and probably misidentified conventional aerial objects. Twenty-three percent, the remaining sightings, defied explanation and were classified as "unknown." A clumsy and careless effort was made in a final appendix to explain away these UFO reports the Air Force had already conceded were unknown. Mostly, Project Grudge officials contradicted their own experts or merely ignored remarkably well-substantiated observations.

The report satisfied the Air Force and it concluded Project Grudge— but the age of Flying Saucers had hardly begun.

It was left to retired Marine Corps Maj. Donald E. Keyhoe to really break the ufological barrier. Writing in *True* magazine, he said:

After eight months of intensive investigation, the following conclusions have been reached by *True* magazine:

1. For the past 175 years, the planet Earth has been under systematic close-range examination by living, intelligent observers from another planet.

2. The intensity of this observation, and the frequency of the visits to the Earth's atmosphere by which it is being conducted, have increased markedly during the past two years.

3. The vehicles used for this observation and for interplanetary transport by the explorers have been identified and categorized as follows: Type I, a small, nonpilot-carrying disc-shaped aircraft equipped with some form of television or impulse transmitter; Type II, a very large (up to 250 feet in diameter) metallic, disc-shaped aircraft operating on the helicopter principle; Type III, a dirigible-shaped, wingless aircraft which, in the Earth's atmosphere, operates with the Prandtl theory of lift.

4. The discernible pattern of observation and exploration shown by the so-called "flying discs" varies in no important particular from well-developed American plans for the exploration of space expected to come to fruition within the next fifty years. There is reason to believe, however, that some other race of thinking beings is a matter of two and a quarter centuries ahead of us.[36]

The article caused a mild sensation and may well have been one of the most discussed magazine pieces ever published. It established Keyhoe as the foremost unofficial ufologist in the country. It is interesting to note that notwithstanding his persistent conviction that the unknowns are intelligently operated interplanetary craft, he is still generally regarded as a UFO man. Since he does not regard the nature of the aerial objects as unidentified, but rather as firmly established extraterrestrial machines, he is, of course, a saucerologist.

Afterward, when he had become even more knowledgeable about the subject, he might have hesitated to state:

The only other possible explanation is that "saucers" are extremely high-speed, long-range devices developed here on Earth. Such an advance would require an almost incredible leap in technical progress even for American scientists and designers.

At another point, Major Keyhoe tells of having consulted the National Advisory Committee for Aeronautics. He writes:

One of their top engineers stated that a disc with a variable-direction jet or rocket nozzles around the rim could rise and descend vertically, hover, fly straight ahead, and make sharp turns. Its direction and velocity would be governed by the number of nozzles operating, the power applied, and the angle at which they were tilted—toward the ground, rearward, in a lateral direction, or in various combinations.[37]

Perhaps later on, Major Keyhoe wondered whether the "saucer" would constitute quite so incredible a leap for other than *American* scientists. German, for instance. As we know, two separate models of saucer-type craft were designed before the conclusion of World War II by the Germans Schriever, Habermohl, and Miethe, and the Italian Bellonzo. On February 14, 1945, the Habermohl-Schriever design was tested and reportedly achieved forty thousand feet in three minutes and a speed of 1,200 miles an hour. It was probably enlisted in the service of Russian science. However, Miethe, whose "saucer" *was* a broad disk, with adjustable jets, came to work for Canada and the United States.[38] Should we not at least consider the possibility that there are Von Brauns of whom we have no knowledge?

A date of importance in ufology is August 19, 1950. Just prior to noon on that day, Nicholas Mariana, owner of the Missoula, Montana, radio station, and his secretary were inspecting the local baseball park. Seeing a pair of UFOs, Mariana raced to his automobile, some sixty feet distant, and got his 16 mm. Revere turret-type motion picture camera. It was loaded with Daylight Kodachrome. He trained the camera on the silver objects to the northwest, which appeared to slow to a complete stop and then float away to the southwest.

The film was processed by the professional Eastman Laboratory and, after showing it to several clubs and other groups, Mariana submitted it to the United States Air Force's Air Technical Intelligence Center, that is to say, to the supposedly disbanded Project Grudge group. According to Al Chop, the subsequent Pentagon spokesman on UFOs, the analytical evaluation was that the film was inconclusive. Ruppelt, who was head of

Blue Book, reported a few years later that the possibility of balloons had been discarded.

Mr. Mariana has said that the film he originally received after processing contained 315 frames, with the first portion by far the clearest. When it was returned by the Air Force, according to R. M. L. Baker, who exhaustively studied the film, this entire initial phase of the film had been deleted.[39]

The public has had numerous opportunities to see the remaining portion of the Mariana motion picture. It was a featured segment of a commercial film which was subsequently produced: *Unidentified Flying Objects* or *UFO*.

The Riddle of the Flying Saucers, later frequently referred to by its subtitle, *Is Another World Watching?*, published in 1950, was the first non-American book on the growing aerial phenomenon to attract attention in this country. Authored by Gerald Heard and published in London, it presents what to this day remains one of the more picturesque theories on the enigma, especially since it frames its arguments in superficially persuasive semiscientific terms.

The first several chapters review the saucerology of the preceding few years, and, to one familiar with the material, the most interesting point is found in a footnote which alludes to Jonathan Caldwell, onetime resident of a Pennsylvania farm,

. . . who did leave a large model of such a craft [flying saucer]. Then he disappeared, and has not been traced. When the decayed model was found, some investigators thought it might be the first sketch for the present discs. It is clear, however, that the investigator [inventor] never brought his craft beyond the model stage, and had not solved any of the real problems of disc flight.[40]

The details of the author's footnote are, to quote the Atlantic City *Press*:

The Baltimore *Sun* tonight quoted an Air Force officer as saying that two battered old aircraft found near here are "definitely prototypes of the flying saucer." The *Sun* quoted the Air Force official as saying that he believes greatly improved models of the two planes found in an abandoned barn are flying now, and are the source of the flying saucer reports of the past two years. State Police found the old machine in a barn near Glen Burnie, about 11 miles south of Baltimore. Their inventor, Jonathan E. Caldwell, dropped out of sight about 1941.[41]

Subsequent reports on the Caldwell machine, accompanied by a photograph of it, located the shed in which it was found at Marley Park, Maryland.[42]

References to anticipators of man-made saucer devices are not uncommon in the literature of this area, although few have such John Galtean overtones as the above.[43] Scully cites Leo Bentz's asserted witnessing of a disc-shaped craft designed by George de Bay in 1928 and a demonstration of Jacques Fresco's "flying saucer" a decade later.

Two-thirds of *The Riddle of the Flying Saucers* is devoted to a recapitulation and affirmations in remembrance of things passed by a variety of pilots, as well as support for more earthbound sightings. However, it is all mere preparation for the introduction of Mr. Heard's personal explanation of UFOs.

The bees did it.

At least, that is the author's theory. Citing various entomologists, as well as specialists in other areas, he first concludes that there is highly developed insect life on Mars; then he attempts to demonstrate that our busy, buzzy little friends are probably at least as bright as man (notwithstanding his concession that they are monomaniacs); and finally he nails it all down by pointing out that only insects could withstand the gravitational stress imposed by some of the UFOs' maneuvering. Unfortunately, the end result is to split the book apart, leaving about 65 percent to UFO reports—and as such it is adequate, but rather threadbare, material today—and the rest to a popular-styled monograph on the habits of the honey bee. Although his bees wax a bit more rational than is quite believable, and he does drone on a bit too long, the final rejection of his apian attitude should probably be based more upon the complete unromanticality of a bee as the super-someone from beyond the stars than anything else. But all such discussions are pointless—that is, basing a speculation on the assertion that only bees are physically capable of handling the aerodynamic demands. As a gentleman from Sussex might well have observed:

"It is quite elementary, my dear fellow—everyone knows perfectly well that, aerodynamically speaking, bees cannot fly."

Chapter 4

UNKNOWNS, UNREASON, AND DECEIT

One of the first major sightings of 1951 occurred on January 20, when Capt. Lawrence W. Vinther, piloting a DC-3 of the Mid-Continent Airlines above the Sioux City Airport, was requested to identify a curious and brilliant light maneuvering above the field. Approaching the UFO, the flying officer was surprised to see it wheel about and dive directly at him, bulleting past the top of the ship. Instantly the unknown, described by both Vinther and his copilot as larger than a B-29 and without any visible means of propulsion, reversed itself and paced them for several seconds.

Foreign sightings were frequent during the years since Arnold's adventure. One of the more interesting of the year was the Mount Kilimanjaro incident of February 19. The regular morning flight to Mombasa was being prepared at the Nairobi West Airport, in Kenya, Africa. The Lodestar craft took off, with nine passengers and a crew of two, into a bright, clear sky. It was 7:00 A.M.

Twenty minutes later, the radio man called Captain Bicknell's attention to a glowing white globe of light suspended above Mount Kilimanjaro. The two observed the UFO for three minutes before calling it to the attention of the passengers, one of whom then proceeded to scrutinize it with a pair of powerful binoculars. Meanwhile, the radio operator hurried off a description of the object and a résumé of the encounter to Eastleigh, the nearest reception station.

The suggestion that it was a balloon was quickly eliminated as the Lodestar occupants continued to examine the clearly defined, bullet-shaped unknown. Some passengers even took photographs. Bicknell detailed the object as metallic, over two hundred feet long, and featuring a tail fin. It remained motionless . . . for seventeen minutes!

Finally, the UFO began to rise with rapid acceleration, reaching an apparent speed of about a thousand miles an hour, and disappeared into the upper, cloudless sky.

Afterward, the captain and D. W. Merrifield, his radio man, stated flatly that the UFO had been an aircraft of some sort. The latter was of the opinion that if, in fact, it was a machine, "it was 500 years ahead of anything we have today." [1]

Saucerologist Max B. Miller pursued this story and was told, via letter, by Publicity Officer H. C. E. Downs of the East African Airways "there has always been considerable doubt as to the truth of the report." Regarding the photographs, the official seemed quite unable to decide on a single course of refutation. First he indicated that some passenger took pictures, but added that his "name cannot now be traced." Then he reported that rumor had it the evidence was destroyed "when they were developed, the chemist obliterating the spots, thinking they were a fault in the negative." Finally, he concluded with the unqualified assertion: "The photographs are non-existent." [2]

The story becomes even murkier, according to Mr. Miller, when one knows that the Natal *Mercury*, of Durban, East Africa, published both a story about the sighting and a photograph purporting to be the UFO. The photographer, Ray Overstreet, reportedly took motion pictures and was on his way to America to try the newsreel market. Rather ominously, Mr. Miller concludes his piece saying that Overstreet never reached his destination and has not been heard from since.

It can hardly be denied that such an ending makes for a more interesting story. Unfortunately, according to James Moseley,[3] who claims he has interviewed several persons involved in the case, there is no mystery. The film exists; it was examined by the Air Force, it was found to be little more than a bouncing bit of light, and it was returned. Obviously, this doesn't disprove Captain Bicknell's, Mr. Merrifield's, and the passenger's story—if the version we have received is reasonably accurate—but it does eliminate the one piece of proof by which those not present might have been influenced, if not convinced.

Look magazine took up the we-have-solved-the-UFO-enigma banner at this juncture. Once waved by *U.S. News & World Report*, it now boasted a new legend.

Dr. Urner Liddel, chief of the nuclear physics branch of the Office of Naval Research . . . [said] "When this project [high altitude Skyhook balloon flights] first began it was kept secret. Now, there is no longer any need for secrecy on a scientific basis. And, certainly, there is no longer any need to keep the public in the dark about what flying saucers are."

The Liddel report is considered to be the most authoritative scientific explanation of the flying saucer phenomenon. As far as Dr. Liddel is concerned, personally he considers his answer incontrovertibly right.

One of the most convincing factors supporting Dr. Liddel's findings is that flying saucers or flying disks were unheard of until the ONR [Office of Naval Research] experiments in the stratosphere began [in 1947].[4]

It need hardly be pointed out that there was nothing scientific in Liddel's "explanation," and, of course, the characterizing of UFOs as phenomena reported only following the inception of the research program is totally without foundation, not that a concurrence of appearance would have proved very much in any event.

The Lubbock Lights sighting may well have been the best of the modest 1951 catalog. It was reported by Dr. W. I. Robinson, a Professor of Geology, Dr. A. G. Oberg, Professor of Chemical Engineering, Dr. George, Professor of Physics, and Professor W. L. Ducker, Head of the Department of Petroleum Engineering, of the Texas Technological College.

Sitting about Dr. Robinson's lawn on the evening of August 25, the four scientifically trained scholars were discussing micrometeorites. At 9:20 P.M. the group witnessed an arc or echelon of blue-green glowing objects flash across the sky. Moving from north to south, the lights numbered between fifteen and thirty, but further details escaped the unprepared professors. Hoping for a second opportunity to observe the phenomena, a careful watch was kept of the sky as their conversation continued. An hour later they were rewarded and were able to verify their previous impressions. The UFO flight differed in only one respect: this time there appeared to be no definite formation, merely a cluster.

It was reasoned that since the UFOs had appeared twice, they might well return again, and so the observers established a watch pattern and were able to monitor the lights another dozen times. The flights specifically checked were timed at three seconds for the entire ninety-degree flight. Always traveling in the same direction, they became observable at forty-five degrees above the northern horizon and vanished at the similar point over the southern one. Only in the first instance was any particular formation discernible; in later sightings the lights, which sometimes passed overhead more than once a night, appeared in no apparent geometric pattern. Efforts to ascertain their altitude were unsuccessful.

Hundreds of persons besides the professors viewed the UFOs during the two weeks of the recurrences. Among these was an amateur photographer, Carl Hart, Jr., who photographed the lights.

On the night of August 31, Hart was lying on his bed near a window. Looking out at the clear night sky, he saw a formation of UFOs arc across it. Hart took up his loaded Kodak 35 mm., set it to f/3.5, at a tenth of a second, and rushed to his backyard. The lights reappeared, and Hart was able to register two pictures. As the UFOs made a third pass, he added three more, for a total of five photographs of the Lubbock Lights. Although not optimistic, because the lights did not seem very bright to his naked eye, Hart had the roll developed the following morning. The results provided what could easily be the most famous group shot in ufological history. A picture of about a dozen and a half lights flying in V-formation, it was published throughout the world and even used as the jacket design of the book[5] by Captain Ruppelt, the well-known director of the Air Force investigation on the subject.

Ruppelt personally investigated the sighting complex. In the course of his inquiry he interviewed a mother and daughter who were driving along a highway out of Matador, Texas, some seventy miles to the north of Lubbock, at about half past noon on August 31. They told him they suddenly saw a "pear-shaped" object almost hovering some 120 feet above the road, about 150 yards ahead of them. The object, which they identified as being comparable to the size of a B-29 fuselage—the daughter had lived near Air Force bases with her flyer husband for a number of years—drifted gradually east at "less than the speed required to take off in a Cub airplane." [6] They observed no exhaust and heard no sound, but it seemed to them that the object had a "porthole." After a while, the UFO, moving into the wind, spiraled upward at an increasing speed until it was out of sight.

On the evening of August 25, the same during which the professors and many others first saw the Lubbock Lights, "an employee of the Atomic Energy Commission's supersecret Sandia Corporation and his wife" [7] saw a huge "flying wing," some 50 percent larger than a B-36, with which both were familar, soaring above them at about a thousand feet. It was moving in a southerly direction and featured six or eight pairs of bluish-green lights along its forward edge, forming a V-shape.

Ruppelt noted that—considering the time elements involved and the distance between Albuquerque, where the flying wing was seen, and Lubbock—if both reports were of the same phenomenon, then it was traveling about nine hundred miles an hour.

After considerable investigation, perhaps as intensive as the head of Project Blue Book ever gave to a single UFO problem, Ruppelt eliminated refracted lights, birds, conventional craft. Other qualified observers dismissed the idea of meteors. Yet, the Air Force ufologist's final conclusion was even more peculiar than some aspects of the case itself. Whereas he generally was quite specific in his explanation of identified phenomena, or, where doubt remained, he quite objectively left the puzzle for further speculation, in this instance he insisted the solution had been found, but declined to reveal it.

Dr. Menzel, with his usual disinterest in ideas expressed by anyone else, even those on his side of the argument, later wrote of "the overwhelming evidence that the original object had been birds." [8]

According to the skeptic, Ruppelt later "asserted without amplification that the lights had been night-flying moths reflecting the bluish-green of mercury-vapor street lights[9]—a surprising anticlimax, in view of his earlier secrecy."[10]

Presenting what he seemed to regard as the solution, Menzel noted that years after the fact, drawing upon second- and third-hand material, much of the best of which came from Ruppelt's personal inquiries, "Maj. (now Lt. Col.) R. J. Friend of ATIC, and Dr. J. Allen Hynek, science consultant, *determined beyond doubt* [emphasis added] that the objects had been plover"[11] (a large bird not uncommon in the Lubbock area).

A subsequent appraisal by a well-known ufologist went to some lengths to support the professorial sightings and discredit the Lubbock photograph, notwithstanding the Air Force's reservations about suggesting it was a simulation. The picture was left no clearer following his criticism, which was directed primarily at the photographer rather than the photograph. Perhaps the most interesting portion of the article read:

According to the professor [one of the Texas Tech four] I spoke with, the lights positively could not have been the result of reflections or temperature inversions —i.e., the theories propounded by the learned Dr. Donald H. Menzel . . . definitely do not apply in this case. The Texas lights, according to the Lubbock professors, were either a totally unknown phenomenon, or else one or more solid craft of some kind.[12]

The Hart photographs were still being attacked thirteen years later as "reflections of street lamps off the oily belly of plovers."[13] It still sounded like a line from Ogden Nash.

In September, 1951, Capt. Edward J. Ruppelt, aeronautical engineer and World War II bombardier, was made the new director of the revivified Air Force UFO investigation. On October 27, the new Project Grudge was officially established. During the weeks which immediately followed, a T-33 jet trainer, over New Jersey, pursued a silvery disc traveling at nine hundred miles an hour,[14] California-based F-86 jets circled below an unknown, unable to achieve its altitude,[15] and a Korean sighting told of a flight of UFOs, radar-tracked by fourteen different ships, which finally departed at more than a thousand miles an hour.[16]

Green fireballs leapt back into the news as November began. Responding to the observation of seven viridescent UFOs in less than two weeks, Dr. La Paz of the Institute of Meteoritics in New Mexico announced:

"There has never been a rate of meteorite fall in history that has been one fifth as high as the present fall. *If* that rate should continue, I would suspect the phenomenon is not natural . . . they don't behave like ordinary meteorites at all."[17] On the following day, an eighth green fireball appeared and was visible as far away as Wyoming.

A fortnight prior to Christmas that year, a conference was held at the Pentagon. The subject: UFOs. Participating were Capt. Edward J. Ruppelt, Col. Frank Dunn, the head of the Air Technical Intelligence Center, Maj. Gen. John A. Samford, new director of Intelligence, Brig. Gen. W. M. Garland, Samford's Assistant for Production, who was also supposed to oversee what was going on in the project, and others.

It was clearly established that it had been confirmed in writing—from on high, apparently—that UFOs were solely the problem of the Air Force. Within the Air Force the complete responsibility fell to the ATIC, which, in turn, delegated the total task to Project Grudge. Ruppelt, in other words, was the man ultimately charged with resolving the mystery.

During this important meeting, Colonel Dunn positively assured Ruppelt that "the United States [did not] have a secret weapon that was being reported as a UFO." [18]

Important years, ufologically speaking, followed the Arnold sighting. In fact, most years had their share of intriguing aerial activity. However, until it happened, there was never a "flap" like that which constituted the UFO history of 1952. It is remembered, with varying reactions, by saucerologists, ufologists, and skeptics alike, and although most identify it with the American excitement of early summer, toward the end of the year the concentration of observations in Europe was impressive.

An important sighting occurred on January 16, when two employees of General Mills—the Aeronautical Division of which "had launched and tracked every skyhook balloon that had been launched prior to mid-1952" [19]—and four persons from Artesia, New Mexico, were monitoring a Skyhook balloon from the Artesia Airport. After about an hour, the group observed two bright flecks of light to the northwest, but decided they were planes. However, almost immediately they realized that the UFOs were "actually two round, dull-white objects flying in close formation." [20] Moving directly toward the Skyhook balloon, the UFO circled it and then returned to the northwest and disappeared over the horizon. According to the witnesses, when the objects banked as they flew around the balloon, it became evident they were disc-shaped, and, measured against the size of the balloon, about sixty feet in diameter.

The Artesia sighting is, as responsible reports go, impressive, but not compared to the adventure of a Navy pilot out of Mitchel Air Force Base, on Long Island, New York.

A lieutenant commander, who had flown in the Second World War, and who was then an Engineer at the Naval Special Devices Center, was taking up a TBM on the morning of January 21. It was about half past nine, and he was circling at 2,500 feet when he observed an object below him which had the appearance of the top of a parachute canopy. A moment later he realized he was mistaken, as the white dome was moving across the wind path. Soon the UFO began to climb and after a few maneuvers over and around the object, the pilot pulled up behind it. He continued to track the semisphere's course, but it was swiftly outdistancing him, and eventually lost him as it disappeared out to sea. He had maintained the observation for at least two and a half minutes.

Subsequently interviewed by Captain Ruppelt, the lieutenant commander made it clear that the possibility of a balloon had occurred to him, but that it was not a balloon—which it could hardly have been, since the object flew faster than the plane. The head of the Air Force UFO project wrote:

> If you want to argue that the pilot didn't know where he was during the chase —that he was 3 or 4 miles from where he thought he was [Ruppelt records earlier that the flier was very precise about the landmarks relative to his, and the UFOs', positions, and marked them carefully on a map afterward]—that he never did fly around the northern edge of the field and get in behind the UFO—that the UFO could have been a balloon . . .
>
> But if you want to believe that the pilot knew where he was all during the chase, and he did have several thousand hours of flying time, then all you can conclude is that the UFO was an unknown.[21]

"I don't know what it was," remarked the pilot, "but I've never seen anything like it before or since—maybe it was a spaceship." [22]

On the twenty-second, the third of the fascinating January incidents was recorded. The location on this occasion was an Alaskan radar installation. Just after midnight, the duty controller, an Air Force captain, and his crew got "three good plots" of a target traveling fifteen hundred miles an hour, at 23,000 feet. An immediate investigation established that there were no planes aloft in the area.

The radar site contacted a fighter base some hundred miles to the south, which responded by sending up an F-94 to check out the reading. Meanwhile, the object maintained its pace. Picking up the fighter plane on the scope, with the UFO, the monitors observed the latter slowing down and reversing its direction. It was heading toward the radar station.

During the activity which followed, the UFO was tracked by the radar equipment on the ground and in the three different F-94's sent up to investigate, although at times both planes and object were too close for the ground station to pick them up, thereby vanishing from the screen. The last of the craft sent up locked on to it, via its radar, and approached to within two hundred feet, but, fearing a collision, swerved away. The pilot made another pass at the UFO, which was very evident on his scope, although not directly visible, passing within two hundred feet once more, according to his radar. The object apparently hung motionless throughout these maneuvers, but then it suddenly seemed to hurtle off to the west and was lost.

Blue Book chief Ruppelt later submitted the detailed report to Capt. Roy James, head of the radar section at Air Technical Intelligence Center. Although not all of the specialists in that group agreed, James's conclusion was that the incident had been caused by "weather."

Subsequently, Ruppelt discussed the matter with an officer and "an ace radar trouble shooter" for the Air Defense Command who had traveled throughout the world "on loan from the ADC, to work out problems with radar." This specialist dismissed Captain James's notion completely.

"No," he said, "I can't believe that those radar targets were caused by weather. I'd be much more inclined to believe that they were something real, something we just don't know about." [23]

March saw the final solidification of the new Air Force aerial-phenomena operation, and in April Al Chop, whose name has become part of UFO history, was made public information officer for UFOs. It was during this phase that "Air Force Letter 200-5 gave Project Blue Book authority to cut red tape, contact any Air Force unit in the U. S. without going through channels; provided for wire transmission of reports to ATIC, followed with details via Air Mail." [24]

Dr. Walter Riedel, German scientist, formerly a major participant in the laboratories at Peenemünde, stated:

"I am convinced that saucers have an out-of-world basis." [25]

He was supported by internationally famous aerodynamicist Dr. Maurice Biot.[26]

The article in which Riedel's comment appeared, titled "Have We Visitors from Space?" which, according to the most reliable UFO research work, *UFO Evidence,* was cleared by the Air Force's commanding general, intimated rather plainly that UFOs might be extraterrestrial.[27]

The unintelligible pattern continued to develop, and in May a group of distinguished guests while being entertained at a lawn party by a high-echelon CIA man observed a diving, soaring light over Alexandria, Virginia. Investigation produced that familiar conclusion: Unknown. About that time Secretary of the Air Force Thomas K. Finletter summoned Ruppelt for a conference. The Cabinet member followed the briefing with an open-end statement to the press:

No concrete evidence has yet reached us either to prove or disprove the existence of the so-called flying saucers. There remains, however, a number of sightings that the Air Force investigators have been unable to explain. As long as this is true, the Air Force will continue to study flying saucer reports.[28]

In June, the Air Force experts were afforded a very immediate opportunity to pursue their inquiry. A UFO which suddenly tripled its speed was tracked at a California radar station.[29] A week later, Dr. Donald H. Menzel offered another solution to Flying Saucers from his bag of astronomical tricks. They were nothing more than light reflections, the Harvardian solon announced.[30]

Project Blue Book was beginning to settle into the new operation. With 60 percent of the submitted reports quickly being proved to be astronomical bodies, aircraft, or balloons, more time was left to examine the sightings initially designated as unknowns. Whatever efficiency was achieved seemed due to Captain Ruppelt, as he coordinated Blue Book with the data available from

the Air Force's Air Weather Service, Flight Service, Research and Development Command, and Air Defense Command, with the Navy's Office of Naval Research, and the aerology branch of the Bureau of Standards, several astronomical observatories, and our own Project Bear [a well-known research organization of several hundred engineers].[31]

Nonetheless, compared to scores of other Air Forces enterprises, it was a sketchily staffed, pound-foolishly financed inquiry. "Only the best reports we received," wrote Ruppelt, "could be personally investigated in the field by Project Blue Book personnel." [32]

Yet, prepared or not, the greatest "flap" up to that time came with the summer. In the entire year of 1948, the Air Technical Intelligence Center received 167 reports; in June of 1952, 149 were recorded. Over the primary four-year period the Air Force had collected 615; during the two months of the "Big Flap" that total was exceeded by more than a hundred. Before the year was over, official Air Force figures[33] would reveal, over 1,500 sightings had been catalogued. Ruppelt would say:

"We were getting an average of 40 reports a day, one third of which were unidentified." [34]

At mid-month, another of the ever-more-frequent briefings was called. When Ruppelt arrived in Washington, he was informed by Maj. Dewey J. Fournet, Jr., who as liaison officer between the project and the Pentagon monitored the Air Force's UFO investigation, that the purpose of the meeting was to establish the significance, if any, of the sharp rise in unknown aerial activity. Apparently the briefing erupted into a rather lively exchange between the more open-minded and the more sceptical cliques present. Little was decided other than that the effort should be continued.

On July 2, at about 11:10 A.M. Chief Warrant Officer Delbert C. Newhouse, of the United States Navy, was traveling along State Highway 30, seven miles north of Tremonton, Utah, when he sighted a group of "gun metal colored objects shaped like saucers, one inverted on top of the other." Racing to the trunk of his automobile, he got his Bell & Howell Automaster 16 mm. motion-picture camera, which was equipped with a 3-inch telephoto lens. He loaded it rapidly, and, setting it for infinity, trained it on the dozen or more UFOs, while his wife and two children watched. At one point he stopped down from f/8 to f/16, a change quite evident when the film (Daylight Kodachrome) was processed. Delivered to his superiors, who forwarded it to USAF-ATIC, the movie was exhaustively examined. Ruppelt wrote that the objects in the Newhouse film were not "airplanes or balloons, and we don't think they are birds."

It should be remembered the officer had a record of twenty-one years in the Navy, two thousand hours flying time as an aerial photographer, and that his story was supported by his family's eyewitness testimony.

A comprehensive photogrammetric analysis of the motion picture by physicist R. M. L. Baker (who had undertaken a similar task with the Montana Mariana pictures) was published in 1956. Scholarly and detailed, the paper concluded:

> The evidence remains rather contradictory and no single hypothesis of a natural phenomenon yet suggested seems to completely account for the UFO involved. The possibility of multiple hypotheses, i.e., that the Utah UFOs are the result of two simultaneous natural phenomena, might possibly yield the answer.

The "flap" was growing in the United States and elsewhere. England was getting a substantial share, as was France. South America was not far behind, while few areas of the world were wholly devoid of fairly solid reports.

The stage was set. What followed would register as the most extraordinary UFO complex since the nationwide sightings of 1896–1897. It was made no less fascinating by Ruppelt's subsequent recollection that a scientist from an anonymous (it is generally conceded the Blue Book head was alluding to the Central Intelligence Agency) government bureau had said:

"Within a few days [things] are going to blow up and you're going to have the granddaddy of all UFO sightings. The sighting will occur in Washington or New York, probably Washington." [35]

From the second week in July on, unknown aerial phenomena were observed around the outer perimeter of the District of Columbia, in Virginia for the most part. A light "too bright to be a lighted balloon and too slow to be a meteor" [36] was seen by the crew of a National Airlines plane on the tenth, and a light converged on, paced, and hurtled off from another airliner three days afterward. Yet few incidents were and remain more mysterious than the Nash/Fortenberry encounter of July 15, 1952.[37]

A Pan American World Airways DC-4 out of New York was approaching Norfolk, Virginia, at about eight thousand feet. It was a clear night—a few thin cirrus clouds about twelve thousand feet above them—and the visibility unlimited. Senior Captain Fred Koepke was back in the cabin, and First Officer William B. Nash and Second Officer William H. Fortenberry were occupying the pilot's and copilot's seats. There were ten passengers.

It was after eight o'clock, the sun had set, the coastline was still perceivable, and the lights of cities sparkled below.

"Suddenly," Nash and Fortenberry recalled,

a red brilliance appeared in the air beyond. . . . We saw it together at practically the same moment. . . . It seemed simply to have appeared. . . .

Almost immediately we perceived . . . six bright objects streaking towards us at tremendous speed . . . they had the fiery aspect of hot coals, but of much greater glow—perhaps twenty times more brilliant [than city lights below] . . . their shape was clearly outlined and evidently circular; the edges were well defined, not phosphorescent or fuzzy . . . the red orange color was uniform over the upper surface of each craft.[38]

The single-line echelon of double-DC-3-sized UFOs then unexpectedly seemed to slow down, with the second and third nearly overpassing the lead light. The pilots thought it

looked very much as if an element of "human" or "intelligent" error had been introduced.

All together, they flipped on edge, the sides to the left of us going up and the glowing surfaces facing right . . . they were much like coins . . . then, without an arc or swerve at all, they all flipped back together to the flat altitude [sic] and darted off in a direction that formed a sharp angle with their first course . . . the change . . . was acute . . . [like] a ball ricocheting off a wall.

Immediately . . . two more objects just like them darted out from behind and under our plane . . . joining the first group. . . .[39]

Shortly afterward, the eight UFO's zoomed off, in single file, to the north, disappearing high above the observers. They disappeared nonsequentially, as individual lights blinked out.

But the climax of the July flap was still to come. It began cresting on the night of the nineteenth. Just before midnight, two radar units at National Airport began tracking eight unknowns southeast of Andrews Air Force Base. The UFOs were also seen by the crews of several airlines, tower operators, and others. Jets were scrambled. Nonetheless, Ruppelt later wrote that Air Force Intelligence was never really aware of what was going on.

The headlines read:
INTERCEPTORS CHASE FLYING SAUCERS OVER WASHINGTON, D.C.
And, shortly thereafter:
AIR FORCE WON'T TALK.
"Thus," recalled the head of Project Blue Book, "intelligence was notified about the first Washington national sighting." [40]

At eleven forty, with one man on the long-range Air Route Traffic Control radar unit at Washington National Airport, about three miles from the capital's center, seven unknowns appeared on the screen. They were located to the east-southeast of Andrews Air Force Base and moved in a slow formation. Suddenly, two of the company accelerated from the collective pace of a little more than a hundred miles an hour to "fantastically high speeds." The possibility that they might have been planes was quickly erased from the operator's mind and he called for his superior. The senior controller took a single glance at the scope and summoned two more men. The quartet unanimously reaffirmed the original evaluation. No planes were responsible for the radar readings.

The controller had technicians verify that the equipment was in perfect working order and telephoned the control tower at Washington National to report the unidentified targets. He was told that they were getting the same radar trackings, and so was Andrews Air Force Base. Each of the other sources agreed with the initially slow speeds, followed by extraordinarily high ones. One UFO registered at seven thousand miles an hour.

Ranging through the Washington skies—even over prohibited areas above the White House and the Capitol—the unknowns were seen by the pilots of two airlines. One captain sighted seven UFOs within a quarter hour.

These remarkable activities continued, and at one point all three radar units—Washington National's two and the one at Andrews—locked on a target demonstrably the same just north of the city. It disappeared from all scopes simultaneously.

Later that night, an even more disconcerting incident took place. The Air Route Traffic Control operator, at National Airport, informed Andrews that an unknown was immediately above its radio station. The tower men at the Air Force Base looked up and sighted a great "fiery-orange sphere" suspended above the field. How this unnerving UFO removed itself from the vicinity is somewhat vague.

Several requests for Air Force interceptors to investigate were made during the night, but not until dawn did a belated F-94 appear. Of

course, the UFOs were gone. Disgusted with the total lack of cooperation, Ruppelt flew back to Dayton.

A week later the ufological circumstance recurred. This time Ruppelt
remained unadvised until he was contacted by a *Life* magazine writer
seeking an official comment. In his book the captain recalls he replied:
" 'I have no idea what the Air Force is doing. In all probability . . .
nothing.' "

At about 10:30 on the evening of July 26, the same radar operators
who had monitored the original sighting seven days earlier picked up
several similar slow-moving objects. They semicircled around the capital
from Andrews Air Force Base to Herndon, Virginia, and were clearly
displayed on the large twenty-four-inch screen. A check with the control
tower and Andrews revealed they were also tracking the UFOs.

When, an hour later, four or five unknowns were being continuously
scanned, jet interceptors were ordered aloft. Again, for unexplained reasons, the two assigned F-94's were delayed, but they finally got airborne
by midnight. All civilian air traffic was directed out of the area, and all
reporters and photographers, who had managed to gain entry to the
radar room, were told to leave, "on the pretext," recalled Ruppelt, "that
classified radio frequencies and procedures were being used in vectoring
the interceptors." [41]

The Project Blue Book chief dismissed the justification as "absurd because any ham operator worth his salt could build equipment and listen
in on any intercept." [42] The truth, he was convinced, was simply that the
persons in control of the radar room expected the sighting to develop
into an historic one and they wanted no press in attendance to witness it
firsthand.

Meanwhile, in the skies above, where visibility was excellent, the jets
moved into the target area. Immediately, the UFOs disappeared from
the radar screens. A brief search was conducted, nothing was found, and
the planes returned to base. Within a few minutes, the UFOs were being
tracked again. Subsequently, rotating lights with varying colors were observed to the south. Soon thereafter, the unknowns reappeared on the
radarscopes around Washington.

An F-94 got up in time to make direct visual contact and zeroed in on
the light. Nearing it, the crew saw it apparently vanish, but they picked it
up on radar. However, as they approached even closer, it seemed to hurtle away and vanish. This radar contact was reestablished and broken
twice more. When the plane lost the UFO the final time, it again became
visible to the monitors at the National airport.

Two interceptors went up and spotted the lights. The unknowns remained visible on the scopes below this time, but whenever the F-94's at-

tempted to close in, the UFO instantly accelerated into invisibility. These maneuvers continued until dawn, when the last unknown vanished and it was all over—except for the explanations.

Major Fournet later told Ruppelt that everyone who had been in the radar room during the prolonged episode had concluded that the trackings had probably been of solid, metallic objects. At the same time, weather targets were frequently seen and quickly recognized by the experts attending.

Headlines bannered the event the next morning.
FIERY OBJECTS OUTRUN JETS OVER THE CAPITAL—INVESTIGATION VEILED IN SECRECY FOLLOWING VAIN CHASE.
JETS ALERTED FOR SAUCERS—INTERCEPTORS CHASE LIGHTS IN D.C. SKIES.
Brigadier General Landry, President Truman's air aide, called at ten, which subsequently resulted in the largest and longest Air Force press conference since World War II, although actual witnesses Major Fournet and Lieutenant Holcomb were conspicuous by their absence.

Contrary to baselessly discrediting analyses by Menzel during the succeeding years, even *Life* magazine—no defender of ufology—in its August 4, 1952, issue noted that the scope blips had been monitored by Barry Barnes, senior controller of the radar room, and the equipment thoroughly examined by two expert technicians. Further, pilots, including C. S. Pierman, sighted six lights. "The attitude of the Air Force . . . was puzzling," remarked *Life*. "[It] stated that it had sent none [aircraft] up." But when confronted by *Time-Life* correspondent Clay Blair, Jr. (who penned an Establishmentarian apologia for the prosecution of James Earl Ray seventeen years later), the Air Force admitted fighters had been scrambled.

Why countless persons behaved questionably during the bizarre period remains, in many instances, unanswered. A classic example of such an experience involved a scoutmaster and three Boy Scouts who claimed to have observed an alien-appearing craft during a nocturnal hike in the woods. The lads were queried as was the scoutmaster, who immediately attempted to auction his story to the highest-bidding editor. Ultimately, it was revealed that he was a saucerographic Svengali who had immersed the Scouts in contact stories and then deceived them with secreted rockets to gain their unwitting support for his alleged confrontation.

The possible motivations for the commission of Flying Saucer, or even UFO, hoaxes are many, among the most obvious being an unrewarded need for attention and either a genuine, if silly, sense of humor, or the desire to deceive rooted in a specific or general social antagonism. In a world of doubters, even the man who *knows* something is not true gains a certain nobility—at least, in his own vision. However, the employment of children, quite young children, to aid in the accomplishment of such ends is a rather more ruthless and serious aberration.

Ohio Northern University, in Ada, Ohio, announced the establishment of "Project A," to investigate reports of unidentified flying objects, during August. The objective was to sift the data on various sightings through various of its departments—Physics, Astronomy, Chemistry, Psychology, *et al.*—hoping that such unofficial, independent inspection might open new avenues of understanding. Unfortunately, although locally publicized, the project received but fifty-four reports in its first seven months of activity. This barren period was not succeeded by a better one, and the university appealed to the responsible Flying Saucer societies for reports suitable for analysis.

William Squires, of Pittsburg, Kansas, was driving on a highway during the early morning hours of August 25. As dawn broke, it suddenly revealed a seventy-five-foot-long, forty-five-foot-wide, and fifteen-foot-thick smooth-surfaced, aluminum-colored craft suspended about three yards over a pasture adjoining the highway. Being but a few hundred feet away, Squires noted that the Flying Saucer had a window, through which emanated a blue glow framing the head and shoulders of an apparently male figure. There were other windows midship, and Squires recalled hearing sounds within, human or mechanical. At the rear of the craft, he saw a set of small propellers turning at high speeds. Finally, the Flying Saucer rose until it was obscured by clouds.[43]

Yet, as interesting as the incident described by Mr. Squires was, it could hardly compare with the extraordinary affair known as The Case of the Flatwoods Monster.

"It looked worse than Frankenstein," [44] reported Mrs. Kathleen May, one of the eight inhabitants of Flatwoods, West Virginia, who claimed to have observed an alien being on September 12, 1952.

The Flying Saucer had been discovered by her sons, Eddie, 13, and Fred, 12, who came to her with a story of a craft having landed on the crest of a hill behind their house.

Gene Lemon, a local youth, announced he was going to investigate the matter, and Mrs. May and several other persons decided to accompany him. The band reached the ascribed location within half an hour and discovered a huge robot, with a crimson face, brilliant green eyes, garbed in a robe and hood resembling that of a monk. Beyond the incredible figure was an enormous glowing sphere.

Most of the group took instant flight, but shortly thereafter A. Lee

Stewart, Jr., of the Braxton *Democrat*, followed by Sheriff Robert Carr, arrived at the scene. Both monster and craft were gone.

"If he walks," an Air Force Project Blue Book man is quoted, "he's an Army problem. Let us know when he flies." [45]

The year of 1952 had provided some exceptional foreign sightings, many in the Orient. One over Japan caused considerable excitement among Far East Air Force intelligence personnel, and, by extension, at Blue Book and the Pentagon.

Two control-tower men, walking across the air field, sighted a brilliant moving light. They raced to the tower and from there viewed the UFO through 7 x 50 binoculars. It appeared circular, constant in intensity, and looked to be "the upper portion of a large, round, dark shape which was about four times the diameter of the light itself." [46] As it was being observed, the unknown seemed to approach, became more distinct in its conformation, and evidenced a second, dimmer illumination along the lower edge of the shadowy under-area.

The UFO moved away and disappeared into the night; then it reappeared; vanished again; returned, this time moving toward the Haneda Air Force Base (now Tokyo International Airport). Beginning at about 11:45 P.M., the UFO was tracked by radar. Shortly after midnight, nearby Johnson Air Force Base scrambled an F-94 to investigate. The interceptor soon got a radar contact, which was maintained for a minute and a half, the target seeming to easily out-accelerate the plane. Simultaneously, the UFO went off the ground radarscope. A few moments later the object was seen again by the tower operators, and it reappeared on the radar screen. Suddenly, the former lost sight of it once more and the radar men reported that it had "broken into three pieces," which spaced themselves about a quarter of a mile apart, vanishing into the northest night sky.

". . . the UFO could not be identified as something we knew about. It could have been an interplanetary spaceship," wrote Captain Ruppelt. "Many people thought this was the answer and were all for sticking their necks out and establishing a category of conclusions for UFO reports and labeling it spacecraft. But the majority ruled, and a UFO remained an *unidentified* [his italics] flying object." [47]

Among the more important developments during this period of reexamination was the decision to investigate the possibility that the motion and pattern of motion of UFOs indicated deliberation and intelligent control.

The Tokyo incident had suggested a definite pattern, according to Ruppelt, but a subsequent sighting over Michigan seemed even more designed. Unfortunately, the Air Force neglected to supply the required men and equipment to pursue this line of inquiry.

On September 20, a silver, spherical UFO was photographed by a newspaper reporter from an American aircraft carrier cruising in the North Sea. On the following day, six RAF jet fighter pilots reported they had tailed a shiny round UFO, but lost it. As they returned to base, one of the fliers noted that the object was following them. Chase was given again, but the Meteor fighter was outdistanced once more.

"I was told" recalled Ruppelt, "by an exchange RAF intelligence officer in the Pentagon," that this, and a sighting at Topcliffe Aerodrome, in England, "caused the RAF to officially recognize the UFO." [48] At that time, the Blue Book chief wrote, the betting at the Pentagon and ATIC was "five-to-three in favor of the UFO."

The files of observations from which the panel was to draw its conclusions seemed extensive. Although Ruppelt wrote that the Air Technical Intelligence Center estimated that it had received reports on no more than 10 percent of all sightings made in the United States, since the first days of summer in 1947, when Kenneth Arnold experienced his historic adventure, about 4,500 had flooded into the Air Force. Almost two thirds of these had suffered automatic dismissal, leaving 1,593 to be analyzed by the succession of investigative groups. In its evaluation of the retained sightings the Air Technical Intelligence Center employed three levels of judgment: *Known, Probable, Possible*. These were applied to several categories: *Balloons, Aircraft, Astronomical Bodies, Other* (searchlight effects, birds, weather conditions, etc.), *Hoaxes, Insufficient Data for Evaluation,* and *Unknowns*. Up until the time of the January, 1953, convocation, the Air Force analysis had resulted in the following breakdown: Known Balloons: 1.57 percent; Probable Balloons: 4.99 percent; Possible Balloons: 11.95 percent; totaling 18.51 percent. Known Aircraft: 0.98 percent; Probable Aircraft: 7.74 percent; Possible Aircraft: 3.04 percent; totaling 11.76 percent. Known Astronomical Bodies: 2.79 percent; Probable Astronomical Bodies: 4.01 percent; Possible Astronomical Bodies: 7.40 percent; totaling 14.20 percent. Other Possibilities totaling 4.21 percent; Hoaxes totaling 1.66 percent; Insufficient Data cases totaling 22.72 percent; and Unknowns totaling 26.94 percent.[2]

Unknowns totaling 26.94 percent. Combined with the Insufficient Data group, this indicated that the Air Force, up until that time, had no answer for almost one half of all the sightings it deigned to evaluate, or about 800. If we accept Captain Ruppelt's assertion that the Air Force was getting in no more than about one tenth of all observations of UFOs made in this country, and then project it against this figure, it can be assumed that, from June, 1947, to January, 1953, 8,000 objects had flown through the skies of America without anyone's having the least idea of what they were. Although, even without such a projection, even without the Insufficient Data cases, over 400 UFOs, for which *no* explanation seems adequate, is something upon which to reflect.

Naturally, the character and source of UFO observations affect our evaluation of them. In the group of unknowns cited, 70 percent were visual air-to-air contacts, 12 percent ground-to-air sightings, 10 percent were recorded by radar, and the remainder were combination visual-and-radar responses. Pilots and aircraft personnel comprised a sixth of the viewers, scientists and engineers more than 5.5 percent, while 12.5 percent of the total came through radar. It is rather interesting to note that of the 1,593 UFO reports analyzed, about two thirds originated with women, but of those which remained unexplained—or unknown—more than 90 percent were submitted by men.[3]

After studying all the available material, including reports on sightings, photographs, films, physical and optical analyses, and educated conjectures, the experts came up with a written report. Captain Ruppelt quotes the opening paragraph in his book.

We as a group do not believe that it is impossible for some other celestial body to be inhabited by intelligent creatures. Nor is it impossible that these creatures should have reached such a state of development that they could visit earth. However, there is nothing in all of the so-called flying saucer reports that we have read that would indicate that this is taking place.[4]

Still, having stated this conclusion, the panel issued these recommendations. It suggested that Project Blue Book be continued and quadrupled in size, allowing it to staff experts in meteorology, physics, electronics, photography, and any other subject applicable to the investigation of Unidentified Flying Objects. Special instrumentation should be provided in all areas where sightings occurred with higher-than-average frequency.

Confronted by a problem it could not solve, even after nearly six years' effort; having established a committee of supposedly superqualified authorities to offer suggestions as to a rational course of action; having provided that group with all the available data; and having received from this group the most carefully thought out recommendations—the Air Force again did the only thing it could do. It ignored the recommendations and went bumbling on for more than another decade. The visionary imagination and intellectual objectivity of Chief of Staff, Gen. Hoyt S. Vandenberg, who had arbitrarily discarded the results of an earlier study, which had concluded UFOs were interplanetary, had not been lost on the service.

On January 24, almost two weeks after the impanelling of the scientific jury, the Air Force was conceding that things had gotten a little out of hand halfway around the world. A minor flap had occurred in Japan. *The New York Times* of that date carried the essence of the official release under the words: AIR FORCE UNCONVINCED. HAS NO EVIDENCE LIGHTS OVER JAPAN WERE SOVIET MISSILES was the subheading.

Four days later, on January 28, papers in this country carried the story of another sighting in the same vicinity. DISK SEEN OVER JAPAN, it said; U.S. FLIER REPORTS IT MADE "PASS" AT PLANE IN DAYLIGHT.

A United States pilot saw at close range a mysterious flying disk make a pass at a Thunderjet plane over central Japan, then speed away, the Air Force said yesterday.

The hitherto secret report from intelligence files said the disk was seen at 6,000 feet on a bright, cloudless day, just before noon last March 29 by Lieut. David C. Brigham of Rockford, Ill. Lieutenant Brigham said the disk was about eight inches in diameter and that it closed to within twenty feet of the Thunderjet before shooting out of sight.

It was the second recent disclosure of mysterious objects in the skies of Japan near Russian-held territory. Last week the Air Force made public intelligence reports of "rotating clusters of red, white and green lights, sighted December 29 by U. S. airmen." [5]

Whether this last observation was the one originally announced on January 24, or whether that was an entirely separate sighting, was not made clear in the American coverage.

However, it was not necessary to unravel the tangled web the Air Force was weaving in the Far East to keep abreast of UFO developments. On the midnight of January 28, the Georgia heavens produced an exceptional encounter.

During a routine base-to-base flight, the pilot of an F-86 was cruising at about six thousand feet when he sighted a brilliant white light above him and to his left. Although the stars were clearly visible and the intensity of the UFO made it easily distinguishable, he decided it must be a star, after all, or another plane. Yet he was not satisfied with his estimate. The object appeared too definite in its circularity.

Climbing toward the light, he passed above the UFO, and it became obvious that it had moved with relationship to the stars. This left only the possibility of an aircraft whose lights were not visible for some reason.

He accelerated and started to close the distance between the object and the F-86. Still, although the UFO increased in size as the distance diminished, no wing lights could be seen. Unexpectedly, the great white light changed color, and was red; then it became white again, then red . . . pulsating several times. Suddenly, the glowing circle re-formed into a brilliant triangle, from which it split into two objects of the same shape, one over the other. Finally, without warning, it vanished.

Realizing that he had consumed a considerable amount of fuel, he decided to forego one of his touchpoints and return to base. Confirming his flight change with the ground, he was surprised to be asked if he had seen the mysterious light. The operator told him that the object had been tracked by radar. It had been classified as a UFO because of its less-than-aircraft speed. As it was being monitored, the F-86 had moved onto the scope, closing in on the light. Radar revealed that, as the plane increased its speed, so did the UFO, just enough to maintain a comfortable lead. However, after a few minutes of this stabilized chase the object accelerated tremendously and disappeared.

On January 26, a letter on Defense Department stationery was sent to the publisher of Major Keyhoe's startling Flying Saucer surveys[6] by Air Force UFO spokesman Albert M. Chop. The final paragraph read:

The Air Force, and its investigating agency, "Project Blue Book," are aware of Major Keyhoe's conclusions that the "Flying Saucers" are from another planet. The Air Force has never denied that this possibility exists. Some of the personnel believe that there may be some strange natural phenomena completely unknown to us, but if the apparently controlled maneuvers reported by many competent observers are correct, then the only remaining explanation is the interplanetary answer.[7]

Still, for all of this seemingly feverish celestial activity, 1953 was one of the quieter years. The National Investigations Committee on Aerial Phenomena's year-by-year breakdown of *flaps* (periods of intensified press coverage) and *concentrations* (periods when the actual number of reports increases) shows that 1953 registered neither to any appreciable degree.

However, if there was a relative numeric lull overhead, here on earth strange appearances were taking place. Space persons were beginning to unmask, admitting their true identity. It must be granted that they were not from the outer reaches of the solar system, but, nonetheless, they were to create a great stir for years to come. They were the original emissaries of the Flying Saucer occupants. They were the first contactees.

George Adamski was unquestionably one of the most important figures to arise in the pantheon of contactology. A self-described "philosopher, student, teacher, saucer researcher," [8] he may be regarded as one of the founding Titans of the mythology of Flying Saucers.

The reports of Adamski's background do not always coincide, but one version has him the son of "a Polish father and an Egyptian mother," who "served two enlistments in the U. S. Army prior and during" the First World War.[9] He appears to have settled in the Los Angeles area in the late twenties, later moving to Laguna Beach, during which time he began presenting himself as an authority, disciple, and even *master* of highly esoteric Oriental philosophy.

The highlight of Adamski's career in Eastern esoterics was the writing and publication of a curious little sixty-seven-page book. Boasting a title page emblazoned with a torch, two clasped hands, the legend "Christ," and a banner with the words "Royal Order of Tibet," all contrived into a centered emblem, it is called *Questions and Answers by The Royal Order of Tibet,* and numbered "Vol. 1." The Royal Order of Tibet, which one suspects had "Professor G. Adamski" not merely as the "compiler" of its holy writ but as its entire membership, is listed as publisher and holder of the copyright of this issue.

While this text, from The Royal Order of Tibet, via "Professor G. Adamski," anticipates some of the later saucerological philosophy of the author, nowhere does it suggest his final and greater career: ambassador for the people from outer space. However, before one is inclined to accept the assurance found in the later work, coauthored, in the early fifties, with English saucerologist Desmond Leslie,[10] namely, that the subject of "interplanetary travel in man-made [sic] ships had never entered [his] mind," it must be noted that Adamski's fiction work *Pioneers of Space* anticipated in time and tale his subsequent Flying-Saucer works.

Around 1944, the practical philosopher took up residence "on the southern slopes of Mount Palomar" in California, only seven miles from the Hale Observatory, with its world-famous 200-inch telescope. It was this accidental, or astute, choice of habitat which caused many of his subsequent followers to infer a connection between the two; an association which, of course, never existed. Yet, Adamski did have a serious interest in astronomy and eventually acquired an impressive 15-inch reflecting telescope which he "housed under a dome."

His baptism in belief occurred on October 9, 1946, conveniently, if belatedly (Adamski's account of his sighting was published a year after *The Coming of the Saucers*),[11] predating Kenneth Arnold's experience by almost a year. As described, the amateur philosopher-astronomer was observing a meteoric shower when he "actually saw with [his] naked eyes a gigantic space craft hovering high above the mountain ridge to the south of Mount Palomar, toward San Diego." The "large black object, similar in shape to a gigantic dirigible, and apparently motionless," seemed to have no "cabin compartment or external appendages." (The resemblance to the historic sightings of 1897 is evident.) As he continued watching, the unknown suddenly "pointed its nose upward and quickly shot up into space, leaving a fiery trail behind it which remained visible for a good five minutes."[12]

Ten months later, in August of 1947, he experienced a second sighting when "a bright light object appeared, moving through the sky from east to west above the mountain ridge to the south. And then another! And another. . . . Suddenly one of the objects stopped in mid-space and reversed its path of travel, and I said to myself, 'This must be what they call a flying saucer.' "[13]

Summoning four witnesses from indoors, Adamski counted 184 UFOs in single file, although he asserted that they were "moving in squadrons of thirty-two." This indicates that there were five groups—each with a "leader," he tells us, plus nineteen stragglers.

A man named Tony Belmonte, and some friends, watched the aerial objects from another angle. They counted 204, which accounts for six squadrons, but still leaves an extra half dozen loners in the sky.

In 1949, Adamski later claimed, he was approached by J. P. Maxfield and G. L. Bloom, "both of the Point Loma Navy Electronics Laboratory near San Diego," plus two other men "from a similar setup in Pasadena," asking if he would cooperate in the collective attempt to get "photographs of the strange craft moving through space." Of course, the results of his efforts have never been publicly accepted as authentic by the official establishment, or a recognized scientific organization, but they have attracted the acceptance of tens of thousands of saucerites around the world and the attention of much of the press and public.

By this time, the money from saucer sources had begun to trickle in. Adamski gave talks before small groups, published an article in *Fate*, the magazine of the improbable, and began selling prints of his curious photographs. By 1953, although having had "700 tries" at catching the elusive objects on film to his credit, he had compiled a file of only 18 really "good" shots (other saucerologists were content with even one).

However, notwithstanding the interest aroused by his original sightings and photographs, Adamski really laid the foundation for his subsequent stature as a saucerological figure on Thursday, November 20, 1952. It was on that date that he made his initial physical contact with the mysterious craft from outer space—and one of its occupants! While not the first contactee, he more than anyone up to that time succeeded in parlaying his purported experience into a personal mythology.

The incident was prefaced by a visit to Palomar Gardens by Mr. and Mrs. A. C. Bailey of Winslow, Arizona, who told Adamski that they and two friends, Dr. and Mrs. George Hunt Williamson, of Prescott, Arizona, would like to observe his next attempt to establish contact with the strange vessels.

Agreeing, the saucerite soon advised the quartet that the event would occur on the early morning of Thursday, November 20, 1952, at a location just west of Blythe, California.

The appointed morning arrived, and Adamski, accompanied by Mrs. Alice K. Wells, owner of the Palomar Gardens café, and Mrs. Lucy McGinnis, met with the others, and the group began to seek out an appropriate site for the desired encounter. Finally, at about 11:00 A.M., they stopped on the road leading to Parker, Arizona, some eleven miles from Desert Centre.

More than an hour passed as the members of the party wandered about the immediate area examining the flora and minerals.

"Suddenly and simultaneously," reported Adamski later, "we all turned as one, looking again toward the closest mountain ridge. Riding high, and without sound, there was a gigantic cigar-shaped silvery ship, without wings or appendages of any kind; slowly, almost as if it was drifting, it came in our direction; then seemed to stop, hovering motionless." [14]

"Take me down the road—quick!" he urged, leaping into the automobile. In moments, he and Mr. Bailey were being driven along the highway by Mrs. McGinnis. Overhead, the great, silent craft followed. After a few minutes, the saucerologist selected what seemed to him a suitable location, and they stopped. The vessel still loomed above.

Instructing his two companions to rejoin the others, Adamski stationed himself and prepared to wait for a possible contact. As the car moved away, the cigar-shaped ship began to drift toward the mountains, crossed over them, and disappeared.

No more than five minutes had elapsed when Adamski caught sight of a "flash in the sky," and almost immediately it assumed the shape of a "beautiful small craft." Without wasting time to focus properly, Adamski set up the camera he had brought with him and snapped shots as rapidly as he could before the scout ship withdrew through the gap in the mountain range through which it had originally emerged.

Waiting, anticipating the possibility of further activity on the part of the spacecraft, his attention was suddenly drawn to a figure about five hundred feet off. The new arrival waved Adamski toward him.

As the distance between them diminished, Adamski noted that the man, for a man it seemed to be, was somewhat smaller—about 5 feet 6 inches and 135 pounds—and considerably younger, perhaps in his late twenties, than he. He wore a chocolate-brown, uniformlike outfit of fine, glossy material. The trousers were similar to ski pants, and no zippers, buckles, pockets, or seams, were visible.

"Suddenly," Adamski later recalled, "as though a veil was removed from my mind . . . I fully realized that I was in the presence of . . . A HUMAN BEING FROM ANOTHER WORLD!" Struck by the visitor's aspect, the saucerologist knew that "the beauty of his form surpassed anything I had ever seen . . . [he] felt like a child in the presence of one with great wisdom and much love."

They touched hands in friendship and immediately Adamski was aware that the "flesh of his hand . . . was like a baby's . . . delicate . . . [but] firm and warm." Long tapering fingers reminded the Earthian of "the beautiful hands of an artistic woman. In fact," he decided, "he could have easily passed for an unusually beautiful woman."

The two strangers having completed their visual appraisals, the *conversation* was begun. As the spaceman spoke no English, this exchange consisted of *telepathy* and sign language. The latter technique sufficed to establish that the pair were on the Earth (which Adamski implies he knew all along) and that the visitor had come from Venus. In response to the contactee's question about the reason for his arrival, the extraterrestrial indicated that his people were concerned "with radiation going out from Earth." A brief dialogue revealed that the nuclear explosions were contaminating outer space, and that we were likely to blow ourselves out of existence, and that, in general, the planets from the blue beyond thought we were putting on an all-around bad show. Needless to say, our man didn't have much of a rebuttal available.

Further exchanges revealed that the Venusian had arrived in a scout ship, a craft of the design most readily pictured in response to the term *Flying Saucer*, and that it, in turn, had been conveyed across immeasurable reaches of space in a supervessel—the great silver cigar-shaped argosy observed earlier by Adamski and his group.

As the time drew near for the spacian to depart, Adamski attempted to get a closer look, and a clearer impression, of the vehicle. He described it as having a translucent quality and speculated that it may have been constructed from a diamondlike material, derived from subjecting carbon to ultraintense heats and pressures. "The splendour" of it, flashing "prismatic colours in the sunlight surpassed every idea [he] had ever had about space craft," as well as impressing "the six others who maintained a steady watch from a distance."

The external aspect of the scout ship seems to have been fairly simple. It was "a beautiful small craft, shaped more like a heavy glass bell than a saucer . . . translucent and of an exquisite colour." The vessel was crowned "by a round ball at the very top that looked like a heavy lens of some kind. And it glowed." Adamski thought this might be "one end of a magnetic pole to draw their power from space as they were moving through it." Also "the top of the craft was dome-shaped, with a ring of gears or heavy coil built into and circling the side wall at the base of this domed top. This, too, glowed as though power was going through it."

Along the outer surface of the scout ship were "round portholes," but they did not completely encircle it; above "one of the balls of landing gear" Adamski observed the vessel's shell was solid. Through one of these windows, which, as differing from the translucence of the body of the ship, were "clear and transparent," Adamski was privileged to catch a fleeting glance of another "beautiful face." He gathered that it was a crew member checking on his companion outside.

Toward the end of the curious exchange the visitor conveyed to Adamski that there were a number of his kind living on Earth, disguised as human, or, anyway, terrestrial, beings. Asked if inhabitants of this planet were ever abducted by Flying Saucers, he is reputed to have "smiled broadly." These two words, sown in the presumably barren desert of Arizona, were later to offer a heavy harvest.[15]

Finally, after the Venusian declined to be photographed and rejected the suggestion of taking Adamski for a joy ride then and there, the ship and crew rose silently, drifted out across the mountain ridge, and disappeared.

Local newspapers carried stories of the adventures of George Adamski and company, but they were not to be compared with the broad publicity given the contactee in later years.

Chapter 6

CONSPIRACIES AND CONTACTEES

"The mystery of the flying saucers is no longer a mystery. The source is already known, but any information about this is being withheld by orders from a higher source . . . we advise those engaged in saucer work to please be cautious," wrote Albert K. Bender, in *Space Review,* the official organ of the International Flying Saucer Bureau, which he had founded. The issue in which the admonition appeared was the last to be published, and it signaled the conclusion of the growing IFSB and the silence of the noted saucerologist from Bridgeport, Connecticut. "A source which the IFSB considers very reliable has informed us that the investigation of the flying saucer mystery and solution is approaching its final stages. The same source to whom we had referred data, which had come into our possession, suggested that it was not the proper method and time to publish this data in *Space Review* . . ." Although a brief mimeo sheet did follow this last edition of the printed magazine, it was not concerned with flying saucers.[1]

Mr. Bender subsequently told the Bridgeport *Sunday Herald*[2] that "three men wearing dark suits" visited his home, identifying themselves as agents of the "higher authority," and questioned him about the operations of the International Flying Saucer Bureau. The conclusion of the interview had the anonymous harbingers of apprehension telling the saucerite "not roughly, but sternly and emphatically" to cease the publication of material pertaining to aerial enigmas. "I was scared to death," recalled Bender, "and actually couldn't eat for a couple of days."

Many members of the IFSB effort, including well-known saucerologists Gray Barker, August Roberts, and Dominic Lucchesi, accepted the report of the "three men in black," as they have since been called. Other inquirers, equally prominent, including James Moseley, editor of the *Saucer News,* have expressed greater scepticism. In 1956, Moseley said:

I was inclined to feel that the alleged hush-up must have been a cover-up for some personal reasons Bender might have had for closing down his club. Perhaps the IFSB was in the red financially; perhaps the paper work involved in running such a large organization had been too much for him, and he had sought a dramatic way to get out from under; or perhaps the man was psychoneurotic in some way, and had misconstrued an innocent visit from government officials, due to a "persecution complex." [3]

Examining the "silence" thesis further, Moseley noted that there had been several other cases of individuals withdrawing from saucer research, noting, in particular, John E. Stuart, of New Zealand, who was supposed to have acquired a UFO fragment, only to have it taken by a stranger; Edgar R. Jerrald, director of the Australian Flying Saucer Bureau, who received a visit from an unknown man and soon dropped from the investigative scene; and Eliot Rockmore, of Brooklyn, who purportedly came upon a craft artifact, was questioned by "some sort of government agent," and abandoned his inquiries. (He, however, returned to the research later.) [4]

After years of implications and innuendos by Gray Barker as to what actually silenced Albert K. Bender and the International Flying Saucer Bureau and as to who the enigmatic "three men in black" might have been, Bender published a book in 1963, revealing the allegedly true explanation of the mysterious machinations.[5] Now Bender knew the solution of the sorcery of the saucers, but he was not permitted to reveal his knowledge, and what hints he scattered only confused his friends.

It was an intriguing manuscript.

Three beautiful women, dressed in tight white uniforms . . . approached me . . . they were physically attractive, even though they had the same glowing eyes [as the male visitors] which . . . seemed to pervade my entire person . . . then my body suddenly became rigid and I could not move a single muscle . . . I became frightened . . . my fright [then] changed to embarrassment as I felt their hands begin to remove my clothing, I . . . could do nothing to stop them, for I was as stiff as a board. [These euphemisms are as frequent as they are obvious.] With great efficiency they removed every piece of my clothing, leaving me as naked as the day I was born . . . [they produced] a vial containing a liquid which they poured over my body. Then the three massaged the liquid into my skin. As they did so my body became warm as if heat were being applied. They massaged every part of my body without exception . . .[6]

In 1967, a Flying Saucer publication suggested that even Morris K. Jessup, well-known ufologist and author of books on the subject, "may have ignored the warning of the dark trio. . . . Jessup was found dead in his automobile in a Florida park in 1959." This demonstrates how far the tentacles of a monster myth will reach. Jessup, who had some severe personal problems, contacted Long John Nebel just before his death, suggesting that he was seriously considering suicide. He requested that, should such a tragic course be pursued by him, a séance be conducted on Mr. Nebel's all-night radio program. The purpose of this plan was to give John, who had assisted him in a number of ways, the incredible story, should such a return prove possible. The program, completely arranged and about to go on the air, was aborted by Mr. Nebel's attorney, who felt that the privacy of certain persons might be violated.

Hoaxes are not unusual in saucerology; among contactees they might even be regarded as common.

On June 8, 1953, an Atlanta barber wagered ten dollars that he could get his name into the community newspapers.

Purchasing a monkey for fifty dollars at a local pet shop, he shaved the poor creature's entire body, bashed in its head, and cut off its tail. He then took the animal's cadaver and, accompanied by two equally ghoulish friends, drove a few miles from town and deposited it upon the highway.

An automobile soon approached and the barbarous barber wildly waved it to a stop, excitedly telling the driver of having seen a Flying Saucer land and three occupants disembark. His arrival had startled the aliens and they had fled back to their craft, he told the motorist, but unfortunately one had been struck by his car. He pointed to the body of the monkey. The saucer, of course, had taken flight just prior to the new driver's appearance on the scene.

Needless to say, the story did make the nearby periodicals, and the morbid prankster presumably collected his ten dollars. He persisted in his hoax for a few days. However, when some scientifically trained observers examined the corpse, it was immediately identified and the barber conceded the fraudulence of his report. A local court imposed a forty-dollar fine for cluttering up a public highway with the body of a dead animal. The financial penalty, plus the price of the monkey totaled at least ninety dollars, not to mention the time and effort expended—all to collect a ten-dollar bet and establish himself as a rather distasteful footnote in the Age of Flying Saucers.[7]

The Age of Flying Saucers was taking even wilder turns. A saucerian magazine report of November, 1953, told of a man named Kames Greer, who lived on a farm near Zanesville, Ohio, being abducted by a "something" in the sky, which disappeared in an explosion of light hurtling northeast. This purported incident was merely another of a long series of "spacenapping" reports found in saucerology long before the widely publicized case of Betty and Barney Hill, which so impressed the saucerologically ill-informed fifteen years later.

An even more elaborate example of this aspect of the Flying-Saucer scene was being discussed before the year was over.

Karl Hunrath and Jack Wilkinson disappeared during November, 1953, in a West Coast mystery comparable to the Bender affair. The James Moseley report on this case may have been the best. The researcher got his version from Mr. Jerrold Baker, who had been personally acquainted with the two men.

Baker first met Hunrath at Adamski's Palomar Gardens home, in November of 1952. Hunrath and George Hunt Williamson were forming an "Adamski Foundation" under the contactee's direction. Hunrath was characterized as the designer of an instrument which could cause breakdowns in Flying Saucers, and consequently force them to land.

As the Adamski Foundation was diverted into metaphysics, Williamson would lapse into trances and allegedly receive space messages in an "unnatural" voice, sometimes speaking in a totally unfamiliar language. Afterward the psychic contactee would interpret the syllables into hieroglyphs based upon "his knowledge of ancient symbology."

In January, 1953, Hunrath, Williamson, and Baker fell out with Adamski and abandoned Palomar Gardens and "foundation," but, according to Moseley, all became convinced that they themselves were spacemen! This was apparently an idea instilled by Adamski, and channeled by Williamson to Baker, Hunrath, and Wilkinson. Baker was *Markon*, Williamson was *Mark III*, etc.

Baker went away, only to return and find that Hunrath and Wilkinson had disappeared, a few days earlier, while flying a rented plane to their saucer rendezvous. Since then, many conflicting rumors have arisen, but allegedly no definite evidence exists that Hunrath, Wilkinson, or their plane was ever seen again. Baker soon abandoned his idea of being a spaceman; however, for a long time he believed that if Hunrath and Wilkinson did not crash on this planet and die, they would be alive on Mars.

"The balance of evidence seems to favor the opinion that the men are dead," concluded James Moseley, who added Hunrath's and Wilkinson's names to those of Captain Mantell and several others ". . . [who] go down in saucer history . . . [as having] lost their lives directly or indirectly due to the elusive flying saucers." [8]

The final month of 1953 began with John Otto addressing the Chicago Rocket Society, on the fourth, on the subject of visitors from other worlds. It concluded with the conviction, on December 29 (according to the Denver *Post*), of Silas M. Newton and Leo A. GeBauer, of Denver University and Frank Scully's book fame, on charges of operating a confidence game.

A new era of ufology had developed into craft-conscious saucerism, which, in turn, began to emphasize landings, extraplanetarians, direct contacts, and rides in spaceships. However, more serious reports continued to flood the files.

The month of February saw important reports in many different areas. For example:

February 1—at Terre Haute, Indiana: sighting by a T-33 pilot;

February 4—at Pittsburg, Kansas: object with blue-light portholes;

February 6—at Rosalie, Washington: UFO with flashing light circled B-36; while at Truk Island, in the Pacific, a glistening, metallic unknown was sighted by a weather expert;

February 7—over Korea: an F-94 pilot lost a chase with an intense orange UFO;

February 13—at Fort Worth, Texas: radar and visual monitoring of strange objects;

February 22—at Erie, Pennsylvania: a one-time Navy gunner and active plane spotter reported a luminous silver disc approximately fifty yards wide.

So the reports rolled in, not merely in February, but throughout the year and the years to come, and because of the frequency of the sightings, no attempt will be made to maintain a full chronicle.

The social aspects of saucerism took active forms. Among the most intriguing were "conventions." The first of these was held in Los Angeles, during August, 1953. This was followed by "The World's First Interplanetary Spacecraft Convention," on April 4, 1954. It was organized by George W. Van Tassel, at Giant Rock, California. Participating were the host, Frank Scully, Orfeo Angelucci, George Hunt Williamson, Truman Bethurum, Daniel W. Fry, and others.

The First Annual Flying Saucer Convention was conducted from June 4 to June 6, in Los Angeles. Presented by the Saucer Research Foundation of Los Angeles, it featured Fry, Angelucci, psychic-phenomena researcher Felix Fraser, and the seer Jeron King Criswell. Various film clips from science-fiction movies were shown at the meeting.

Dr. Harold Percy Wilkins, F.R.A.S., Director of the British Astronomical Association, one of the foremost living astronomers,[9] recorded that, while a confirmed unbeliever, on June 11, 1954, during a flight along the eastern seaboard of the United States, he personally saw over a period of two minutes an oval, clearly defined, goldish, metallic-looking UFO, about fifty feet in diameter, and moving at speeds of more than two hundred miles an hour. He subsequently wrote that if, in fact, such UFOs are solid objects, functioning aerodynamically as they appear to, "then they must have been devised and [be] operated and controlled by intelligence superior to man."

The British Air Ministry, on July 2, was reportedly investigating a story that had an English commercial plane being escorted for eighty miles, off Labrador, by a large dark unknown of indeterminate and/or varying shape, which was attended by half a dozen lesser objects. The London *Daily Express* accompanied the report with the observation that "Mars is closer to the Earth this week than at any time since 1939."

On the fifth, Berliners watched the flight of three small circular objects, while, in Canada, two days later, a stranger tale was being told.

A report out of Garson, Ontario, had a young Canadian miner describing a Flying Saucer and three occupants, each over a dozen feet tall, with "ears like spurs" and a triple set of arms. The twenty-five-year-old Ennio LaSarza reputedly told a Royal Canadian Air Force investigator that he saw the craft land and the crew exit from it. "They fixed me with a hypnotic stare until I fainted," he asserted, "when I came to they said the ship had vanished."

Across the border, later that month, Dr. Frank Halstead, astronomer at the Darling Observatory in Duluth, reportedly told a newspaper reporter that "many professional astronomers are convinced that the saucers are interplanetary machines. . . . I think they come from another solar system, but they may be using Mars as a base." [10] And on July 9, a supervisor of the Ground Observer Corp, a civilian auxiliary to the Air Force, revealed that more than one hundred UFOs had been registered over Wilmington, Delaware, during the previous two years.

British Air Marshal Lord Dowding, RAF leader during World War II, wrote in July 1954, for a British newspaper.

"I am convinced that these objects do exist and that they are not manufactured by any nation on Earth. I can, therefore, see no alternative to accepting the theory that they come from some extraterrestrial source." [11]

As a matter of fact, even as early as 1954, saucerists had reached the stage of having developed a sense of humor. The August issue of *Nexus* that year carried a several-page report titled "I Spoke with an Earthman," by Melvin Morbid, Flight Leader 669, Squad 8, planet Masar (Code 3), which described a sometime space pilot taking a brisk spin to the planet Filth, and an encounter between the Masarian and "John Adams Sky," an obvious parody on George Adamski, and happily spoofed the entire contactee cult. Outside the sphere of saucers, treating the subject in any but a ridiculing way was likely to prove hazardous. In the summer of the year, famous long-time Mutual Broadcasting System commentator Frank Edwards was fired by his sponsor, The American Federation of Labor. Years later, Frank told the author that he had been advised to abandon his interest in saucerology, at least as broadcast material, and he had no doubt that his refusal to do so had been the reason for the incident.

The second half of 1954 provided saucerites with a wealth of foreign sightings, and, of more interest, landings and contacts.

Cesar Feriera, a landowner of Castelibranco, Portugal, claimed that on September 29 he saw a "flying cup" land and "two eight-foot giants clad in pocketless metallic suits" emerge, collect vegetation, and return to their craft and hurtle away. The Madrid newspaper *Arriba* purportedly identified Flying Saucers as merely missiles, planes, and bombs of the United States, unless, that is, they originated in the Soviet Union. In Rome, a zeppelintype object, flying at three thousand feet, was reportedly viewed by several thousand people while simultaneously being tracked on radar. Drifting slowly at first, the silver-and-red craft was said to have plummeted toward the Earth at one point, and then vanished into the upper atmosphere at a tremendous speed. And France was not to be outdone. . . .

Maurice deWilde, a French steelworker, asserted he saw thirty-six-inch, wide-shouldered, armless, space-helmeted creatures conducting a "black mass" near his home. Approaching them, he was blinded by an emerald light from their craft, into which they fled and in which they disappeared in the night sky. However, at this point the French were excelling in such contactee stories. In Chatterault, a man named Yves David claimed to have been caressed and green-rayed into partial paralysis by an extra-Earthian who abandoned him for an outbound saucer. In Bugeat, Antoine Masaud supposedly was accosted, kissed, addressed, and deserted by a similarly affectionate spaceman. The stories from France that year were legion, if not legend.

The English, naturally, constructed their episodes on less volatile themes. In London, John Foster Forbes gave a lecture in August and proposed that his listeners attempt to establish a telepathic tryst with Venusians. On the appointed day, September 19, the Venusians, reflecting the tasteful restraint of their hosts, succumbed to no tawdry flamboyance of flashy landings which might have reduced the serious intent to a carnival atmosphere.

However, such social delicacy was not to interfere with Gallic escapades. On October 8, M. Garreau, of Chaleix, France, encountered khaki-clad saucer occupants who admired his dog. A week later, Damien Sigueres, a resident of Perpignan, contradicted the "caninephilic" characterization in his story of a large red sphere and a pilot, in a diver's-type suit, who fled to his craft and took off at the sight of the Frenchman's dogs.

In Montluçon, a railroad worker supposedly caught the pilot of a four-yard bullet-vessel filching diesel oil from the yard tank. The Earthian was later unable to state positively whether the visitor was coated with long hair or wearing a long hairy overcoat.

The French reports were endless, fascinating, and amusing. "I'll be seeing you," cried one extraterrestrial, leaping into his saucer, while another wore an enormous moustache and spoke Latin. A third, notwithstanding his being described as zebra-striped, was also supposed to have varied color from yellow to green, as if subject to continual chemical transition. Literally scores of communities claimed nearly as colorful visitations. Even *Le Figaro* carried a story of the initial saucers seen on the Riviera, *France Soir* told of spacecraft flying between Poitevin, Marais and La Rochette, and the *Paris Presse* told of a moustached Martian weekending in Vienna.

Perhaps the variety of French attitudes was best summed up by the order issued by the mayor of Châteauneuf-du-Pape, on October 27, which forbade the landing of flying saucers and directed the impounding of any spacecraft ignoring injunction, while in Brittany, an innkeeper advertised a reward of $35,000 for a live Martian.

The Age of Flying Saucers was reaching all around the world.

Dr. Marcos Guerci, chief of the Argentine Meteorological Service, Carlos Bassoli, a control-tower operator, and numerous others reported that on November 25, two luminous UFOs, one apparently semicircular and the other circular, hovered over Córdoba, in Argentina, for almost an hour. According to a Reuters dispatch sent from Nairobi on October 15, 1954, Dr. G. Duncan Fletcher, vice-president of the Astronomical Society of Kenya, reported observing a craftlike object which, the report said, the astronomer suspected to be an extraplanetary machine.

In the Middle East, Tehran's leading daily newspaper *Ettela'at* carried a report, on October 15, of a hemispherical, rainbow-radiant saucer descending near Mahallat. This was followed by another story, from Shamsabad, India, of a device resembling a brilliant star. In the latter instance a laughing pilot was observed. However, neither of these was to be compared with the occurrence in Amireah Street, in Tehran itself.

According to the newspaper, a man named Ghaseme Fili saw a glowing object from the second story of his house. Inside the strange craft, Mr. Fili perceived a black-garbed man boasting an improbable mask with a trunk like that of an elephant. He recalled that, standing on his balcony, he "suddenly felt as though . . . being drawn up towards the object as though by a magnet." [12] The Earthman's terrified protestations aroused his neighbors, and the luminous craft flashed into the oblivion of the night heavens.

Curiously, the description of a trunk mask was not unique. Such characterizations are found in reports from various parts of Europe, as well as elsewhere.

Needless to say, the fascination with Unidentified Flying Objects steadily increased in the United States. A poll conducted by *Saucers* during the autumn of 1954 concluded that enthusiasts regarded Major Keyhoe as the "best author of flying saucer material," according him two thirds of the vote; Adamski, Leslie, Scully, and Fry, in that order, shared the remaining third. Keyhoe's *Flying Saucers from Outer Space* collected half of all the ballots in the "best book" category, with the Adamski/Leslie *Flying Saucers Have Landed* and Bethurum's *Aboard a Flying Saucer* each garnering 16.5 percent. Frank Edwards was overwhelmingly commended, by 75 percent of the voters, as the newsman giving the best flying-saucer coverage, and Keyhoe, Adamski, and Scully shared equally as the "personalities" who had done most for the subject of Flying Saucers.

Two of the more intriguing aspects of the growing world of saucers—especially contactology—were the emergence and ranking of messianic figures, and the constant maneuvering and battles, though camouflaged, for positions and disciples. One, eventually to be consigned to a tertiary tier among the saucer peerage, was John Otto.

Appearing on WGN, a Chicago radio station, on November 28, Otto requested that the program moderator deliver an announcement at precisely 11:15 A.M., "Chicago Earth time," which the saucerite had prepared. In part, it read:

This is Jim Mills. I invite you and those in flying discs . . . to stand by for a message from . . . Earth! We desire to communicate with you. . . . Earth listeners . . . maintain complete silence at 11:25 and report anything you hear or see to me, Jim Mills, WGN Chicago, by letter or postcard. Thank you.

Shortly thereafter, report has it at 11:25, Mr. Mills cued in the visitors from other worlds.

"One second—two—three—zero! Come in, outer space." It is recorded that the station was flooded with calls, but nothing of pertinence seemed to arise from the experiment. Well, *almost* nothing, according to Otto. Apparently, enlisting the aid of Mildred and Marie Maier, he had prearranged to wire-record the program, and upon replaying the broadcast, he says, a powerful television kind of transmission, with musical overtones, virtually obliterated the program and the moderator's voice.

Others are supposed to have subsequently heard this remarkable recording and found it to sound like a teletype transmission, with harmonic grace notes.

Truman Bethurum, a much more important figure in the hierarchy, broadened his base considerably in 1954, with the publication of his adventure under the title *Aboard a Flying Saucer.*

The contactee was born at Gavalin, California, August 21, 1898. He attended school irregularly, was employed in a defense plant during World War II, was married in July, 1945, and, following the war, did construction, repair, and maintenance work. Although Bethurum characterizes himself as a construction engineer, analytical researcher, and "reader, analyst and appraiser of unseen human vibrations," [13] his professional allusions are rather casual.

According to the contactee, he "first became initiated into what might be called 'The Saucer Seers' on the night of July 28, 1952, while out one evening collecting sea shells in the desert." [14] The effort proved tiring, and Bethurum decided to nap in the cab of his truck. Shortly thereafter he was awakened by "about eight or ten small sized men . . . from four feet eight inches to about five feet tall." [15] They were well developed, with faces of taut olive skin, and each wore a uniform. One approached Bethurum, addressing him in alien speech. Failing to communicate, he tried again.

"You name it," he suggested.

"My God! You can speak English too," exclaimed the welder, only to be assured that extraterrestrials "have no difficulty with any language." [16]

Bethurum descended from his truck and saw a type of Flying Saucer, which he later discovered the visitors called "Clarion's Hollow Wheels." It was a great, round wonder of burnished steel, measuring about three hundred feet across and eighteen feet deep. Encircled in a yard-wide rim of beveled steel, and featuring no wings or other appurtenances, it hovered silently a few feet above the scruffy desert brush.

One of the saucerians invited the contactee to meet "our captain in our scow." As they approached the floating vessel, it tilted to make the entrance steps, which suddenly appeared, accessible. Bethurum had observed no transmission of instructions and therefore concluded the reception had been motivated telepathically. The earthman and the alien boarded the craft, moved along a narrow companionway, and entered an elegantly furnished captain's quarters.

A beautiful woman, commander of the scow, was awaiting their arrival. Her skin was olive, her eyes brown, her cropped hair black, and she wore a short-sleeved, fitted bodice of black velvetlike material and a "radiant red" pleated skirt of a woolly texture.

Responding to a question from the contactee, she explained that she and her crew were interplanetarians, whose initial arrival on this planet was of recent date. She identified her vessel as an "Admirals' Scow," but one of many. The subsequent conversation was singularly unexciting, considering the participants were a knowledge-seeking Earthian and an alien from outer space, but the captainess smiled a lot and was properly enigmatic, and that seemed to satisfy our man in the desert. At dawn, the scow disappeared into the bright sky "like a vaporized pearl."

A second sighting followed a week later. On this occasion Bethurum discovered that the aliens' home planet had no illnesses, doctors or nurses, nor mechanics, nor laborers, as "they only mean trouble, so you see they are all taboo." The captain also dismissed dams, lakes, rivers, automobiles, airplanes, cities, farms, all military organizations, atomic devices, politics, and taxes. Her comments on voting reflected one of the ubiquitous threads running through almost the entire tapestry of contactology: "With so many politicians, voting seems hardly worthwhile."

The scow's third visit, on August 18, afforded the welder an opportunity to finally ascertain his Circe's name. It was Aura Rhanes. It seemed about time, since he regarded her "as tops in shapeliness and beauty," notwithstanding her revelation that she was a grandmother. Aura Rhanes explained on a subsequent visit that her planet, Clarion, was "entirely invisible from earth, since it was [unvaryingly] on the other side of the moon." [17]

All of Bethurum's experiences with Captain Aura Rhanes were not confined to the Flying Saucer. Once, when he approached her drinking orange juice in a restaurant, she ignored him. Before he departed, however, the waitress delivered a message of acknowledgment. On another occasion, while the virtually bald Mr. Bethurum was getting a haircut, he noted her passing by the window. Subsequently, she assured the contactee that Clarions never kill anyone, they just teleport them away; that she spoke all languages (she read a note in French and wrote one in Chinese); and that he was going to have an opportunity to travel on the Admirals' Scow and vacation, with friends, in her world.

The last several of Bethurum's encounters with the craft from Clarion were definitely anticlimactic. As a final fillip, Bethurum included a visit with "Professor" George Adamski in a manner intended to constitute an imprimatur of the other California contactee.

Mr. Bethurum, in a letter to the author many years later, called attention to the point that "when I went to DeVorss to get my book 'Aboard' published in the Fall of 1953 a man who owns an air line [nonscheduled] went with me and told Mr. Andress of the DeVorss Co. that 5 of his pi-

Chapter 7

OF ALIENS AND ATTITUDES

Daniel W. Fry was born in Verdon, Minnesota, a small Mississippi River steamboat landing, on July 19, 1908. Orphaned at nine and reared by his grandmother, his higher education was obtained in the Pasadena Public Library. We are told that at the time of his extraordinary encounter, in 1950, Mr. Fry was engaged in arranging test instrumentation for high-powered motors at the White Sands Proving Ground, New Mexico.

On July 4, Fry had planned to go into nearby Las Croces to celebrate. Instead, missing the last town bus from the proving grounds, he retreated to his room and a book. But the insufferable heat indoors, caused by a breakdown in the air-conditioning system, soon forced him out for a walk onto the semidesert.

Daylight was virtually gone, and the sky was already dappled with stars. Surprisingly, as he gazed upward, some of the gleaming lights seemed to be extinguished. When the stars failed to reappear, Fry discarded the explanation of a passing plane or weather balloon.

Finally he perceived a silent "ovate spheroid about thirty feet in diameter . . . [and] about sixteen feet" deep, with no propellers or other external devices. Recognizing that it might "appear to be saucer-shaped," Fry actually saw it as "more like a soup bowl inverted over a sauce dish." He noted that it was not the dark-blue color it had originally seemed but a polished silver metal of slightly violet iridescence.[1]

Nearing the Flying Saucer, which hovered just above the ground, he stroked it with his fingers and discovered the slightly warm surface to be extraordinarily smooth, like "a large pearl . . . covered with a thin soap film," which gave off a slight tingling sensation.

"Better not touch the hull, pal, it's still hot!" snapped a voice out of the air.

The sudden shattering of silence unnerved Fry and sent him sprawling on the sand.

"Take it easy, pal," the words came again, "you're among friends."

"You could have turned the volume down," retorted Fry, "you scared me out of a week's growth." [2]

The voice apologized, explaining that proximity might have caused death, not by radioactivity but from a force-field shield that was "very powerful at molecular distances but diminishes by the seventh power of the distance so that the force becomes negligible a few microns away." The contactee was informed that the saucer came from unexplored recesses of outer space. Its controller had never set foot upon the planet Earth, although he had studied English for two years and would be forced to wait twice that before becoming acclimated to the atmosphere and gravity.

An invitation to a brief excursion in the saucer seemed quite natural to Fry. The vehicle was described to him as a "cargo carrier" remotely controlled from a "mother ship" nine hundred miles above the surface of the planet.

An aperture opened. Fry entered and found himself in a nine-by-seven-foot compartment, with a ceiling six feet high. The walls curved at the corners; they were without angles and beveled at top and bottom; four contour chairs, two behind two, were in the center of the room. The rear wall featured a lens affair projecting a soft diffusion of light. The cabin was hyperfunctional—and in Fry's words, it looked "like a cell."

The trip began and Fry found himself at ten thousand feet within less than half a minute. Continuing upward, the saucer leveled off at about thirty-five miles altitude. Alan, as Fry's distant host identified himself (actually A-Lan to his own people), was forced to restrict himself to the simplest explanations. Any revelations of specifics, he noted, would require that he instruct the Earthian in "an entirely new groundwork in Basic Physics." Projecting a telepathic cross-section diagram of the major mechanics of the ship, he spoke in a musical, hypnotic voice:

"The large drumlike structure just above the central bulkhead is the differential accumulator. It is essentially a storage battery which is capable of being charged from any of a number of natural energy differentials which may be available. By the word 'charged,' I merely mean that a potential difference is created between two poles of the accumulator. The material of the poles has available free electrons in quantities beyond anything of which you could conceive. The control mechanism allows these electrons to flow through the force rings which you see at the top and bottom of the craft." [3]

According to Alan, his ancestors originated on the planet Earth at a time when it was hostilely divided by two great world powers, Lemuria (or Mu) and Atlantis. The conflict sparked, the conflagration started, ultimately destroying human civilization. Only a handful of survivors congregated, with six aircraft, "on a high plateau, in what is now the country of Tibet," to determine what, if any, reasonable course of action yet remained. It was recognized that the Earth was virtually uninhabitable, and so the thought of flight to other planets was presented, although no such attempt had been made in the past. Still, with practically no options, and Mars in closer than usual conjunction, a vote was taken. Four of the crews decided for the planetary gamble; two resolved to take their chances on the towering, still uncontaminated, peaks at the top of the world. "The Great Lesson," the early history of Alan's race, recorded that three of the spaceships reached their destination and began again. Intriguingly, the fate of the fourth remains unknown throughout the ages to this day.

After the trip, which had given Fry magnificent views of many cities—St. Louis, Cincinnati, Pittsburgh, and New York—Fry was returned to the White Sands Proving Ground.

The year of 1954 introduced another volume of saucerological interest, *Flying Saucers on the Attack*,[4] by Harold T. Wilkins. It opted for the idea that spaceships coming to Earth might be hostile. Still, Wilkins was not one of the saucerites, nor was he a chronicler of recent sightings, after the style of Donald Keyhoe in his successive contributions. Like Keyhoe, however, his was not a purely reportorial approach, but rather one of highly editorialized reportage. Or, in the Englishman's specific case, predilected history.

Attempting to establish that the arrival of extraterrestrial craft appeared in early human records, the author included a chapter titled "Flying Saucers of Other Days." Yet, as interesting as some of these reports are, Wilkins seemed inclined to grab at positively anything not nailed down, even contradicting reasonable explanations of phenomena. Of course, Mr. Wilkins was not examining the sociopsychological development of the Age of Flying Saucers, but, rather, was posing the question—to quote the cover of the 1967 paperback edition of his work—"Are [UFOs] friendly visitors from outer space or invaders planning conquest?"

"It is my thesis that flying saucers are real and that they are space ships from another solar system,"[5] wrote the famous German scientist, sometimes called the father of the V-2 rockets, Professor Oberth, in the fall of 1954.

I think that they possibly are manned by intelligent observers who are members of a race that may have been investigating our earth for centuries.

I think that they have possibly been sent out to conduct systematic, long-range investigations, first of man, animals and vegetation, and more recently of atomic centers, armaments and centers of armament production.

They obviously have not come as invaders, but I believe their present mission may be one of scientific investigation.

Dismissing explanations relying on autohypnosis, hallucinations, optical illusions, fireballs, and meteors, Oberth states that none "meet scientific standards." He further rejects, for scientific reasons, speculation that the unknowns are man-made.

"While believing that the saucers are a reality," he continues,

I do not conclude, as some investigators have, that they come to us from one of the other planets in our own solar system. It is my theory that they are directed by living beings from another solar system, or more than one other solar system, and I call this race of visitors "Uranides." I have taken the liberty of making up the word from the Greek word for heaven, *ouranos*.

The scientist holds that, notwithstanding the immense difficulties, "a journey from one system to another is theoretically possible, once an unlimited source of power is developed." However, he rejects completely the possibility that extraterrestrials would bear any physical resemblance to Earthians.

Arguing that the failure of alien visitors to communicate with man (and he accepts no kind of contact story) is based upon an as yet unexplained difference between "their sense organism" and ours, he ventures that an interchange may initially be achieved through "anything from a ray to a parapsychological power." Mathematical symbolism appears to offer the most likely first step, Oberth conjectures, wondering if the ultimate result might not be the disclosure to us of "secrets that otherwise we might not lay bare for a hundred thousand years." [6]

The beginning of each year was highlighted by new UFO sightings, and, as the modern Age of Flying Saucers burgeoned, curious cases seemed to compete for earlier and earlier recognition. In 1955, a singular observation was recorded at 9:45 P.M. on the evening of New Year's Day, in Sydney Harbour, New South Wales. Three persons aboard the local ferry noted a glowing, somewhat globular cloud above them descend slowly to the right and vanish. Seconds thereafter, a brighter, bell-shaped cloud appeared, shifted to the right, and fragmented into four smaller units which continued moving in the same direction and suddenly were gone. Concluding the episode, a third cloud became evident, apparently turned luminous, and divided into a pair of ovoids which also disappeared.

Some hours later, when night was descending on Peru, fifty residents of Lima watched a flight of five iridescent silver saucers for at least five minutes before the strange craft were absorbed by the outer reaches of celestial darkness.

The Telonic Research Center came to public attention before spring did that year. Established as a nonprofit organization by George Hunt

Williamson, and devoted to the new science of saucerology and space visitation, its specific purpose was reported to be attempts at communication with Venus, Mars, Saturn, Jupiter, the craters Plato and Tycho on the moon, and UFOs in the immediate vicinity. The impression was given at the time that Telonic Research and the European L'Association Mondialiste Interplanétaire, which will be discussed shortly, had established some sort of practical reciprocity.

Still, the Earth was not without inhabitants who saw that Flying Saucers must be fought with "flying saucers."

Charles D. Lennon, of St. Petersburg, Florida, revealed in February that he had obtained a United States patent for his revolving-wing aerial craft, which, he asserted, would be capable of flying several times the speed of sound. The "Lennoncopter" was reportedly operated by cyclonic action related to gyroscopic principles, the combination of which created a field of etheric matter along the wing surface, eliminating the prevalent air pressure. Designed to be driven probably by an atomic-force source, the observable operation of the craft consisted of the outer circle of wing spinning about the central cabin. Unfortunately, civilian and military authorities did not wax overly enthusiastic about Mr. Lennon's device, because the inventor declined to reveal the mysterious principle permitting it to achieve its great speeds.

In Toulouse, an Italian claimed to have created a saucercraft as early as 1938. His plans, he said, were given to the military in Berlin. (According to James Moseley, a small prototype was constructed and successfully tested in the Heinkel-Dornier plant in Germany, in 1939.) It was the Italian's further contention that he saw a larger model, nine meters in diameter, in 1941, but having been denied any further association with his creation, he was sent to the front.

On June 24, Adolph C. Peterson, of Edina, Minnesota, was issued patent number 2711295 for a high-speed, disc-shaped, airfoil craft, designed to ascend vertically and carry passengers or cargo. In Paris, around the same time, aeronautical designer René Couzinet announced that test flights for his *aerodyne à ailes multiples* were scheduled for the following spring. The craft was said to have the appearance of two soup plates, stuck bottom to bottom, to have tremendous speed and maneuverability, and to be driven by three 135-horsepower engines. A model of the vertical takeoff plane was exhibited to reporters in the City of Lights.

George Van Tassel conducted his Second Annual Spacecraft Convention on the weekend of March 12 and 13, 1955. Among those who spoke at the Giant Rock and Space Port, which is also the general site of the College of Universal Wisdom, were Orfeo Angelucci, George Adamski,

Dan Fry, Truman Bethurum, Frank Scully, Dick Miller, Dr. Charles Laughead, generally known as Dr. Doomsday, Williamson, and others. Reputedly present, but of a somewhat different category, were Captain Ruppelt, former Blue Book head, and Air Force Intelligence and FBI men. A thousand-person attendance was claimed for the first day, and three hundred for the second, and the high point of the conference was the appearance of Dick Miller, new to the West Coast, who told of his twelve-hour saucer trip over the Detroit area.

Some Earthians were not as passive as the cult conventioneers; they sought immediate participation in the other planets—or, at least, the moon.

Harry Hall, agent for extraterrestrial real estate, came into direct conflict with the Interplanetary Development Corporation in 1955. He claimed that the New York corporation, established to market lunar plots, was a claim-jumping operation, as he had been selling one-hundred-acre properties on the moon since March, 1955, and had already disposed of, and legally filed, two thousand such claims. The northeastern firm countered by announcing that they had located 4,500 persons willing to participate in the high-in-the-sky scheme, at a dollar per acre. From a practical point of view, it would seem that Hall's offer was the better of the two, as his fee was also only a dollar per acre. However, Interplanetary was promoting deeds that included mineral rights and other extended coverage. At the time the story broke, neither company had a scheduled date of departure for a customer survey of purchased property.

The gentle lunacy created an amusing situation many years afterward when the United States landed men on the moon. Leona Bishop, of New Orleans, among others, relocated her misplaced deed for an acre of moon-land and announced her claim to the press. Robert R. Coles, president of the Interplanetary Development Corporation, from whom she had acquired her "rights" to a lot "in the northeast quadrant of Crater Copernicus," explained that the entire project had been something between a promotion stunt for a liquor company and a joke.[7]

The preceding selenitic disputes seemed parochial, however, compared to the interspacial contretemps threatened by Chicago industrial designer James T. Mangan in the fall of 1957, when he issued a public protest against the introduction of a Russian satellite into Celestia, a domain established and proclaimed by him in 1950, which comprised all unoccupied space beyond earth. Claiming that he held a legal charter, although neglecting to identify by whom it was issued, he stated flatly: "I refuse to issue any licenses to Russia for use of outer space. Neither Russia, the

United States, or Great Britain [sic] has any claim to space except through my nation, Celestia."

Meanwhile, halfway around the world, the island of Majorca, in the Mediterranean, recorded almost forty sightings during the first half of the year.

A fascinating report reached the United States from Great Britain during April, in the form of a newspaper article on the Air Ministry's five-year probe into Flying Saucers. According to it, the question "Do flying saucers exist?" was answered in the negative; however, no details were to be revealed. Nonetheless, Dorothy Kilgallen wrote on May 22:

> British scientists and airmen, after examining the wreckage of one mysterious flying ship, are convinced that these strange aerial objects are not optical illusions or Soviet inventions, but are actually flying saucers which originate on another planet. The source of my information is a British official of cabinet rank, who prefers to remain unidentified. "We believe on the basis of our enquiries thus far, that the saucers were staffed by small men—probably under four feet tall," my informant told me. "It's frightening but there is no denying the flying saucers come from another planet."

A spokesman for the British Ministry in London completely denied the entire report.

During the year, Col. Gernod Darnbyl, officer of the Norwegian Air Force, announced that a UFO had crashed near Spitsbergen. "It has—this we wish to state emphatically—not been built by any country on this earth," the flyer was quoted as having said.[8] "The materials used in its construction are completely unknown to all experts who participated in the investigation." Although he stated a complete report was soon to be released, none ever was.

The World Interplanetary Association (L'Association Mondialiste Interplanétaire—AMI, a French acronym for "friend") was founded on October 28, 1954, at Lausanne, by Prof. Alfred Nahon, with the usual journals and other courtesies being offered for a price. AMI held its first Interplanetary Assembly on July 16, 1955, at which time it sent word to the Big Four—presumably England, the United States, the Soviet Union, and France—explaining that it had convened to weigh the problem of aliens "who have delivered a final warning to the world." In support of this gesture, Mr. Nahon, identified as a professor of psychology and philosophy (at which institution, or where he received his degree, is not clear), directed a petition to the United Nations, suggesting that body, in the name of major powers, renounce atomic energy, reveal the truth about Flying Saucers, and move toward total disarmament. According to the latest report, neither the United Nations nor the Big Four appear to have replied.

Meanwhile, in the United States, many people were being converted to the belief that the leprechauns of outer space were landing everywhere. Although countless prominent saucerologists of the day dismissed the popular idea of little green men, saying that although many tales of extraterrestrials existed, none specified visitors of such verdant pigmentation, the truth is that there were several such descriptive reports. The J. C. Sutton family of Hopkinsville, Kentucky, is supposed to have encountered a commando group of a dozen or more emerald aliens on the night of August 23. The miniature marauders, who purportedly glowed in the dark, sent the family scurrying in their two cars to the local police station, where they told of the incident. The story had the strangers from the sky returning on the following evening to cavort over trees and across the roofs of houses. Although the police discovered shotgun holes in the house—the family admitted shooting at the invaders—they missed the aliens themselves. Nonetheless, another person, Mrs. Glenie Langford, claimed to have seen them from her parlor window. She said, "Those green things are worrying me to death." [9]

Finally, the United States with its power and resources relented and revealed its accumulated wisdom on the mystery of our age, oracularly setting the heavens straight. The Air Force issued Press Release No. 1053-55 on October 25, 1955. Based upon Project Blue Book Special Report No. 14, of May 5, which summarized the results of its eight-year investigation of unidentified aerial objects, it contended that "no evidence of the existence of the popularly-termed 'flying saucers' was found." Further, it quoted Secretary of the Air Force Donald A. Quarles as saying, "No object such as those popularly described as flying saucers have ever overflown the United States . . . [however] we are now entering a period of aviation technology in which aircraft of unusual configuration and flight characteristics will begin to appear." Therefore, it said, we should not be unduly disturbed by observations of improbable aerial phenomena.

The original full report of 316 pages, titled *Analysis of Reports of Unidentified Aerial Objects* and subtitled *Project No. 10073—Project Blue Book Special Report No. 14,* disclosed that the Air Force had received approximately 4,000 sighting reports, of apparently inexplicable events, from July 1947 to December 1952, although it noted that few supplied reliable measurements or physical characteristics. Approximately 800 submissions were dismissed as too contradictory or vague, and about 1,000 were characterized as duplications of previously reported unknowns. The remaining 2,200 reports were divided into 1,766 Knowns (balloons, aircraft, astronomical miscellany, birds, etc.) and 434 Unknowns, which is to say UFOs whose descriptions and maneuvers fitted no recognizable object or phenomenon.

The 2,200 sightings with which the Air Force dealt appeared to indicate no pattern or trend, although they were evaluated in terms of six major characteristics: color, number, shape, duration of observation, brightness and speed. It was argued that a similar percentage distribution regarding each characteristic in the Knowns and Unknowns would strongly suggest that there was no basic difference between the groups. However, various statistical techniques failed to prove anything.

The Air Force then subdivided the Unknowns into 186 daylight and 248 night sightings, and then they subjected all of the former and 5 of the latter to further examination. The second sifting brought officialdom to the conclusion that about 80 might have been misinterpreted conventional objects; 20 seemed to be definitely unfamiliar objects, whereas the remaining number, nearly 90, continued to be regarded as Unknowns primarily because of behavioral characteristics. These latter were considered of minimal interest, as the possibilities for inaccuracies in such visual observations were very great. In conjunction with the chi square and other tests, this reevaluation caused the Air Force to conclude that the majority of the Unknowns easily might have been known objects. (Obviously, this did not account for the large remaining number of unexplained night sightings.) Of the 434 sightings classified as Unknown, only a dozen were described in some detail, and according to the Air Force, no consistent configuration of a Flying Saucer could be deduced from a comparison of them.

The Air Force observed that ". . . it can never be proven that flying saucers do not exist . . . [but] it is considered to be highly improbable that any of the reports of unidentified aerial objects examined in this study represent observations of technological developments outside the range of present-day scientific knowledge." These conclusions were based on the lack of patterning, the absence of a uniform "saucer-type" design emerging from best reports, and the failure of any physical evidence to be obtained which was demonstrably from an unidentified flying object.

The Air Force evaluated 425 sightings in 1953, 429 in 1954, and 131 in the first half of 1955, but the conclusions drawn were the same. The substantial Air Force report on UFOs contained some 60 pages of text, 39 of charts and graphs, and 218 pages of tables and miscellaneous material. It was written to a great extent in officialese, which naturally served to obscure emphasis, and any nuances, and inferences which might have been drawn by those willing to elicit from the work its actual implications. Regrettably, there was more than one inconsistency between the press release and the report from which it was derived. For example, the public announcement suggested very strongly that Flying Saucers do not exist, in contradistinction to the report, which concedes that it simply cannot prove whether they do or not. The report has been interpreted in a variety of ways by saucerites and saucerologists, ranging from regarding it as an attempt to hide the fact that UFOs are American-built and -piloted devices to the conviction that its purpose is to obscure the fact that the Air Force knows the phenomena to be extraterrestrial and is probably in direct communication with the occupants thereof, but refrains from so informing the world public for fear of mass hysteria, economic collapse, or for more ominous reasons.

Such suspicions found ample and eloquent support in the writings of popular saucer researchers—especially Donald Keyhoe.

The Flying Saucer Conspiracy, published around this time, was intended to update the Marine Corps major's chronology of prominent saucer sightings. As with his previous two books, the material is well researched and its presentation lucid. However, digressing from pure ufology, this Keyhoe book reflects considerable concern for life-on-the-moon theories and antigravity explanations, and rather surprisingly, in speaking of recently discovered satellites—origin and identity undetermined—suggests they might be "mother ships" monitoring our civilization. On the other hand, he dismisses all contacts, little men, and earth-built saucer stories. Keyhoe's main underlying thesis is the "conspiracy" one, which postulates a "silence group" within the Air Force whose purpose it is to prevent the public from acquiring any legitimate information regarding the phenomena above. Nonetheless, it was an interesting addition to his continuing index of major UFO sightings.

Still pursuing the Fortean fancy, Harold T. Wilkins' *Flying Saucers Uncensored*,[10] which appeared concurrently, also managed to help amplify the apprehension syndrome. Much like his previous volume, the later one describes curious objects—ice, stone, metals, lights, fires, and unknown matter hurtling through the sky, and tells of abductions and disappearances, with the general understanding that everything is a Flying Saucer unless the opposite is proved beyond a reasonable doubt. Reflecting the esotericism of such ethicists as Steiner, Gloria Lee, the Borderland Science Research Associates, of San Diego, and other pseudomystical individuals and groups, Mr. Wilkins implies that Flying Saucers are mutations from an abstract, abstruse, fourth-dimensional world—which would seem to suggest time travel, but apparently not to him. Intimating they can vary virtually all of their characteristics—shape, color, size, opaqueness—at the least flexing of their hyper-Will, the reader is left to infer their purpose is to save us from the folly of our infinite fissions. Unfortunately, the mystical ufologist counters this conviction by making it quite clear that he believes other Flying Saucers also permeate the stratosphere in pragmatic, concrete, and three-dimensional forms, and these are prepared to erase mankind from the face of the earth. He suggests the hostile craft may come from Saturn, which might lead one to draw an interesting mythical analogy, if only men were Titans. That they are not may well explain why they wait for Flying Saucers. He who would be god, but isn't to the hierarchy born, must wait until a deity arrives who may at least confer on him some small accouterment of immortality.

Yet, excluding the more extravagant contact recitals, it is likely that no prominent figure during this period of the Flying Saucer Age offered more stimulation to the imagination than Morris K. Jessup. Regardless of certain tangential aspects to his participation in the droll drama, his attitudes would come to influence many of the more esoteric saucerologists. Some of his ideas boasted a degree of originality, some were patently derivative, but few were dull.

Charles Fort is one of the most popular patron saints of Saucerdom, and his technique of chronicling extraordinary occurrence in interminable and uncatalogued sequences laid the foundation for many of the research-oriented books on the subject. *Oddities* and *Enigmas,* the earlier books of Frank Edwards, Wilkins, Leslie, and even Vallee, are prime examples of works influenced by the quaint collector of newspaper clippings. One of the foremost of this school was the late Morris K. Jessup. This energetic researcher, who in personality and psychology probably more resembled Fort than any other of the master's disciples, presented his theories, and the research upon which they were based, in a 1955 work, which subsequently became a minor classic in the field, *The Case for the UFO.* Jessup's approach to the investigation of Flying Saucers was even less "scientific" than that of some of his confreres. For example, he warned that we must "segregate paranormal experiences into groupings having some family likenesses," since such segregation serves two purposes: "It simplifies our problem of analysis because it helps to bring order out of chaos" and it permits us to give additional strength to any of our historical sources which are "too weak to stand alone." [11]

"Two elements of importance in our study of the antiquity of intelligence [are] the proof that superior beings have been here longer than mankind has been civilized and the demonstration that forces were at work in those millennia, the magnitude and nature of which are only suspected today . . . the vast amount of material from the past shows clearly that *intelligence exists in space* [his italics]!" [12] Jessup admonishes mankind to conceive of "intelligence" in new terms. *Mind* he restricts to the definition of the function of the brain and lower animals, but *"intelligence"* he conceives of as "an ability to think, construct, direct, analyse, plan, navigate, laugh, etc., which is not necessarily a part of, or associated with, a carnate brain . . . it may be and probably is superior to our own, and it may inhabit physical entities of a discarnate nature such as nebulus or cloudlike bodies." [13] Generously conceding that "nobody knows the precise nature of this spatial intelligence, much less the nature of the physical body within which it resides," he concedes to the overmind a relative omnipotence which indulges in obscure and inexplicable behavior such as whipping up localized storms for purposes as yet to be decoded. And although hypothesizing the "spatial intelligence" [14] on the basis of wholly unsupportable premises, Jessup liked to offer artifactual and/or artifanciful evidence of its existence, especially where he assumed it anteceded the development of civilized man. His most famous "example" was probably "the little piece of meteoric iron which was found deep within a tertiary coal bed. The locale and the findings are authentic. [However, he fails to cite same in his book.] The shape is purely artificial. It is but an inch or so square, practically a cube. Four sides are squarely faced, and the other two are convexly shaped, with complete symmetry. Around the four surfaced sides runs a groove, geometrically contrived." [15] Jessup asked whether "this gadget" could have been the product of an indigene or is evidence of extraplanetary visitors. His answer is basically yes to both questions, sifted through an Atlantean sieve. Like Fort, Edwards, and others, Jessup is willing to accept any kind of mysterious occurrence or strange phenomena as being probable, providing it can be woven into the scheme of his predisposition. It is therefore not surprising—even expected—that he too should list endless disappearances, purported abductions, falling ice, stones, animal and organic matter, water, seemingly manufactured objects, and rubbish to support his thesis; not to forget unusual clouds, storms, legends of levitation, strange marks and shapes in stone, various celestial happenings, as well as a potpourri of other material covering a score or more of categories.

Notwithstanding Jessup's inclination toward mysticism, he does present interesting ideas concerning the possible origin and nature of Flying Saucers. Regarding the seemingly explicable nature of UFOs, he made an imaginative suggestion.

Suppose that some intelligent entity was [sic] directing a concentration of potential which could make small volumes of rarefied air rigid, could set up a sort of island in the gravitational or magnetic field, moving the island about as the *spot* of a searchlight is moved on thin clouds . . . in moving the *island* would simply "freeze" on the advancing edge and "thaw" on the trailing edge . . . it could have almost infinite velocity, and also acceleration . . . only the force beam would move, not the air.[16]

Recognizing that a single beam would not achieve the proposed effect, since it would require the "freeze" to extend along the entire shaft of force, creating a masslike column, he theorizes that his notion could be made functional by the use of a pair of intersecting beams, arguing that "it is possible that the three-dimensional volume enclosed within the intersection of *two* beams might create such a congealed island [his italics]."[17]

Another aspect of Jessupian conjecture centers about the purported enormous "mother ships," which usually hover hundreds of miles above the earth, serving as ports for the frequently observed scout ships and, perhaps, large expeditions of explorers and/or colonizers from alien areas of the universe. These supercraft are often described as, or suggested to be, hundreds of yards to hundreds of miles in length. Although vastly outnumbered by the smaller saucers, the monumental mother ships are seldom thought to be so rare as Jessup thought they might be when he wrote that "these constructions are few in number, not *many* (there is some possibility, in fact, that there *may* be only two of them) [his italics]."[18]

Mother ships are generally described as zeppelinlike in shape, but, again going off on his own tangent, Jessup sees them "usually globular, sometimes spindle-like." However, of considerably greater interest is his assertion that they are "an indigenous part of the earth-moon binary-planet system."[19] He goes on to explain that he believes "that these space islands probably use both earth and moon for their convenience," suggesting that "their most natural and permanent habitat is at the gravitational neutral of the earth-sun-moon, three-body system which is well within the orbit of the moon."

Yet, at times, the saucerologist felt required to introduce somewhat more "scientific" explanations for the manner in which erstwhile extra-terrestrials overcame practical problems. On these occasions he appeared to forsake Fort in favor of Fry. "Any force," explained Jessup, "which would simultaneously accelerate every molecule of either the living body or the mechanical structure would avoid all such stresses (as would be encountered in rapid acceleration), and both the living and the mechanical could undergo any amount of acceleration without the slightest damage or discomfort!"[20] Dan Fry, in his earlier book, quoted Alan as saying (with regard to the saucer in which Fry was riding), ". . . the force which accelerates the vehicle acts not only upon every atom of the vehicle itself but also acts equally upon every atom of mass which is within it, including the pilot or passenger." [21]

However, although the two approached by different paths, both were antigravitationists. Jessup might make a momentary concession to science-fiction science (and not good science fiction, at that), but nothing more clearly delineated his antireason attitude than his contention that "it should be obvious to all engineers and scientists that rocket propulsion will never solve the problems of space travel, not only because of the unavoidable problems of acceleration, but because of the impossibility of transporting the necessary fuel. . . ." [22] Like Fry, he ultimately reverted to the ancient alchemy of nullifying gravity as an explanation of the powers of space propulsion.

Perhaps the most fascinating aspect of his exposition was an imaginative extrapolation from material he discovered in the October, 1946, issue of *Intelligence Digest,* which carried an article alluding to Russian projects involving cosmic rays. Apparently something in the piece indicated (at least to Jessup's satisfaction) that the scientists had developed a "method of freezing large areas of ground to sub-zero temperatures, killing everything therein." [23]

From this he inferred the possibility that "the Russians [had] captured a space ship" or that "space people [had] taken over the Red Empire." [24] Subsequently, Jessup gravitated more and more toward the mystical, finally producing the second of his two best-known works, *The UFO and the Bible.* [25]

The vast preponderance of UFO sightings are viewed by a limited number of persons, under limited conditions of observation, for relatively brief periods of time, but the Cincinnati sighting of March 21, 1956, was an exception. Appearing to the naked eye as an intense blue-white light, some thirty degrees above the horizon, the unknown was witnessed high over that city by a large number of residents for more than forty-five minutes. Under the survey of strong binoculars, the UFO seemed to be a compact complex of bright lights slowly revolving about a hypothetical center. According to some citizens, the widely reported sighting was the third appearance of the phenomenon (phenomena) over consecutive nights. The only explanation offered was drawn from the Air Force vernacular, *i.e.,* the UFO was Venus.

Approximately two weeks after the Cincinnati affair, another sustained sighting was reported, one of similar duration. Flying out of New York City, destined for Buffalo, veteran American Airlines pilot Raymond E. Ryan spent forty-five minutes on the evening of April 8 pursuing a rather explicit unidentified aerial light. Picking up the object over Schenectady, at about 10:15 P.M., Ryan pulled abreast of the glow. It responded with intense acceleration and hurtled westward at what Ryan estimated to be close to a thousand miles an hour. The mysterious luminescence reduced its speed at a point some eight miles distant and began monitoring the plane. Ryan contacted the tower at Griffiss Air Force Base and two jets were scrambled, while he was instructed to keep the object under surveillance. The UFO was followed to the shores of Lake Ontario, with the plane never approaching closer than three miles, and then it shot northwest over the water toward Canada. Although observed in Albany, Watertown, and the Griffiss Base near Rome as well, no further observaton of the UFO was made.

Chapter 8

IN THE LEGEND OF THE UFO
THE CONTACTEE IS KING

The National Investigations Committee on Aerial Phenomena was created in 1956 in Washington, D.C., by Thomas Townsend Brown, a fifty-one-year-old physicist, with the support of seventy responsible persons. The heralded intentions of the group were broad in scope and seemed serious in purpose, and ultimately it was to become the most influential and probably best known independent agency for inquiry regarding UFOs in the United States.

The beginning of 1957 saw the house of NICAP assume a semblance of order when, on January 15, the board of governors, chaired by Admiral Fahrney, dispensed with the services of most of the remaining old guard and appointed Major Keyhoe temporary director, a position later made permanent. The "shakedown" cruise was over, and the National Investigations Committee of Aerial Phenomena was underway.

Among the more interesting books of 1956 were Michel's *The Truth about Flying Saucers*[1] and Jessup's *The UFO and the Bible.*[2] The former, written by a French science writer and channeled to this country through the efforts of the Civilian Saucer Intelligence (society) of New York, was an attempt to present a serious, if obviously proselytizing, evaluation of a limited aspect of the mystery. Weighing a number of commonly known American sightings, the performance of the United States Air Force, and a collection of then relatively new European reports, Michel attempts to put them into what he regards as the proper perspective. His efforts are quite detailed and frequently designed to discredit the explanations of sceptics by demonstrating the practical or scientific implausibility of such solutions.

A follow-up to his preceding books, Jessup's *The UFO and the Bible* exhaustively examines biblical events which might possibly be interpreted as having some relationship to UFOs. It is a highly researched and dedicated volume, but it is basically an attempt to prove the author's widely known convictions by providing pseudohistorical and generally mythic evidence for events of his own day. Since the source material quite evidently is for the most part historical distortion or pure allegory, only a few examples may be regarded seriously.

A number of the peripheral works were coming out around the mid-decade. Two were of representative interest. *There Is Life on Mars,*[3] whose author has been described as a fellow of the Royal Astronomical Society, the Royal Geophysical Society, and the Royal Society of Anthropologists, attempted to reverse the post-Lowellian, post-Pickerellian thesis of a noninhabited Mars by postulating the opposite contention—suggesting that because life *might* exist on the curiously channeled planet, it necessarily *does.* The second of the pair was *Strangest of All.*[4] Although only tangentially touching upon saucerology and more reflecting volumes like *Enigmas,*[5] or a selection of Forteanisms translated into anecdotes, it has its place in the subject library because so many of the highly curious occurrences alluded to in it are held by many saucerites and saucerologists to be explicable only in terms of alien visitors of semiomnipotence.

The gallery of contactees boasts an amazing assortment of unlikely portraits. Virtually all are extravagantly conceived, usually in semiscientific or pseudomystical terms. However, there are a few iconoclasts among archetypes, individuals drawn with a different brush. Such is Denver-born, ranch-raised, road-wandering Ozarkian Buck Nelson. Emphasizing rural simplicity in his denim shirts, old-fashioned overalls, and sturdy work shoes, he is a contactee of a different color, bearing little, if any, resemblance to the suburban, business-suited Van Tassels, Williamsons, and Frys, or the Tythanian-uniformed Prince NEosom. Still, his claims, which first appeared in a Springfield, Missouri, newspaper, are cut from a rustic portion of the widely woven whole cloth. His entrance into national contactology coincided with the publication of his experiences under the title *My Trip to Mars, the Moon and Venus,*[6] which was published toward the end of 1956.

Flying Saucers first came to Buck Nelson on the afternoon of July 30, 1954. Disturbed by a ruckus in the barnyard, Nelson logically collected his camera and flashlight and went to investigate. Above, "a huge big disc-like object" hovered; at a far greater elevation two companion craft waited. The sighter, soon-to-be-contactee, snapped three photographs and signaled with his flashlight. The response was immediate. Nelson was rayed "down behind a barrel" by a light "brighter and hotter than the sun." Yet, lest ye misinterpret, the results were the elimination of lumbago and neuritis conditions from which he had suffered for fifteen years, and so great an improvement in his eyesight that his spectacles were abandoned.

The first actual landing occurred at about midnight, on March 5, when the craft opened to permit the disembarkation of three men and a positively enormous dog. The visit lasted about an hour, with the space travelers investigating all of Nelson's simple necessities with great interest. One of them burned his hand on an oil stove and could not understand why it was hot; general confusion was expressed by the electrical arrangements, since "they plugged their lights and appliances into the radio for power." Two and a half weeks later, the visitors came and went again, and on April 24, again at midnight, the opportunity was afforded the contactee to join the joys of saucernautics. It was at this time "The Twelve Laws of God . . . on Venus" were given to Buck Nelson. The code of the clouded planet bears a reassuring resemblance to Mosaic commandments, in most cases reiterating them verbatim.

The contactee provided his followers with a few simple illustrations relating to his adventure. Some of the drawings described the interior of the spaceship in which he traveled, but as they appeared to be excerpts from one of the more obstruse designs of the noted engineer Rube Goldberg, a verbal description is difficult, if not impossible, to provide.

Change characterized the Age of Flying Saucers, as it did the conditions concurrent to it. The noted English saucer-writer Cedric Allingham died of tuberculosis in a Swiss sanatorium in the autumn of 1956, while in New York the Civilian Saucer Intelligence group, whose membership included former *True* editor John DuBarry, Lex Mebane, and others, struggled on.

In London a somewhat more conservative defender of liberal scientific thought, British astronomer H. P. Wilkins, resigned from the moderate British Astronomical Association, announcing his intentions of establishing a more free-thinking celestial society. Simultaneously, in the United States, astronomer E. C. Slipher, of the Lowell Observatory, was quoted in a December 14 press release as having claimed that his observations with sophisticated visual instruments indicated that the controversial "canals" of Mars were artificially constructed. The astronomer echoed the oft-repeated speculation that a Martian civilization had once existed, passing into oblivion when the planet ceased to be inhabitable.

Meanwhile, on the ground, the indefatigable George Hunt Williamson, having dissolved his Telonic Center, had a new operation functioning before the snows of winter came. After an apparently uneventful trip to Peru, word was relayed to the initiated in this country that he had inaugurated The Brotherhood of the Seven Rays, a sect consisting of the newest beneficiaries of his mystical munificence. Although supposedly consisting of fewer than ten persons from the United States, and possessed of purposes not quite clear, there was little doubt, in the hearts of those who knew him, that the neo-Peruvian had great plans for his new colony.

But if one contactee forsook the limelight temporarily, another was always waiting anxiously in the wings to do his turn.

The intimations of strange pressure groups, purportedly intent upon obscuring the true meaning of Flying Saucers, began arising in the early 1950's, the most famous of these being the "three men in black" and the "silence conspiracy," which Major Keyhoe and others regard as an ominous element functioning within the Air Force. During the summer of 1956, *Saucer News* editor James Moseley postulated an addition to this enigmatic company in the June, 1956, issue of his magazine. Theorizing that Flying Saucers were originally being researched by the United States in 1946, were capable of speeds exceeding four thousand miles an hour, and were operating from a supersecret subterranean base below a southwestern state, he continued:

> The whole project is so highly classified that ordinary military pilots and even the Air Force's saucer investigators on Project Blue Book could not possibly know about it. In fact, this type of saucer is not built by the American Government as we ordinarily understand the word "Government." As fantastic as this might sound . . . these saucers are actually built, operated, and maintained by an organization which is entirely separate from the military and political branches of the Government that we know about. Although a handful of people at the very top of the Government know about the existence of this project, they have no direct contact with it. . . . I shall call this secret project "The Organization." [7]

Moseley considerably elaborated on the activities of this shadowy cabal with some very extravagant revelations.

The first decade of the modern Age of Flying Saucers was approaching its conclusion, and from the fluttering blips perceived by Kenneth Arnold over the Cascade Mountains had emerged a vast and complicated—if not generally accepted—aspect of contemporary life. Of course, as has been detailed, the appropriate climate had preceded the myth in the making, but nonetheless, it was remarkable that so slight a sighting could have developed into the sociopsychological complex that it did. Religions were formed from it, and philosophies as well. It fostered theories about extraterrestrial life, space mechanics, parochial astronomy, quintuple dimensionality, inorganic intelligences, botanical aliens, and scores of others. The conversations of millions were colored by it, comic strips and books drawn from it, and radio broadcasts, television programs, and motion pictures inspired by it. It was the conceptual sponsor of toys, advertising campaigns, poor jokes, and clever cartoons. And although many of these manifestations of the Age of Flying Saucers did not fully burgeon until later, as the period completed its first official decade, the seeds had been sown.

It must be conceded that notwithstanding the wide success of the Adamski and Keyhoe books, the era was yet to reach its height. To a very great extent the more fervent acolytes were concentrated on the West Coast, and elsewhere the subject was still somewhat peripheral. Then the phenomenon burst from the confines of California and flooded along the eastern seaboard and onward to the Mississippi. An infidel appeared and virtually invented Flying Saucers for millions of Americans. His name was Nebel.

Long John Nebel arrived upon the madness scene in 1956, and if the Flying Saucers had become a circus, there could be no question that, in the ex-pitchman turned all-night radio personality, they had found their Barnum. Of course, John had been broadcasting, in a smaller way, for several years, and certainly UFOs were widely talked about; however, the melding of the two forces seemed to create something new—something different. It may have been that John Nebel was the coagulating factor, the coalescing element, that turned a thousand tales of unlikely possibilities into a cohesive psychosocial consciousness. This is not to say that Long John single-handedly, or even very intentionally, took up the endless threads and wove them into the vast mythic tapestry that would eventually appear as one of the fascinating mysteries of our time, but merely that he drew together the dozen major figures into an unbalanced central group about which lesser personalities could be gathered, and beyond which the interminable background could be sketched.

John Nebel came out of Chicago something more than fifty years ago. His father was an advertising executive for a major candy firm and his mother a successful dermatologist. During his early life he collected occupations in the manner he was later to collect characters, and before he moved into broadcasting, he had peddled merchandise door to door, managed piano stores, ushered at the New York Paramount, been assistant manager at the Winter Garden, operated a string of department-store concessions, played tenor banjo, toured the outlands with an eighteen-piece band (the height of which tour was following Rudy Vallee into a split-week ballroom booking), Svengalied the career of a set of Siamese twins, done a modest magic turn, and worked night clubs with a mind-reading act, until he finally found the natural outlet for his extraordinary verbal talents: He became a pitchman. It was the times, not the inclination, that sent him merchandizing in the streets, and before long he had scored with high pitches and low, rolled with carnivals dispensing Old

World Herb Tea, and distributed Chinese Corn Punk along the side-walks of the city. Finally, he ended up establishing the first of the vast New Jersey highway drive-in emporia, a twenty-five-thousand-square-foot installation that sported across its roof a 41-by-32-foot sign that read: LONG JOHN. This enormous banner caught the eye of a New York radio executive, and he stopped to hear the pitch of the auctioneer whom *Argosy* identified as "the man who can sell anything," and discovered they were right. What he could do with hundreds, he could do with millions, it was ventured, which reasoning began the radio career of the "man who invented saucers."

In 1956, Long John Nebel inaugurated what was to become the most successful radio talk show in America. It emanated from the small chief engineer's office at the Carteret, New Jersey, transmitter of New York radio station WOR. These somewhat makeshift arrangements were necessitated by the fact that there were no formal broadcast studios in the rather remote location, which had been selected for Nebel's all-night-every-night conversation piece, rather than the regular facilities at 1440 Broadway, in the city, because it reduced production costs to something fractionally higher than zero.

In the beginning, Long John conducted his taped interviews from his Tudor City apartment, and a number of the initial guests helped lay the groundwork for the later superstructure of his program, at least the more *outré* aspects thereof. During one of these parlor recording sessions, a minor messianic figure of a quasi-philosophic self-help cult made reference to "flying saucers." It was not a subject about which he seemed to know a great deal, but what he had picked up he was able to integrate into his thesis. As Long John had yet to develop any expertise of his own in the area, he was happy to decorate his shows with whatever tales his guest could tell. After a few stories, the broadcaster decided he would like to hear some of the amazing adventures from the mouths of the persons who had experienced them, and he asked his guest if any of the California contactees ever visited New York. He was assured they did. As a matter of fact, remarked the modified mystic, one was due in the city for a lecture within two weeks. His name was George Van Tassel.

The contactee did arrive shortly thereafter and happily appeared on the program, contributing a fascinating interview to Long John's series. Van Tassel told of his Flying Saucer center at Giant Rock Airport, in California, of the convocations of saucerologists held there, of séances and ethereal communications with aliens through interplanetary telepathy, and of his encounter with an extraterrestrial.

Solganda first appeared to George Van Tassel at about two in the morning on August 24, 1953. The saucerite and his wife were sleeping on the desert that evening, as was their wont during the hot months of the year, when George suddenly awakened to see a strange man a half dozen feet away. The shadowy figure said,

"My name is Solganda. I would be pleased to show you our craft." [8]

Attempts by Van Tassel to rouse his wife were unsuccessful, and he deduced that the alien had placed her "under some kind of control." [9] Van Tassel got up, garbed only in a pair of shorts, and followed along to view the ship from outer space. It was a brief trek, and soon the contactee was able to discern a pearly, opalescent disc about thirty-six feet across and nineteen high. Moments later he found the interior, which featured a 360-degree series of portholes, arranged over a nearly continuous shelf, about halfway up the rounded sides. The principal element of the circular cabin was a column thrust from ceiling to floor, presumably extending beyond to aid in the craft's operation. The Earthian was then treated to a look at various instruments of celestial navigation, "the power generating room," and other interesting physical aspects of the Flying Saucer. Solganda and three companions Van Tassel encountered within stood about five foot seven inches and were of medium frame. The four appeared to constitute the entire interplanetary crew.

The tour consumed about twenty minutes, and then Van Tassel was escorted back, Solganda vanished across the desert, and the alien ship shafted upward into the oblivion of outer space.[10]

The Council of the Seven Lights,[11] an exposition of some of Van Tassel's philosophy, wisdom and adventures, was published in 1958. Although recounting his meeting with Solganda in condensed terms, the book was essentially a presentation of various of the author's contentions regarding the origin of man, his purpose in the universe, and a scattering of cosmogony, cosmology, and cosmography.

"Man was created," Van Tassel concedes, but not on Earth. He was, it seems, made and distributed through "millions of solar systems to serve as an instrument of God's doing." [12] Further, it did not all begin in Eden, since "Adam was not a single man, the Adamic *race of Man* was the first people to inhabit the Earth." [13]

Mr. Van Tassel's expositions on the place of Jesus, Mary, and Joseph in the spacial hierarchy were not confined to lunar-astral interchange. Asserting that Christ "was the last space teacher to be introduced to Earth via normal birth," [14] he contradicts the further contention that "Joseph was a foster father. . . . There was no blood of Joseph in Jesus." [15] Elsewhere the saucerite argues that "Mary volunteered for the assignment[!] of bringing through birth—to the Earth—a true son of the Adamic race [space people]. Jesus also accepted the assignment knowing beforehand what his earthly birth would entail. Mary became pregnant and was landed on the Earth by one of our ships." [16]

There is a lot of such hitherto scarcely perceived material in *The Council of the Seven Lights,* including some first-rate stuff about the Great Pyramid, which was constructed 25,836 years ago (but not by the Egyptians), as well as sex, the spirit, and other subjects to intrigue the serious scholar of extraplanetary interpersonal relationships.

Actually, the contactee has penned several volumes, but in at least one case the dedication is infinitely more compelling than the text. In the book *Into This World and Out Again* it reads:

This book is dedicated to the people from other life levels in space. The 4th density center of the Quadra-Sectorm Blaau. The Council of the Twelve Lords in our solar system. The Council of Seven Lights on Shanchea. The Space Station Schare and all its complement of guardians. Also the active participants in the reception of this information at the College of Universal Wisdom.[17]

George Van Tassel's endeavors have been so varied and engrossing, it is very difficult to attempt to present any sort of full picture of him and his activities within the very limited space available to report on him. However, omitting comment on his work in the field of rejuvenation would be unforgivable. The saucerite had for some time been interested in the infant science of age arrest, or even regression. From his friends from the vast beyond he received instructions as to how a machine might be erected which would permit the subject to pare away a number of years, perhaps as many as a score. However, it was a highly complicated device which, upon completion, would be of considerable size. To house the rejuvenating machine, Van Tassel began to collect funds to finance the several-story housing necessary to it. By the early sixties, reports had it nearly completed at a construction cost of seventy or eighty thousand dollars. The device would revivify the subject, possibly reconditioning him to enjoy the perfection of health enjoyed twenty years earlier, but the rejuvenation was to be *entirely internal.* The subject would never be embarrassed by having friends know he had undergone the recapture of youth, with all the incumbent explanations, gibes, and knowing looks.

During one of George Van Tassel's earliest appearances on the Long John Nebel program, while the contactee was expounding on astral mediumship and the cabalistic ceremonies conducted in the cavern at the foot of the four-story natural totem which gave Giant Rock Airport its name, the interviewer asked why there appeared to be such a congestion of contactees in southern California, already well known as a magnet for those preoccupied with esoteria and mysticism.

Van Tassel assured John that such remarkable happenings were not confined to the West Coast. Visitations of a similar order were actually occurring within the greater megalopolis surrounding them; Long John's own environs boasted a representative of spacial aliens. Immediately John sought the identity of this singular individual, but the California contactee declined on the basis that the unknown gentleman had not accorded him permission to reveal his name. However, *sotto voce* calls were made, mysterious agreements formed, and finally the anonymity was lifted to reveal the first, and still most important, East Coast saucer figure—the now famous High Bridge, New Jersey, contactee, Howard Menger.

Menger's initial stories were extravagant and entertaining. Virtually without effort, but almost solely through the good offices of Long John Nebel, Howard Menger became a sociopsychological phenomenon. An erstwhile simple sign painter, he found people wanting to convert his home into a shrine, and proposing the raising of tablets honoring where he walked. Of course, to this day, no one knows which among these proposals surprised Howard and which reflected him. Nonetheless, it was a high point of an era, and the Atlantic seaboard would never produce his like again.

Howard Menger was born in Brooklyn, New York, on February 17, 1922, where he lived until he was about eight, when his parents moved to High Bridge, New Jersey. Shortly thereafter, he and his brother Alton "began to see discs in the sky," [18] one of which finally came to rest in the meadow where they were playing. It was three yards across, considerably smaller than the one they also observed high above. The boys approached, but, when within about twenty-five feet, the disc commenced vibrating and swiftly spun into the sky.

Two years later, during a soft summer day in 1932, when Howard was ten, he was visiting a glade in woods near his parents' home. Unexpectedly, he came upon a beautiful, sensuous, long-haired blond girl, revealing "the curves of her lovely body . . . through the translucent" ski-type suit as she reposed on a rock by a crystally brook. "Even though very young," recalled Howard later, ". . . a tremendous surge of warmth, love and physical attraction . . . emanated from her to me." The rapturous vision explained that she had " 'come a long way,' " adding, " 'We are contacting our own.' " [19] Following a few more revelations, she departed, leaving the first of the publicized child contactees sobbing a farewell as he ran out of the woods.

A decade later, having completed high school, Howard entered the army. During his initial service, while attached to a tank unit on maneuvers in the Southwest, he again began to see saucers in the sky. One evening, while on a pass in Juárez, a taxi drew up beside him as he strolled along the pavement. "I have something to tell you, would you get in the cab?" said a bronze-skinned man, with long blond hair, in the rear seat.[20] Menger declined the invitation. A subsequent contact identified the passenger as a spaceman, but added that the alien's companions had warned him to trim his tresses if he intended to wander around contacting Earthmen. The new extraterrestrial informed Howard that many Mexicans were aware of Flying Saucers and had been initiated into interplanetary intercourse "long before the . . . Conquistadores made contact with the Aztecs." [21] Marvelous inventions and secrets had been bestowed on other civilizations, the stranger said, but, as in the case of the victims of Cortez, they were destroyed or forsaken by invading warlike races.

A short time after this episode, Howard was shipped to Hawaii as a draftsman at Battalion Headquarters. One evening, having completed his assignments, he succumbed to an impulse and, borrowing a jeep, drove to some caverns located near the base. Intuition indicated he would have another rendezvous with a creature from beyond this world—and he was not to be disappointed.

Near one of the caves, he suddenly perceived the figure of a beautiful woman with long dark hair and darker eyes, semidressed in a flowing, pastel-pink tunic, with under-pantaloons to match. Both pieces of apparel being, as seemed invariably the case with the females of the species, translucent, Howard later wrote that "this girl [like the one on the rock] . . . exuded the same expression of spiritual love and deep understanding . . . but not without a strong physical attraction one finds impossible to allay when in the presence of these women." [22]

All of Howard's impulses did not lead him to such pleasant trysts. On the next occasion he discovered not a space-person at the end of his jeep ride but three Japanese soldiers, whom he dispatched in high cinematic style. Afterward he wept. However, on the next evening, he had a proper *tête-à-tête* with a chap from the planet Venus.

Yet, in reality, all of the contactee's experiences were preparatory, for his relationship with the spacians didn't achieve its true pace until he had returned to the United States and established his sign-painting business near Washington, New Jersey. About a year and a half after the war, in June of 1946, Howard was touched with the impulse to see his old High Bridge saucer haunt once more. Driving to the location of his childhood wonderment, he found that the enchantment had dissipated, and, in disappointment, turned toward his automobile to leave. Suddenly, there was a great flash of light and heat as a fireball hurtled down across one section of the lea. The enormous, whirling, bell-shaped craft spun to earth, and an aperture in its surface opened allowing two remarkably handsome, fair-skinned, blond men, in metallic-colored ski suits, to exit.

Behind them came a woman of similar coloring and beauty, dressed, like her companions, in a somewhat translucent costume. Immediately Howard recognized her as the girl on the rock, from the halcyon interlude of fourteen years before.

"But you're no older—"

"Oh, but I am. Guess, Howard, how old I really am."

The contactee could not imagine.

"I'm more than 500 years old." [23]

A mildly sexual conversation ensued, and soon the girl from Venus left.

In the fall of 1947 a pair of extraplanetarians introduced Howard to "Field Location No. 2." It later became evident to him that the glade in which he had his initial meeting was "Field Location No. 1." These would be the sites of many subsequent encounters between Menger and the spacians.

Saucerologically uneventful years followed, but they were barbed with tragedy. His son Robert became very ill in 1954; his younger brother Alton, who had shared his earliest childhood saucer experience, died in the fall of 1955, followed weeks later by the death of Howard's mother. In 1957, Robert died, and before the end of the year the contactee's father followed. A fateful three years for the young man from High Bridge, filled with more than enough sorrow to make one seek elsewhere, than on this earth, for peace.

The encounters appear to have been renewed by March, 1956, when "telepathic invitations to contacts started again," [24] and Howard began what may have been the most amazing of his contactological years.

Acting on behalf of the space people of both sexes and from various planets, he purchased clothing (one group of alien girls tossed brassieres back at him through a saucer door, giggling they didn't wear such things), dark glasses (occasionally with red lenses), and other required items; he cut their hair, briefed them on customs and colloquialisms (they usually acquired two or three formal earth languages within a couple of weeks), delivered to them special food; and, in general, made himself useful.

Howard Menger procured his first Flying Saucer photograph on an evening in April, 1956, while visiting Field Location No. 1 in response to a mental message. He leapt from the car as he arrived just in time to get a picture of an approaching spacecraft flashing in a cycle of colors, from white to green to red to white. . . .

And the tale goes on. . . .

Chapter 9

THE AIR FORCE AND THE ENEMY

Saucerology is many-tiered, but the major levels are based upon the degree of intercourse one has had with aliens. Rank is reserved for those who have seen UFOs, i.e., apparently aerodynamic phenomena—whether in flight, hovering, or on the ground—that defy natural or scientific explanation. Next, there is the stage upon which are gathered those who have seen Flying Saucers, i.e., obviously intelligently controlled craft seemingly (by virtue of any of several characteristics) from beyond the Earth; there is a slightly superior recognition accorded those who have observed the usually gigantic, zeppelin-shaped "mother ships," rather than one of the smaller "saucer types." Measurably higher are placed those who claim to have come upon a landed Flying Saucer, especially if they assert they have actually approached, or even touched, the vessel. These persons might be regarded as semicontactees. Still, none of the foregoing can be granted the respect due those of the second division of saucerites—the true contactees. Of course, within this more elevated echelon there are degrees, but the group collectively is quite set apart from their more Earth-oriented brethren. A few contactees have not seen a Flying Saucer. They claim to have been accosted, often in the most plebeian locations, by extraplanetarians who were physically indistinguishable from any terrestrial. Like the "telepathic" contactees, who maintain nothing more tangible than a psychic communication with aliens, they are not too common, nor very interesting. The majority of contactees begin, as was the case with Howard Menger, by seeing UFOs, or often Flying Saucers directly, followed by an encounter with a landed vessel. After this they are permitted a meeting with an occupant and, then, accorded access to the interior of the craft. The privilege of riding in a Flying Saucer ascends through four main classes: a brief whirl near the Earth; a phenomenally swift trip to another portion of the world; a journey to another planet, sometimes known, sometimes unheard of on this one; finally, the kind of experience described by Orfeo Angelucci—but more about that later.

Howard Menger first flew in a vehicle from outer space in August,

1956. The interlude was of the first class described above, a very limited spin above the Earth. This excursion was followed, a few days afterward, by a more lengthy trip, during which the Earthian was shown and told many secrets. Not the least of these was information concerning a "man from Yucca Valley, California" [1] (the area of George Van Tassel's Giant Rock Airport), who was conducting some extremely advanced scientific experiments. This man, said the spacians, would soon be lecturing in New York. "Just to make it a pushover for you to find him, take this down," [2] Howard was told, as they gave him the name of a hotel, and room and telephone numbers.

The events of 1956 became more and more momentous, and in September he was taken aboard a Flying Saucer "for a trip beyond the earth's atmosphere." It was of this occasion that Menger wrote:

. . . we were actually flying a few feet above the surface of a beautiful planet. Immediately I saw it was not Earth, and my question had been answered: Venus!

The scene shifted rapidly. Sometimes we were about 10 feet above the scene below; at other times . . . possibly a hundred. . . .

The planet was fantastically beautiful. I did not get the impression of cities; instead, I was reminded of suburban areas . . . on our own planet. . . . Buildings were set in natural surroundings. . . . I saw forests, streams, large bodies of water. . . . People dressed in soft pastel colors moved about. . . . Vehicles moved . . . seemed to float slightly above the ground. [3]

Soon, Howard was invited to bring others to view a landing. Immediately he prepared for this major event, which would provide some witness to his remarkable relationship with the space people. On the first occasion the Flying Saucer arrived and landed, and some of the crew appeared. These visitors were about seven feet tall, one of which was "leaping and at the same time giving the appearance of gliding over a fence five feet high and covering a distance of 20 or more feet in an abnormally short time."

The legend of Howard Menger continued to grow. He learned to teleport, not only himself, but objects as well; he learned to distinguish and describe thought discs (telepathic projections manifested as small circles of light), bell-shaped Saturnian crafts, mother ships, Venusian scout ships, and protective green fireballs. He spent four days on the second planet from the sun and experienced many other phantasmagoric things, but I will mention only a few more elements in the incredible compound of his tale.

A brief, but intriguing, episode concerned Howard's "moon potato," which admittedly appeared to be a stone to everyone present the night Howard brought it up to Long John's studio. However, the contactee, who conceded he had obtained the object from another interested Earthian, explained that this confusion was caused by the fact that the potato was "dehydrated." Unfortunately, one had to accept the word of Howard's benefactor regarding this, since the key to "*rehydrating*" it was not given with the unearthly vegetable. According to the guest of the evening, a laboratory had analyzed the matter, finding it to consist of moisture, ash, fat, and " 'N' as Protein (N X 6.25) = 15.12%," which, as is commonly known, is about six times as great a protein content as is found in our own potato—*un*-dehydrated, of course.

Another of the odd evidential and scientific visits Howard made to the show was even more delightful. The contactee had brought along a small model of a machine based upon specifications provided by the space people. If memory serves, it was either an "energy accumulator," the full size of which was intended to accelerate crafts from planet to planet, or a miniaturized perpetual-motion device; whichever, Howard set in motion whatever aspect of the little machine was meant to move. Suddenly, one element of the engine, reflecting the rarefied scientific advances of the civilizations from other worlds, fell off the body proper. An embarrassed silence obtained, until Howard sagely nodded and made one of the classic observations in the history of saucerology and interspacial physics.

"I guess the glue came apart."

Few aspects of the Menger story are more extraordinary than his encounter with Marla Baxter, who, despite the fact that he was married at the time of their initial meeting, was to become his wife. The occasion was one of Van Tassel's private lectures at Howard's home in High Bridge.

"I noticed a slim, attractive, young blond woman raptly listening to the lecture, and I knew at once who she was," wrote Howard later.[4]

"My mind flashed back to a prediction the woman from Venus had made. She said I would meet a young woman who closely resembled the girl I had met years before, as a child, in the forest [the girl on the rock]. She said her name would be 'Marla.' "

Howard Menger writes:

I do not remember all my life as a Saturnian, but I recall . . . I was a spiritual teacher who instructed the young. I had at my disposal a space craft which I used for traveling to different planets. . . . I taught . . . the positive use of telepathic projection, and the story of God's Universal Laws. . . .

On one of my trips . . . I stopped on Venus, and there I met Marla for the first time . . . tall, lithe, with long, blond wavy hair cascading around her shoulders. . . . Our love on Venus was intense . . . but it was fated [that] . . . I must travel to Earth and complete a mission . . . my day of birth on that planet.

. . . when I arrived at the portals of Earth a one-year-old boy by the name of

Howard Menger had just died. . . . . I, Sol do Naro, watched, and communicated with the soul leaving the little body. . . . I then entered the body . . . as this blob of light I entered the Earth body.[5]

The reunion of Howard, the Saturnian, and Marla, the Venusian, was ultimately resolved.

A book recounting some of the radio and television adventures of Long John Nebel, published half a decade later, gave a highly condensed, but stimulating, account of the dramatic reunion of the two displaced planetarians, from Marla's viewpoint. In her version, she refers to the contactee as "Alyn," which, as has become obvious, is a very popular name (although the spelling tends to vary) among the saucerities.

One evening, sometime after their initial meeting, Marla was lying naked on her bed, with a small towel tossed casually across her body. Unexpectedly she sensed a presence in the room, but, looking about, confirmed she was alone. However, later, while conversing with Howard, he complimented her on her loveliness and confessed he couldn't resist astrally projecting from time to time.

" . . . the very next sentence was a soul-searching kiss." As they embraced, [Marla] tells of how he "began to grind his teeth, and turn and twist and stretch. . . . He appeared to be getting taller and stronger . . . his voice was different— deeper and lower. . . . He had ceased to be Alyn [Howard] and had become a Saturnian. . . . After a short time, there was a short exhalation of breath, and he grew weak and sort of collapsed to his regular height . . . and he was himself again." [6]

Howard Menger made his first appearance on the Long John Nebel Show on October 30, 1956, and many times thereafter. However, elsewhere, countless other adventures were being related, positions taken, and saucerology advanced.

Naturally, having found out where the brass rings were being made, Long John was not about to abandon the merry-go-round. His position and influence in the field grew rapidly, and soon everyone in the business, legitimate or not, wanted access to his unexpurgating microphones. John Otto reappeared on the scene with Nebel on Easter morning, April 21, presenting a new invitation to those extraterrestrials who might be monitoring the broadcast, suggesting a contact be made on the thirtieth of that month. Subsequently, it was claimed, although no reliable records of quantitative coverage exist, that the press review of this particular overture was extraordinarily extensive. Since Lake Michigan was the locale offered as a rendezvous point, the Midwest newspapers were especially attentive. The Chicago *Daily News, Tribune, Sun-Times,* and the Waukegan *News-Sun* reportedly contributed a combined total of 235 column inches to the chronicles of contemplated encounters.

Actual contact stories were circling the world almost as swiftly as the saucers themselves were supposedly doing. The northern French hamlet Beaucourt-sur-Landre was the source of a report of a back-road landing of a curious craft which expelled a quartet of gray-garbed aliens. Although dismissed by provincial gendarmes as group hallucination caused by the flashing lantern of a farmer's wife, a half dozen persons attested to the reality of the ruddy-colored vessel and its crew.

The chorus of more sober voices in support of unknown aerial craft, or at least inexplicable UFOs, was also growing. In May, the former United States Ambassador to Switzerland, Henry J. Taylor, revised his 1950 contention that the phenomena were American secret weapons, saying that they were serious and not easily explained. *Flying Saucers* magazine said on June 7 that the United States Air Defense Radar Station had traced over one hundred unknowns approaching this country from across the Atlantic Ocean. Although no explanation was rendered, assurances were given that the blips were neither Russian planes nor missiles.

A month later found Capt. Wallace W. Elwood, assistant adjutant at the Air Technical Intelligence Center in Ohio, conceding that Air Force pilots had opened fire on UFOs, or what they thought to be UFOs, when the objects were caught in commission of acts assumed to be hostile to the United States. It need hardly be stated that the illogicality of denying the existence of something and then proceeding to evaulate the non-existence's acts and attacking the non-it on the basis of its non-existence is too highly ciphered for the layman to decode—without, of course, getting zero.

However, the ufologists, and a few saucer researchers of less extravagant natures, were firmly convinced by the beginning of the second decade of the Age of Flying Saucers that persons in extremely high positions were infinitely more informed about that mystery than had been suspected. In most cases the thesis was broad enough to include high officials of several other governments. Our British allies, for example.

"In room 801 of what was once the Hotel Metropole, Britain's Air Ministry is investigating flying saucers—and that's official," said one 1957 report.

At airfields all over Britain fighter planes are kept ready to intercept, and if necessary engage, any unidentified flying object within combat range. . . . [The room's] existence was admitted last night by an Air Ministry spokesman. He disclosed that it has been investigating flying saucers since 1947.[7]

Rarely was the interplay between officialdom and serious researchers made so public as on the night of September 27, when Major Keyhoe appeared on the *Night Beat* television show, moderated by John Wingate.

As the program progressed, the director of NICAP was queried extensively on the subject of Flying Saucers, then, as the broadcast drew toward its closing minutes, Wingate suddenly announced:

"This afternoon, the Air Force gave *Night Beat* an official statement . . . [saying] that as Director of NICAP you have been given *all* the information in the hands of the United States Air Force, and that any claim to the contrary is absolutely untrue!" [8]

"Mr. Wingate, NICAP asked Secretary Douglas to let us see those solved reports. Here's the Air Force's answer," replied Keyhoe, holding a letter before the camera. "As you see, it reads:

" 'We must decline your offer to review and publish the Air Force reports on this subject.' "

"You mean the Air Force lied to *Night Beat?*" exploded Wingate, rather rhetorically.

"Let us say they gave a false statement," concluded Keyhoe.

Autumn of 1957, especially November, produced one of the most interesting flaps of the later part of the decade. Curious, although difficult to place properly in the puzzle, was a conversation between Major Keyhoe himself and an associate, which occurred on October 31. He records the following exchange:

"Mr. Healey, has the Air Force given you those four hidden documents?"

"No, but I'm to get a summary of the January, 1953 conclusions, after the Pentagon conference."

"Why only a summary?"

"Well, it's a classified document, and it's the CIA, not the Air Force. . . ."

"Then we were right! The CIA does control the [flying saucer] investigation." [9]

His associate made no comment.

Centered amid the great flap of that fall was the Levelland, Texas, complex of inexplicable events. The overture of the long-argued series of sightings and encounters may have been scored by John Wolfe, of San Rafael, California, who reported, on November 1, seeing an immense ovoid object, as large as a "harvest moon" and so bright he found it blinding. However, the first movement began on the following evening, when hundreds, if not thousands, of people of western Texas and New Mexico were witness to an extraordinary oval object of vivid red arcing across the sky.

A few minutes before eleven, Officer A. J. Fowler got one of the earliest reports. Pedro Saucedo, accompanied by a friend, José Salaz (sometimes spelled Salav, Palav, or Salvaz), were proceeding along Texas Highway 116 in a farm truck when they saw a glowing unknown plummet to the ground nearby.

"We didn't think much about it," Saucedo said, "but it rose up out of the field and started toward us, picking up speed. When it got nearer, the lights of my truck went out and the motor died . . . the thing passed directly over the truck with a great sound and a rush of wind. It sounded like thunder, and my truck rocked from the blast. I felt a lot of heat." [10]

Saucedo observed the departing object and described it as torpedo-shaped and about two hundred feet long.

Similar reports were subsequently made by James Wheeler, José Alvarez, Newell Wright, Frank Williams, James (Jesse?) D. Long, Ronald Martin, and many others of the vicinity, each describing a glowing UFO which caused the electric components of their automobiles to fail until it had passed. By early morning, Sheriff Weir Clem and Deputy Pat McCullough, on assignment to investigate the remarkable stories, noted the object shooting through the air lighting "up the whole pavement in front of us for about two seconds." [11]

On the early morning of the third, at about 3:00 A.M., Corp. Glenn H. Toy and Pfc. James Wilbanks, both of the military police, reportedly observed a radiant vermilion disc slowly descend to within fifty yards of earth near the White Sands Proving Grounds. The object, which was about two miles from their position, appeared to be nearly three hundred feet in diameter.

"It came down very slowly to about fifty yards," reported Toy. "It stayed there three minutes, giving off a brilliant reddish orange light. Then it came to the ground fairly fast. It looked like a completely controlled landing." [12]

The "MP's told the Intelligence officers they believed it [the UFO] was a controlled machine from outer space," records Keyhoe. [13]

Specialists Richard Oakes and Henry Barlow described a sighting which took place at eight o'clock the next evening as of similar breadth but shaped like a long, thin projectile. Their unknown was noted hanging above the earth, slowly rising until it appeared to be a star, and then vanishing. Newell A. Wright of Abilene, Texas, recalled seeing a 120-foot, neonlike luminescent ovoid take off from a highway surface and disappear into the night. Don Clark, a civilian radarman at Holloman Air Force Base, reported a cigar-shaped object west of Alamagordo, New Mexico.

The reports of two Army patrols were of particular interest. They identified a UFO suspended above an abandoned technicians' bunker, which had been used during the first atomic tests in 1945, at the White Sands Proving Grounds—a location nearly identical with that cited by contactee Dan Fry as the point at which he encountered the extraterrestrial craft that spirited him to New York and back in half an hour. A similar observation was made by James Stokes, a missile engineer at Holloman. According to this witness, an iridescent oval object stalled ten or more automobiles along Highway 54. Coming from the northeast, it swept in a shallow pass across the sky, moving toward the Proving Grounds to the southwest, radiating a great wave of heat as it soundlessly passed overhead. Reports were even coming in from north and south. In Elmwood Park, near Chicago, two police officers told of a glowing, iridescent rocket nearly the length of a football field cruising three hundred feet above their patrol car. Dispatcher Daniel de Giovanni and his companion monitored the unknown object until it outdistanced them. Meanwhile, at 5:10 A.M. on the morning of November 5, as the Coast Guard cutter *Sebago* was cruising about in the Gulf of Mexico, veteran radarmen began tracking an unidentified flying object as it swiftly circled about the ship for ten minutes. The scope showed it wheeling around, suddenly stopping, hovering motionlessly, and then plummeting off at speeds near a thousand miles an hour. Visual observation of the brilliant object was made by Lt. Donald Schaefer, Ensign Wayne Schottley, Q.M. Kenneth Smith, and Seaman Radioman Thomas Kirk, among others.

Hundreds of persons reported sightings throughout the entire Levelland complex, scores recounted having their automibile engines and/or headlights extinguished by the presence of the phenomena. The incidents occurred across a fairly wide area, actually several hundred square miles (including the vicinity of Lubbock, of earlier overflight fame), and were characterized in very much the same language, except for the one or two reports distinctively different, emphasizing "cigar-shaped" craft.

Today the Levelland sequence is as much of a mystery as ever, notwithstanding the typically absurd explanations offered by religiously dedicated debunkers like Donald Menzel, most of whom finally settled on "ball lightning," an entirely inadequate solution if all of the observations recorded are weighed. Needless to say, the ball-lightning theorists, as was the usual practice among professional—if highly ineffectual—dispellers of doubt, merely selected those few sightings the descriptions of which seemed to fit their preconception and discarded the remaining reports. Since, as even Menzel concedes, the Air Force contributed but a single investigator for only seven hours to examine the situation, the sites, and the witnesses—which, quite obviously he did not, could not, do—it is perfectly understandable that officialdom is as ignorant of the true meaning of the Levelland enigmas as it is of most major UFO puzzles. A decade had taught it nothing, except, perhaps, to be even more superficial in practice and dense in interpretation than had been its original inclination.

Yet, although the Levelland complex was the most concentrated aspect of the great November flap, sightings were flooding in from all quarters. Capt. Clyde C. Russ, of the Beaumont, Texas, police force, five of his men, and reporter Paul Smith, saw an apparently controlled UFO; a trio of men from the Alton & Southern Railroad watched two silvery ovoids; an enormous unknown was reported by three Atlanta, Georgia, firemen; Illinois State Police chased a glowing object for fifteen miles, near the town of Danville; an oval UFO was seen by an Episcopal minister, newspaper editor William Stewart, and several others in Spooner, Wisconsin, and in Chicago by a number of law officers; a group, including an Air Force major, told of sighting a half dozen glistening unknowns over the Municipal Airport, near Long Beach, California; and scores, if not hundreds, more such observations were made before the fall "flap" of 1957 slowed down to the usual sighting pace throughout the United States.

Single-tracked skeptic Dr. Donald Menzel, head of the Astronomy Department at Harvard, who usually discounted UFO reports as meteors, birds, and other natural phenomena, decided the Levelland complex would not fall before such an explanation and so came up with another solution—mirages. He was never to rationally apply this thesis to the effect the phenomena seemed to have on automobile engines, headlights, and other electrical devices. Later, without reference to his initial evaluation, he supplanted his psychological solution with a more physical one, which had been popularized by other skeptics. By 1963 he had tagged his endorsement to the contention that "the evidence, however, leads to an overwhelming probability: the fiery unknown at Levelland *was* ball lightning." [14] As is usually the case, Menzel's deductions are more than adequate comments on themselves.

The Mount Stromlo Observatory in Australia offered one interesting contribution when four of its astronomers tracked a luminous object across the sky on the early morning of November 8. "It is the first time that the observatory has sighted what might be called an unidentified flying object," recounted Dr. A. R. Hogg, who added that the phenomenon was too slow for a meteor and was neither Sputnik I nor II.[15] Elsewhere in the scientific community Dr. Lincoln La Paz, Director of the Institute of Meteorics, University of New Mexico, originally characterized the Levelland incidents, and other concurrent happenings, as fireballs; however, later he reversed his position and said that they could not possibly be explained as fireballs or other celestial phenomena.

The various occurrences described, although improbable, seem quite believable when compared with a further report from Brazil, as made by Dr. Olavo T. Fontes to the Aerial Phenomena Research Organization in

Phoenix.[16] According to this researcher, the Brazilian Army fortress Itaipu at São Vicente, in the State of São Paulo, was approached on the moonless, tropical evening of November 4, 1957 while all but two sentinels of the garrison were asleep. This pair was suddenly startled by the appearance of an iridescent object above the fortification. A star and an airplane were eliminated as possible explanations because of the speed and aerial gymnastics of the apparition. The UFO achieved the air over the fortress at great acceleration and then abruptly arrested its motion, drifted slowly down to an altitude of less than two hundred feet, and hovered. The sentries, were immobilized as a burning sensation engulfed them. One man staggered, gasped for air, and blacked out. His companion, terrified, began howling frantically, racing about like a trapped animal. Suddenly, the communications were dead, the emergency circuits failed, and, most peculiar of all, all the clocks in the barracks, which had been set for 5:00 A.M., began to ring simultaneously.

Shortly thereafter, the facilities were restored, and a rapidly reorganized fortress spread to battle stations to defend against the unknown enemy who was surely attacking. As they came into position, a number of officers and soldiers perceived an orange light in rapid vertical ascent, which then changed direction and bulleted into the stratosphere at a tremendous speed. The two sentinels were found near their posts, one still unconscious, one huddled in a corner mumbling and bereft of his senses. Immediate medical examination established that both had suffered first- and second-degree burns over more than 10 percent of their bodies.

The entire unbelievable episode had, according to the report, taken little more than three minutes.

On the following day, the commanding colonel forbade his men to discuss the incident. Intelligence officers appeared, assuming control of the case. The fort came under martial law.

An addendum to this fascinating story was written by the appearance of a U.S. Army Military Mission, which suddenly arrived to question the pertinent witnesses, especially the sentinels, who had been transferred to a maximum-security hospital ward. Along with a thousand other cases, this one has no conclusion—it merely stops.

However, if startling UFO sightings were becoming almost common, contactological contentions kept pace.

Reinhold O. Schmidt, a small-time businessman from Kearney, Nebraska, was responsible for one of the more interesting contact stories of 1957. According to his report, November 5 found him driving southeast of the community, at about two thirty in the afternoon, under a cloudy gray sky. Something brilliant suddenly flashed, and a short distance beyond he saw what he subsequently described as "a large silvery ship of some kind of metal . . . [which] appeared to be solid . . . without portholes or windows. . . . [It] must have been about 50 feet long and 30 feet wide and about 14 high. . . . [It featured] a large tube about 12 feet in diameter in each end of the ship, [and] in each of these tubes was a large 8-to-10-foot bladed fan." [17] The contactee recalls he was invited to enter the vehicle, within which he found "four men and two ladies." Mr. Schmidt was to later expound at length on the characteristics of the ship and its occupants, but best remembered was his contention that while they all spoke fluent English, in every instance the accent was German, and that, among themselves, they spoke nothing but *haut deutsch.*

Following Mr. Schmidt's purported adventure along the banks of the Platte River, local radio and television stations and newspapers broadly announced that spaceships had landed at Kearney, Nebraska. The contactee was widely interviewed and continued to provide elaborations of his original story. Subsequently, he made contact with Wayne Aho, a curious individual who appears in numerous saucer situations, and proceeded to give talks to small groups about his adventure. While his tale had certain amusing aspects, Mr. Schmidt was never able to achieve a place among the first- or even second-rank figures of contactology; yet he remains of sufficient importance in the history of UFO sightings to deserve at least a passing glance from anyone interested in the subject.

Three days after the supposed Schmidt encounter, Hank Mollohan, Jr., of Holly, West Virginia, claimed an adventure—also at two thirty in the afternoon—with a cigar-type ship, forty feet long, displaying about a dozen portholes. However, notwithstanding a fairly lengthy interview, Mr. Mollohan added little more to that simple report than that the device had landed and he thought he had seen a shadowy three-foot figure wandering about.[18]

Mrs. Cynthia Appleton, of Birmingham, England, meanwhile perfected her own phantasizing. According to this twenty-seven-year-old mother of two, a pair of alien tourists strolled into her home, ensconced themselves, and chatted with her for some time about their intentions for the planet Earth. And if Reinhold Schmidt had heard his ultramen conversing in fluent German, Mrs. Appleton was somewhat less chauvinistic. Her spacemen were "tall and blond like Greek athletes." According to one source, both her husband and two clergymen of the Church of England believed her story, certainly reflecting a heartening faith on the part of all.

On November 10, two Cherokee Indians, in Cherokee, North Carolina, reported seeing a hundred-foot-wide, glowing red globe crusing above the highway. Approaching it in their automobile, they recalled that it descended behind trees and disappeared. Offering a somewhat different explanation than that usually encountered, they characterized the apparition as a "skillie," a human, according to Cherokee lore, who through magical ritual has achieved the ability to transform himself into an animal, vegetable, mineral, or energy—in this instance, light.

Photographs from this period were, of course, rarely worth comment. However there was, at least, one exception. This intriguing saucer picture was allegedly taken sometime in early December, 1957, at the mysteriously recurring point in time, two thirty in the afternoon, by British radio officer T. Fogl, of the S.S. *Ramsey*. It presents a quite clearly defined craftlike object with protuberances that appear to be landing gear or jets. Fogl subsequently conceded that he had read Adamski's book in 1954, observed another saucer while sailing on the Panamanian ship *Eagle* in 1955, and in general was receptive to the possibility of interplanetary visitations. Nonetheless, his two photographs are interesting.[19]

The Olden Moore saga commenced on November 6, 1957, when that Lake County, Ohio, gentleman was driving along Route 86 and noticed in the sky a luminous unknown that had "stopped when it got to the center of the driver's half of the windshield."[20] At that point it "split into two pieces, [and] one part went upward,"[21] as the remaining segment brightened even more. Later, the sighter was to recall that the disc-shaped object was about fifty feet across and about a third that thick. It was topped with a conic effect, which may have doubled its total height, seemed bathed in a blue-green mist, and appeared to be smooth-surfaced, without any apertures.

After some time, Moore left his automobile and began to walk the several hundred feet separating him from the device. However, having traversed about half the distance, he decided to retrace his steps, retreat from the field and find another witness. Unfortunately, by the time he brought his wife to the site, the vessel had vanished.

The incident was reported the following day, at which time the local Civilian Defense director Kenneth Locke and Lieutenant Reinek, of the Ohio 5th Area Civilian Defense unit, examined the area visually and with a Geiger counter. They allegedly found footprints "coming from nowhere and going nowhere," as well as what appeared to be tracks from spiked shoes. The roentgen reading taken registered about 150 in the center of the cited area, dropping to approximately 20 at the outer perimeter. A second scanning several hours later revealed that the middle ground peaking of 150 had subsided to between 20 and 30, and the circumference, to zero. There was no question of the response being due to mineral deposits.

On November 10, according to Moore, he was visited by Geauga County Sheriff Louis Robusky, a deputy, and an Air Force lieutenant who requested that he accompany them to Youngstown, where he could make a full statement and answer whatever questions seemed appropriate. Assured he would be back by evening, he was surprised when his companions first drove him to the sighting location, where an Air Force helicopter waited. He was flown to Youngstown, exhaustively interviewed, and finally returned to his home a little before midnight.

One week afterward, two Air Force officers arrived in an officially marked automobile, and requested that he come with them to Washington, D.C., for a few days for even more detailed interrogation. Leaving him time to pack a few essentials, they departed and reappeared in an hour. Moore was driven to a plane which immediately took off. At Wright-Patterson Field, at Dayton, they set down to deposit one officer and enplane another, finally arriving in Washington in the evening. Moore was driven from the airport to a building, in which, he recounts, he was domiciled during his entire stay. Subsequently shown photographs of various buildings in the capital, to which he had never been before, he is supposed to have identified the United States Court House, on Constitution Avenue, as one of those in which he had been queried.

Much later, Moore says, he was visited again by Air Force representatives. These officers assured him that what he had seen in 1957 had been only a giant fireball. In 1962, researcher James W. Moseley, while writing of a field trip to Blue Book headquarters at Wright-Patterson Air Force Base, said that Col. Robert J. Friend, then directing the evaluating operation, had dismissed the entire matter.

According to Colonel Friend, the Air Force went to inverview this man and asked him "politely about these wild claims [about the Washington, D.C., trip]. The fellow [Moore] admitted in private that they were not true. Apparently he had merely strayed from home for a few days and needed a good story to tell his wife." [22]

Nonetheless, almost a year later, Moore was quoted as saying:

"I know I saw a solid object that night, because I was close enough to it to see the reflection of the moonlight on the object's mirror-like surface. It wasn't any fireball. I know what I saw and nothing they said could change my mind." [23]

The year concluded with the issuance of an Air Force "fact sheet" titled "Air Force's 10-Year Study of Unidentified Flying Objects."

It, following the usual official pattern, dismissed virtually all of the recorded UFOs as "balloons, airplanes, vapor trails, jet afterburners, stars, planets, meteors, comets . . . Venus, Mars, Jupiter seen through haze, fog, or moving clouds, sundogs, spurious radar indications, hoaxes, fireworks displays, flares, fireballs, ice crystals, bolides, etc. . . ."

Keyhoe interestingly points out that the 1956 analysis specified 778

Chapter 10

FACT, FRAUD, AND FANTASY

The Brazilian Navy incident—a complex of sightings, topped by a gallery of photographs, which well may have been the most important sighting series of its time—began toward the end of November, 1957, and concluded almost a year later.

Commander Carlos Alberto Bacellar, directing a Brazilian Navy task force, was operating in the waters around the island of Trindade, about seven hundred miles into the Atlantic. The purpose was to establish an International Geophysical Year research activity under the supervision of the Hydrography and Navigation Division of the Ministry of the Navy. Bacellar himself was a highly qualified officer, a technician, a recognized expert in meteorological and atmospheric phenomena, and the initiator of a radio-sonde system in his country (a broadcast technique in which sensitive instruments are sent up in usually unmanned balloons to record and report to the ground humidity, temperature, pressure, and other data). Accompanying Bacellar were a number of carefully chosen specialists.

A meteorological balloon was sent aloft on a clear, sunny morning in November with a crew monitoring it, waiting for the moment when, according to schedule, it would parachute its instruments. Unexpectedly, a new radio signal intruded, while, simultaneously, visual observation identified another object in the sky near the balloon. The unknown appeared silvery, highly mobile, and capable of tremendous speeds. Immediately the azimuth and elevation of Venus were verified and found to bear no relationship to the object of attention. To quote the report of well-known ufologist Dr. Olavo T. Fontes, carried in the Aerial Phenomena Research Organization *Bulletin*:

Com. Bacellar took over the theodolite [a surveying instrument which measures horizontal and vertical angles, equipped with a telescope] and found the balloon still there, whereupon he immediately abandoned it and picked up the unidentified object as it came out of the sun. Through the 20-power scope, the UAO [Unidentified Aerial Object] presented a distinct oval-shaped outline and was about three times as long as it was wide. It was silvery-white in color and reflected sunlight with what looked like a metallic shine. It appeared to change shape according to its position in space in relation to the observers. [Of course, anything would except a sphere.] Sometimes it seemed round, or looked like a planetary disk.[1]

The object was described as having no projections, no vapor trails, and no rotary motion, although, at times, some oscillation was suggested. After the remarkable stay of three hours, it began to move away until the technicians tracking it found it gone. Since Bacellar dismissed two earlier reports—including a landing on Trindade Island—this is regarded as the first of what became a series of extraordinary happenings in the area.

The second sighting occurred on December 5, the third on the last day of the year, the fourth on the following day, and the fifth on the evening of January 2. A Brazilian Navy tow ship named *Triunfe,* cruising some four hundred miles from Trindade, was circled for nearly ten minutes by the enigmatic craft as the entire crew watched.

The next instance of the UFO was on the sixth of the month, on a hazeless morning with a bright, clear sky featuring a lone cumulus cloud just overhead. Unexpectedly, the signal of the weather balloon, which was being tracked visually and via its radio-sonde, began to fail, and then went silent. Commander Bacellar immediately went out for a personal observation and saw the balloon high above, still ascending, passing the point at which the instruments were supposed to be parachuted. As it rose, it came closer and closer to the isolated cumulus cloud. Suddenly, it was sucked into the cloud, disappearing. Out of sight for ten minutes, the balloon finally moved into sight again, continuing its upward flight. However, now the instrument package was gone. It had entered the fluffy condensation with its equipment and exited without it.

Moments later another object emerged from the cloud: the UFO. Spotted by a technician with a theodolite, the silvery, aluminum-looking device moved slowly through the sunlight. Bacellar examined it with powerful binoculars and then monitored it with the theodolite for thirty minutes. Switching to a sextant, he continued his scrutiny until, just after noon, it moved toward and behind a bank of cirrus clouds, ending the incident for the day.

The climax of the event was the photographing of the UFO on January 16, 1958.

The Brazilian Navy ship *Almirante Saldanha,* a former training vessel converted for special hydrographic investigation associated with International Geophysical Year researches, under the command of Comdr. Sadanha da Gama, was in the waters of the island of Trindade, preparing for its return trip to Rio de Janeiro. At twelve fifteen in the afternoon, a strange object in the sky was observed by a number of persons on deck. The aerial unknown swiftly approached the island, hovered near it for a brief time, vanished behind a small mountain peak, and reappeared on the other side. During these maneuvers a professional photographer and former newspaperman named Almiro Barauna photographed the mystery craft five times. In reply to questions put to him, these are some of Barauna's comments and conclusions:

I was on the deck . . . the sea was agitated. The weather was cloudy, clear, with no shadows. I had my Rolleiflex 2.8, model E, which was kept inside an aluminum box for protection against the corrosive effects of water and salt . . . the deck was full of sailors and officers. Suddenly, Mr. Amilar Viera [a member of the federal CACEX Research Division] and Captain Viegas called me, pointing to a certain spot in the sky and yelling about a bright object which was approaching the island. At this moment . . . Lieutenant Homero—the ship's dentist— came from the bow toward us, running, pointing out to the sky and also yelling about an object he was sighting . . . it was coming over the sea . . . I lost about thirty seconds looking . . . but the camera was already in my hands, ready, when I sighted it clearly silhouetted behind the peak . . . my camera was set at speed 125, with the aperture at f/8, and this was the cause of an over-exposure error, as I discovered later.

The object remained out of sight for a few seconds . . . reappearing bigger in size and flying in the opposite direction, but lower and closer than before, and moving at higher speed. I shot the third photo . . . [subsequently as] it was moving again toward the sea, in the same direction from which it had come, and it appeared to stop in mid-air for a brief time. At that moment I shot my last photo.[2]

Barauna concluded:

I am absolutely certain it was a controlled object—either directly or by remote control—but very well operated, in any case. The general impression of the people aboard the ship was the same: it had come to make a close observation of the ship.[3]

"The object sighted in the skies of Trindade," recounted Comdr. Paulo Moreira da Silva, of the Hydrography and Navigation Service, "was not a weather balloon, neither an American guided missile. . . ."[4]

Mr. Amilar Vieria Filho, a member of the federal research operation CACEX, noted: "What I saw, in fact, was an object of gray color and oval in shape when first sighted, which passed over the island and then— emitting a fluorescent light it didn't possess before—went away toward the horizon . . . it looked like an object with a polished surface and uniform color. I am sure it was not a balloon, an airplane, or a sea-gull."[5]

Soon after his original comments, the Commander stated flatly that "the photos are authentic, and the film was developed on the same occasion [as they were taken], aboard the NE *Almirante Saldanha*—and also that the image of the object on the negatives was verified, at the same opportunity, by several officers. . . ." [6]

Admiral Gerson de Macedo Soares, the Navy General Secretary, was quoted as saying: "I do not see any reason to doubt the reports of reliable witnesses. Personally, I believe in the reality of the flying saucers, even if they come from another planet." [7] The Minister of the Navy, Admiral Alves Camers, meanwhile told a correspondent that he "didn't believe in flying saucers before, but after Barauna's evidence [he] was convinced." [8]

However, the peculiar behavior of the Pentagon and the Air Force was never more clearly highlighted than during the *Armstrong Circle Theatre* broadcast on the subject of Unidentified Flying Objects, offered over CBS television on January 22, 1958. Originally the show—"UFO—Enigma of the Skies"—was apparently conceived as a balanced survey of the mystery, presenting various points of view, and to this end Maj. Donald E. Keyhoe, Capt. Edward J. Ruppelt, Capt. C. S. Chiles, Kenneth Arnold, Prof. Donald H. Menzel, and several Air Force spokesmen were to appear.

Shortly after the invitation was delivered to Keyhoe, he was again contacted by Irve Tunick, liaison man for the *Armstrong Circle Theatre.* Tunick told Keyhoe that after some unspecified negotiations the Air Force had agreed to participate; however, they insisted that they be permitted to see Keyhoe's script in advance and that assurances be given that no ad libs would be permitted. Obviously, this indicated they expected to have approval rights over anything the NICAP head intended to reveal. And this was not the least of the imbalance. Keyhoe was told that he was to be accorded seven minutes and the Air Force and associates twenty-five. Further, the Air Force had banned the screening of the Utah UFO film, calling the phenomena shown sea gulls.

Disenchanted, the director of NICAP proceeded to prepare his script. He submitted the material and assumed it to be his final version. However, when it was returned to him for broadcast use he discovered that it had been eviscerated, and that all the essential points had been deleted. Upon objecting to the program, he was told that it had been too long, although he had repeatedly timed it before submission and found it easily readable within the brief, but allotted, seven minutes. It was about this time he was informed that both Ruppelt and Chiles had reversed their previous decisions and had no intentions of appearing. The word was that they had been forced to succumb to Air Force and/or economic threats.

When rehearsal day arrived, Keyhoe had retained one brief item of interest:

> There is an official policy, believed in the best interests of the people, not to confirm the existence of UFOs until all the answers are known. Captain Edward J. Ruppelt, former chief of Project Blue Book, has confirmed the existence of four important documents that should be noted. In 1948, in a "Top Secret" estimate, the ATIC [Air Technical Intelligence Center] concluded the UFOs were interplanetary spaceships. In 1952, an Air Force Intelligence analysis of UFO manoeuvres brought the same conclusion . . . interplanetary. In January, 1953, a report by a panel of top scientists at the Pentagon reached this conclusion: There is strong circumstantial evidence, but no concrete proof that UFOs are spaceships. They recommended intensifying the investigation and telling the American people all the facts. . . .[9]

This, he was quickly informed, could not be used.

"Then the Air Force *is* censoring this program," exclaimed the head of the National Investigations Committee on Aerial Phenomena, reiterating a charge he had made several times earlier.

And so, under blatantly obvious censorship by the Air Force, the program stumbled along, bearing little relation to the actual mystery, let alone the facts, surrounding the subject of Unidentified Flying Objects. Eventually Arnold dropped out as well, and little was left but Keyhoe and the Establishmentarian propaganda.

The show hit the air and it was absurd, with ridiculous references to contactees and spacemen pilots by Air Force, or Air Force–oriented, spokesmen. When Keyhoe appeared with his vacuous, disemboweled script, little could be done to contravene the nonsense which had preceded him. Suddenly, total exasperation exploded within the director of NICAP, and he abruptly veered from the teleprompting text:

"And now I'm going to reveal something that has never been disclosed before . . . for the last six months we have been working with a Congressional committee investigating official secrecy about UFOs," but, by now, although the audience could see that Keyhoe was still speaking, the producer had already cut the audio off the air. The public was never to hear him as he continued and concluded: ". . . if all the evidence we have given this committee is made public in open hearings it will absolutely prove that the UFOs are real machines under intelligent control."[10]

Should there be the slightest doubt as to the control maintained over every aspect of the program by the Air Force, NICAP's files contain the following concession, made by the CBS director of editing, Herbert A. Carlborg:[11]

> This program had been carefully cleared for *security reasons*. Therefore, it was the responsibility of this network to *insure performance that was in accordance with*

predetermined security standards. Any indication that there would be a deviation from the script might lead to a statement that neither this network nor the individuals on the program were *authorized to release.* [Emphasis added.]

One thing, at least, emerged from the Armstrong show, an involuntary restatement that, as the Air Force entered its second decade of dealing with the problem of Unidentified Flying Objects, it had no more intention of telling the truth than it had during the preceding ten years.

The year 1958 was of particular interest to the serious student of the Age of Flying Saucers because of the involvement of Dr. Carl Jung, onetime associate of Sigmund Freud and among the leading psychiatrists and analysts in the world. His name came up as a result of an announcement made by APRO (Aerial Phenomena Research Organization), which quoted Jung as having allegedly said:

If the extraterrestrial origin of saucers should be confirmed, this would prove the existence of an intelligent interplanetary relationship. What such a fact might mean for humanity cannot be predicted. But it would put us without a doubt in the extremely precarious position of primitive communities in conflict with the superior culture of the white race.[12]

The Swiss psychiatrist's *Flying Saucers* was originally published as *Ein Moderner Mythus von Dingen die am Himmel gesehen werden.*[13] He wrote it in part to correct what he regarded as a misinterpretation of his position, as expressed in an interview for the Swiss journal *Die Weltwoche* in 1954, the belated result of which was to identify the analyst as a "believer" in Flying Saucers. His issuance of a correction four years later suggesting that "something is seen, but one doesn't know what" went unnoticed. Dr. Jung conceded that UFOs (Unidentified Flying Objects) were real, but suggested studious avoidance of "wild speculation," such as prematurely concluding they were Flying Saucers. However, his book tended to substantiate the contention that Jung was a "believer," rather than to mitigate, or contradict, it—not merely of UFOs, but Flying Saucers, as well.

Despite the large library of material regarding UFOs which accumulated during the late forties and early fifties, in the beginning of his volume the psychiatrist regards their physical reality as "very problematical," especially since the apparently complex phenomena had an inescapably psychic aspect. In speculating about the presumably physical UFOs, which were frequent in *appearance*, on the one hand, and completely inexplicable, on the other, Jung admits that one had no way of knowing whether the viewer had actually observed a real object and followed it with a psychological response or had been the subject of an initial fantasy that manifested itself in ufological illusions. The third alternative offered is that such sightings were in some manner "synchronistic," or "meaningfully coincidental." Disqualifying himself, as being unequipped, from considerations of UFOs in terms of the physical sciences, Dr. Jung proceeds to examine "their undoubted psychic aspects."

Confronted with the obvious initial reaction to UFOs, that of automatic rejection, he begins by considering them as "rumours," that is, as "psychic products," and attempts to analyze them as such. Since they are seen, he defines the phenomena as "visionary rumours" and relates them to other cases where seemingly impossible occurrences have been observed, i.e., the incident at Fatima.

Dr. Jung explains that a prerequisite for "visionary rumours" is "always an *unusual emotion*." Suggesting that the yet unexplained sightings during World War II (the *ghost rockets* of Scandinavia, the *foo fighters* familiar to Allied pilots, etc.) had been grafted, in the minds of some of the American public, to the famous prewar Orson Welles radio version of H. G. Wells's *The War of the Worlds,* the author feels that the extraterrestriality of the invaders of the broadcast was attributed to the unknown aerial phenomena, resulting in the original "rumours" being interpreted as intelligently controlled craft from outer space. Notwithstanding the fact the UFOs demonstrated no hostility, thus indicating that their presence was due to curiosity or reconnaissance, people felt spied upon, felt as if they were being subjected to a vast, almost ubiquitous, voyeurism. This disquiet, as much as anything else, led to the establishment around the world of various national and independent agencies to investigate the mystery on a more organized and efficient basis.

Jung considers various physical descriptions of UFOs and accepts the rumor-objects as not conforming to any recognizable flight behavior. Rather he compares their reported activities to "tourists unsystematically viewing the countryside." He mentions, but does not dwell upon, how variously the contactees picture the occupants of these *craft*, especially with regard to height. Some of the extraterrestrials, he notes, are supposed to stand about three feet high, while others range as tall as fifteen feet. However, regardless of their appearance, they are generally purported to possess immeasurably terrible and destructive weapons, capable of destroying mankind, but are usually assumed to be so superior intellectually that their advanced wisdom would preclude their being a danger to inhabitants of Earth.

Referring to those many scientific authorities who deny any possibility of Flying Saucers, the psychiatrist counters that if the phenomena are instances of "psychological *projection*" they must derive from a *"psychic cause."* It is his opinion that no rumor so worldwide could be "purely fortuitous" and wholly unimportant; therefore, the countless individual reports must have some common, or at least relatable, causal basis. He deduces that the ubiquitously present element, one conceivable as the basis of such broad-scale rumor is *"emotional tension,"* that is, the distress and apprehension of people everywhere with regard to international affairs and the ever-present shadow of martial holocaust.

Jung holds that such illusory rumors arise in the individual between a conscious attitude and the unconscious. This separation presents the conscious mind with an inexplicable situation which cannot be assimilated and, therefore, indirect expression is sought, such frequently taking the form of improbable convictions, "beliefs, illusions, visions, and so forth." In this state persons see things in an exaggerated or fictionalized way, or translate normal occurrences into omens and signs from the unknown or unexplained. Often conditions of this nature manifest themselves as crowd hysteria, or separate, but collective, responses, and not infrequently as wholly independent, but parallel, attitudes.

Where the atmosphere is conducive, it is often found that individuals who have always been unbelievers, or agnostics, suddenly convert and *see* whatever the rumor is, and because of their previous scepticism they are viewed as exceptionally credible witnesses. Projection is nowise unique, or even unusual; it is common in mental illness, advertising, theatrical popularity, and political propaganda. Of course, Jung adds, it has "different ranges," depending upon its source and the conditions surrounding the subjects.

The psychiatrist states that "collective contents, such as religion, philosophy, political and social conflicts, select projection-carriers of a corresponding kind—Freemasons, Jews, Jesuits—" but that "projection-creating fantasy soars beyond the realm of earthly organizations and powers into the heavens, into interstellar space, where . . . the gods once had their abode."

Remarking on the "camera-mindedness of Americans," yet the rarity of convincing UFO photographs, the author concludes that the phenomena are not photogenic, regardless of their explanation. Nonetheless, he classifies the celestial sightings as a *"living myth."*

Among the factors presented by the analyst as the most important in the mystery, especially from the psychic-rumor perspective, are the apparently uncontrollable population explosion and the ensuing congestion and diminution of per-unit living space. As the earth's size is reduced for all practical purposes, it appears inevitable that it will become too small to support the entire human family. Add to this the Damoclean threat of nuclear catastrophe, and we have a perpetually increasing cluster of prisoners who know they may be facing death, but never how or when. The result: fear.

However, since no solution seems likely to be discovered on Earth, or by its inhabitants, many minds are receptive to the idea that mankind, or at least they, may be saved by extraterrestrial intervention. Dr. Jung explains that "from a fear whose cause is far from being fully understood and is therefore not conscious, there arise explanatory projections which purport to find the cause in all manner of secondary phenomena, however unsuitable."

"Mass rumour," the author states, especially when accompanied by "collective visions," cannot be dismissed with obvious and convenient conclusions, but deserves serious analysis. This is all the more necessary, he feels, since any phenomenon so worldwide must have a basic cause rooted in the very fundamentals of our existence. He concedes that broadly accepted fantasies occurred much earlier in history, citing the prophecy of the end of the world at the conclusion of the first millennium, but contends that such projections were always metaphysical, mystical in origin. So highly ephemeral hypotheses would gain little acceptance in the middle of the twentieth century, he suggests, but minor miracles based upon the modern religions—science and/or the psychological (psychic)—might receive a much warmer welcome. Having abdicated the hard-science approach to others more qualified (although, at times, he falters in his restraint), Dr. Jung continues his investigation of the "psychic aspects of the phenomenon."

Pausing to admonish psychologists, he cautions them to carefully appraise "mass phenomena like UFOs," since their very improbability suggests to the reasonable individual that their explanation might lie in the mind, as well as the eye, of the beholder.

Dr. Jung subcategorizes UFOs into two basic types: round and cigar-shaped. He mentions the obvious phallic implications of the latter in a footnote, but then concentrates his analytical attention on the disc-shaped and spherical phenomena. "The figures in a rumour," he assures the reader, "can be subjected to the same principles [as] dream interpretation." In the case of round rumors the psychiatrist sees a "symbol of totality well-known to all students of depth psychology, namely the *mandala* [Sanskrit for *circle*]," which is "found in all epochs and in all places, always with the same meaning."

As well as being a classical totality symbol, encompassing and protecting the psyche, the mandala is a unifying device for inner conflict and, as such, is "a distinct *individuation symbol.*" Combining this with the ancient concept that the "soul" is sphere-shaped, Jung updates and translates the symbolism into the patois of our time, and the UFOs are defined as "a totality of the individual" symbol, a "spontaneous image . . . a symbolical representation of the *self,* by which I mean not the ego but the totality composed of the conscious *and* the unconscious."

The author argues that if the round UFOs are to be viewed, as he has recommended they should be, i.e., as "visions," one cannot avoid regarding them as "archetypal images . . . involuntary, automatic projections based on instinct" which cannot be ignored.

Extending his thesis even further, Jung calls attention to the fact that the circle has appeared in all ages, not only as the soul-symbol, but also as a "God-image." " 'God is a circle,' " he quotes, " 'whose centre is everywhere and the circumference nowhere.' " Or, as he sums up, the "totality symbol *par excellence.*"

Returning to the original rumors, bringing his conclusion with him, Jung expectedly observes that "UFOs could easily be conceived as gods."

The condition of the world was "as never before" conducive to the stimulation of hopes for some great, Earth-saving event. The great "emotional tension" had created an ideal atmosphere for such a projection. (It might be pointed out that Dr. Jung was writing in 1958 and about the international situation as it existed at that time and immediately before. One is inclined to wonder if his reliance upon the worldwide psychological strain thesis is quite so applicable to the initial period of modern ufology, that is, from the afternoon of Kenneth Arnold's original experience until Russia's detonation of a nuclear explosion more than two years later.) In such circumstances, Dr. Jung concludes, such a projection "thrusts itself to the forefront in the form of a symbolic rumour, accompanied and reinforced by the appropriate visions, and in doing so activates an archetype [the mandala, in the form of round UFOs] that has always expressed order, deliverance, salvation, and wholeness."

Reaffirming his position that "the apparently physical nature of UFOs creates such insoluble puzzles . . . one feels tempted to take them as a 99 percent psychic product [a type of reverse reasoning not uncommon to Dr. Jung] and subject them accordingly to the usual psychological interpretation." He cautiously adds that even if "an unknown physical phenomenon" is the actual basis for his "myth," it would in no way effect his theory, since many myths have external causes which are not necessarily, in themselves, explanations thereof. Thus the author concludes the first section of his book *Flying Saucers* (wherein he almost invariably uses the term "Ufos," suggesting that his more commercially conscious publisher may have selected the title), which is devoted to the phenomena as rumors.

The second part of the work is titled "Ufos in Dreams" and, while it interestingly reflects the analyst's attitude toward dream interpretation, it has very little to do with the study, history, or nature of saucers, no more than nightmares of flying squirrels have to do with zoology. (Although dreams wherein the subject conceived of himself *as* a Flying Saucer might offer a fascinating parallel to certain zooanthropic mental disorders.)

Unfortunately, as is the case with the preceding section, the descriptions of the dreams and the commentaries which follow suggest strongly that Dr. Jung had a very spotty knowledge of the history of Flying Saucers/UFOs, only a superficial acquaintanceship with the nature and variety of reports *and* observers, and but a sketchy familiarity with the literature of the subject. As a matter of fact, these weaknesses are even more evident in the chapter "Ufos in Dreams" than in his exposition of his "rumour" thesis.

The author's highly speculative dream commentaries are so studded with learned allusions, citations, and cross-references that the subject of UFOs is abandoned for pages at a time in favor of entertaining digressions—Mercurius, the magician, Heraclitus, Zosimos of Panopolis, Christ, Leibniz, Freud, the *summum bonum*, Moses, Horus, Set, Osiris, Nietzsche, Adler, Oedipus, Dr. Rhine, Faust, Jupiter, Charon, Venus, Balder, Wotan, and so on, for many pages. None of these allusions are necessarily inappropriate of themselves, but, in this instance, they do not merely explain and elaborate the theme, they become it.

"Ufos in Modern Painting," the following chapter, is another example of Dr. Jung's grafting a few unconvincing hypotheses onto ufology. The paintings used to illustrate his arguments are of no interest within the context of the subject, and very little outside of it. In actuality, these pages merely serve as an extension of the previous chapter, with a minor switch from sleeping visions (dreams) to waking ones (painting). However, there is one comment which deserves mentioning, especially in terms of properly evaluating Dr. Jung's explanation of UFOs. The same thought is suggested in two places. Firstly, where the analyst concedes that he had encountered "very similar dream-visions" thirty years "before Flying Saucers were heard of" (at least, by Dr. Jung); secondly, in a footnote where he calls attention to the fact that van Gogh's "Starry Night" (1889) has large, shining disks in the sky, unlike anything ever seen, and says that this painting was supposedly inspired by a dream. If these observations are intended, however obliquely, to refer to UFOs, they further undermine his nuclear-age-tension proposition; if not, they seem to have no place in the book.

Dr. Jung then offers a very fragmentary "Previous History of the Ufo

Phenomenon," in which he deals with four examples of reports of curious celestial activity in 1561, 1566, and the twelfth and seventeenth centuries. These are not without interest, particularly the earliest, which is illustrated with a picture showing a *relationship* (represented by an umbilical-like tentacle) between a square balloon, filled with eyes and circles, and an unborn infant in its mother's womb. It is rather reminiscent of some of the symbolism used by certain saucer sects in the 1950s.

The concluding chapter of Jung's work is titled "Ufos Considered in a Non-psychological Light" and introduces a modification, if not a reversal, of the posture previously taken by the author. After reiterating that "it was the purpose of this essay to treat the Ufos primarily as a psychological phenomenon," he now belatedly admits that "there are good reasons why the Ufos cannot be disposed of in this simple manner." He bases his back-tracking on what "remains an established fact," that UFOs have been observed visually, scanned by radar, and recorded photographically. These convictions derive from his reading of the works of Captain Ruppelt and Major Keyhoe, plus Professor Menzel's failure "despite all his efforts, in offering a satisfying scientific explanation of even one authentic Ufo report."

The frailty of this argument is overwhelmingly self-evident, logically speaking, but some of the more obvious flaws might be mentioned. One can hardly regard as an "established fact" the very essence of the mystery one is investigating, especially since direct sightings, radar observations, and Flying-Saucer/UFO photographs have been all contested collectively and, in most cases, individually. Further, if one is convinced that Ruppelt and Keyhoe "leave no room for doubt in [the previously itemized] regard," it seems rather pointless to have presented the lengthy argument for UFOs as visionary rumors, rather than concentrating upon the physical reality of the phenomena. Finally, although Dr. Menzel has, for reasons of his own, spent a great deal of time attempting to disprove the existence of Flying Saucers, objectively viewed it is the claimants who must establish their case, not the sceptics.

Posing a hypothesis as interesting as the UFOs themselves, Jung winds up the foregoing with the alternatives "that either psychic projections throw back a radar echo," or actual objects *occasion,* not specifically cause, the mythological projections.

Continuing to wander about in a sort of disorganized speculation, the analyst notes that the only thing we *know for certain* regarding UFOs "is that *they possess a surface which can be seen by the eye and at the same time throw back a radar echo.*" He does concede, however, that "*we do not know, either, whether they are manned machines or a species of living crea-*

ture which has appeared from an unknown source." (Here only, in this entry, are emphases within quotes added.)

In drawing his book to its conclusion, Dr. Jung shifts ground a few more times with mercurial *pronunciamentos* like ". . . if these things are real—and by all human standards it hardly seems possible to doubt this any longer . . . ," finally introducing, in the penultimate paragraph, one of the most intriguing (although not original) ideas yet to arise regarding UFOs. In Jung's words: ". . . there is a third possibility: that Ufos are real material phenomena of an unknown nature, presumably coming from outer space, which perhaps have long been visible to mankind, but otherwise have no recognizable connection with earth or its inhabitants."

Appended to the main body of the work is an "Epilogue" devoted to the writings and person of Orfeo Angelucci, Jung apparently having just become acquainted with that famous contactee's volume *The Secret of the Saucers*.[14] Appended to the "Epilogue" is another (?) epilogue given over to expressing the psychiatrist's enthusiasm for astronomer Fred Hoyle's science-fiction story *The Black Cloud*.[15] Finally, a "Supplement" is tacked on to permit Jung to offer a critical commentary on *The Midwich Cuckoos* by John Wyndham.[16] Neither of the latter two have any more to do with Flying Saucers/UFOs than hundreds of other science-fiction or fantasy fables; Angelucci's books are, of course, *classics* in the library of contactology.

Flying Saucers by C. G. Jung is important in the bibliography of ufology, and, to a lesser extent, in that of saucerology and its subcategories, because it is one of the very rare attempts at a serious appraisal of the phenomenon, rather than fictionalized exploitation or real and pseudo-reportage. Although the importance of the entire subject-complex is glaringly apparent from the social, psychological, historical, and religious points of view, it has been thoroughly ignored by most major figures in such fields. When this author once attempted to elicit opinions and theories from prominent persons in psychology and psychiatry on the subject of Flying Saucers/UFOs, most replied in the tone of Dr. Theodor Reik, who explained that he had never given the subject any thought.

Jung's *Flying Saucers* derives most of its value from its uncommonness, for, with the exception of some portions of the chapter "Ufos as Rumours," it is superficial, vague, and founded on many misconceptions about sightings, persons involved, methods of investigation, and so forth. Regrettably, Dr. Jung, who had the broad, flexible attitude from which might have emerged a really exceptional analysis of Flying Saucers/UFOs, simply didn't know enough about the subject in question, and so he left it where he found it—in question.

Chapter 11

THE OTC-X1 AND ORFEO ASCENDING

Among the most persuasive of all sightings during the beginning of the second decade of ufology took place on the evening of February 24, 1959, from 8,500 feet in the air. The American Airlines DC-6 Flight 713, nonstop from Newark to Detroit, was passing over Bradford, Pennsylvania, at nearly half past eight. In command was Capt. Peter W. Killian, a fifteen-year, four-million-mile veteran; his copilot was the highly experienced First Officer John Dee. The sky, through which the ship was cruising at about 350 miles an hour, was crystal clear on all sides and above; some three thousand feet below were scattered clouds.

Later, the Detroit *Times* quoted Killian:

We were lying around 8,500 feet between Philipsburg and Bradford, Pa., at 8:45 P.M. when I looked off to the south and saw three yellowish lights in a single horizontal line overhead.

At first, I thought it was the Belt of Orion [a group of stars in a constellation] but then I took a second look and saw both the Belt and the foreign objects.[1]

The unknowns, wrote Keyhoe later, drawing from NICAP interviews with Killian,

were huge—not only larger [than Orion stars] but brighter. Their color, too, was different, an intense yellowish white. Abruptly, one flying object . . . came toward the plane [but] . . . slowed some distance away, apparently observing the DC-6. Killian now knew it was a UFO—some unknown machine, under intelligent control. He could not be sure, but it seemed at least triple the size of the plane. Swiftly . . . the UFO rejoined the formation. Not until then did Killian tell First Officer Dee about the objects. While Dee watched them, Killian cut in the intercom . . . and made a calm announcement to the passengers regarding the aerial phenomena.

Subsequently, as the plane's occupants observed as they seemingly were being observed, one of the UFOs again approached Flight 713, and then returned to its group. Killian went on the air to check whether any pilots were monitoring the strange objects. Immediately, another American Airlines captain revealed that he had been participating in the sighting for at least ten minutes; then a second veteran from a third American Airlines flight radioed that he was tracing the UFOs. The unknowns were lost as the planes descended to the Detroit airport.

It had been Killian's intention to turn in his report to the company and let them handle it from there. However, soon after landing, Mr. N. D. Puncas (Puscas?) brought to the surface even more startling information. The UFOs had also been observed by three other United Airline crews. It was agreed that they had been no known aircraft.

Major Keyhoe diligently pursued this exceptional multiple-pilot sighting. Contacting a long-time Washington newsman, he asked:

"Could you find out what the Air Force is going to say? If there's a cover-up, and we could tell certain congressmen——"

"Who you working with now?" asked his source.

Keyhoe told him, then added, "Also, we've promised the names of key witnesses and proof of the censorship to the Senate Preparedness Committee."

"Meaning Senator Lyndon Johnson?"

"Yes. Nothing definite yet, but his staff is looking into it." [2]

The question was: What would the Air Force do? Its first action was to provide an answer for all the airborne persons who had seen the UFOs. The blazingly incompetent solution was that "airline pilots who reported flying saucers last Tuesday were actually seeing stars through broken clouds" [3] (Orion), notwithstanding the fact that the constellation and the unknowns had been seen simultaneously, that the oversky was absolutely clear, that—it was not true.

"There is no astronomical explanation of the reported sightings. I know of nothing that occurred in the skies last night that could account for the objects described," stated Dr. Orren C. Mohler, assistant director of the McMath-Hulbert Observatory of the University of Michigan.

On March 1, the New York *Herald Tribune* carried a new Air Force reply to the mystery, through the person of an unnamed spokesman. It asserted that it could hardly be bothered by claims made by "people who can't remember anything when they sober up the next day" [4] nor by persons who were deluded, incompetent, or barefaced liars. Considering that the witnesses included a dozen seasoned pilots with many millions of hours airtime among them, it seemed a viciously slanderous and reckless rebuttal.

Flying Saucers: Top Secret carries a telephone exchange between Killian and Keyhoe which is particularly pertinent to this record.

"I never drink before or during a flight," he said flatly. "The Air Force knows it's a strict airline rule."

"What do you think of the Orion answer?"

"It's not true," said Captain Killian. "In the first place, the clouds were 3,500 feet *below* us. Second, we saw the UFO's and Orion at the same time, repeatedly. Even if there had been broken clouds, no experienced airline pilot would be deceived like that." [5]

Moments later, Keyhoe asked about a quote attributed to him by the New York *Herald Tribune*. It read:

"I am sure there are people on other planets who have solved the problem of space travel. I sincerely believe their vehicles are coming close to the earth."

"Is that correct?" inquired Keyhoe.

"Yes," said Killian, "that is what I believe." [6]

Hugh McPherson, radio personality on WCHS, Charleston, West Virginia, taped an interview with Killian, during which the pilot reiterated the experience. Long John Nebel presented First Officer John Dee to his listeners, and they heard the details from an eyewitness. Bob Barry, Director of the Aerial Phenomena Investigations Society, of upstate New York, meanwhile received a letter in response to an inquiry regarding the affair. It was from Maj. Lawrence J. Tacker, well-known UFO spokesman for the Air Force, and assured Barry that what all the pilots and passengers had seen had been nothing more than "a B-47 type aircraft accomplishing night refueling from KC-97 tankers." [7]

Major Keyhoe flew to New York to speak directly with Captain Killian and arrange for him to testify before a group, to include Senator Barry Goldwater, which was being scheduled by Representative Sam Friedel, of Maryland. To quote the words of the NICAP director:

I checked into the hotel and called Killian's. His wife answered. Then the blow fell.

"Captain Killian has been silenced by the Air Force," Mrs. Killian told me. "He's under strict orders. He can't meet with you or talk to anyone [not, apparently, even a Congressional committee] about what he saw." [8]

The Air Force always gets its man—well, almost always.

Early 1959 saw the reemergence of accusations directed toward another, considerably more puzzling, aspect of the government—the Central Intelligence Agency. Although to this day few persons have ever related the ultraespionage United States establishment to UFOs, Dr. Leon Davidson presented a carefully construed argument for the existence of "electronic countermeasures (EMC)," designed to obviate air defenses, which assertedly could "pick up the enemy's radar impulses, amplify and modify them, and send them back" so that they would "cause the 'blip' on the [enemy's] radar screen to have an incorrect range, speed, or heading." Pointing out that such equipment was featured on our more sophisticated bombers as early as 1950, he quoted *Aviation Research and Development:*

A new radar moving-target simulator system, which generates a display of up to six individual moving targets on any standard radar indicator, has been developed . . . [and] can . . . simulate . . . realistic flight paths. . . . Speeds up to 10,000 knots (about 11,500 mph) are easily generated. . . . The target can be made to turn left or right . . . [and there are] adjustments to provide a realistic scope presentation.[9]

Contending "that the CIA, since 1951, has caused or sponsored saucer sightings for its own purposes," the author explains that "by shrewd psychological manipulation, a series of 'normal' events has been served up so as to appear as quite convincing evidence of extraterrestrial UFOs. Some of this 'normal' activity includes military use of EMC on a classified basis. . . ."

To support his thesis, Davidson cites some ambiguous remarks made by the Director of Air Force Intelligence on June 29, 1952, that "the jet interceptors which guard Washington [D.C.] were moved from Andrews Air Force Base (4 miles away) to New Castle, Delaware (90 miles away) . . . during the month [July] of the [1952] sightings in Washington." Further, he calls attention to Ruppelt's report that

a few days prior to the [July 19, 1952, Washington, D.C.] incident a scientist, from an agency [CIA] that I can't name . . . said that he thought we were sitting right on top of a big keg full of loaded flying saucers. "Within the next few days," he told me, and I remember that he punctuated his slow, deliberate remarks by hitting the desk with his fist, "they're going to blow up and you're going to have the granddaddy of all UFO sightings. The sightings will occur in Washington or New York," he predicted, "probably Washington." [10]

On April 1, 1959, various explosions were reported around the Seattle area, just prior to a UFO sighting, at approximately 7:45 in the evening, by Mr. and Mrs. Sam Snyder, of Graham, Washington. They saw a brilliant aerial unknown, followed by another a few moments later. Shortly thereafter, a C-118 Air Force transport crashed near Mount Rainier, reportedly the victim of a mysterious missile which removed a portion of a stabilizer. Four men were killed. Why the craft turned away from, rather than to, McChord Air Force Base, for a forced landing, is not understood.

Some five months later, on August 24, a number of blinking lights were seen across the sky of Bremerton, Washington. They persisted for about three hours. McChord Air Force Base was supposed to have been notified by the local law, but reportedly never was.

The Maury Island affair, fully detailed earlier, had begun McChord AFB on a long and enigmatic relationship with Unidentified Flying Objects, and it was continuing more than a dozen years later.

On March 11, Rear Admiral George Dufek, of the United States Navy, made a surprisingly open-minded statement:

"Some of the supposed meteor explosions in our atmosphere might be saucers from Venus or other planets, driven by intelligent creatures. I think it is very stupid for human beings to think that no one else in the universe is as intelligent as we are." [11]

An entirely new aspect of saucerology was now being developed into a unique episode of the golden age. It began much, much earlier, however.

Otis T. Carr was born on December 7, 1904, in Elkins, West Virginia, the son of Marion and Edda Jane (Watson) Carr. His father was a skilled laborer and a part-time lay preacher.

In 1925, Carr arrived in New York and enrolled at the Art Students' League. At the same time, he gained employment as a checkroom clerk at the Hotel Pennsylvania in New York. According to O.T.C., the great scientist Nikola Tesla was in residence at the impressive hostelry opposite the New York Main Post Office. A warm bond was woven by the inventor's loneliness and the clerk's willingness to run errands. For these services, Carr was to explain years later, he had had revealed to him incredible secrets unveiled by the master's mind, but not then sufficiently refined to present to the scientific community. Since Tesla went to his death without publishing these phenomenal electromagnetic aerodynamic mysteries, the world was forced to wait upon the creative powers of Carr to perfect them. As a matter of assertion, he once stated, "We believe our theories and discoveries to be superior to those of Dr. Einstein . . . [whose] theory of relativity was just the first crack in the Shell of Awakening." [12]

In 1957, he announced that his invention was ready for mankind—or perhaps he said Man was ready for his invention. It was described by Carr, according to Gosnell's later notes, in the following lucid fashion:

I have invented a fourth dimensional space vehicle. This Circular-Foil Spacecraft has as its source of power my discovery and invention, a revolutionary Utron Electric Accumulator, which is completely round and completely square and generates and regenerates electrical energy, operating in unison with the free energy of the universe. My vehicle can be launched from earth and does not have to be blasted into space by jet propulsion. The basic design was brought to the attention of the United States Government and a patent [was] filed by me in 1949. [13]

While it would be a few years before Carr, riding the allegorical winglessness of the OTC-X1 Circular-Foil Spacecraft, would achieve the pinnacle of his ascent, he was already well on his way when he managed to capture the interest of Wilfred C. Gosnell, a highly successful Maryland businessman and former war hero. OTC Enterprises, Inc., was situated in Baltimore, on an attractive residential street. The structure had once been a modest white brick home with tasteful furnishings. It featured numerous rooms and apparently housed various departments and in general suggested a successful operation.

It was, of course, inevitable that Carr and company should eventually gravitate to the microphones of Long John Nebel, and when the entrepreneur of UFOs was contacted regarding such an appearance, he happily acceded. How, after all, could one resist the opportunity of conversing with the man who had issued "Information Bulletin No. 3," which specifically stated:

> Any vehicle accelerated to an axis rotation relative to its attractive inertial mass, immediately becomes activated by free-space energy and acts as an independent force. We have shown that a charged body, so accelerated, indicates polarity in a given direction. The dip-needle points, say, upward toward the top of the body. But mount this whole rotating body, with its spindle, on another platform and rotate this platform on a spindle, then, if the counter-rotation is greater than the initial forward rotation of the body, a dip-needle on the second platform will point *down* while the first dip-needle points *up,* indicating the *complete* relativity of polarity. When the exact counter-rotation matches the forward rotation, the body loses its polarity entirely and immediately becomes activated by free-energy (tensor stresses in space) and acts as an independent force.[14]

The projection for the première OTC-X1 Circular-Foil Spacecraft had it forty-five feet in diameter and fifteen feet through the center. It was designed to accommodate three passengers and have a cruising range of about a thousand miles—straight up. Subsequent models were mentioned, ranging from a ten-foot-wide version—a "family-sized" convenience to replace the automobile—to one a hundred feet in diameter. Deliveries of the forty-five-foot-style were assured within twenty-four months, and the price was $20 million. However, this price applied only to the first models. All later purchases could be arranged for a mere $4 million a unit.

By the winter of 1959, Carr had intrigued a number of businessmen in Oklahoma City with his flights of fancy—the only kind anyone had yet seen him take—and he had moved his operation to this fresh, fertile field, having pretty well harvested the Baltimore, and even New York, crop. The consummating moment was approaching: The OTC-X1 was to have its actual air debut. Not broadcast air, stratospheric air. For the occasion, he invited Long John and seven of his regular panelists, and a few other interested persons to what was variously called "Space, Oklahoma," "Space City, Oklahoma," and—its non-Carrian name—"Frontier City, Oklahoma." Here, in an amusement park operated by Sam McCoy, the six-foot prototype of the OTC-X1 was to be revealed and, after suitable examination, launched on its experimental demonstration of the aeronautical feasibility of the Utron Electric Accumulator principle.

Long John and company arrived very late Friday night. The OTC-X1 was secreted in an otherwise deserted warehouse a few miles away. The group drove up in front of a shadowy gray, dimly lighted corrugated-steel building decorated with large block letters saying: "SOONER Sheet Metal and Roofing." Answering to pounding on the door, a semigiant announced that the building was "classified" and that no one could be admitted.

"In that case," countered John, "you can tell Otis that I'm flying back to New York on the next plane."

This seemed to be the secret pass phrase, and they were ushered into the center of the warehouse where rested the OTC-X1. The top had been removed, or not been placed on, and the interior of the quarter-ton, four-foot-deep, six-foot circle was a science-fiction motion-picture set designer's dream—of what a Flying Saucer should look like upon inspection following a severe crash landing on Pluto. Wires askew, coils canted, batteries unconnected, unidentifiable elements creating cipherless mechanical codes . . .

"My belief in Otis' saucer had always been nil," observed Long John later. "At that point it lost considerable ground."

All inquiries regarding the officers of the operation proved unsatisfactory. Carr was nearby but "unavailable." Notwithstanding the great man's retreat into seclusion, he was quickly traced to the local Mercy Hospital, where he was supposedly being treated for some sort of throat disorder. On Saturday, April 18, Nebel strode into the private room where Carr, resplendent in an abbreviated nightdress, stood chatting with an attractive young nurse.

His visitor's "Hello, Otis," struck with considerable impact, causing the scientist to hurtle forward onto the bed and under the covers to the melody of grievous grunts of pain and disenchantment with his lot. A rapid recovery ensued, however, permitting Carr to proceed with a tape-recorded interview.

On the following Sunday afternoon, press and public clustered in considerable number about the pad specified as the planned departure point. Takeoff was announced for three o'clock, suggesting, perhaps, that the craft would be delivered to the site by two. It failed to arrive that early. Or by three. Or four or five.

Evening rose, and the scientific community—resident and imported—of Frontier (Space) City dispersed.

The delay had been caused by a "mercury leak" and/or failure of the "superior housing unit to fully true-set with the craft body."

The flight was rescheduled for December 7, 1959, but somehow all interest seemed to have evaporated long before that date, in spite of Carr's guarantee that he would personally function as flight captain.[15]

Over the years, many investors had come to complain that they never saw any results for their participation, let alone rewards. Yet Carr was able to keep clear of the Security Exchange Commission and various legal agencies. It couldn't last forever.

Finally, Mr. Gosnell, who asserted he had been duped of many thousands of dollars, contacted the SEC and explained his problem, contending that, in total, Carr had been the recipient of from a quarter to a half million dollars over the years in return for stock in the several aspects of his company. The Commission's investigations eventually brought Carr to court, and in the late spring of 1959 he was enjoined against any further OTC Enterprises, Inc., activities and fined for five thousand dollars.

Many of the Flying Saucer figures have had distinctive personalities. George King commanded the aloofness of a Puritan minister; Adamski could have been a kindly country doctor; Van Tassel projected the personality of the president of a modest-sized harvester company; Dan Martin was not unlike a sheriff I once knew in Oklahoma. But Orfeo Angelucci was something else. Of all the members of the myth I ever met—and I met most of them—only he truly presented the impression of a man who spoke with visitors from outer space. By this, I do not necessarily mean to impugn the claims of his co-contactees; rather I am merely stating that of all the clan he was the most "unearthly."

A small, slender, almost fragile man, Orfeo had dark, wavy hair, trusting eyes, and a delicate, semi-ascetic face. It was frequently reminiscent of a saint's head by da Vinci. He had suffered frequent illnesses, by his own admission, and the softness of his voice reflected the quality of quiet perseverance.

Orfeo differs from all the other Titans because, whether regarded as fact or fancy, his fables are fascinating—certainly the most beautiful of the mythology of the Age of Flying Saucers. One of the most extraordinary of his tales tells of the adventure he encountered at Twentynine Palms, California.

The Secret of the Saucers,[16] an early book, had earned Angelucci some reputation when he decided to move into the desert to work.

In December of 1954, Orfeo decided to drive a short distance down the road to a diner.

I opened the door, and my eyes fell at once upon a young man sitting alone at a center table. . . . Our eyes met in an intense gaze as we made a brief appraisal of one another, and an inner communication passed between us, as though we had always known one another. . . .
"Hello, friend."
"Hello, Orfeo," he replied immediately.
"I know you only as well as you know me. Please, just call me Adam, and do not ask my real name."

The stranger had ordered dinner for two, which arrived at this moment. Orfeo observed that there were three glasses of water.
"Are you expecting someone else?" inquired Angelucci.

Adam said he wasn't and appeared to be puzzled when his companion pointed out the extra glass of water. . . .

Offered a bottle of beer, Orfeo declined, preferring water. In response, his new friend smiled and produced "an oyster-white pellet" from a pocket.
"O.K., Orfeo. Then how about some very rare champagne?"

Accepting the ivory ovoid, the contactee dropped it into his glass of water, which bubbled, assumed a pale amber color, and effused an exhilarating aroma. The delicious flavor was familiar; he had tasted it in an earlier adventure. Writing later, Angelucci skillfully expressed his reaction:

My sudden excitement had taken me from earth number one to earth number two . . . from the mere recognition of the nectar. . . . No wonder Adam had expected me. . . . He was in the protective care of others . . . not of earth, not of our solar system. . . . No longer was I in Tiny's cafe in Twentynine Palms. It had been transformed into a cozy retreat on some radiant star system. . . . Adam glanced at the empty glass, that third glass at the place on the table where no other person was expected to sit. His puzzled look betrayed the fact that he was asking himself . . . why it was there. . . .

"In the final analysis, Orfeo, there is only one virtue; the love of pure learning," his companion said. He then identified himself as a medical doctor, formerly of Seattle, who a very short time before had found it necessary to forsake his practice because he had only nine months to live.

"I flailed out, trying to grasp as much of life as could be packed into each day. . . . I came to be interested in all things pertaining to the universe. . . . I went to hear a talk on flying saucers in Seattle [where] I obtained your book *The Secret of the Saucers.* . . . I found a kindred spirit. . . . You had mentioned Twentynine Palms. . . . So here we are. . . ."

Adam elaborated on his story by telling how, after arriving in the small community, he rented a cabin in the desert, began a period of introspection, and arrived at certain philosophic convictions on the temporality of men, aspects of mortality, and the nature of cosmic identity. "We are directly observed by the Space Visitors," he asserted. Then, in Orfeo's words:

We lingered over our dessert. . . . I was fraught with expectancy. . . . Were my ears deceiving me? What was that music I heard coming from the direction of the glass? . . . Indeed, the fluid in the glass was being used as a radio. . . . It was so faint that only ears made sensitive by [the nectar] . . . could hear it.

Then slowly I looked again at the glass and was held in amazement. A miniature young woman was dancing in the nectar! Her golden-blond beauty was as arresting as the miracle of her projection in the glass. . . .

Her arms moved in rhythmic motion with the graceful thrusts of her dancing body. Her feet were so light and responsive that the music itself seemed to emanate from them. The expression on her face was that of . . . bliss and eternity among the angels. . . . Her eyes . . . had not shifted their gaze from Adam's eyes. . . . Why would she not cast just a passing glance my way?

. . . I could see tears pouring down his cheeks. Except for these, his face seemed frozen into a handsome mask. . . .

Adam's initial encounter with aliens overtured an even more extraordinary adventure. It began with his moving to the isolated retreat in the desert, a cabin without electricity, water, and gas. On the third night, he later told Angelucci:

". . . the very firmament seemed strangely different. . . . I was sweeping into me all the cosmos, or else, it was enfolding me. Then there was this music. . . . At last something moving . . . a star had decided to roam the heavens. . . . Soon a circle was completed and the light went out. . . . It appeared again much larger . . . changing from its previous amber to a yellowish green. . . . The light grew steadily larger . . . spiraling down. . . .

"This was no star . . . no meteor. . . . Its light pulsated from green to orange-yellow, getting faint, and flickering. . . . I could still hear the faint music. . . .

"Suddenly, I realized . . . it was a space ship of some sort. . . . At that instant the light went out completely . . . the music increased in volume. . . . I was swept emotionally into a depthless, unendurable emptiness. . . . Then a feminine voice sweet, musical . . ."

Magically, before him, there appeared an insubstantial, slowly congealing, silvery, dome-shaped craft, beside which stood a slender, beautiful woman. Adam entered the flying saucer.

The two companions of different worlds sat side by side in the blue-hazed iridescence of the interior of the intergalactic vessel, which began to translate into opacity as it pulsed in a dim-bright cycle. Soon, the lovely alien told Adam to address her as "Vega" and proceeded to explain some of what was happening. They had just passed through the ionosphere, she began, continuing:

"The molecules of our craft were tightened a little so that the ionized layer around earth would not cause a glare inside. . . . To confirm what you already know, our ship can adjust itself to . . . electrical and magnetic conditions. . . ."

Adam came to understand that the vessel, which was a remote-controlled scout, was being impelled by a magnetic and gravitational force directed by a distant mother ship.

"Before my eyes was the earth in all its daylight glory . . . surrounded by the stars beyond like jewels around the head of a majestic being. . . . Its atmosphere made an auroral halo of rainbow colors. . . . The stars remained fixed. . . . The earth light dazzled a bit, flared, and then flashed. . . . Then it became just like a huge star, brighter than all the others, larger, and falling back rapidly. . . .

"Suddenly . . . our field was so broad we were seeing the moon, also. . . . It, too, seemed to recede rapidly. . . ." [17]

Chapter 12

THE PROPER STUDY OF GODS IS MAN

The new decade was not without a new theory, or, at least, a variation on an old one—that not only were Flying Saucers not originating from beyond the farthest reaches of our planet, they were being expelled from within it. In December, Ray Palmer wrote a lengthy article elaborating his intricate and imaginative thesis, and prefaced it with the assertion that he was prepared

> to prove that the flying saucers are native to planet earth; that the governments of more than one nation [if not all of them] know this to be a fact; that a concerted effort is being made to learn all about them, and to explore their native land; that the facts already known are considered so important that they are the world's top secret. . . .[1]

The continuation of his contention reads:

> . . . is there any area on Earth which can be regarded as a possible origin for flying saucers? There are . . . four . . . the two major, in order of importance, are Antartica [sic] and the Arctic . . . the two minor areas are South America's Matto Grosso and Asia's Tibetan Highlands.[2]

Palmer eliminates the latter two because the locations are too easily and too frequently overflown.

After considering the traversing of the top of the world by submarines, he concluded that "apparently the sort of base necessary for the UFO mystery in its entirety does not exist in the North Polar regions." [3]

"But there is an area of doubt," says Palmer, explaining that Admiral Richard E. Byrd made the following comment, in February, 1947:

"I'd like to see that land beyond the Pole. That area beyond the Pole is the center of the great unknown." [4]

The author then fills in some of the details of the puzzle.

> When [Byrd's] plane took off from its Arctic base, it proceeded straight north to the Pole. From that point, it flew on a total of 1,700 miles beyond the Pole, and then retraced its course to its Arctic base. As progress was made beyond the Pole point, iceless lands and lakes, mountains covered with trees, and even monstrous animals moving through the underbrush, were observed and reported via radio by the plane's occupants. . . .

. . . calculate the distance to the Pole from all the known lands . . . a good portion of them are well within the 1,700 miles. But none of them are within 200 miles of the Pole. Byrd flew over no known land . . . after 1,700 miles over land, he was forced by gasoline supply limit to return, and he had not yet reached the end of it! He should have been well inside one of the known areas mentioned . . .

That land, on today's maps, CANNOT EXIST. But since it DOES, we can only conclude that today's maps are incorrect, incomplete, and do not present a true picture of the northern hemisphere!

On April 5, 1955, the U.S. Navy announced an expedition to . . . be headed by Admiral Richard E. Byrd. It consisted of five ships, fourteen airplanes, special tractors, and a complement of 1,393 men. The stated purpose . . . "to construct a satellite base at the South Pole."

Once again we have penetrated an unknown and mysterious land which does not appear on today's maps . . .

. . . the actual announcement carried by press and radio on February 5, 1956: "On January 13, 1956, members of the United States expedition accomplished a flight of 2,700 miles from the base at McMurdo Sound, which is 400 miles west of the South Pole, and penetrated a land extent of 2,300 miles beyond the Pole."

And on March 13, Admiral Byrd reported, upon his return from the South Pole: "The present expedition has opened up a vast new land."

Finally, in 1957, before his death, he reported it as: "That enchanted continent in the sky, land of everlasting mystery!" [5]

In support of his contentions, Palmer remarks that the "musk-ox migrates north," that Arctic explorers have observed bear heading north into an area where there cannot be food for them," that "foxes also are found north of the 80th parallel, heading north," that "butterflies and bees are found in the far north, but never hundreds of miles further south," and that "southern Eskimos themselves speak of tribes that live in the far north. . . ." He concludes this aspect of his thesis saying that "only Admiral Byrd's 'mystery land' can account for these inexplicable facts and migrations." [6]

However, needless to say, as imaginative as Palmer's reasoning is, it is only his pathway to a cause. That he poses in the following fashion:

Since the mapped area of the spherical Earth does not allow sufficient room in which to place our two mystery lands, can it be that the Earth is of a different shape, one that allows us to place these lands on that portion of it which does not come under the category of "spherical"?

. . . arguments for a perfectly round Earth are not based on fact, only on assumption . . . based on a brand of astronomy no longer acceptable to the scientist. Today the nebular theory of formation of planets, suns, even galaxies, is looked upon favorably. The condensation of nebula into stars and planets is accomplished by whirling motion. The whirling motion more often produces the "spindle" shape, round at the "equator," and projecting at the "pole;" or the "doughnut" shape, with flattened poles and holes through the middle. Since the Earth so formed, it may well be that it is either shape. . . .

. . . the "spindle" shape possesses many specific arguments against . . . the bearings taken point to the "doughnut" shape.

The evidence is extremely strong, and amazingly prolific in scope and extent, that the Earth actually is shaped in this fashion. And if it is hollow, then we no longer need to look for the saucers from outer space—but rather from "inner space!" . . . Byrd flew 1,700 miles over the inner edge of the "doughnut hole," and the Navy flew 2,300 miles over the opposite inner edge. Both flights went a partial way into the inner Earth. And if this is all true, then no doubt extended flights to 10,000 miles and beyond have been made since 1957 into this hollow Earth, for we have the planes to do it!

The Flying Saucer has become the most important single fact in history. The answer to the question raised in this article must be answered.

Flying Saucers come from this Earth! [7]

If the seeming science-fictionization of aerial history by Mr. Palmer strained credulity, even hard science appeared to have its moments of enchantment. As the new decade began, Soviet Master of Mathematical Sciences M. A. Argest was quoted as having suggested that "Sodom and Gomorrah might have been destroyed by a nuclear explosion set off by invaders from Outer Space," [8] arousing considerable excitement among the ufologists of the Western world. Unfortunately, the actual article, which appeared in the *Literary Gazette,* was little more than a recapitulation of old theories.

The outer peripheries of saucerology continued to grow, and, by 1960, the theatrical world began to feel the ring close about it, too.

The arrival of a letter from a man called Ottmar Kaub was the first time most people heard of Marlo. This epistle established the writer as "Secretary to Dr. George Marlo, Director of U.F.O. Research, with 60,000 members world-wide, who has been on space ships known as flying saucers more times than most of the contactees of the world." [9] In essence, the missive was an invitation for Jack Benny, Jack Paar, Arthur Godfrey, Art Linkletter, Long John Nebel, Gray Barker, and Ray Palmer to join "The Brothers and Dr. Marlo" on an excursion in an alien craft. [10] Who ultimately actually received the letter is not clear, but it definitely reached Long John Nebel, and the published record of aspects of his remarkable career alludes to the episode. [11]

Unfortunately, the flight which was to circuit the country to collect various famous persons and then deposit them for a visit on a nuclear-war-proof island off the coast of Brazil was eventually rescheduled and finally canceled.

Soon afterward, on February 5, 1960, a group of interested persons gathered about the microphones of Long John Nebel to weigh the matter. Actually, the meeting consisted of a conference call, with Nebel and noted news commentator Frank Edwards in New York studios, publisher of contactee tales Gray Barker speaking from Clarksburg, West Virginia, and television star Jackie Gleason from his home in Peekskill, New York—the latter two being tied into the program by telephone. One exchange featured a classic question in the catechism of contactology. The comedian asked Barker to explain celestial selection.

Gleason: Why do you think they [space people] pick a sign painter [Menger] and a guy that's been in the clink a couple of times [Schmidt] to impart this *very important* information to the world? Why don't they step down and pick a guy like, ah—Stevenson? Governor Stevenson, who's a nice fella', speaks nice English. . . .

Barker replied that it had been rumored that highly placed persons had been the recipients of such social largesse, but that the elite of Earth had disregarded the spacial overtures.

Gleason: You mean to tell me, Gray, that you really believe that if Stevenson was contacted by a flying saucer, and he knew it was a flying saucer, and he knew these were legitimate people, that he wouldn't run out in the street immediately and shout this information?
Barker: I don't believe he would—
Gleason: Why?
Barker: I think that he would be afraid. First of all, people wouldn't believe him.

Gleason countered that intelligent spacians would provide such chosen representatives with some concrete evidence of the meeting. Then Frank Edwards joined the conversation.

Edwards: Why would people believe Menger if they wouldn't believe Stevenson?
Barker: Well, a great many people haven't believed Menger, including Jackie Gleason, I believe—and it invites ridicule when you say anything.
Edwards: Are we talking about Adlai Stevenson?
Gleason: Yes, that's who I'm speaking of.
Edwards: Well, I think that he's fully as credible a witness as Howard Menger, although there may be some lack of ability on his part to paint signs.
Gleason: I think he's even more credible, Frank—
Edwards: Well. That's possible.
Gleason: —because his wife was never married to a Saturnian.[12]

However, the comedian did not always treat the subject of contactology lightly. The book on Long John Nebel's career as the midnight ringmaster of the airways, *The Way Out World*, tells of the initiation of a somewhat less humorous exchange between Gleason and "the voice of Interplanetary Parliament," George King. The contactee was appearing on the program at the time, the night of February 19th.

On a previous occasion . . . Jackie had made an offer of $10,000 cash to anyone who could produce conclusive evidence that there was higher intelligent life on other planets. Without mentioning the famous comedian's name, I told King that such an offer had been made and that if he could fulfill its demands I'd have that small fortune for him by noon the following day. First King asked what I meant by "evidence," and then said that it made no difference, since he could not accept the challenge even if ten million was offered. At this point a call came in on my private line and I had it transferred to the "beeper phone" [an arrangement which permits both sides of a phone conversation to be broadcast]. It was Jackie Gleason wanting to discuss the entire matter with the English contactee.[13]

The entire broadcast exchange, as heard by Nebel's fascinated audience, went as follows:

Gleason: How are you?
King: Very well, thank you.
Gleason: Are these people from outer space good friends of yours?
King: I believe that they are friends of mine, yes.
Gleason: Could you call upon them for assistance? For instance, if you were in some sort of legal difficulty, embracing some part of their recognition of you, would they come to your aid?
King: Under those circumstances, they would help, yes.
Gleason: If I were, for instance, to say to you that you are a bare-faced liar, now you know you could sue me for libel, right?
King: Yes, yes.
Gleason: Now do you think that you could get any legal assistance from them in a case like this?
King: No, I don't.
Gleason: Why?
King: Why should they help?
Gleason: Well, you're championing their cause.
King: No, no, I'm not. I'm trying to give a spiritual message, which I believe to be good for all people. . . .
Gleason: Why do we need a spiritual message from someone in a flying saucer? Don't we have enough from Christ, Buddha, Moses . . . men like that?
King: Do we live by those teachings?
Gleason: Yes, I do.
King: You do? Then you're the first Christian I've ever seen.
Gleason: You mean that no one lives by the laws of Buddha, or Christ, or . . .
King: I never met anyone.
Gleason: By the way, do you know that every time you are uncertain when you say something, you cough. Do you know what that means psychologically? In other words, you cough every time you tell a lie.

King: Do I?

Gleason: Now, George, look at the juicy opportunity you have. Here's a guy that you're talking to that's got a lot of dough. You can sue me for maybe a million dollars . . . and maybe get it. And all you have to do to get it is to bring one of your friends from Mars to O.K. this thing. And then you win.

King: I've already answered this question. There isn't a man on Earth who could do this.

Gleason: In other words, you have absolutely no proof from these people whom you are championing? You have absolutely no backing from anybody from outer space for what you say?

King: Just a moment, please. Just one minute.

Gleason: I'm waiting . . . and cough a little bit.

King: I shall put this phone down in a moment.

Gleason: Yes?

King: I'm a guest here, you see.

Gleason: Not in my house, you're not a guest. I think you're a phoney!

King: C L I C K ![14]

This former London cab driver has convinced his disciples that he was originally called to the spiritual life in May, 1954, when, as he stood in the small kitchen of his modest flat washing dishes, he heard the summons from on high instruct him:

"Prepare yourself, you are to become the voice of Interplanetary Parliament."

Eight days afterward he was visited by the astral presence of an august figure who explained that the direction was merely an overture, and that King had been chosen to act as the ambassador, on Earth, of the aliens from space. Soon the semicontactee, who asserts he had never heard of Flying Saucers before the disembodied voice and the disembodied body, was propagating the word, by way of trances, in the context of public lectures. The Aetherius Society, named for the primary source of King's extraterrestrial expositions, sometimes called the "main communicator," rapidly evolved from these programs and was followed, shortly thereafter, by the organization's official publication, titled *Cosmic Voice* and subtitled *Mars and Venus Speak to Earth.* This tract featured thirty-two pages and occasional photographs and was devoted to the presentation of messages from and about the spacians with whom George King and his mother, Mary, were in contact.

The not infrequent suggestion that George is King, the Christ, if not literally Christ, the King, reincarnate, the manifestation of the Second Coming, accompanied by his mother, Mary, is too patent for even his naïve troupe to overlook.

Following his appearance on the Long John broadcast, a conversation highlighted by many messianic intimations, King wrote to the talkmaster that he would "like to refute a statement made by you on your programme last night. You said that I hinted that I was a Re-incarnation of Jesus. This is not in any way correct. I made no such hint.

"I hereby state quite definitively, that I am not a Re-incarnation of Jesus. . . ." [15]

Succumbing to the pilgrimage pattern of so many cultists, and occultists, the messianic Englishman eventually moved to America and set up salvation in southern California, where he continued to make his marks.

The submyths became more and more entangled, but the serious reports continued to roll across the researcher's desk, although it must be conceded that mere dots darting about the sky attracted less attention than in previous years. Still, notwithstanding the diminution of interest in simple "sightings," a great many observations, especially of the air-to-air variety, proved as fascinating as their predecessors.

Earl W. Miles, an Eastern Airlines pilot, and crews of two other flights monitored a UFO over Virginia on March 15. One report of the pilot's account of the incident went as follows:

The object was clearly visible, including the outline of its shape and certain details. The shape of the entire object was identified by all of us to be like the fuselage of a plane except many times larger than any plane we ever saw. From the back of the fuselage streamed a tremendous white flame that from our distance appeared to be a quarter of a mile long. It had no wings, and there were no protrusions on the body that could keep it balanced or directed. We estimated from what we know of flight speed that the thing was travelling in excess of 6,000 miles per hour. [16]

The first book to represent the official Air Force position, since Captain Ruppelt's, [17] appeared in 1960, under the name *Flying Saucers and the U.S. Air Force*. Establishment spokesman Lt. Col. Lawrence J. Tacker opened the defense with a description of a UFO sighting by several air crews near Honolulu. The object of this sighting complex is quickly classified as a bolide for no apparent reason other than that the author was forced to concede that it was not a balloon and that the UFO *might* have been a meteor. [18]

Ironically, *Flying Saucers and the U.S. Air Force* repeatedly cites Prof. "Joseph A. Hynek [sic], prominent Astrophysicist and the head of the Ohio State University Observatory [who] worked under contract with the Air Force Air Materiel Command on an intelligence investigation of flying saucers sightings. . . ." [19] Of course, Hynek later severely modified his professional skepticism, suggesting that there was considerably more to the entire picture than had ever been accurately sketched by the misdirecting pencil of the Air Force.

Flying Saucers and the U.S. Air Force offered the latest official positions on several of the more famous ufological incidents. Among the "classics" treated is the case of Capt. Thomas Mantell, Jr.

"The final conclusion of the Aerospace Technical Intelligence Center [formerly Air Technical Intelligence Center; later Foreign Technology Division] was that Captain Mantell had chased a [Skyhook] balloon on that fatal day." [20] Then he adds, however, if that wasn't the case, he may have, as suggested by Dr. Menzel, mistaken some form of aerial phenomena, such as a mock sun, for a flying saucer. Obviously, Tacker was willing to accept any suggestion offered, providing it did not exceed Air Force imagination. On the other side, it may be added, Tacker, after a reasonable description of the Chiles/Whitted sighting, granted that the object they saw from their Eastern Airlines DC-3 "is still carried in the Air Force files as unexplained." [21] Of course, the issue is somewhat confused by the assertion of Donald Menzel to the effect that more than a decade earlier, "Dr. J. Allen Hynek, astronomer consultant to ATIC, in his report of April 30, 1949, identified it as an undoubted meteor." [22] and that "The Air Force officially accept[ed] this solution" [23] in 1959.

The usual feeble explanation of the Washington flap in mid-July, 1952, is offered. While conceding that at least two commercial pilots made air-to-air sightings of the objects monitored by experienced radarmen at National Airport, CAA traffic control, and Andrews AFB, Tacker insists "the solution for these sightings was relatively simple and quickly found. . . . [They] were due to temperature inversions." [24] Tacker's explanation of the Killian episode is equally authoritarian.

A considerable number of letters identified as inquiries sent to the Air Force are reprinted, including one which inquired about—

"A 1947 ATIC document concluding that UFOs were real," and "a 1948 ATIC document concluding that UFOs were spaceships," and "an Air Force document analyzing UFO maneuvers concluding the same," and, finally, "a 1953 report conducted by the CIA and made by a panel of scientists concluding that the Air Force quadruple its project and release all their information to the public." [25]

Tacker added his comments, which asserted that the first three documents never existed and that the fourth only said the "public should be informed on this subject and the aura of the mystery . . . should be minimized." [26]

However, as always, the Air Force is revealed as inconsistent, at least, and as persistent purveyors of duplicity, more likely. In direct conflict with Tacker's contention is a flat statement by the best researcher his service ever had, Capt. Edward J. Ruppelt, who wrote in 1955:

"On September 23, 1947, when the chief of ATIC sent a letter to the

Commanding General of the Army Air Force stating that UFO's [sic] were real, intelligence committed themselves." [27] Without dwelling on each item, attention might be accorded the final passage which reveals Tacker's reply to be in direct opposition to the statements of Ruppelt, who was there. The latter wrote that the scientific panel had recommended increased research activity, noting:

> . . . the expansion they recommended would require a considerable sum of money. The investigative force of Project Blue Book should be quadrupled in size . . . and it should be staffed by specially trained experts in the fields of electronics, meteorology, photography, physics, and other fields of science pertinent to UFO investigations . . . and lastly, they said that the American public should be told every detail of every phase of the UFO investigation. . . .[28]

Attention need hardly be called to the blatantly obvious discrepancies between the testimony of Ruppelt and that of public-relations officer Tacker. Ruppelt, who established Project Blue Book and directed it for some time, and who, to strike at the core of the matter, was there where it was happening, later wrote the initial "official" book on the subject, which incidentally was much longer, detailed, and better written and substantiated than the subsequent effort.

Yet notwithstanding the growing failure of the Air Force to offer a rational explanation of the twenty-year mystery, the era of aerial wonders was beginning to show a touch of weariness and wear. On May 28 and 29 the Giant Rock Flying Saucer Convention attracted two thousand persons, more than the previous annual event but only 20 percent of the number of people who had attended the pilgrimage a half-dozen years before.

The sightings continued to flow in, the Air Force continued to discount them, individuals and groups persisted in their criticism of the official policies, and the establishment untiringly replied.

Foreign accounts began to attract industrious ufologists even more than those at home, doubtless caught up in the ancient truism that distance lends enchantment. Italy was honored with an outstanding sighting on the evening of July 18, when a greenish oval or globular object, with varying-color afterburn, moving at speeds up to 12,500 miles an hour, was scanned by radar, and directly observed over Rome, Trieste, Bolzano, Genoa, Florence, Trento, and Verona. Dedicated audiences of such sightings, regardless of their location, touted them and their alleged suppression, irritating the Air Force into occasional retorts. On July 21, for example, it issued a release, which in part stated:

> The Air Force is charged by many private UFO groups with possession of classified information which concludes or proves that space ships from other

planets exist and are visiting our atmosphere. Nothing could be further from the truth. The Air Force possesses no information, classified or unclassified, which proves this contention.[29]

Elsewhere, however, the Air Force felt required to call attention to its position that "most individuals fail to recognize the fact that there is such a thing as legitimate classified security information." It is these amendations which cause perceptive ufologists to infer that such "legitimate classified security information," relating to the aerial mystery, actually exists.

A convocation of the clan under the aegis of Gabriel Green and his Amalgamated Flying Saucer Clubs of America, Inc., purportedly another "non-profit organization conducting research on the subject of Flying Saucers, interplanetary travel and communication, and related subjects," occurred in August. It was convened to inaugurate a campaign by Green, previously announced at an August 9 press conference, for the Presidency of the United States. Unlike Van Tassel's superficial lapel-pin/bumper-sticker gesture, the convention, AFSCA's second, held in the Shrine Auditorium in Los Angeles, had definite if unusual political overtones. "The Space People's Choice," supported by "proponents of the New Age," was distinguished by organization, at least some serious money, and elaborate promotional material. Yet despite financial disclaimers, the AFSCA gave every indication of being among the most commercial of all the saucerological operations.

Politicians were as much concerned with Green's and Van Tassel's natural province as the saucerologists were with theirs. Capitol Hill was witness to accelerated interest in the great aerial mystery. Congressman Leonard G. Wolf, of Iowa, a member of the House's Science and Astronautics Committee, conceded, on August 31, that there was "real concern about UFOs by many members of Congress."[30] His colleague, William H. Ayres, of Ohio, offered the fragile assurance: "Congressional investigations are being held on the problem of UFOs. *Most of the material is classified; hearings are never printed.*"[31] (Emphasis added.)

Debunkers were not helped any when, sandwiched among sightings, Convair Aircraft engineer Tom Hemphill, head of the San Diego lunar observation team, was quoted as saying: "I am convinced that a huge mystery satellite is orbiting the earth."[32]

Such pronouncements were actually conservative by this time, even from highly qualified, scientifically trained individuals. Regardless of the sarcasm or distortingly oblique reportage of the majority of the press, television, and radio, trained, responsible men were voicing open-mindedness toward, and even tentative acceptance of, the thesis that there was something in the skies which might be intelligent and might have come from someplace other than the Earth.

During the year, various astronomers were added to the list of those with sighting attributions: James Bartlett, Washington, D.C., Frank Halstead, former curator of the Darling Observatory, Duluth, Minnesota, Director Robert Johnson, of the Adler Planetarium, Chicago, and others. Professor Robert G. Brown, of Connecticut State College, allegedly felt that a UFO sighting might "be a visitor from another world," [33] and Dr. Frank D. Drake, head of the National Observatory, Green Bank, West Virginia, directing the government's Project Ozma, a search for intelligent signals from beyond the earth, said that "we may intercept messages from space probes, launched by other civilizations in space." [34] Even astronomer Donald H. Menzel reputedly granted that he might have based his debunking evaluations of important earlier sightings on insufficient evidence.[35]

Dr. Clyde W. Tombaugh, discoverer of the planet Pluto, top natural-satellite government expert, and UFO sighter, remarked:

> These things, which do appear to be directed, are unlike any other phenomena I ever observed. . . . Other stars in our galaxy may have hundreds of thousands of inhabitable worlds. Races on these worlds may have been able to utilize the tremendous amounts of power required to bridge space between the stars.[36]

"We must now accept it as inevitable—there are other worlds with thinking beings," [37] stated former Harvard Observatory director Harlow Shapley.

Now, as serious scholars of the heavens were speculating more and more about UFOs, some of the saucerologists were broadening their scope to include precognition. Richard Ogden, described by James Moseley as "a rather notorious saucer researcher," made a number of dramatic prophecies in 1960, based upon "mental communications with a scientist from the planet Neptune." [38] He stated that "if these predictions come true, you will know that space people do exist." [39]

Forecasting that Stevenson and Nixon would be nominated, Ogden selected the latter as the winner. One correct projection out of three possibilities. However, it was not without interest to the receptive that he asserted that "the president elected in 1960 [note the phrasing does not say Nixon] will die in office during his first term." [40]

At the final moment, the psychic contactee revised his prognostication regarding the Democratic nominee, deciding upon Kennedy. Unfortunately, the remainder of his many prophecies were left intact, including the tenth, which warned that "the beginning of World War III" would be initiated in West Germany in 1966.[41]

A rather unusual story, dated November 27, highlighted the autumn annals of ufology. Seven residents of the Caravan Trailer Court, in Chula Vista, California, including the managers, Mr. and Mrs. Robert Cameron, Mr. Alex Koff, Mr. and Mrs. Donald Carter, and amateur astronomers Mr. and Mrs. Lewis Hart, began monitoring a remarkable red-ball UFO at about seven thirty in the evening. Olive Hart sent their collective report to the Air Force, a portion of which read:

> First, I wish to make it clear to you that we are competent observers . . . have been amateur astronomers for many years . . . are well acquainted with all the constellations and planets . . . have seen many varieties and many spectacular meteors . . . are also very used to jet plane sightings, weather and observation balloons, satellites, helicopters and all the other things, including inversions, that are often mistaken for UFO's. We have watched all the sputniks and Echo.
>
> . . . we were sitting watching television when the manager of this trailer court knocked on the door and asked us to please come out and see if we could identify the strange thing they were watching in the sky. So we seized our binoculars and rushed out to see a staggering sight. It was an object a bit redder than Mars (orange-red) and was describing huge circles in the air. Then it would come to a sudden stop and hover. Through the binoculars it closely resembled a planet, but it had something connected with it a planet does not have. The best way I can describe it is to say it looked like a 4th of July sparkler connected to the side of the object and appeared to go in and out. Then the red-orange glow went out and the sparkler part kept right on making dashes at terrific speeds. It went away down into Mexico and then circled some more and then returned and from where we were viewing, it went out over North Island and hovered some more. Kindly remember that seven people (three with binoculars) were viewing this object for a long time [seven for twenty minutes, two for a half hour]. Then it vanished. And did not reappear.[42]

The report was received and answered by Lt. Col. Lawrence Tacker, who dispatched a forty-two-question U. S. Air Force Technical Information Sheet to the observers for additional data. Lloyd Mallan, long-time investigator, wrote regarding the amendations to the original account:

> She (Olive Hart) made three points that were not included in her letter. One was that the planet Mars was in the sky, often near the strange UFO, so an accurate comparison could be made of the UFO's size and color. Another was that when the object sped down past San Diego over Mexico, its size and magnitude resembled those of the planet Mercury. The third point was in answer to question 38: "In your opinion what do you think the object was and what might have caused it?"
>
> The Harts' answer: "It was unquestionably some kind of intelligently controlled air or space vehicle."

The Project Blue Book evaluation of this sighting concludes:

Object has many characteristics of a refracted astronomical object, but the movement from east to west and the high elevation angle tends to rule out this possibility. Witnesses indicated they were watching object through binoculars; therefore a balloon or aircraft should have been recognized, and 30 minutes is a long time for an aircraft to be in sight if flying in any one direction for any length of time. This case is classed as an "Unidentified." [43]

Interesting. Yet, there may have been more to it. About a hundred days later, on March 13, 1961, two Air Defense Command Naval pilots, Lt. William Friel and Ensign James Jocanin, both attached to the All-Weather Fighter-Interceptor Squadron, based on North Island, made a ground-to-air sighting, aided by binoculars. The observation covered nearly ten minutes and was described by Lieutenant Friel.

What intrigued us was the light from this object. It wasn't the kind of light you see from a reciprocating engine exhaust at night or from a jet afterburner. The nearest you can describe it is to say that it looked like a steady stream of electric sparks. Something like a sparkler on the 4th of July." [44]

Yet, if endless UFOs flashed by the window of the Unknown, one door was slammed shut. In 1960, the man who could have revealed just what the Air Force had been all about in those early years was gone. Capt. Edward J. Ruppelt had died.

It need hardly be noted that, even to this day, many believers argue that the age of saucerology burns as brightly as it ever did, but the truth is that the golden glow was going bronze, the great contactees had come and spun their spells and then declined, either into repetition, oblivion, or, in several instances, along with Ruppelt, death. The West Coast maintained a concentrated cluster of the names in southern California, but the clearing and hearing house of the most prominent remained the Long John Nebel Radio show in New York City. However, even it was beginning to find fewer and fewer fascinators pounding at its doors. The "classic" figures made from one to half a dozen appearances on the forum annually, and most of these programs were repeated several times for the devout, but the ranks, as has been said, were thinning, and rarely did an unknown contactee appear. Throughout ensuing years, accounts from imitative lesser lights drifted to the surface of the subject, and much later one or two well-publicized, but very secondary, or even tertiary, claimants caught the public's fancy. The Hills were an example; also, of a somewhat different nature of contactology, monsterism took an upward turn, but the god-myth-makers, the ultra-dream-merchants, were well on the wane. Among the final of the "classic" group, although certainly not among the primary figures of the pantheon, was Dan Martin, of Texas.

In the tradition of most contactees, Martin claimed primacy, or at least near-primacy, for his inaugural relationship, in 1940, with the other-worlders. In terms of historicity, however, this first revelation was admittedly telepathic in nature. Martin dates his initial physical encounter sometime in August, 1955, at which time he was on a trip to visit his mother about a hundred miles from the Texas-Mexican border.

He was crossing the Nueces River, he recalled later, when he became aware of a tingling sensation throughout his body. Pulling his automobile to the side of the road, he stopped, and almost immediately was conscious of an object roaring up on the opposite side of the highway. He observed it had "somewhat the appearance of an R. R. Diesel locomotive . . . about eight inches off the ground . . . no landing gears of any kind." [45] While no portholes or other apertures were visible, one great window wrapped around the stern and through it Martin observed male occupants. The entire affair seemed to be more than a dozen feet in diameter and four or five times that in length.

Approaching the craft, he saw a hatch open and a modestly attractive woman descend, greeting him by name. They chatted for a few moments, but soon Martin conceded that he "couldn't think of anything sensible to ask" this creature whom he accepted as an extraterrestrial. At last his natural chauvinism asserted itself.

"Why is it that you," he inquired, "being a woman, are sent to speak to me when I can see that there are men aboard the craft?" Responding that she alone spoke "his language," [46] the alien explained that she and her associates were from the planet Mercury. After a brief additional exchange, Martin's well of curiosity ran dry once more— "I couldn't think of anything more to ask her," [47] he subsequently admitted—and she reentered her vessel and it departed.

Fortunately, he was to be given a second access to some of the extraplanetarian mysteries about a year later.

On June 11, 1956, there came a tap at his back door, and opening it he found a man and woman who said, "You are Mr. Martin, Dap O'Day." (The latter is a phrase by which he frequently identifies himself, and which he has incorporated into a personal emblem of some mystical implication.) Grasping him by his elbows, the pair levitated Martin to the upper atmosphere, where he felt surrounded by blackness and stars. Then he suddenly became aware of having come to a hover beneath a vast canopy, the center of which was a tube, multiple-shuttered like a camera lens. Martin and his companions were drawn up into a control room with buttons, levers, dials, and the other accepted "scientific" accouterment. Shortly, he was moved into a vast hall about the length of a football field, where another female addressed him as "Mr. Martin, Dap

O'Day" and led him into a smaller chamber, where sat "a man the like of which I had never seen before except, in an asteral [sic] experience. . . ." [48]

Martin was seated on a couch next to the girl guide, who, in spite of being the male's mate, apparently insisted on rubbing thighs with the contactee, notwithstanding his withdrawing in "an act of modesty." Following a brief résumé of his various lives, some of the history of the Flying Saucer, apparently of the mothership type, was unfolded for him.

"This ship . . . named for the Prince of Princes, MICHIEL, or as you know JESUS THE CHRIST OF GOD . . . has been on active duty in and around the atmosphere of this Earth for more than six thousand years," [49] wrote Martin later, explaining further that at the time of his inspection it traveled nine hundred miles above the earth, at approximately eighteen thousand miles an hour. Of special importance was its "gravity neutralizing machine," which rendered any object weightless. Among its many attributions and achievements, the MICHIEL was spoken of in the legend of Enoch,[50] effectuated the Noachian Flood, "was employed in the construction of the Great Pyramid of Gaza [sic]," [51] appeared as the biblical pillar of fire, and the stabile sun of Joshua. It was MICHIEL which thrust back the Red Sea and was "described as the Star of Bethlehem that was present at the time of the birth of Jesus and it was the voices of its crew which was [sic] heard by the shepards [sic] as they sang that famous song 'Peace on earth and good will toward man [sic].' " [52]

Generally, such expositions conclude on a religious note, often providing rough outlines of the theocratic political structure of the solar system, the galaxy, or even the universe. Martin's was no exception. Whether in pamphlet or in person, if a potential disciple pressed forward, he would eventually discover all sorts of immortal truths, not the least of which was that

the word Christ means an office, just like the word [sic] "presidency of the United States" or "office of president." It *is* authority, you understand, but there is a personality there, a president with a name. Christ is an office and has a personality called Jesus who is in authority. Spiritually his name is Michael although we call him Jesus here,

elaborates Martin, concluding that Jesus "is now on the planet Venus. . . ." [53]

However, even at his most perverted religiosity, Dan Martin was never able to achieve the sacrilegious extravagance of the messianic George King.

PART II
GÖTTERDÄMMERUNG

Chapter 13

THINGS UNKNOWN PROPOSED

A curious wedding notice appeared on New Year's Day, 1961, in the San Luis Obispo, California, *Telegram-Tribune.* It read in part:

"Among the guests were HRH Prince Michel d'Obrenovie-Obilic van Lazar, Duke of Sumadija, and his wife and son, Marc, of Paris. The prince is the noted anthropologist with the pen name George Hunt Williamson."

The variety of the saucerologist's activities seemed infinite, even when he edged outside the yields of extraterrestriality. Apart from mysterious alleged expeditions to Peruvian jungle mountaintops and the like, he was engaged for about a year working in the Noblesville, Indiana, offices of Soulcraft, a group created by William Dudley Pelley, a former fascist who had spent some eight years in prison on a sedition conviction. A spiritualistic, paramilitary organization, Soulcraft claimed mediumistic communication with Abraham Lincoln and George Washington. Neither transdeathism nor right-wing politics is foreign to Flying Saucer circles. As a matter of fact, a great many of the contactees purvey philosophies which are tinged, if not tainted, with totalitarian overtones.

Still, if the paramilitary permeated contactology, the injection of the ufological into the official military was equally frequent.

"A Polaris missile was fired [January 10, 1961]. . . . The missile was on its way up when an 'unidentifiable flying object' came over the range," wrote Maj. Donald E. Keyhoe.

The UFO was evidently so big and maneuvered so close to the Polaris that automatic tracking radar on the ground, set to follow the Polaris, locked onto the UFO by mistake. The UFO eventually flew out of the radar's "sight." It took trackers 14 minutes to find the Polaris again.[1]

Needless to say, this incident was not very widely dispersed; such seldom were. It was not without full justification that House Majority Leader John W. McCormack remarked:

I feel that the Air Force has not been giving out all the information it has. . . . These UFOs must be in a very high state of development and perfection.

Whether they come from some other planet, we don't know. . . . So many expert witnesses have seen these objects that you can't disregard so many unimpeachable sources.[2]

Across the Atlantic, Bruno Ghibaudi, an Italian writer, was making a splash for himself with UFO photographs he asserted were taken on April 27. As a number of magazines reproduced his pictures, he claimed that over two hundred thousand *"dischi volanti"* had been sighted up to that point, with at least two hundred landings proven. Ghibaudi, like most ambitious saucerologists, moved quickly once underway, and by September 27 he had produced motion-picture footage of aerial unknowns and contended that he had experienced personal contact with aliens.[3]

Still, few foreign alienologists could compete with our domestic contactees. Dan Fry revealed to the impatient world that he had had bestowed on him a doctor of philosophy degree from St. Andrews College, of London—not for contacteeism, but for his "scientific" speculations in the book *Steps to the Stars.*[4]

The devotees of Flying Saucers have always appreciated symbols of authority, however intangible. Fry supplied a bit of "science," Adamski traded in "philosophy," King's ware was "religion," Van Tassel, and some others, had a fairly mixed and balanced bag of enchantments. In April, a very peculiar tale arose, and it was one of the few to draw its authority from the law, but even stranger was that it extracted its essence from the culinary.

The tale told Judge Frank Carter by an Eagle River, Wisconsin, plumber named Joe Simonton was that just before noon, on April 18, Joe had encountered a ten-yard wide, four-foot-deep, "brighter than chrome" hovering saucer with an opened hatch, through which he observed two occupants in tight, gray, hooded uniforms. One of the aliens, who "appeared to resemble people of Italian descent," gesticulated that he wished a shallow bowl he produced to be filled with water. Simonton accommodated the request from his property well and perceived another crew member busy over some cooking apparatus not unlike a grill. Samples of the alien cuisine—greasy, grayish pancakes—were dropped into Simonton's hands as the door to the craft closed. The vessel then rose, sailing out beyond the horizon.

Judge Carter, who thought the spacial crepes suzette had the aroma of "goose grease," sent a sample to Major Keyhoe's National Investigations Committee on Aerial Phenomena, requesting an analysis, which reportedly forwarded the specimen to the newly dissolved Civilian Saucer Intelligence in New York. A trio of Air Force officers appeared to interview the country plumber, and Prof. J. Allen Hynek was said to have taken a personal interest in the peculiar case. Upon receiving no reply from NICAP, the provincial jurist sent an exhaustive and critical letter to Keyhoe, elaborating on the details of the alleged incident and complained of the seemingly cavalier treatment his report had been accorded by the Washington inquiry group.[5]

Analyses by the Food and Drug Administration and the Physics Laboratory of the Materials Central at Wright-Patterson Air Force Base, as well as the conclusions of Civilian Saucer Intelligence all indicated the pancake to be composed of terrestrial ingredients, but this did not prevent Simonton from hying himself to the lecture road to relate this and subsequent electrifying events.

Early in 1961, Richard Ogden proposed that Major Keyhoe's interminable battle with the Air Force on the matter of UFO had in reality been deftly puppeteered by the intelligence service to the end of convincing saucer-conscious elements of the public that the inexplicable objects hurtling about the skies really were extraterrestrial. Among Ogden's primary arguments was his assertion that Keyhoe had always had far greater access to Air Force files than any other investigator, and has been accorded much gratuitous publicity from officialdom.[6]

Around this time, Lt. Col. Lawrence Tacker was replaced as Air Force UFO spokesman by Maj. William Coleman.

The sightings continued, although there seemed to be fewer flaps, and the contactees continued to spin their spells, but even these grew more and more threadbare. The most interesting development during this period was the increased receptivity of "serious" scientists to the possibility that there was life elsewhere, and, possibly, life that somehow might have, at some point, reached here.

A number of Soviet scientists were cited for remarks relating to the Flying Saucer mystery in an article appearing in July, 1961. Physicist Prof. V. Krasovsky is said to have taken the position that "the reason for probing the cosmos is, above all else, to unlock the secrets of outer space —of past and present cosmic civilizations, if they existed or still exist." [7] Another physicist, Dr. I. S. Shklovsky, reputedly argues that Mars was once inhabited, but suffered a thinning of its atmosphere. To accommodate some of the population, it constructed and launched two hollow, erratically orbiting satellites, Phobos and Deimos. "The creation of such satellites," Dr. Shklovsky is quoted as saying, "is not an insoluble engineering problem for intelligent creatures. There is no doubt that in centuries to come, we shall have such satellites around our own planet." [8] Mathematician M. M. Agrest has suggested that Earth may have been visited by an enormous space vessel in biblical times. He has wondered whether the Baalbek Terrace of Lebanon, an architectural marvel consisting of immense stone slabs up to sixty feet long and four million pounds in weight, might have been erected by aliens as a return launching platform for their craft.[9]

Unfortunately, if new voices were being raised, others were silenced. Ruppelt was gone, and he was followed by noted English researcher Arthur Constance, author of *The Inexplicable Sky*.[10] Also, Meade Layne, founder of the very esoteric Borderland Science Research Associates, died of brain cancer, and Riley Crabb, who had already assumed direction of the group, was permanently ensconced. The ranks had not thinned enough to deplete the personality roster of the saucer symposia, however. On the other hand, the gathering of both publicity and disciples had become increasingly more of a problem. The 1961 Space Convention, at Giant Rock, California, bannered appearances by Fry, Bethurum, Williamson, Angelucci, Max Miller, James Moseley, Gabriel Green, and Van Tassel, but the response was in no way comparable to previous occasions.

Echoing certain characteristics of several of the sightings which formed the great 1897 complex, when, over a period of six months, UFOs were reported from coast to coast, the account of two Drake University seniors, Tom Phipps and James B. Furkenhoff, both twenty-one, was of interest to those familiar with the early American episode. On August 12, the Kansas City pair told investigators they saw a 150-foot long bobsled-shaped vessel sailing overhead. Described as having a series of lights along each "runner" and an enormous tail fin, it took several minutes to pass out of sight.[11]

Another reminiscent report was registered by a British Overseas Airways Corporation captain, piloting a Boeing 707. R. A. Griffin told of encountering a doughnut-designed craft over the Pacific, at about 40,000 feet, on September 21. This UFO, which fit the description of the Maury Island devices, as well as several others, was also observed by a Pan American flight in the area. Both planes radioed Wake Island and Honolulu with details of the incident.[12]

Women, while occupying definitely secondary, even tertiary, positions on the descending tiers of saucerology, have nonetheless made names for themselves. Among these was Gloria Lee (Byrd), a one-time child actress, model, singer, and airlines stewardess who had married William H. Byrd, an aircraft designer, and mothered two children. In the 1950's, Gloria Lee had sighted a flying saucer, and not only became a follower of the cult, but, in a small way, a leader.[13] During this period, in September, she was the absentee high priestess of several small quasi-religious-telepathic contact lectures in the Great Northern Hotel in New York. It was toward the end of the Long John Nebel television series, which had, over a period of two years, presented about all the major Flying Saucer personalities. About a year earlier, Howard and Marla had faded from the scene, and not even the emergence of the contactee's book, *From Outer Space to You,*[14] caused them to return to the public stage. Then, unexpectedly, Nebel was informed that Howard Menger wanted to come out of his seclusion and appear on the television program. The ringmaster of the saucer circus assumed that he had been involved in, or had single-handedly evolved, a completely new odyssey of outer-space adventures.

Several days prior to Menger's televised return, George Adamski was scheduled to appear on Long John's all-night radio program. When the Californian arrived, it was revealed that he was scheduled to give a major lecture on the night Howard was to appear on the television show. Needless to say, this created a great conflict in the saucer community, as Adamski and Menger were two of the handful of really major figures in the field. It was solved in an appropriately imaginative way. The Adamski lecture, in the ballroom of a New York hotel, began with an introduction by popular saucerologist Courtland Hastings and moved directly into the opening segment of George's address. Then the audience's attention was called to a number of television sets distributed about the vast hall, and within minutes all were watching *The Long John Nebel Television Show,*[15] featuring the second coming of Howard Menger. The lecture was completed after the program.

It was one of the historic crossroads of contactology. Menger, to the astonishment of supporters and opponents alike, recanted the vast majority of his personal legend, suggesting that all of his experiences may well have been "psychic" (a kind of reneging generally regarded as the most unforgivable in the contact community). It was an intriguing broadcast, but there can be little question that its impact upon the speciality of alienology was disastrous. Later, Howard Menger returned, rather tentatively, to the carnival of confusion, but it was never to be the same again.

The following year saw the United States begin to move into outer space, in the wake of the Soviet Union's Vostok I and II, commanded by Maj. Yuri A. Gagarin and Maj. Gherman S. Titov, respectively, which had orbited the earth on April 12 and August 6 and 7 of 1961. The Gagarin flight had circumnavigated the planet once, Titov's seventeen times. However, on February 20, 1962, Col. John H. Glenn piloted a Mercury capsule around the world three times; then Lt. Comdr. M. Scott Carpenter duplicated the feat on May 24, and Comdr. Walter M. Schirra raised it to six orbits on October 3. Observations made by Glenn are not inappropriate in a study of Unidentified Flying Objects:

The strangest sight of all came with the very first ray of sunrise as I was crossing the Pacific toward the U.S. I was checking the instrument panel and when I looked back out the window, I thought for a minute that I must have tumbled upside-down and was looking at a new field of stars. I checked my instruments to make sure I was right-side-up. Then I looked again. There, spread out as far as I could see, were literally *thousands* of tiny luminous objects that glowed in the black sky like fireflies. I was riding slowly through them, and the sensation was like walking backwards through a pasture where someone had waved a wand and made all the fireflies stop right where they were and glow steadily. They were *greenish yellow* in color, and they appeared to be about six to ten feet apart. I seemed to be passing through them at a speed of from three to five miles an hour. They were all around me, and those nearest the capsule would occasionally move across the windows as if I had slightly interrupted their flow. On the next pass I turned the capsule around so that I was looking right into the flow, and though I could see far fewer of them in the light of the rising sun, they were still there. Watching them come toward me, *I felt certain* they were not caused by anything emanating from the capsule. I thought perhaps I'd stumbled into the lost patch of needles the Air Force had tried to set up in orbit for communications purposes. But I could think of no reason why needles should glow like fireflies, nor did they look like needles. As far as I know, the true identity of these particles is still a mystery.[16]

Carpenter not only saw the objects but photographed them as well. His pictures show some to be shaped, at least as the profile aspect reveals, fairly close to the classic saucer design.[17] It was Carpenter's contention they were ice crystals flaking off the craft; however, Glenn's response to this explanation was to reaffirm his own impression, which included the fact that the objects were moving *toward* him and were greenish yellow.

Brothers, published by the Cosmic Brotherhood, edited by Dr. Yoshiyuki Tange, and covering a wide range of saucer subjects, emerged from Japan in the spring of 1962. Tending toward mystical interpretations, it nonetheless featured legitimate astrophysical speculations and representations of the AVROCAR. The second issue was centered about the June 24 Special International Flying Saucer Sighting Day.

The year also offered a prosperous UFO, Flying Saucer, and even contact harvest for Italy. Perhaps it would never match the quantity or variety of the production of some other foreign countries, e.g., Brazil and France, but it was building a bumper crop.

Eugenio Siragusa, a minor government official, reported that he had encountered two spacians on Mount Manfee, near the volcano Mount Etna, on April 30. The duo was said to have delivered to him a message of peace for President John F. Kennedy, Premier Khrushchev, Elizabeth of England, De Gaulle, Pope John, and President Segni, of Siragusa's own country. The contactee conveyed the cosmic billets-doux and reportedly actually received a courtesy note from a De Gaulle aide. Siragusa later made another contact and returned with a drawing of the Flying Saucer.[18]

On the same day as Siragusa met his extraterrestrials, top American test pilot Maj. Joe Walker hurled the experimental X-15 aircraft along in the upper atmosphere at speeds exceeding two thousand miles an hour, a rear-view motion-picture camera, attached to the plane, monitoring the area behind him. Walker brought his ship in and the film was developed. It revealed "a group of five disc-shaped or cylindrical objects. Most of the time they were flying in echelon formation." [19] Major Walker alluded to them in a television interview and the strip was shown. The Air Force dismissed the phenomena as "ice flakes;" prints of the film were never released; Major Walker never mentioned the incident to unofficial questioners again.

The endlessly recurring theme of persons being silenced by the Establishment—both in the exotic outer reaches of contactology and among the most serious researchers—has puzzled countless investigators and, to a great degree, been responsible for the Air Force's poor reputation in this area. An instance of a step up from the X-15 film matter might be the Air Force activity allegedly surrounding a sighting in Berlin, New Hampshire, on June 14. According to ufologist Ralph Rankow, the unknown was sighted by two members of the staff of radio station WMOU and subsequently carried as an item on the station's news broadcast. Immediately, WMOU received a call from the Pease Air Force Base, close by in Portsmouth, New Hampshire, asking that no further reference to the sighting be made until official investigators arrived. Air Force officers appeared shortly thereafter and questioned the UFO viewers, Michael Saunders and Lillian M. Jeskey, exhaustively. "No further information on this case has ever been broadcast," [20] observes Rankow ominously.

Throughout the year the Italian sightings continued and contacts burgeoned, until, as Christmas approached, they were inescapable. Antonia Candau told of meeting two saucer pilots, who spoke an unintelligible language, on December 9;[21] Francesco Rizzi encountered a yard-high spacian on the eighteenth;[22] and Italo Magri met a slightly smaller alien on the twenty-second.[23]

However, North America and Europe were not the only areas to boast such strange accumulations of observations and encounters. As has been noted before, South America was developing a considerable UFO and Flying Saucer history. Casual researchers in the United States were aware of this but tended to believe that nearly all of the stories were originating in Brazil. Yet Argentina was close behind, and the great flap of 1962 caused considerable excitement among more deeply probing investigators.

One case had two astronomy students, of the University of Cordoba, taking fifteen photographs of a circular unknown, jetting a crimson exhaust, wheeling about at approximately two thousand feet. The report was dated March.[24]

Four months later, a seventeen-year-old motorcyclist reported that during the evening of July 26, while on a deserted side road near Parma, he encountered a melon-headed, three-eyed, six-foot creature who snatched his scarf from him and walked off toward a light hanging low in the sky, disappearing in the dark.[25]

Jacques Vallee noted the following report:

The Director of the Corrientes Airport at Camba Punta, Argentina, and Dr. Gustavo Revidapte, a judge . . . saw a strange object coming toward the runway from the west. It emitted flashes of green, white and red light. . . . Six other persons, including several policemen . . . observed the object as it stopped at the end of the runway, spinning and emitting beams of light. When the witnesses got into a truck and drove toward the object it left at great speed.[26]

A vast, zeppelinlike luminescence was observed near Buenos Aires, by Pedro Attili, on the very early morning of August 6, while across the border, in Santiago, Chile, a score of swift, brilliant UFOs were watched by numerous persons only a week later. This incident was followed on August 16 by a sighting of several smaller unknowns flashing from a "mother ship," which was under the surveillance of two or three dozen persons.[27]

The adventures of a physician and his wife were recounted in a periodical of Formosa, Argentina. According to the journal, the couple saw a classic-styled Flying Saucer land on the night of August 21, from which descended two light-haired, bulging-eyed, six-foot figures. Jamming the accelerator of his automobile to the floor, Dr. Gazcue fled. One week afterward, José Bellantoni supposedly photographed an iridescent, twenty-five-yard-diameter UFO near the town of Dolores.[28]

Farmer Juan Sosa, of San Juan, reported a September 3 vessel landing, and a large group of residents testified to the appearance of an unknown near La Matacos, on October 4. Another cluster of the population described an object twice the size of the moon, which hung above them for a while on the evening of October 14.[29]

Among the more interesting of the Argentinian adventures was carried in a Tucumán newspaper. It asserted that an Italian truck driver, Pier Livio Quaia, almost rammed a highway-straddling UFO on the evening of November 5. The glowing, ovate, approximately fifteen-by-forty-foot object was circled with small windows, through which red-and-green lights were visible. The craft's belly featured a yard-wide transparent window, bright with white illumination. Quaia was later joined by two additional night drivers. The trio surveyed the scene for about an hour, until they decided it was not going to do anything more interesting than merely *be* there, and they left.[30]

The Aerial Phenomena Research Organization's South American investigator, Dr. Olavo T. Fontes, called attention to an extraordinary adventure. The narrator of, and alleged participant in, the incredible episode was twelve-year-old Raimundo do Aleuia Mafra, of Duas Pontes, Diamantina, in the Brazilian state of Minas Gerais. According to the boy, on the night of August 19, as the entire family, consisting of his father, his two younger brothers, and he himself, was sleeping, eerie footsteps sounded in the house. Inconsistently, shadows accompanying the curious noises floated above the floor—bringing to mind the levitational proclivities of Albert K. Bender's Three Men in Black, a story hardly likely to have come within the compass of a youth in a relatively remote Brazilian village.

Shouting by the family elicited no response from the presences, but strange, threatening voices were overheard, as well as a warning of the impending murder of the father, Rivalino. Although sleep was eschewed for the remainder of the night, daylight delivered no cessation of the terror. In Raimundo's obviously well-edited words:

In the morning, still afraid, I had the courage to go outside to get my father's horse . . . but then I sighted two balls floating in mid-air side by side, about three feet from the ground, one foot from each other. . . . They were big. . . . One of them was all black, had a kind of irregular antenna-like protuberance and a small tail. The other was black and white, with the same outlines. . . . Both emitted a humming sound and appeared to give off fire through an opening that flickered like a fire fly. . . .

I called my father . . . out of the house. . . . He walked toward the objects . . . stopped at a distance of two meters. At that moment the two big balls merged into each other. There was only one now, bigger in size, raising dust from the ground and discharging a yellow smoke which darkened the sky. With strange noises, that big ball crept slowly toward my father.

I saw him enveloped by the yellow smoke and he disappeared inside it. I ran after him into the yellow cloud, which had an acrid smell. I saw nothing, only that yellow mist around me. I yelled for my father but there was no answer. Everything was silent again.

Then the yellow smoke dissolved. The balls were gone. My father was gone. . . . I want my father back. . . .[31]

Raimundo was thoroughly interrogated by Lt. Wilson Lisboa, police chief of Diamantina, by Father José Avila Garcia, who doubted the account, and by psychiatrist Dr. Joan Antumes de Oliveria, who told the press:

"I do not wish to discuss the case further. The facts are beyond my competence. But I can tell you that the boy is normal and he is telling what he thinks is the truth."[32]

Testimony of a corroborative nature was offered by several persons. Antonio Rocha, a minor postal official and a friend of the priest, said he had seen two ball-shaped objects near the house in question. Dr. Giovani Pereira, a town physician, reported a brilliant UFO disc in the vicinity. Four days later, half a hundred persons saw a similar object pass across the sky. Also, Lieutenant Lisboa found local prospectors who swore Rivalino told them he had seen little yard-high strangers digging holes in the area a short time earlier.

Material in various media continued to be published in the field, as represented by the privately issued *Challenge of Unidentified Flying Objects,* by Prof. C. A. Maney and Richard Hall, and the production of Dr. Frank Stranges's book, *Flying Saucerama,* as a film titled *The Earth May Die Tomorrow.* It was claimed the motion picture was budgeted at nearly a quarter of a million dollars, but most saucerites were more willing to believe that the clerical-collared gentleman had actually met Thor Valiant, from Venus, in the heart of the Pentagon, as he asserted.

Gloria Lee, who had founded Cosmon Research, offered the government some spaceship blueprints bestowed upon her by the alien entity "J. W." but was rebuffed. In response, on orders from her Jovian master, Gloria Lee (Byrd) began a fast on September 23 which was to be continued until a "light elevator" arrived to convey her to Jupiter. By November 28 she was unconscious. The promised celestial transportation apparently arrived four days later; the thirty-seven-year-old metaphysical contactee died on December 2.

Saucerology, at best, is hardly a repository of good taste, and the commercialization of Gloria Lee's demise exemplified its more tawdry aspects. Prior to her death Mrs. Byrd had engaged in a brief relationship with the Mark-Age MetaCenter in Miami, Florida, a group specializing in more abstract forms of alienology; following it, Mark-Age published a newsletter, titled *Gloria Lee Lives,* which purported to contain messages from the deceased transmitted through the instrumentality of one "Yolanda." It was a crudely composed tract, ranging from "Hello everybody, this is Gloria," to an account of her meeting with the late Marilyn Monroe. Perhaps it was not, after all, so inappropriate a conclusion to the esoteric career of Gloria Lee.

Chapter 14

WORLDS WITHOUT END

The world stands out on either side
No wider than the heart is wide;
Above the world is stretched the sky—
No higher than the soul is high.
                    —"Renascence," Edna St. Vincent Millay

The hope, at least among ufologists, that the Establishment or the Air Force would ever invest either financing or dedication in the investigation of Unidentified Flying Objects had pretty well been abandoned by 1963. Nevertheless, The National Academy of Sciences' Space Science Board opened the new year with a report (#1079) urging that a search for extraterrestrial life "be proclaimed the top-priority scientific goal of our space program." [1]

Unknowns certainly appeared to have forsaken no part of the world. In Livron, France, two field hands told of a luminous aerial disk revolving above them on January 26, which remained visible for nearly a minute;[2] a half-dozen residents of Modesto, California, spent several times that long watching a round UFO, about one hundred yards in diameter, on February 2;[3] Charlie Brew, an Australian farmer, turned in an account of a thick disk, with reflecting rims and scuttle-like appendages, which appeared overhead on February 16, frightening his livestock;[4] according to Amos Biggs, of Montana, a silver saucer, with a small compartment, eased down to the frozen surface of Crystal Lake on March 9, its hatch opened, nothing happened, its hatch closed, and it flew away.[5]

Elsewhere—A black airborne sphere startled Alwyn Green, of Hurchor Bluffs, New Zealand, on the afternoon of April 23. Yolando and Miriam Curas, residents of Cardona, saw an elongated red-, green-, and yellow-streaked UFO flash across the highway, near Oncativo, Argentina, on May 12. Farther along, seeing the object had come to rest fairly near the road, they were able to note it had a "reddish hut-shaped" canopy and portholes.[6] The Reverend R. Dean Johnson, and his wife, dur-

164

ing a drive near Lake Michigan, reported seeing an enormous round object, with a double row of square windows, about two hundred feet above the road exactly a week later. They estimated it to be fifteen feet high and five times that in diameter.[7] On the twenty-first, a seventeen-year-old in southern Australia paced a UFO at sixty miles an hour for several minutes.[8] Chicagoan Janice McKay attested to having seen an aerial unknown, with five small windows or lights, spinning across the sky on the night of the twenty-first.[9] Four days afterwards newspaperman Richard Pothier, of the Quincy (Massachusetts) *Patriot-Ledger*, took 35 mm. photographs of an orange-and-white UFO. Dozens of other sightings of similar description were reported throughout the state.[10]

The succeeding month, in terms of English sightings, was of special interest, in spite of that country's being the source of many remarkable accounts. An immense torpedolike ship "as big as four-terraced houses" was viewed by Frank Selwood, of Parkstone, on Sunday morning, July 14. It hung about a hundred yards overhead, not far from his home, and emitted an undulating blue-white light and whistling motor sounds before it moved off at a tremendous rate.[11]

Two ten-year-old boys, Michael Lee and John Duffy, of Kentwood Approach, Leeds, told their parents of a dully metallic-looking saucer, with a cockpit, which descended from an overcast sky on July 24 and then rapidly sped away.[12]

The next night proved to be an active one for the entire English Midlands. Accounts from Birmingham centered about an object possessing a powerful searchlight, which suddenly began to glow red and swept out of sight as swiftly as it had appeared. Two inhabitants of Bloxwich, named Dunn and Cape, also told of a UFO featuring a great beacon, in this instance flashing on and off. It first seemed bluish-white and then graduated into red, vanishing southward. A number of other reports from the area came in that evening.[13]

Roy Blanchard's discovery of a crater in his potato patch suggested the opening passage of a space-age children's story, but it inaugurated an intriguing episode in English saucerology. The primary excavation was almost two yards wide and one deep, it was surrounded, to the distance of forty feet, by large lumps of scattered earth, and spokelike impressions radiated from the axis pit. Concurrently, craters began appearing with alarming frequency. Among the many communities to report them were Middle Moneynut, East Lothian; Dufton Fell, Westmoreland; Flamborough Head, Yorkshire; Sanquhar, Dumfriesshire; and Southerness, Kirkcudbright.

The flow of reports certainly didn't cease, although it may have subsided somewhat. On August 1, for example, a former RAF pilot and practicing flying instructor observed the familiar triangular unknown for a considerable period of time before it climbed beyond view. The object was also monitored by an air-traffic controller four miles away.[14] Two weeks later, ". . . for the second night in succession, scores of people telephoned the Air Ministry and the BBC to report a mysterious triangular-shaped object in the sky over London and the Home Counties," recorded the London *Daily Sketch.*[15]

In the United States, while numerous reports continued to flow across official and unofficial desks, there was little question the reports were less frequent than during earlier phases, especially as compared to the high points in the fifties.

Illinois underwent a minor flap during the initial two weeks of August, apparently starting with an unnerving experience suffered by Ronald Austin and his girl friend, Phyllis Bruce, on the night of the fourth (some reports have the third). The couple were returning from an evening at a drive-in movie when Austin's automobile was buzzed, at about tree level, by a glowing white UFO, which continued to pace the car, even as it accelerated, sometimes approaching to within a hundred feet. At one point in the chase, the unknown passed the two terrified young persons, cutting in front of them, although they reported they were racing at nearly 120 miles an hour at the time. Side effects did not help to make the episode less frightening as the radio screeched static and the motor missed at the very high speeds. Austin finally got to his home, where his state of shock required medical sedation. Sheriff Harry Lee of Wayne County, who monitored a light for several hours, said it is unclear whether it was clearly established that it was *the* light, but that it moved and was "high in the sky and bigger and brighter than any star." [16] The National Investigations Committee on Aerial Phenomena suggested that what the officer saw might have been Jupiter,[17] but that certainly does not account for the original hair-raising incident.

The September issue of *Flying Saucers* touted a rarely considered hypothesis when it suggested that the disaster of the submarine *Thresher* might have been caused by a UUO—an Underwater Unidentified Object.[18] It was speculation tossed upon the waters of reader imagination, hoping, no doubt, a biblical return, but as it appeared *sans* argument, few results were realized. Actually, it seemed like little more than another attempt to introduce a stimulant to the body saucerological, which was finding that it had almost inbred itself into a mythologically hemophiliac state. If there was any doubt remaining regarding the debilitated condition of certain branches of the second- and third-generation enthusiasts of the world of Flying Saucers, one had only to attend the

Tenth Annual Giant Rock Spacecraft Convention, still under the direction of George Van Tassel. Originally the most successful of all such convocations, attracting many thousands to hear its prophets and philosophers, in 1963 the paying participants probably numbered fewer than four hundred.

The autumn records of reports seemed to reflect an increasing decline and even outside of the United States the pattern continued to be irregular. Argentina, for instance, was eschewing little aliens for giants, as with the tale related by Eugenio Douglas. The contactee told investigators that he was driving between Monte Maíz and Isla Verde when he encountered a brilliant light straddling the road. Emerging from his truck, he could ascertain that the iridescence was a circular metallic saucer about thirty-five feet high. As he watched, the door to the craft opened and several men, whose height exceeded thirteen feet, descended to the ground. They wore skintight uniforms and a headdress which seemed to provide for, or featured, antennae. The saucer crew sighted Douglas and flashed him with a red ray, which instantly seared his flesh. Snatching a revolver that he carried on these lonely trips, he fired three times at the monsters, and turned and fled toward Monte Maíz. The red ray followed him along the road and into the village, and when it struck the local street lamps their yellow glow translated into a violet, then green, color and emitted a gassy odor. Douglas raced up to the home of the Ribas family, whose male head had just died, where a wake was in progress. The crimson beam went with him, causing the ritual candles and the electric lights to react as had the street lamps. Finally, apparently, the ominous effulgence dissipated, and Douglas was escorted to the police station to relate his experience. His scorched skin was examined by Dr. Dabolos, who remarked it to be similar to radiation burns. On the following day, the area of the original encounter was investigated and the truck was found to seemingly have suffered some sort of heat damage. However, the denouement was the discovery of footprints. Reputedly they were nineteen and a half inches long.[19]

It is possible that the Socorro, New Mexico, incident of April 24 elicited a more favorable response from hardheaded researchers than any report of its emphasis in the late phases of saucerology. A composite sighting/landing/semicontact, it came as close to the tales of the contactees as any report accorded any credence at all.

Lonnie Zamora, an officer of good reputation in the Socorro Police Department, was described by Air Force investigator Dr. J. Allen Hynek in the following manner:

> Zamora, although not overly articulate, is basically sincere, honest, and reliable. He would not be capable of contriving a complex hoax, nor would his tem-

perament indicate that he would have the slightest interest in such. He was simply a cop on duty, relinquished on discharge of that duty [chasing a speeding car] for another which he thought was of more immediate importance [investigating the possible explosion of a dynamite shack]. His fright was genuine, and his feeling that he had seen something truly unusual attested by the fact that he asked whether he should speak to the priest first before saying anything.

Any question of hallucination seems clearly out. He is a non-drinking man, and is a solid, well-built, physically healthy individual. He is a cop who looks as though he could be pretty gruff with his customers, and in fact his complaint about the UFO sighting was that it did not allow him to give out his full quota of tickets for the day.[20]

At about 5:45 in the afternoon, as he drove the Socorro patrol car 2, he observed a speeding automobile and gave chase. At one point, when the pursued vehicle was still three blocks ahead, Zamora was distracted by a great noise. In his words:[21]

At this time, I heard a roar and saw a flame in the sky to the southwest, some distance away. . . .
Noise I heard was a roar, not a blast, not a jet. It changed from high frequency to low frequency and then stopped. The roar lasted possibly ten seconds. . . .

Proceeding toward the "roar and flame," Zamora came over a rise in the road and started down the other side into a gully.

Suddenly I noted a shiny-type object to the south about 150 to 200 yards. It was off the road. At first glance, I stopped. It looked, at first, like a car turned upside down. Thought some kids might have turned it over. Saw two people in white coveralls very close to the object. One of these persons seemed to turn and look straight at my car and seemed startled—seemed to quickly jump somewhat.
At this time, I started moving my car towards them quickly. . . . The object was like aluminum—it was whitish against the moss background, but not chrome. It seemed like it was oblong in shape. . . .
The only time I saw two persons was when I had stopped, for possibly two seconds or so, to glance at the object. . . . These persons appeared normal in shape —but possibly they were small adults or large kids.[22]

Later, he cast doubt on the humanoid aspect of the story.[23]

The officer continued along the road approaching the object as he called to the sheriff's office in Socorro. At that time, Sergeant Sam Chavez picked up the message and proceeded to the location. Zamora was still speaking on his radio when he brought his prowl car to a stop. Signing off, he emerged from the vehicle and moved in the direction of the arroyo in which he knew the object to be located. He later recalled that he had

hardly turned around from my car when I heard a roar, a very loud roar. . . .
The object was starting to go straight up—slowly up. [The] flame was light blue and at the bottom it was sort of an orange color. . . .

The object was smooth—no windows or doors [visible]. As the roar started, it was still [on] or near the ground. I noted red lettering of some type, like an insignia, about 2¼ inches high and about two inches wide. Insignia was in the middle of the object.[24]

The symbol was reportedly a "V" or "crescent" slashed by three strokes.

The saucer then rose above the level of the squad car, moved off over the shack, and disappeared over Miles Canyon Mountain.

The Sergeant Chavez came up and asked me what the trouble was because I was sweating and he told me that I was very white, very pale. I asked the Sergeant to see what I saw and that was the burning brush [in the area where the object had been]. The brush was burning in several places.[25]

Considerable physical evidence was apparent to those who inspected the site, although, of course, they had no way of being certain of its cause.

The matter was investigated by the state police, the Federal Bureau of Investigation, and the Air Force, which sent its top man, Hynek, accompanied by Sgt. David Moody, from Project Blue Book, at Wright-Patterson Air Force Base. An initial survey of the alleged landing location revealed considerable scorching, as well as four wedge-shaped impressions which seemed to coincide with the position of the vessel's legs. However, by the time Hynek arrived, most of the physical factors had been obliterated or obscured by previous examiners and the curious.

Hynek devoted most of his attention to Zamora, with whom he conversed for many hours, and whom he had reenact the entire episode. While conceding the report to be unique among those he had investigated during his years of inquiry for the Air Force, the astronomer was unhappy at the lack of radar confirmation (noted newsman Frank Edwards was to assert that the nearest "radar wasn't working"[26]) and/or other witnesses.[27] But with regard to the latter complaint, at the time he was not in possession of following supporting data and testimony.

Opal Grinder, manager of Whiting Brothers' Service Station, also immediately north of Socorro, reported that shortly before the time of the Zamora sighting an unidentified driver had stopped for gasoline and remarked on a curious craft which had overflown him, adding that he had noticed a police car heading in its direction. Unfortunately, this witness may never have been located.[28]

Ultimately the Socorro sighting, even with the supportive reports which followed it closely, must rest on whether one believes Lonnie Zamora or not. Apparently Hynek did, and Dr. Lincoln La Paz, "America's foremost authority on meteorites,"[29] who allegedly attributed the patrolman's experience to an experimental United States craft, in spite of the Air Force's rejection of all such explanations, says: "I have had contacts with Officer Zamora in my work and he is a thoroughly dependable observer." [30]

The New Mexico affair did not end there.

Soon after midnight, only hours after the police officer's alleged encounter, Orlando Gallegos, who was visiting his father's house near the small village of La Madera, claims he observed a grounded craft of an ovoid, metallic appearance and about five yards in vertical circumference. He said it "looked like an egg-shaped butane tank . . . as long as a telephone pole and about 14 feet in circumference." [31] After approaching to about two hundred feet, caution and the spokes of blue flame spurting from radiating jet nozzles precluded closer investigation. Reportedly a large charred area, which was examined by local lawman Nick Naranjo, who notified his captains Vigil and Kingsbury, and Air Force personnel, later on, testified to the nocturnal visitation. Coral Lorenzen wrote that while interviewing State Police Capt. Martin Vigil, he had told her of strange markings at the allegedly new landing site. "He told me the impressions were four in number, each was wedge-shaped at the bottom. They were three to four inches deep, 12 inches wide, and eight inches across." [32] These were very much like some of the impressions discovered at the Socorro location. Additionally, Vigil said that "rocks in the center of the area were split, a bottle was melted and green brush had been set on fire, evidently by intense heat." [33]

On Sunday night, April 26, George Mitropolis, of Albuquerque, was traveling north along Route 85, at about half past ten, when his eye was attracted to a low-flying, slightly luminous object, having something of the look of "an upside down bathtub, gliding out across the desert. No lights were evident, but he saw an exhaust-like underglow and heard sounds "like muffled jets." [34]

The supporting testimony of Don Adams, of Edgewood, Texas, was even more dramatic. As he drove along the highway shortly after midnight on the morning of April 28, he became aware of the presence of a twenty-five-foot-long emerald unknown drifting a hundred feet above his automobile. In a lusty Wild West fashion he took a .22-caliber pistol from his vehicle and fired a half dozen times at the curious craft, hearing the bullets ricochet off a solid surface. Reloading—for one can't keep an irrepressible American twenty-year-old frustrated when he wants to kill something—he shot six more times. Eventually either he or the spacians drifted off to some other activity. [35]

However, the flap had hardly begun. Briefly, here are a few of the more interesting accounts to be recorded during this southwestern resurgence of ufology.

Ten-year-old Sharon Stull, of Albuquerque, saw a "weird-looking thing bobbing about in the sky," [36] an ovoid about the size of an aircraft[37] as she stood in her schoolyard at lunchtime on April 28. The five-to-ten-minute observation damaged her eyes and face. The physician whom her parents, Mr. and Mrs. Max Stull, called in is said to have remarked that normal daylight "would usually be considered insufficient to cause the burns and inflammation caused by longer exposure to the sun." [38]

That afternoon, Napoleon Green and his wife observed a pair of unknowns, plane-sized egg-shapes north of Socorro.[39] Also on the twenty-eighth, a group of children and adults witnessed a white globe in the sky near Hobbs, New Mexico.[40]

The extraordinary concentration of sightings continued unabated. Before the day was over, a highway patrolman, Paul Arteche, a private pilot, and several port-of-entry employees, located near Las Cruces, monitored a luminous UFO, which flew an erratic pattern.[41]

It is doubtful the twentieth century ever provided as fertile a field for fraud as The Age of Flying Saucers. And truly, hoaxes abounded. Some malicious, some amusing, some commercial, some political; they ranged from the small and parochial to the vast and complicated. One of the better-known examples of the relatively harmless, but imaginative, deceits occurred in New Jersey as summer ended.

On September 4, a woman and two adolescent girls were entranced by a glowing skyborne light as they walked through the early fall evening. On the following day, an eleven-year-old boy named Ward Campbell, Jr., and his brother, who was three years his junior, were approached by a young man as they fished on the banks of Lake Segri, New Jersey. The stranger told them that a Flying Saucer had landed nearby on the previous night, and he indicated approximately where this irresistible event had come to pass. The boys rushed to their father, who, coincidentally, happened to belong to the local chapter of the National Investigations Committee on Aerial Phenomena, and related their adventure. Mr. Campbell informed the police and McGuire Air Force Base.

The location given the boys was a secluded clearing of about thirty by forty feet. Here, examination disclosed, were to be found three distinct holes, one less than a yard across and nearly half that deep, the other two, some 50 percent smaller. A possible fourth, lesser, hole was barely perceptible. These major depressions were surrounded by a triangulation of minor ones. The branches of many of the encircling trees were broken downward.[42]

A week after the episode, a New York newspaper[43] carried a story saying that the Air Force investigators had interpreted a gum wrapper, remains of a cherry bomb, and a sneaker footprint, found in the clearing, as conclusive indications that a hoax had been attempted. The inference to be drawn was obviously directed at the Campbell boys.

The case did, indeed, prove to be one of fraud, but it was not perpetuated by the discovering lads. Elaborately contrived with the aid of potassium nitrate, sulfur, radium dioxide, suitable equipment, imagination, and two credulous pawns, an eighteen-year-old college student had contrived the entire scheme. Ultimately he revealed himself and attempted to market the story of his deception to the press. He was charged with being a disorderly person and fined $50 by Municipal Judge Lawrence E. Meyers. His Honor waived the mulct, letting the boy and his friends go with only $10 in court costs to pay.[44]

The Age of Flying Saucers was still declining. Ufology, however, at least during this period, seemed to have been revivified. George D. Fawcett, frequent contributor to magazines of this genre, offered an enlightening survey of 1964–1965 sightings. He had cataloged forty-six landing reports; thirty-four from this country and a dozen terrestrially deriving from Canada to Venezuela, from Australia to Austria. Humanoids were noted in fourteen of his cases, evenly divided between domestic and foreign attributions. Fourteen—nine and five—specific radar trackings were recorded, and a dozen plane pursuits, seven above the United States. Radiation evidence was cited in seven instances, only once overseas, while photographs and motion pictures were acquired eleven times here and six times elsewhere. Nine automobile chases were listed, one each occurring in New Zealand and Venezuela. Five burns, four in the United States, were reported. On three occasions—in Washington State, New Mexico, and Venezuela—sighters fired guns at Unidentified Flying Objects.[45]

Horace Burns is a gunsmith of Harrisonburg, living at Grottoes, Virginia. On December 21, as he was driving toward Waynesboro, a few miles east of Staunton, he saw an enormous object sweep from the sky, cross Route 250, and come to rest in a small meadow about a hundred yards off the road. Simultaneously, the motor of his station wagon sputtered and died, and he guided the vehicle along the shoulder until it stopped and then got out. The inverted-top-like device was immense; over forty yards across and nearly thirty high. The conic conformation featured a half dozen tiers of concentric circles decreasing in size from base to dome. The lowest, twelve to eighteen inches wide, emitted a bluish iridescence. No door, hatch, window, porthole, seam, or landing gear was evident.

Suddenly, the saucer ascended for several hundred feet and vanished to the northeast.[46]

Professor Ernest Gehman investigated the story and the alleged landing site. Nine days after the incident date, he reported, "A preliminary testing with a Geiger counter revealed radioactivity of over 60,000 counts per minute." [47] His readings were checked and verified by two engineers employed by the nearby DuPont installation, Harry Cook and Mr. Funk.[48] The equipment used for the test was a model 2612 Portable Survey Meter, with a Model P15 probe.

January 12 found Technical Sergeant David Moody and Staff Sergeant Harold Jones, of Wright-Patterson Air Force Base, interrogating Burns and Professor Gehman, and examining the landing location.[49] In reviewing the official inspection, Gehman left little doubt that he regarded the two sergeants' conduct of it as extremely questionable. He wrote later that Sergeant Moody's Model 2586 Beta-Gama Survey Meter repeatedly indicated significant radiation—more than three weeks after Burns's purported encounter—but that the Air Force man falsified the reading by adjusting his instrument to reduce the indication to zero.

The three-page report was extremely incomplete and contained numerous inaccuracies, according to Professor Gehman, and he has clearly and convincingly cited these inadequacies and discrepancies, not the least of the former being that the two engineers who participated in the original examination of the vicinity for radioactivity were never questioned, although they reaffirmed that the area was very "hot." Among outright errors in the report were the description of 38–44-foot powerline poles as 75-foot telephone poles, a difference of $2\frac{1}{2}$ hours as to the time specified when Moody visited Gehman, a specified angle of direction, which was noted as 60 degrees when it is 45 degrees, and the fact that there were no other witnesses, when fourteen-year-old Kenneth Norton and his mother, a father and his son, and another man all offered circumstantially supportive sightings,[50] which were detailed in the local press only a few days after Moody's arrival on the scene.

Virginia was the source of a rather more improbable tale as 1965 began. A woodcutter, working at Brand Flats (elsewhere recorded as Lynchburg), on the late afternoon of January 19 (elsewhere January 23), allegedly became aware of two landed saucers some distance from him, although he had not been conscious of their having landed.

"While he stared in amazement at the two things," wrote saucerologist John A. Keel, "three tiny beings came out of the smaller one and slowly walked toward him, he reported. He estimated that these creatures were from 35 to 37 inches tall. They were shaped like human beings and dressed in uniforms. . . ." [51]

Regarding an incident dated July 7, the Argentinian Secretary of the Navy issued a press release to the following effect:

The Navy garrison in the Argentine Antarctica, Deception Island, observed on July 3, at 19:40 hours local time, a giant, lens-shaped flying object, solid in appearance, mostly red and green in color, changing occasionally with yellow, blue, white, and orange shades. The object was moving on a zigzag trajectory toward the east but several times it changed course to the west and north with varied speeds and without sound. It passed at an elevation of forty-five degrees over the horizon at a distance estimated to be about ten to fifteen kilometers from the base.

During the maneuvers performed by the object, the witnesses were able to register its tremendous speeds and also the fact that it hovered motionless for about fifteen minutes at an altitude of about three miles. The meteorological conditions for the area of the sighting can be considered as very good for this time of the year: clear sky, some strato-cumulus, moon in the last quarter and perfect visibility.

The object was witnessed by the meteorologist together with thirteen members of the garrison and three Chilean sub-officers visiting the base. The observation lasted for twenty minutes and photographs of the object were taken.[52]

One of the better and best known UFO photographs was supposedly taken on August 3, by Rex Heflin, a highway accident investigator for the Los Angeles County Highway Commission. Using a Polaroid, a tool of his occupation, and 3,000 ASA-rated film, he rapidly shot three pictures, through the windshield, of an object that appeared ahead of him above the road. The results were what would be regarded as excellent UFO photographs—clearly something apparently in the air, of a conformation acceptable as a craft, and yet not so defined as to reveal itself as some other specific object—that is, a picture which, if there are such devices, might be of a Flying Saucer.

According to Heflin, the original prints (keeping in mind that the camera was a Polaroid) were requested by an investigator from NORAD, and he relinquished them. That organization and the Air Force subsequently denied any knowledge of them. Nevertheless, the latter denounced the pictures as a hoax. On the other hand, as chronicled by newsman Frank Edwards, Ralph Rankow, a photographic analyst, Clay T. Miller, Chief Photographer for the Santa Ana *Register,* and several other informed persons, rejected the condemnation.[53]

The Air Force, of course, continued to explain sightings—let alone photographs—away, but if many doubted Flying Saucers, the credibility of Project Blue Book was hardly more substantial. One California newspaper, among a good many others, voiced its complaint eloquently:

According to Air Force spokesmen a powerful assortment of police officials, sheriff's deputies and other individuals, including even some members of the Air Force itself, were suffering a mild form of anomia—the loss of ability to name an object correctly, as evidenced by their failure to recognize such obviously common objects as weather balloons, planets, comets, etc., when they spotted them in the skies over an area of some eight states. They saw the objects plainly enough of course, but their error lay in terming them unidentified flying objects, more commonly called flying saucers.

Just how the Air Force spokesmen were able to tell that hundreds of reports of UFO's from an area the size of Free Europe were faulty—and especially how they were able to do it within 24 hours of the time the reports came in—ought to rank as one of the most remarkable examples of lightning-like mass diagnosis of all time.

That is, it ought to if the Air Force spokesmen were actually correct.

However, it now appears that—as countless thousands of well-informed persons have suspected for years—the Air Force spokesmen were wrong again. According to a UPI story from Houghton, Michigan, this past weekend, personnel at the Air Force Radar Base on the Keweenaw Peninsula reported "solid radar contact" with 7 to 10 Unidentified Flying Objects moving in a "V" formation over Lake Superior. The objects were moving out of the Southwest and were heading North-Northeast at about 9,000 miles an hour, at elevations ranging from 5,200 to 17,000 feet.

What distinguishes that story from many others involving Air Force personnel during the past several years is that it was not accompanied by a paragraph "explaining" that the objects had finally been identified as a flight of ducks, comets, balloons or something else equally commonplace.

Why wasn't it?

The most likely reason is that the Air Force spokesmen, whose duty is to explain away the seemingly improbable in terms of the commonplace, have been getting such a workout lately that either they are starting to break down or their superiors are coming to the conclusion that they are making the Air Force appear ridiculous.

Of the two, the latter seems more likely. The business of attempting to protect the public from panic—as the obvious reason for the Air Force's traditional policy of identifying flying objects as weather balloons, etc.—is something that cannot be indefinitely sustained, particularly when the source of the presumed potential panic is a mass of peculiar things that persist in flying around where large numbers of persons can see them. To do that is no more possible than it is for the panic to be sustained by individuals for more than a few hours at most. It's too exhausting. One can flee a horde of little green men from outer space only so long. Presently one gets tired and decides to do something else, even if it is no more than sitting down.

But whatever the reason may be why the Air Force spokesmen are becoming less vocal, the time is long overdue for the Government to disclose to the public all that it knows about UFO's.

It is now generally admitted in the scientific fraternity that Earth is not the only heavenly body to have intelligent life, and since we ourselves are now invading outer space, it would be nonsensical to suppose that inhabitants of other worlds have not already done so.

In other words, it should surprise no one today to learn that the UFO's are spacecraft from elsewhere in the solar system—or beyond. In fact, it would be even more surprising to learn that they were not. Hence, the only way in which the public interest may be served in this matter is for the Government to disclose what it knows about these phenomena.[54]

Some, of course, found themselves convinced by encounters rather than arguments. Ray Hoffman, a pilot of thirty years' experience and owner-operator of the Shamokin Flying Service, was an example. He saw his first UFO on August 13 and pursued it in his plane, but was outpaced. "If I ever had any doubts about reports of mysterious flying objects," he granted, "they are gone now."[55]

An interview with three top members of the staff of the Cerro Calan Observatory, in Chile, produced an intriguing explanation of UFOs. "There is scientific evidence that strange objects visit our planet . . . it is lamentable that governments have drawn a veil of secrecy over all this," wrote Prof. Gabriel Alvial. The director of the observatory, Prof. Claudio Anguita, remarked: "We are not alone in the universe." A Russian scientist, Dr. Mitrovan Zverey, working with the aforementioned, agreed that "something unknown to our understanding is going around the earth."[56]

An incident reported out of Exeter, New Hampshire, on September 3, received the attention due an interesting sighting during the months following its occurrence. However, subsequent publicity—mostly through articles and a book by John G. Fuller—ballooned a very interesting and persuasive sighting into an importance considerably beyond that which, as relative to other major sightings, it should have been accorded.

Fuller's newness to the field of saucer research is evident.[57] Yet one or two additional points might be made regarding Fuller's presentation, in that he also demonstrates the inadequate approach of the charming amateur (and John Fuller is a delightful man) in a field actually or potentially fraught with delusion and deception. At one point he observes that the fact that "most of the population," including he himself, had never seen a UFO "still didn't prove that UFOs were nonexistent. How many people have seen an albatross, a white whale, a plover's egg, a pair of Siamese twins, or a cyclotron? An infinitesimal fragment of the population. Yet no one contests their existence."

The actual episode began at 2:24 A.M. on the warm, moonless night of September 3, 1965, when Norman Muscarello rushed into the Exeter, New Hampshire, police station, pale and trembling.

Muscarello claimed that walking along the highway he had passed an open field, where he saw "the Thing," as it came to be called after his designation. (One need hardly point out the echo of the carrot-from-outer-space motion picture of a few years earlier.) Larger than a house, perhaps ninety feet in diameter, according to the witness, it emerged from the night sky, brilliant and pulsating crimson lights around its perimeter. Wobbling and shifting flight position, it descended silently, gently, directly toward him. In terror, Muscarello flattened along the edge of the road, and the UFO seemed to hesitate, recede slightly, arrest its flight over a nearby house, finally moving farther away.

Slamming his fists on the door of the cottage elicited no response, and he fled back to the road, where he was picked up and brought to the Exeter police station.

Naturally, Officer Reginald Toland, who heard his story, was somewhat sceptical. Still, the intensity and excitement of the young man made him decide to recall Patrolman Eugene Bertrand, in Cruiser #21, to the station. This police officer had his own odd tale to tell upon his arrival. An hour before, the Korean War veteran had encountered an extremely distraught female driver on the highway who said an enormous aerial object had paced along behind her, only a few feet away from the rear of her automobile. Finally, she told Bertrand, the UFO had flashed upward and was absorbed by the night. Patrolman Bertrand drove Muscarello back to this sighting location. They arrived around three in the morning. The officer radioed in to Toland, still in the station, that he and his charge were leaving the prowl car, and told him not to be concerned if he could not reach them.

The two walked several hundred feet from the highway, approaching the corral of the Carl Dining farm. Suddenly animals—horses, a nearby dog, hanging bats—became frenetic.

"I see it! I see it!" [58] cried Muscarello. Bertrand watched a brilliant, soundless UFO rise from beyond a pair of tall pine trees and approach them, engulfing the ground in bloody light. The Dining house and the Russell one close by turned crimson. Both men raced for the squad car and its radio. Bertrand shouted into the microphone:

"My God. I see the damn thing myself!" [59]

The altitude of the object was estimated at about thirty yards and its distance from them at three times that. It gave the impression of rolling back and forth on its axis, the fluctuating rim lights were dimming in a seeming cycle, and, because of its brilliance, it was difficult to ascertain its actual conformation.

Eventually the UFO slowly moved off to the east in an erratic flight. Almost concurrent with the unknown's retreat, Patrolman David Hunt, in Cruiser #20, who had overheard the radio exchange between Bertrand and Toland, arrived at the scene. Fuller quotes him as saying:

I could see that fluttering movement. It was going from left to right, between the tops of two big trees. I could see those pulsating lights. . . . Then it started moving, slow-like, across the tops of the trees, just above the trees. It was rocking when it did this. A creepy type of look. After . . . a B-47. You could tell the difference [between the UFO and an aircraft]. There was no comparison.[60]

Immediately following the incident, Toland was told by a night telephone operator in Exeter that a hysterical man had called, raved about a Flying Saucer plummeting at him, and then was cut off. Supportive sightings were to follow, as they almost invariably do. Ron Smith, a senior in high school, was supposed to have observed a UFO resembling the earlier one.

I was riding with my mother and aunt [Fuller quotes him as testifying]. I guess around eleven-thirty P.M., and this was just about two or three weeks after the officers here saw this object. All of a sudden, my aunt said, "Look up at the sky!" . . . I saw a red light on top and the bottom was white and glowed. It appeared to be spinning. It passed over the car [which he had stopped] once and when it passed over and got in front, it stopped all of a sudden in midair.[61]

"Stopped in midair?" asked Fuller.

"Stopped in midair, went back over a second time, stopped again. Then it headed over the car a third time and took off." [62]

Mrs. Virginia Hale, a reporter for the Haverhill, Massachusetts, *Gazette*, also submitted a report, saying she had clearly seen a similar UFO for at least five minutes, probably in the first week of October.

A number of witnesses to other, possibly supportive, sightings were discovered by John Fuller and are detailed in his exhaustive reportage of the *Incident in Exeter*,[63] which, while reflecting a certain prosaucerism, deriving from the author's newness in the field and his assumption of narrative license, unquestionably provides the most comprehensive account of an individual, isolated sighting now available.

It should be noted that many regard the Exeter affair as one involving five separate, baseball-sized lights, rather than a single large object with small rim lamps.[64]

All things considered, the multiple sighting in Exeter[65] was probably the highlight of that year—upon well-publicized reflection; however, as a convincing sighting, one reported out of Texas on the same night is noteworthy.

It was about one in the morning as police-school graduates Chief Deputy B. E. McCoy and Patrol Deputy Robert Goode, working out of the Angleton Sheriff's Office, drove along the dark highway. The quiet night was abruptly interrupted as their attention was snared by an enormous aerial object, highlighted by the bright moon. They agreed the object must be about two hundred feet long and a quarter that at center thickness, diminishing in circumference at either end. The forepoint radiated a purple light; the tail glow was a blinking blue.

Turning, they retraced their path toward Damon, something less than a mile, and then pulled onto the shoulder to watch the extraordinary phenomenon. As they scrutinized the UFO, they alternately used the binoculars they had in the squad car. Without warning or altering its pace, the object swooped toward the automobile, in a manner identical to actions described by Muscarello and numerous others, until it was no more than a hundred feet away. Its shadow raced along the ground, matching, in effect, the apparently real attack of the substance. Goode was conscious of considerable heat, which he deduced was being emanated from the purple headlight, now less than fifty yards behind them. Finally, getting the car into gear, the two officers fled off along the highway at speeds as high as 110 miles an hour, until the UFO abandoned the chase. Shaken and unnerved by the experience, Goode and McCoy courageously decided, after a few miles of additional breathing time, to return to the original site and attempt an investigation.

Nothing had changed for the better. As they approached the location, they clearly saw the lights of the vast vessel altering in the fashion that had preceded its previous attack, and they, very understandably, hurtled off down the road at a speed which did justice to their earlier escape.

A full written report was delivered to the Sheriff and to Ellington Air Force Base investigator Maj. Laurence R. Leach, Jr. Incredibly, as far as can be ascertained, Project Blue Book itself did not get involved and Hynek, for example, never interrogated McCoy and Goode.[66]

Across the border, Cleamente Gonzales Infante, a Mexican sign painter following in the steps of Howard Menger, forecast that three thousand Flying Saucers from Venus would fly over his city at nine in the evening of October 1. They failed to arrive, as did Gonzales, according to reporters who came to see both.[67]

About a month earlier, on the night of September 6, crowds in Kosice, Czechoslovakia, saw red-and-black UFOs pass over their town.[68]

While it is still quite popular among even semiserious researchers to suggest that the great November 9 electrical power failure of the United States Northeast may have been caused by Unidentified Flying Objects, it is a most tenuous argument, even for saucerites. Attempting to interrelate blackouts with the presences of UFOs is not restricted to that particular debacle. There is a report out of Cuernavaca, Mexico, of a power failure which was preceded by the arrival of an aerial unknown.[69] Allegedly, when the UFO moved off, the power inexplicably returned. After the total power failure in the Northeast the Indianapolis *Star* editorialized that UFOs should be considered as a possible cause.[70] Of course, there were a number of sightings before the blackout,[71] but then, if one researched any date, support for such a claim could probably be found.

Although 1964 saw the publication of two versions of Laura Mundo's alienology—*Flying Saucers and the Father's Plan,* which was almost coherent, and *The Father's Plan and Flying Saucers,* which wasn't remotely —and Gray Barker's rather ominous book regarding the death of well-known astronomer and UFO researcher Prof. Morris K. Jessup, a slightly earlier volume attracted more attention. It was *The World of Flying Saucers,* authored by dedicated antisaucerite Dr. Donald H. Menzel and a female science-fiction writer who once penned an article suggesting that Jonathan Swift might actually have been a transplanted Martian. By 1965 a considerably more interesting work by Jacques Vallee, titled *Anatomy of a Phenomenon,* was published, but there was also the loss of the most famous of all British UFO periodicals, *Uranus,* as well as the less important *Interplanetary News,* which went when Mrs. Mundo's Detroit operation dissolved.

In the early stages of the Age of Flying Saucers, sightings by the young were not too common, and sightings by children almost nonexistent. The enormous increase in reports originating with adolescents and persons even younger was fascinating to watch, although space does not permit particular examination of the sociopsychological phenomenon here. However, for the purpose of recognizing the extraordinary variety and nature of some of the accounts delivered by individuals below twenty, the following unlike examples are cited.

Takashi Fujii, a twelve-year-old Sky Scout, his mother and grandmother, all of Kobe, witnessed a round red UFO, twice the size of a star, moving across the mountains.[72] The sighting occurred on November 9. A similar observation took place in Kozu, on the seventeenth, while on the twenty-first an incredibly swift golden saucer was reported. December 12 gave rise to a blue UFO in Osaka, and the twenty-fourth to a yellow one, in Gifu. While the color aspect alone of these additional Japanese sightings would make them well worth mentioning, the specific point is that in each case adolescents were involved, the ages being thirteen years (Kozu), probably about twelve (golden saucer), thirteen (Osaka), and seventeen (Gifu).[73]

The second example is found in the allegation that two seventeen-year-olds repeatedly shot a rifle at an Unidentified Flying Object seen near Rio Vista, California, on September 21.[74]

Ranging over into an intriguingly different account, we have that of Claudette Cranshaw, who claimed that she was walking along the beach near Blanca, California, one evening, in the autumn of the year, when she saw a strange luminescent globe land. A half-dozen eerie semihumanoids emerged, garbling horrible sounds at one another. The sextet caught sight of, and began pursuing, the girl. She was swiftly caught, overwhelmed, and raped by the six monsters—twice each! Subsequently, the nineteen-year-old is supposed to have given birth to a blue-skinned, seven-fingered, web-toed baby.

In Lima, Peru, on August 1, fifteen-year-old Alberto San Roman Nunez saw a saucer on the roof of his house. From it emerged a three-and-a-half-foot creature with "greenish light on his skin which made him look like a frog." [75] The recurrent amphibious characteristics are of considerable mythopsychological interest, especially when found in sightings related by persons who have spent their entire lives inland.

However, little men had not yet seen their grandest manifestation. James Townsend, a nineteen-year-old Long Prairie, Minnesota, radio announcer, alleged that on October 23, he saw alien occupants of a tiny spaceship who were shaped like tin cans on miniature tripods. They were six inches tall. [76]

The children must have their hour in saucerology, as elsewhere, and in the mid-sixties, in the United States and around the world, they had it.

Chapter 15

FINAL ARGUMENTS
AND A DIRECTED VERDICT

The fantasy was fading, and only the facts remained; theory was obsolete, only reputable testimony was pertinent. Still, while the unsubstantiated allegations and allegories of esoteric contactees had become less and less frequently heard, all of the romance was not gone—especially beyond the confines of the United States, where the mythic aspect of The Age of Flying Saucers had, for the most part, apparently served its purpose.

Nonetheless, strong, multiple, if possible, sightings were the focal point of interest in most investigative circles. One occurred early in the year.

On January 11, Patrolman George Dykman reported "a large, bright, white object over the north end of the dam" [1] at Wanaque, New Jersey. "It moved like one of those low-flying private planes . . . [but] there was no sound to it. . . ." [2] The attention of other officers was called to the UFO, which was monitored as it circled above the six-mile-long reservoir, hovered for several minutes, at one point descending to so low an altitude that it was reflected in the ice, and, finally, moved off. The next morning, investigators are alleged to have discovered a circle melted in the frozen surface in the area above which the UFO had hung.

Fred Steimes, employed at the reservoir, saw the phenomenon as a crimson-tinted moon-form; Civilian Defense Director of Wanaque Bentley Spencer recalled "it was a big ball of light . . . reddish on the inside, bluish on the outside. It was hovering, dancing, and dipping across the reservoir. It was moving from right to left, swinging like a pendulum. It cast a bright reflection on the ice." [3]

Throughout the spring, summer, and early autumn, the series of reports continued.

The story broke open again on the evening of October 10[4] (October 11[5]).

Mrs. Robert J. Gordon, a member of NICAP, sighted a "disk-shaped object about the size of an automobile" pass over her Pompton Lakes house, disappearing in the direction of the Wanaque Reservoir.[6] Summoning her husband, a police sergeant who was purported to metaphorically view the entire local flap, as well as his wife's interest in UFOs with a jaundiced eye, Mrs. Gordon pointed at the sky.

Robert Gordon told investigator Lloyd Mallan the following story:

> My wife had seen a very bright object up in the sky, above a nearby TV antenna. The antenna is five hundred and some feet in the air and this object was high above it. The object was *very* bright. It appeared to be the size of a softball, or a grapefruit. It was moving in a north-northeasterly direction. It came from my left and moved to my right. How can I describe its brightness? It wasn't like looking at a streetlight, or a strobe light, or anything like that. It looked just as though there were a hole punched in the sky. There was no actual beam from it. . . .
>
> I . . . phoned Headquarters. One of the police officers drove over, and just as he got to our house, the thing disappeared from our view.

Mallan has written on the Air Force's relationship vis-à-vis Wanaque in an exchange with Sgt. Robert Gordon. The officer said:

"No. It was no aircraft. I've seen a lot of aircraft. In fact, there were aircraft all over the place after this thing disappeared. But nobody knows where they came from. There were seven helicopters and, I would say, ten or twelve jets." [7]

"Oh? Were these U.S. Air Force aircraft?" asked Mallan.

"I don't know."

"You don't know where they originated? They just came on the scene?"

"Right on the scene!" the officer affirmed. "It was only fifteen minutes from the time we had spotted the thing. And the Air Force claims they didn't get any report on it. And they didn't send any aircraft into our area. But I don't know. They seem to be holding something out on us. I just don't know. Now I've never seen seven helicopters at one time in this area in all my life—and I've lived here for forty years." [8]

Checking on these jet and helicopter overflights, nearly concurrent with the exceptional sighting, investigator Mallan contacted U.S. Air Force officers at Project Blue Book, Wright-Patterson Air Force Base, and at the Pentagon; officers of the U.S. Navy at Lakehurst, New Jersey, Floyd Bennett, New York, and Willow Grove, Pennsylvania, Naval Air Stations; plus many other possible origins, official and private. He learned nothing. Fortunately, if the Air Force did not know, or was not willing or able to reveal the answer, someone was.

"I know the secret of the flying saucers," wrote Maj. Donald E. Keyhoe in January. Supporting his boast, the noted researcher said, in part:

> The answer is *antigravity:* artificial gravity fields and control of gravity power. Control of gravity is something that men have been dreaming about for centu-

ries. Now it appears that we are on the threshold of achieving it. Its value, to the country that first attains it, is incalculable. Our government, hoping for a technical breakthrough, has set up 46 different research projects on various aspects of gravity control. The Air Force is running 33 of these projects and the others are divided among five other agencies.

Included in the 46 government projects are experiments and research at two Air Force Laboratories (Flight Dynamics and General Physics Research), Radio Corporation of America, Massachusetts Institute of Technology and several technical engineering centers. In addition, official projects are being carried out at Barkley and Dexter Laboratories, Fitchburg, Massachusetts; Israel Institute of Technology, Haifa; Stevens Institute of Technology; the universities of California, Denver, Harvard, Indiana, Manchester (England), Maryland, Michigan, Minnesota, Ohio, Purdue, Stockholm (Sweden), Syracuse, Texas, and two New York schools—Queens College and Yeshiva Graduate School of Science.

And, of course, some government agencies have projects so secret that they are not publicly registered and cannot be revealed without permission.

Private industry is also looking at the question of gravity control with new seriousness. A large number of giant corporations, including Bell Aerospace, General Electric, Hughes Aircraft, Boeing, Douglas and many others, have set up gravity projects.

If you add up all the known gravity programs being run by the government and private industry, you get somewhere between 65 and 70 projects. This means there is a heavy concentration of scientific and engineering brains working on the problem.

One leading scientist who is convinced that UFO's are spaceships using gravity control is Dr. Hermann Oberth. Doctor Oberth, a recognized authority, was co-designer of the V-2 rocket and later a U.S. special consultant at Huntsville, Alabama, one of the installations where important antigravity research is now under way.

"With ordinary propulsion," Doctor Oberth told me in 1961, "such violent accelerations and maneuvers would endanger the ship. Also, the force would crush any creatures aboard against the rear or sides of the machine. But with an artificial gravity field the force applies simultaneously to the passengers and the spaceship. Even in swift changes of speed and direction, the ship is not strained and the passengers feel nothing." [9]

"At least 40 persons, including 12 policemen, said today that they saw a strange flying object guarded by four sister ships land in a swamp here [Ann Arbor, Michigan] Sunday night, March 18," stated a *New York Times* article.[10] Frank Mannor and his son Ronald approached to within five hundred yards of the automobile-sized, football-shaped craft. They saw a pulsating blue light at one end and a white one at the other. Washtenaw County Sheriff's Deputies Stanley McFadden and David Fitzpatrick saw the UFO pass over their patrol car moments after the Mannors saw it ascend.[11]

Officer Robert Hunawill and others apparently saw the UFO before dawn on Monday and Wednesday.[12]

However, on the night of the twenty-second, the sightings wove into a perplexing pattern. "87 Coeds Saw a Flying Object Near Michigan Col. Dormitory," [13] read the boldface lead. The story revealed that Mrs. Kelly Hearn, for seven years a newspaper reporter (and at that time Assistant Dean of Women, Assistant Professor of English, and a dormitory housemother at Hillsdale College), accompanied by more than four score students, monitored the UFO for over four hours. William Van Horn, Hillsdale County director of civilian defense, who said that "it was definitely some kind of vehicle," [14] remarked that the object, which almost unanimously was described after the fashion of the earlier UFO, dimmed its lights when approached by police cruisers and intensified them again when the cars withdrew.

The Air Force dispatched Dr. Hynek to the scene and he set up operations at Selfridge Field, Mount Clemens, Michigan. By the next day, he was in the field conducting his investigation, which by that time had come to include the claim of a Dexter farmer that a "ghost ship" had landed in the vicinity.

Hynek called a press conference and announced that at least two hundred persons who had observed the Michigan UFO, over the several-day period, had been deceived by "marsh gas." However, it was the general understanding that Hynek had merely suggested this as a possible explanation for one or two of the great many sightings in the Michigan complex, but that the military head of Project Blue Book, Maj. Hector Quintinella, had insisted this position statement be made.[15] Allegedly, Hynek, after eighteen years as the Air Force consultant on UFOs, even threatened to abandon the responsibility, but he eventually resigned himself to the assertion of the improbable rather than assert himself in an improbable resignation.

A considerable number of sightings continued to be recorded in that area.[16]

On March 25, House Republican Leader Gerald R. Ford, of Michigan, called for a Congressional inquiry into the problem of Unidentified Flying Objects, to be conducted under the auspices of the Armed Services Committee or the House Space Committee.[17] It certainly seemed justified, since according to Air Force pronouncements, the previous year had seen the third-greatest number of reports (886) in its investigative history, exceeded only by 1952, with 1,501, and 1957, with 1,006.

Soon after, the *Special Report of the USAF Scientific Advisory Board's Ad Hoc Committee to Review Project Blue Book* revealed little knowledge of its subject, commended the Air Force on its thoroughness over the period of nineteen years (during which its UFO resources had consisted of a trio of a middle- or low-ranking officer, a sergeant, and a secretary), and suggested a Condon-like inquiry.

More aggressive attitudes were also being expressed.

"It is pure ignorance to assume that earth is the only inhabited planet in the universe," contended Charles Harvard Gibbs-Smith, aeronautical historian for the Victoria and Albert Museum, London, in May. "Certainly there are other civilizations, perhaps thousands of times older and wiser. And I believe intelligent beings from these civilizations are visiting us in spacecrafts—and have been for years. It is only natural fear and human arrogance that makes some authorities say saucers don't exist."[18]

In the spring, *Saucer News* claimed to have been the first ufology periodical to have carried material on the Barney and Betty Hill story[19] (reputedly deriving from a 1961 experience), which John Fuller was to make famous.[20] Of course, many newspapers had presented elements of the case considerably earlier.[21]

The incident occurred on the night of September 19, 1961. Barney Hill and his wife were driving through the mountains from the Canadian border to their home in Portsmouth, New Hampshire, when Betty's attention was attracted by a star of unusual brightness, and then by an even more brilliant star or planet which had risen past it. When she brought it to her husband's notice, he thought it appeared "like a star, in motion."[22]

They drove on through the night, through the mountains, once stopping to walk their dog, and the object remained in sight.

Suddenly, at about midnight, as they were approaching the dark mass of the Cannon Mountains, the strange light abruptly swung off course and began to move in their direction. Through their binoculars, Betty saw the unidentified aerial phenomenon to be cigar-shaped, with flashing blue, green, amber, and red lights. Later the object drew quite near to the automobile and Betty perceived a double series of windows on the structure, which, itself, appeared to be immense.

The object moved to within a hundred feet, and two huge fins, dotted with a ruby light apiece, slid from the body proper. The windows, now clearly to be seen, swept the rim of the disk, glowing white, after the fashion of the usual description of this order.

Responding to what he subsequently described as an "irresistible impulse" (which brings to mind *Anatomy of a Murder* more than *Anatomy of a Phenomenon*), Barney Hill, grabbing up the binoculars, raced toward the craft until he was about fifty feet from it. Aided by the field glasses, he could see that beyond the windows at least a half dozen black-uniformed crewmen were staring at him. Terror seemed to engulf Hill, and he turned and fled back to his wife and car. Leaping into the vehicle, he raced down the road. Betty, looking back at the wake of their escape, could no longer see the craft. It seemed to have vanished. Then the beeping began, and the car seemed to have been caught up in a vibration, an irregular rhythm. *Beep. Beep. Beep.* The two began to feel strange and seemed to have succumbed to some sort of spell. It was an unknown period of time later that they became conscious of the beeping again, the dizziness passed, and they seemed to be in full command of themselves once more.

Subsequently, the Hills put themselves in the charge of Dr. Benjamin Simon, a Boston psychiatrist and neurologist, who commonly employed hypnosis as a medical technique. In trance, as ascertained by Dr. Simon, the Hills told of having been "aboard a Flying Saucer," the subtitle of John Fuller's later book on their alleged experiences, and also, unfortunately, the title of a well-known—among serious saucerologists—book by contactee Truman Bethurum. The resulting tapes, which constitute the greater portion of the book *The Interrupted Journey*[23] are discussions of race and prejudice, anxieties, sex, the physical examination of Betty, and diet; it tells little of the craft, the personnel, or anything else having to do with a possible spaceship.

To examine a few points, let us understand that Betty Hill was Flying Saucer–oriented. In Fuller's words: "Earlier Betty's sister . . . had told about seeing an unidentified flying object . . . and Betty tended to believe the story." After her own alleged incident Betty telephoned her sister to share *her* experience.

The argument is made that the concoction and coordination of such a tale would be difficult, although it has been accomplished countless times by amateur pranksters and theatrical professionals. In the commentary on Hill's claims, folie à deux, dual delusion, is rejected because of the "absence of other characteristics of this rare psychosis." As a matter of fact, the Hill case possesses several attributes sometimes associated with such a disorder. Gralnick, who analyzed 103 such cases, observed: "In folie à deux there is a close association of two or more persons and the transfer of delusional ideas from one to the other by *some means yet unexplained* [emphasis added]." The second most common relationship between such individuals was found to be that of man and wife. None of which is to suggest any of the foregoing explains the Hill case but merely to note that it is quite apparently beyond the area of expertise possessed by the evaluators.

Yet, as the citizenry became more jaded, there seemed little increase in skepticism. Dr. Gallup's Institute of Public Relations Poll reflected that

96 percent of Americans had heard of Flying Saucers, with 20 percent of the women believing they had actually seen one. Forty-six percent—far more of them women than men—were convinced they were "real," while 34 percent accepted that there are people "somewhat like ourselves" living on other planets in the universe. Researcher George D. Fawcett published another of his informative breakdowns in October. The 1966—up to September—landings and contacts had dropped considerably from the previous year. Landings were down a third, to twenty-one, and contacts fell off almost 50 percent, to four.[24] The Air Force's scientific advisory board of the spring appeared to be having some effect by mid-September. The New York *World Journal Tribune*[25] asserted that "several universities have turned down a Pentagon grant of one million dollars to investigate flying saucers. No school wishes to leave its reputation in the hands of the Government, because the results of the probe would be classified—whatever the results might be." [26] While the dubious institutions might well have been justified in their skepticism, on October 7 Dr. Edward U. Condon, of the University of Colorado, was contracted to conduct an "objective" review of the entire Flying Saucer enigma. The program was allotted eighteen months and $318,000 to achieve its proclaimed purposes.

An appropriate presentation of the Condon effort was offered by James W. Moseley in his *Saucer News:*

> The new project's headquarters will be on the Colorado University campus at Boulder, Colo., but *the Air Force will help with personnel,* and will transport investigation teams to sighting sites. Project Blue Book will continue to operate, as before, at Wright-Patterson Air Force Base in Dayton, Ohio; *but the base will notify the University of events which seem to merit special investigation,* and allegedly, no pertinent data regarding past or future sightings will be withheld from the University.[27] [Emphasis added.]

The number of scientists who are open-minded, or even convinced of the extraterrestrial intelligence factor behind the mystery of Unidentified Flying Objects, is considerable; the number who have had the courage to publicize their convictions is small. Among the latter group is physicist Dr. James E. MacDonald, professor of meteorology and senior physicist at the Institute of Atmospheric Physics at the University of Arizona.

In an address to the District of Columbia Chapter of the American Meteorological Society, Washington, D.C., on October 19, 1966, he subdivided the possible explanation for Unidentified Flying Objects into eight categories:[28] (1) hoaxes; (2) hallucination/hysteria phenomena; (3) misinterpretation of natural astronomical phenomena; (4) observation of experimental craft, satellites, etc.; (5) misinterpretation of natural physi-

cal phenomena; (6) misunderstood psychological phenomena; (7) extraterrestrial probes; and (8) messengers of salvation and occult truth. Of
these possibilities, he remarked (from a summary paper, not verbatim):

> There appears to be a general agreement among all who have seriously studied
> the past 20 years of UFO reports, here and abroad, that Categories 1 through 4
> do indeed account for a substantial number of reported "unidentified aerial phe-
> nomena." However, when such cases are eliminated, there remains a still-sizable
> residium of unexplained reports from credible observers.
> . . . I would emphasize that I now regard Category 6 as the only important al-
> ternative to Category 7. . . . Category 8 is accepted by a distressingly large and
> vocal group outside the scientific community, but I am not aware that supporters
> of that Category 8 have shed useful light on the basic problem. My own study of
> this problem has led me to the conclusion that Category 7 now constitutes the
> *least unsatisfactory hypothesis* for accounting for the intriguing array of credibly
> reported UFO phenomena that are on record and that do not appear to fit ac-
> ceptably into the first six categories. . . .
> My study of past official Air Force investigations (Project Blue Book) leads me
> to describe them as *completely superficial.* They have, for at least the past dozen
> years, been carried out at a very *low level of scientific competence* as a very low
> priority (one of about 200 within the Foreign Technology Division, Wright-Pat-
> terson AFB). Officially released "explanations" of important UFO sightings have
> often been almost absurdly erroneous.[29]

The remainder of the summary, and the address itself, continued along
the same lines. In covering Dr. MacDonald's comments two days later,
The New York Times, noting that the speaker held degrees in physics,
chemistry, and meteorology, reported his announcement that he had
found evidence that the Central Intelligence Agency, in 1953, had requested that the Air Force discredit saucer observations.[30]

Countering with a response that left unexplained the period from
World War II through 1966, the CIA stated that "*presently* [emphasis
added] the subject of U.F.O. is a responsibility of the Air Force and we
have absolutely no interest either in building up or debunking any information regarding, or views on, U.F.O.'s." [31]

One of the major contact stories of the year centered about the activities of Woodrow Derenberger, of Parkersburg, West Virginia, who, while
driving along a highway on the night of November 2, saw a "long dark
object" pacing his small truck. Then, according to the report, the UFO
swung in front of him and stopped, hovering less than a foot above the
road.

The door to the vessel opened and an alien emerged, with whom Derenberger reputedly conversed—by extrasensory perception. Among the
more interesting aspects of the exchange was the saucerian's name,

"Cold," and his modest concession that he came from "a country much less powerful" than the United States.[32]

Kathy Reeves, sixteen years old, told of seeing "three little stumps that walked across the pasture," near Newport, Oregon, and before the year was over, more than twenty-five persons of that area claimed to have seen Cyclopean giants in the nearby hills.[33]

The monsters had begun to walk—and fly.

John Osborne told of a hirsute, seven-foot wayfarer, in British Columbia, on July 21, and the report was echoed by Don Gilmore, of the same town of Richmond, on the following day.[34] As the creature encounters continued, reports came in from Eire on several occasions, and in August five persons of Malvern, Arkansas, swore to having seen an eight-foot luminous humanoid, who flushed red, subdued to orange, faded to yellow, and then reversed the spectraumatic performance.[35]

However, of even greater interest was the ascension of the mothman into the hierarchy of the aliens. To quote John A. Keel, who has specialized in the investigation of monster reports, primarily within the framework of contactology:[36]

On September 1st, Mrs. James Ikart, of Scott, Mississippi, phoned a local paper to report a man-shaped object fluttering about the sky . . . several other people said they had seen it. John Hursh, a local meteorologist, solved the mystery by calling it a weather balloon.[37]

On November 15 [near Point Pleasant, West Virginia] . . . it was seen again by four young people who were driving through a local park, the McClintic Wildlife Station. They were astounded to see a tall, man-like figure with wings standing in front of an old, abandoned power plant. Its eyes were a blazing red, some two inches in diameter, and it thoroughly terrified them before waddling into the building.[38]

Steve Mallatte and three companions drove out of Point Pleasant, West Virginia, one night around mid-November. As their automobile moved over a rise, it came upon an apparition with crimson eyes, which were shining at them from the roadside shrubbery. They passed on, assuming it to be an animal common to the vicinity. However, shortly thereafter, they saw the creature again, and more clearly. It was a six-foot, humanoid monster, with no arms, a face resembling a penguin, and radiating vast wings ("like an angel")[39] of ten-foot span. As they raced back toward the town, at over a hundred miles an hour, the creature followed, flying above and immersing them in its shadow. "No matter how fast I went, it kept gliding over the roof, sort of moving from side to side. We could hear a flapping noise."[40] The quartet was to claim afterward that the monster soared across the automobile, screaming sounds like a great amplification of a rat's call.[41]

The mythology of alien monsters extends into the remotest recesses of prehistory, permeating the earliest cultural symbologies. In modern times, they have been evoked by the medium Hélene Smith, who told of encountering tiny-eyed and -nosed, large-handed, yard-tall inhabitants during her astral projections to Mars.[42]

"The Flatwoods Monster," or, as it was less frequently called, "The Braxton Monster," is said to have appeared on the night of September 12, 1952, in the small community of Flatwoods, West Virginia, a village of some three hundred persons. A United Press story of the following morning read, in part:

POLICE SAY BRAXTON MONSTER PRODUCT OF "MASS HYSTE-RIA" Sutton, Sept. 14—(U.P.) Seven Braxton County residents vowed today that a Frankenstein monster with B.O. drove them from a hill-top near here, but police figured the smelly boogie-man was the product of "mass hysteria." [43]

The thing, described by witnesses as "half-man, half-dragon," had not been reported since Friday night, but residents of the area said a foul odor still clung to the hill-top yesterday.

The strongest aspect of this totally improbable case was the number of witnesses, notwithstanding the reappearance of the adolescence factor. They were Mrs. Kathleen May, a beautician, her two children—Eddie, thirteen, and Fred, twelve—Gene Lemon, seventeen, Neil Nunley, fourteen, Ronnie Shaver, ten, and Tommy Hyer, ten.[44] Sooner or later all were interviewed, some several times, and Mrs. May, Gene Lemon, and a local newspaper editor, Lee Stewart, appeared on the television program *We, the People* to relate the incident.

Gray Barker, who personally investigated the matter for some time, recorded the following description of the initial encounter:

The first thing they saw was a huge globular mass down over the other side of the hilltop, to their right, about 50 feet away. "It was just like a big ball of fire," Nunley said, which seemed to dim and brighten at regular intervals. He didn't know how large it was; some of the others said it was as "big as a house." It is not clear whether a complete sphere was seen, or a hemisphere, resting on the ground.

Nunley heard no noise. Others said it made a low thumping or beating sound, "like someone hitting canvas. . . ." [Barker does not attribute this quote.] [45]

However, the later "flapping noise" [46] of the mothman tale was to be reminiscent of it.

The report from Barker on the actual contact reads:

Distracted by the globular mass Nunley did not see a huge figure standing to their left. Lemon said he thought he saw animal eyes in the tree and flashed his light on them.

Fifteen feet away, towering over their heads, was a vast shape something like a man. The face, everyone agreed, was round, and blood red. No one noticed a nose or mouth, only eyes, or eyelike openings, from which projected "greenish-orange" beams of light. These light beams pierced through the haze pervading the scene. In the excitement some of the group thought the beams of light were focused upon them, but Nunley was specific that they were not. "They went out over our heads."

Around the red "face" and reaching upward to a point was a dark, hood-shape. The body was seen only from the "head" down to the "waist." It appeared dark and colorless to Nunley, though some said it was green. . . . No one is sure whether the shape rested on the ground or was floating.

The "monster" could not have been more than fifteen feet tall, for it was under the overhanging limb of a tree; and the limb was of [at] that height.

Originally the group said the strange, nauseous odor resembled burning metal, or burning sulphur . . . finally [it] was described only basically as sickening, irritating to the throat and nasal passages. "It seemed to grip you in the throat and suffocate you." [47] [The final quote is not attributed by Mr. Barker.]

While A. Lee Stewart, Jr., of the Braxton, West Virginia, *Democrat,* and Sheriff Robert Carr visited the site immediately thereafter, they were unable to offer any substantiating testimony, other than to confirm that an unpleasant odor pervaded the atmosphere.[48]

Jim and Coral Lorenzen, founders and directors of the oldest of all extant research organizations, Aerial Phenomena Research Organization, have unearthed—or is it "extraearthed"?—an amazing number of fascinating reports. In the category of "monsters," few are more curious than that received through Richard Grenwell, who was put in touch with the contactee by the Instituto Peruano de Relaciones Interplanetarias, of Lima, Peru.[49]

Dated approximately 1949, it is the purported experience of a fully mature Peruvian male, who witnessed the late afternoon landing of a bus-dimensioned vessel along the coastline. Creature(s) then emerged who (which)

didn't have a defined form. They looked like those mummies. They had the profile of human beings but their legs were joined. They did not have two legs but one "double" one—like twins. . . . They had no exterior sign of sex, ears, or eyes. A body, a head, and legs joined together . . . have you ever seen twin bananas? You see the form of both bananas but they are joined together . . . one large foot . . . they moved as if they were, I don't know, dancers . . . they had arms but their hands consisted of a group of four fingers stuck together and a separate thumb. . . . The head had no features at all, except at about the height of the eyes there was an oblong substance like jelly with a sort of bubble in the center . . . no ears, no mouth, no nose, nothing. . . .

The story is detailed in a dialogue-styled interview in *UFOs over the Americas.*[50]

In December, Dr. J. Allen Hynek wrote a refreshingly objective article in the *Saturday Evening Post.* Among the most interesting observations were the following:

> During the next few years I had no trouble explaining or discarding most of the cases referred to me, but a few were baffling enough to make me wonder—cases that the Air Force would later carry as "unidentified." Let me emphasize the point that the Air Force made up its own mind on each case; I merely submitted an opinion. I soon found that the Air Force had a tendency to upgrade its preliminary explanations while compiling its yearly summaries; a "possible" aircraft often became a "probable" aircraft. I was reminded of the Greek legend of Procrustes, who tried to fit all men to his single bed. If they were too long, he chopped them off; if they were too short, he stretched them out. . . .
>
> Gradually I began to accumulate cases that I really couldn't explain, cases reported by reliable, sincere people whom I often interviewed in person. I found that the persons making these reports were often not acquainted with UFO's before their experience, which baffled and thoroughly frightened them. Fearing ridicule, they were often reluctant to report the sighting and did so only out of a sense of duty and a tremendous desire to get a rational explanation for their irrational experience. . . .
>
> Then, from 1958 through 1963, the UFO reports began to diminish in quality as well as quantity, and I felt that perhaps the "flying saucer" era was at last on the wane and would soon vanish. But since 1964 there has been a sharp rally in the number of puzzling sightings. The more impressive cases seem to fit into a pattern. The UFO's had a bright red glow. They hovered a few feet off the ground, emitting a high pitched whine. Animals in the vicinity were terrified, often before the UFO's became visible to the people who later reported the incident. When the objects at last began to disappear, they vanished in a matter of seconds.
>
> A very real paradox was now beginning to develop. As the Air Force's consultant, I was acquiring a reputation in the public eye of being a debunker of UFO's. Yet, privately, I was becoming more and more concerned over the fact that people with good reputations, who had no possible hope of gain from reporting a UFO, continued to describe "Out-of-this-world" incidents.
>
> In July, 1965, I wrote a letter to the Air Force calling again for a systematic study of the phenomenon. "I feel it is my responsibility to point out," I said, "that enough puzzling sightings have been reported to warrant closer attention than Project Blue Book can possibly encompass at the present time."
>
> Then, in March of this year, came the reports of the now-celebrated "swamp-gas" sightings in Michigan. . . .
>
> The press conference, however, turned out to be no place for scholarly discussion; it was a circus. . . . When I handed out a statement that discussed swamp gas, many of the men simply ignored the fact that I said it was a "possible" rea-

son. I watched with horror as one reporter scanned the page, found the phrase "swamp gas," underlined it, and rushed for a telephone. . . . I got out of town as quickly and as quietly as I could. . . .

I would like to suggest two more steps to help solve the UFO problem:

First, all of the valuable data that we have accumulated—good reports from all over the world—must be computerized so that we can rapidly compare new sightings with old and trace patterns of UFO behavior.

Second, we need good photographs of UFO's. Although the *Air Force has probably spent less on UFO's so far than it has on wastebaskets* [emphasis added], I realize that it is impractical to expect the service to set up a costly "flying saucer" surveillance system across the country. When a UFO is spotted, the terrified witness usually picks up the phone at once and calls the local police, who have missed dozens of opportunities in the past to record the phenomena on film. I recommend that every police chief in the country make sure that at least one of his squad cars carries in its glove compartment a camera loaded with color film. The cameras, which could also be used for regular police work, might be furnished by civic or service groups. (I carry a camera in my briefcase at all times.)[51]

Further, according to the London *Evening Standard,* Hynek began to move on the basis of his reevaluation of the subject of Unidentified Flying Objects.

An impressive nucleus of respected scientific talents is now prodding NASA into action. This group is led by Dr. J. Allen Hynek, an astrophysicist, near Chicago, and the official consultant to the U.S. Air Force on UFOs.

For almost two decades, Dr. Hynek was a leading member of the special scientific establishment, inclined to dismiss the UFO phenomenon as a product of a study and undisciplined public imagination.

Today he is so impressed with the enormous collection of testimony from reliable witnesses that he has begun to organize an international association of responsible scientists to assemble and analyse evidence on flying saucers from all over the world.

"I've called this group the Invisible College," Dr. Hynek told me. "It's very much like the early days of the Royal Society in England, when it was not too savoury to admit any interest in science."

Membership of the Invisible College is limited to those educated at least up to the degree of doctor of philosophy, and a number of prominent British astronomers and physicists, all too shy to reveal their names for publication, have been admitted.[52]

While Hynek appeared to some to be moving to a near prosaucer position,[53] Dr. McDonald's positive stance grew firmer: "I have absolutely no idea where the [UFOs] come from or how they are operated, but after ten years of research, I know they are something from outside our atmosphere." [54] Some presumed scientists were still maintaining an ossified Menzelian position, in spite of their having no reputations for ever having studied the subject or possessing any knowledge of it. For example, Dr. Edward Ney, professor of astrophysics at the University of Minnesota, is reputed to have bluntly stated that "respectable scientists don't even discuss UFO's in serious terms." [55] The tragedy is that "respectable" scientists have rarely ever done anything but mouth self-protecting platitudes, ridiculing Galileo, Einstein, Goddard, Von Braun, or anyone else who ever saw beyond the reach of their security-blanketing blindness. Needless to say, the quote and the comment are not necessarily meant to be related, for, in truth, as the good astrophysicist has doubtless never heard of the author, the author has never heard of him prior to researching this work. Yet it seems very likely both of us have heard of Dr. Herman Oberth, one of the founders of modern rocketry, and author, forty years ago, of *By Rocket to Interplanetary Space,*[56] who believes Flying Saucers to be intergalactic. The great scientist said, in part, as the year 1967 began:

> *Science should regard anything as possible so long as it cannot be proven impossible by facts based upon observations.* Each explanation should be considered valid as a working hypothesis until observations are presented to contradict it. [Emphasis added.]
> According to information available to me, there exist more than 70,000 eyewitness reports of UFOs. . . . Eleven percent of these reports cannot be easily explained. They should not be lies or hoaxes because they involve responsible senior Air Force officers or radar readings or photographs from responsible sources.
> Their speed can be enormous. Radar measurements have shown up to 11.8 miles a second! [57]

When feeling that such speeds are utterly ridiculous, it behooves one to remember that in 1829 an unloaded steam-engine locomotive proved it could go almost thirty miles an hour; within a little more than sixty years, this figure was raised by more than 250 percent, to $112\frac{1}{2}$ miles an hour. In seventy-five years, men were flying at two hundred and fifty *times* that speed and almost a *thousand times* as fast as one hundred and forty years earlier. To achieve "42,000 miles per hour!" man need not even double the speed he has achieved; he has but to raise it by two-thirds. What will he be doing in seventy-five years if he has formed another series of new propulsions and is going two hundred and fifty times faster than he can today? Flying over six million miles an hour?

Dr. Oberth remarks on UFOs in particular:

> A. They are not built by human beings . . . today we cannot produce machines that fly as UFOs do.
> B. They are flying by means of artificial fields of gravity. This would explain the sudden changes in directions. . . . This hypothesis also would explain the pil-

Chapter 16

THE CULTURAL IMPLOSION

There is a great tendency for certain tales in saucerology, as in other cultural myths, to be endlessly repeated in only slightly varying forms. A classic example of this echo ethos may be found in the September, 1967, issue of *Orbit*,[1] which describes the appearance of two mysterious children in the Spanish hamlet of Banjos one afternoon in August, 1887. Little need be detailed other than that the young boy and girl emerged from a cave, spoke an unintelligible tongue, possessed green skin, and could not be explained. Credit was given to Dan Fry's publication *Understanding* as the previous source, and to John Macklin writing in *Grit* before that.

The story is, of course, virtually identical to the twelfth-century legend of the children of Wolpittes, which varies hardly a syllable from the recent version, except that it took place in England under the reign of Stephen, or possibly Henry II.

Early in 1967, a general magazine, the *Saturday Review*,[2] featured two segments of a debate on the subject of UFOs, ufology, and Flying Saucers. The participants were John Fuller and John Lear. Fuller, a longtime columnist for the periodical, whose affiliation with it had been severed, was replying to a prior article by science editor Lear, which had been Menzel-like in its anti-UFO attitude, in general, and caustic about aspects of Fuller's work on the subject in particular.

The exchange was heated and little marred by objectivity on either side; however, of the two positions assumed, Fuller's was more open-minded, if only slightly so.

Meanwhile Maj. Raymond Nyls, base-operations officer, an amateur astronomer, at Selfridge Field, in Mount Clemens, Michigan, evaluated a UFO photograph of an apparent craft as "the best I've ever seen." He further noted that in a January 9 picture, taken by Dan and Grant Jaroslaw ". . . you can even make out what resembles an antenna on its back."[3] Dr. Hynek said of the hamburger-like object, as represented by a set of wire photos: "I have no knowledge yet whether the pictures are authentic; in all honesty, at this moment, I cannot call them a hoax." On the twenty-second, after two weeks of Air Force and personal study,

Hynek ventured that a hoax, while not completely eliminated, seemed increasingly less likely.[4]

The striking thing to me [said the Air Force consultant] is the similarity of these pictures to other photos I've seen, and also to verbal descriptions I've taken from ostensibly reliable people. To the best of my recollection, even the "antenna" shown on the back has been previously reported, as has the "tail" structure.[5]

The perpetual indirect intimations and the direct accusations that "silence" groups were attempting to mute many witnesses to UFO sightings and even some who claimed to have accomplished contacts with extraterrestrials was given some seeming substance from an unexpected source in the spring of 1967. Appearing in newspapers throughout the United States, as well as in foreign publications, the statements made by a Pentagon spokesman were, all things considered, extraordinary revelations. He said:

Mysterious men dressed in Air Force uniforms or bearing impressive credentials from government agencies have been "silencing" UFO witnesses, according to Col. George P. Freeman, Pentagon spokesman for Project Blue Book.

"We have checked a number of these cases," Freeman said in an interview this week, "and these men are not connected with the Air Force in any way."

He cited one recent case in which the police officers and other witnesses at the UFO sightings in Wanaque, N.J., were allegedly collected together by a man wearing an Air Force uniform. They were told that they "hadn't seen anything" and that they shouldn't discuss the incident.

"We checked with the local AFB," Freeman declared, "and discovered that no one connected with the Air Force had visited Wanaque on the date in question. Whoever it was, he wasn't from the Air Force."

Another mystery man, this one bearing credentials from the North American Air Defence (NORAD), turned up at the home of Rex Heflin, a man who had taken a series of UFO pictures in California in 1965, and demanded the originals. Later NORAD denied having anything to do with the incident.

Major General M. M. Magee, NORAD's chief of staff, later told Rep. James B. Utt, R-Calif., that "for your information NORAD does not have the responsibility for the evaluation of UFOs and therefore would not knowingly be in the business of collecting UFO pictures for evaluation. In addition, the office of primary interest for UFO matters is the Department of the Air Force."

Heflin's photos have never been returned and the Air Force has never been able to determine the identity of the mystery man who took them.

Similar mystery men, according to other sources, have turned up and confronted UFO witnesses in the states of Washington, Texas, Connecticut, and on Long Island, N.Y.

In February, 1960, Joe Perry, a restaurant owner in Grand Blanc, Mich., took a series of UFO pictures and was soon visited by two men posing as FBI agents. They seized a photo of a dome-shaped object with a green tail.

More recently, a man claiming to represent "a government agency so secret that he couldn't give its name" appeared in a school in Norwalk, Conn. and grilled two 12-year-old boys for two hours about the disc-shaped object which they said had pursued them at ground level in April, 1966.

"We haven't been able to find out anything about these men," Freeman admitted. "By posing as Air Force officers and government agents they are committing a federal offence. We would sure like to catch one."

When asked if any efforts have been made to track down the elusive imposters, Freeman replied: "Unfortunately, the trail is always too cold by the time we hear about these cases. But we're still trying."

Freeman also commented on the numerous reports of sightings of low-flying unmarked planes over areas where UFOs had recently been seen. "That's a federal offence, too," he said. "All Air Force planes are clearly marked. We don't know anything about these unmarked planes. We'd like to catch one of them too."

Many witnesses swore that they saw several Air Force helicopters manoeuvering over Wanaque reservoir following a UFO sighting last October. Freeman said that a careful check had been made and that no formation of helicopters had been in that area at that time. "Besides," he continued, "most Air Force bases have only one or two helicopters for rescue work. I just don't know where a whole formation of them could have come from." [6]

Officer William Fisher reported a boxcar-size UFO had hovered for several minutes at about two thousand feet above Moline, Illinois. A second object was supposed to have joined the first as he watched. The Associated Press item said that "the objects also reportedly were sighted by two nuns and about 40 students at the Sacred Heart elementary school."

March heralded the revivification of the Wanaque story, as UFOs were reported over the reservoir for several consecutive Sundays. According to Sgt. Ben Thompson, of the installations police, "the unknown object was circular and ringed by the glow of bright lights that seemed to come from inside of it.

"It had a red glow and stayed there going up and down like a yo-yo for about 15 minutes. It would almost touch the water and then go back up to about 40 feet."

Four staff members of the New York *World Journal Tribune* stood and watched a UFO on the night of March 30, from the roof of the building housing the publication's offices. Calls describing an unknown of red, green, and gold had sent them scurrying up. Then a "mysterious red light" scored the sky. Unfortunately, experimental rockets fired from Wallops Island, Virginia, to test electrical fields and wind direction were the cause of the furore.[7]

Notwithstanding so much ado about nothing, astronomer Dr. Clyde W. Tombaugh, discoverer of the planet Pluto and UFO sighter, continued to press for concentrated exploration of space.

Dr. James E. McDonald continued his series of thought- and, no doubt, in some areas, temper-provoking comments. In an April interview by Nyla Crone, he said among other things:

Contrary to the feelings that quite a few scientists have, there are a number of possible scientific approaches to the problem. The first and most important single technique will be radar. . . .
Secondly, records indicate that close-range UFO's disturb the magnetic field in some manner. This has been observed on magnetic recording devices, ship's compasses and hand compasses. There are a large number of cases on record where automobile engines were stopped by what appears to be some form of electromagnetic disturbance from a nearby UFO. That strongly indicates that some kind of electromagnetic sensing device could be designed to detect UFO's if only the problem were given serious scientific attention. . . .
NICAP and several other independent and private groups unofficially have been investigating the problem for many years, and I regard their methods and results as vastly superior to those of project Blue Book within the United States Air Force. Incidentally, I have made this same statement to the Air Force. . . .
One of the most puzzling questions that comes to anyone who seriously has studied the problem is the following: If these things are some kind of extraterrestrial probes, why don't they contact us? As soon as that's asked, I think it ought to raise in the mind of a discerning person the pitfall of homo-centrism. We tend to think that we're so important that anything else in the universe would also regard us as important. We also tend to think of "contact" in purely human terms, but this is obviously a logical and scientific fallacy. The nature and extent of any contact to investigate this planet might take forms utterly unknown to us. Some persons have suggested that maybe we already have been contacted; others have suggested that it's impossible. Still others have suggested that the time scale in which contact could be made is beyond our comprehension. If I personally were to say anything about "contact" I'd be forced to point out that the evidence suggests a curiously casual reconnaissance by the UFO's. I do want to emphasize that all this sort of speculation is premature until the extraterrestrial hypothesis itself is much more carefully scrutinized by many level-headed scientists. . . .
There are hundreds of good cases in the Air Force files that should have led to top-level scientific scrutiny of this problem years ago, yet these cases have been swept under the rug in a most disturbing way by Project Blue Book investigators and their consultants.[8]

On April 22, 1967, Dr. McDonald gave a detailed and singularly informative address before the American Society of Newspaper Editors, in Washington, D.C. It was titled "UFOs: Greatest Scientific Problem of our Times?" [9]

Man-made craft have always been one of the explanations for some of the saucer sightings. By 1967 a variety of officially developed vehicles had been constructed. The Ling-Temco-Vought XC-142A was the largest of the V/STOL (Vertical or Short Takeoff and Landing) planes. A 37,400-pound, tilt-wing transport, it featured a rotating wing with four 15½-foot propellers and an 8-foot tail rotor. Five were built, but by April, 1967, three had crashed. Bell produced two X-22A's: ducted tilting propeller, 15,000-pound, four-engine planes. One crashed. Of two similar Curtis-Wright XV-19A's, one crashed. Of two Lockheed XV4A "Humming Birds," with multiple nozzles, one crashed. Two Ryan XV-5A's were built, with two fans in the wing and one in the nose and two turbojet engines, and both crashed. A Canadair CL-84, somewhat like the Lockheed "Humming Bird," was still being tested in the winter of 1967. Six of the British Hawker P-1127 Kestrels—in the United States, XV6A—were also still undergoing tests.[10] In 1968, the impressive craft was the subject of a fascinating short film demonstrating its ability to make totally vertical takeoffs and landings, fly forward, backward, or sideways, revolve on its own axis, and hide like a bird under tree branches.

In April, newspapers carried stories of a hypersonic transport (HST) plane, designed by Republic Aviation, projected to travel about 8,500 miles an hour, or four times the speed of sound.[11]

However, technology found it difficult to keep up with the best of English sightings. Among the most intriguing of these was one featuring eight experienced coast guardsmen monitoring an enormous glistening cone for over an hour. The UFO was circumnavigated by a plane and sketched by Brian Jenkins, who said of the June 22 experience: "I don't know what it was, but it was unlike anything I had ever seen before—and I have been watching this coast for five years." [12]

A Ministry of Defence spokesman was said to have conceded that "our experts are examining the sketches [of the Brixham Coast Guard Station UFO], but we don't know what it was the coastguardsmen saw." [13]

Jenkins, the thirty-two-year-old lookout, situated on a cliff, had the supporting observations of Station Commander Harry Johnson, and furthermore of Charles Dunn, Tom Sowerbutts, and Max Cawse, all mature men in their fifties and forties. And, as if that were not a sufficiently persuasive contingent, District Officer Ralph Rowland, Area Inspector Arthur Shaw, and the Deputy Chief Inspector of Britain's Coast Guard, Lt. Comdr. John Douglas, were present on an inspection tour.

All saw the gleaming cone, it is said. In Jenkin's words:

At about 12:30 I saw a plane—it must have been a jet because it gave off a vapor trail—approaching the cone.
The jet seemed to be an aircraft like the RAF Lightning, and from the size of this compared with the cone, I estimated the cone's size to be about 150 feet wide by 200 feet high.

The jet circled the cone once, then flew off.[14]

Unfortunately, the plane's insignia could not be ascertained because of its altitude.

Station Commander Johnson affirmed that "all of us looked at the cone through field glasses and saw the shape that Jenkins described. We have all been in the Coast Guard service for a long time—at least three years for each of us—and I have been in for 22 years. Not one of us had ever seen anything like that object before." [15]

"I can confirm that," said the second-highest-ranking officer in the Coast Guard, Lieutenant Commander Douglas. "At first we all thought it might be a balloon, but after watching it carefully, we decided that it was out of the question. But what it could have been, I don't know." [16]

The official log recorded the sighting, the townspeople of Brixham allegedly watched it by the hundreds. The RAF controller at Plymouth, Flight Lt. David Smith, forwarded the report to the Ministry of Defence Headquarters in London, saying he had no knowledge of a plane having been sent to investigate, and would have, had one been so dispatched; nor had the airfield's radar revealed an Unidentified Flying Object.

Conclusion: None.

It seems that the decline of religious security was one of the important elements in the rise of the Age of Flying Saucers. An April 12, 1967, Gallup Poll indicated: "A majority of Americans—57 percent—say religion is 'losing' its influence on American life." [17] Of course, it cannot be proved that there is a direct correlation between the loss of religious persuasion and a move toward agnosticism or atheism, or that such evidence, if available, could be positively related to the sociopsychological phenomenon of preoccupation with mysterious and/or messianic extraterrestrials. However, it is certainly legitimate circumstantial data.

One of the most dramatic shifts in the American scene the survey found was that the proportion holding this view was four times as large in 1967 as it had been ten years earlier (the admission of this fact may have taken at least a decade to surface), when only 14 percent felt the impact of religion was diminishing.

Carl Sagan, of the Smithsonian Institution Astrophysical Laboratories, prepared an article for the *Encyclopedia Americana*. Here are some of the points he stressed:

> In the Harvard Meteor Project performed in New Mexico during the period 1954–1958, extensive photographic observations were made by Super-Schmidt cameras, with a 60° field of view. In all, a surface of about 3,000 square miles (7,700 sq km) was observed to a height of about 50 miles (80 km) for a total of some 3,000 hours. Visual and photographic observations were made which could

detect objects almost as faint as the faintest objects visible to the naked eye. These observations by professional astronomers were made in a locale and period characterized by extensive reports of unidentified flying objects. No unexplained objects were detected, despite the fact that rapidly moving objects were being sought in a study of meteors. Similar negative results, obtained by large numbers of astronomers, help to explain the general skepticism of astronomers toward flying saucer reports. . . .

Intersteller space flight is far beyond our present technical capabilities, but there seem to be no fundamental objections to it. It would be rash to preclude, from our present vantage point, the possibility of its development by other civilizations. But if each of, say, a million advanced technical civilizations in our galaxy launched at random at interstellar spacecraft each year (and even for an advanced civilization, such a launching would not be a trivial undertaking), and even if all of them could reach our solar system with equal facility, our solar system would, on the average, be visited only once every 100,000 years.

UFO enthusiasts have sometimes castigated the skeptic for his anthropocentrism. Actually, the assumption that earth is visited daily by interstellar spacecraft is far more anthropocentric—attaching as it does some overriding significance to our small planet. If our views on the frequency of intelligence in the galaxy are correct, there is no reason why the earth should be singled out for interstellar visits. A greater frequency of visits could be expected if there were another planet populated by a technical civilization within our solar system, but at the present time there is no evidence for the existence of one.[18]

Dr. Sagan constantly blunders when he strays from straight astronomy or astronautics. He is totally unaware of the difference between UFOs and Flying Saucers and does not know that "contacts" and "landings" are not the same (alleged) phenomenon. He writes that "it is noteworthy that in the contact tales, the spacecraft and their crews are rarely pictured as hostile." Apart from the absurdity of "hostile" machinery, the hostility factor is not only quite common, but of early origin. In our own time Mantell and Gorman were but two subjects of "pictures" of conceivable hostility, and James and Coral Lorenzen and others have written entire books on the potential threat of Flying Saucers.

Sagan is not quite as inept as Howard Margolis, however, associated with the Institute for Defense Analysis in Washington, D.C., who was responsible for a propagandistic overture to the Condon report which featured such egregious errors as contending that UFO phenomena cannot be separated from the idea of visitors from other planets, although numerous alternative explanations have been introduced, among which are the sequestered-terrestrial-site, inner-earth, other-dimensional, animal-organism, intelligent-energy-field, and etheric-expression hypotheses. Margolis goes on to warn that the Condon clique might be condemned for not looking into "the right cases." Actually, it examined fewer than sixty, offering no explanation for many. He also raises the dubious analogy of another field, spiritualism, in which he appears equally ill-informed, pontificating that "all great mediums were shown to be frauds," a statement which is totally false, whether, in truth, all of them were suspect or not.

Warren Rogers, writing slightly more objectively in *Look* magazine, summed up the entire investigative attitude of the "scientific" establishment when he pointed out that the Air Force was willing to invest in the projected (Condon) UFO inquiry less than the cost of a single B-52 strike in Viet Nam.

According to Major Keyhoe, in 1959 NICAP had "promised the names of key witnesses and proof of the censorship to the Senate Preparedness Committee [Senator Lyndon Johnson]. . . . Nothing definite, but his staff's looking into it. . . .[19] They're worried about Lyndon Johnson," he reports a Washington newsman told him, "—afraid he might order hearings before they can knock down these airline reports [primarily Killian's]." [20] Regarding Congress, at least eighteen Senators and fifty Representatives have expressed their interest in UFO and/or allied research.[21] The Gallup Poll quoted previously refutes the alleged disinterest of the public.

On June 7, the United Nations Outer Space Affairs Group heard an address by Dr. James E. McDonald, on the subject of Unidentified Flying Objects, during which the physicist summarized his views.

Certainly of interest in terms of the possibility of other life in the universe was the announcement by the Soviet Union that the mirror for the largest (236-inch) reflecting telescope in the world had cooled, was being ground, and would soon be ready for installation.[22] Of even more immediate fascination was the June 14 fly-by of Mariner 5 and the Russian Venus probes, both due to scout the blue planet in October.[23]

New York's initial major Flying Saucer convention—The 1967 Congress of Scientific Ufologists—which was attended by Dr. Edward U. Condon, convened on June 23 in the Commodore Hotel. Unfortunately, the festivities were considerably dampened by the death of one of the oldest and best investigators in the field, Frank Edwards.

On June 27, an International Sky Watch was conducted in England to commemorate the original Kenneth Arnold sighting a score of years earlier.

Sightings in England continued unabated.

The village of Hedley-on-the-Hill was the source of a report which echoed, in essence, many others recorded. Mr. Brian Ford, while sitting on a slope watching foxes on the evening of July 18, observed six gray objects with orange centers hovering over a nearby rise. Retracing his steps homeward, he soon returned with his wife and a friend to find that the UFOs still hung above the hill. Then the unknowns broke formation, and, as is often asserted, "played tag" before departing.[24]

A considerable flap occurred in northern Europe on the following night. Objects—according to some estimates, as many as three hundred —seemed to flash up from the Mediterranean area, cross France eastward toward the German border, and moving north again, vanish over the English Channel. According to astronomer Jean Muller, of the Meudon Observatory: "These things could be disintegrating chunks of the Soviet satellite Cosmos 168 . . . they could also be shooting stars, meteorites, or new space vessels launched by the Americans or Russians. In fact, anything—except flying saucers." [25]

Among the more widely publicized hoaxes of the year was perpetrated by two aviation students in England. It caused lead stories throughout the world, even the front page of the second section of *The New York Times*.[26] Christopher Southall and Roger Palmer, both twenty-two, built a "flotilla of whirring, beeping, 'flying saucers,' " which were supposedly seen sailing through the skies—although they were hundred-pound devices designed to confound on the ground and incapable of flight. One of their stated goals—to "give the police an exercise in dealing with alien spacecraft, because it could happen one day"—appeared to have been achieved, as the constabulary summoned defense experts to ascertain if it was safe to investigate the devices.[27]

The autumn of the year found more articles on the probability of life beyond our solar system. Speaking to the World Book Encyclopedia Science Service, Dr. Harrison Brown, professor of geochemistry at the California Institute of Technology and foreign secretary of the National Academy of Sciences, raised the following questions regarding such extra-earthian life:

> What is the probability that life exists on such ["medium-type"] planets? Where on the probability spectrum does the question lie? Is it closer to zero or closer to unity [a near certainty]?
>
> The more we look into it, the more we discover that it's close to unity, that given these [previously specified] conditions, life will inevitably emerge.

Dr. Harrison contended that the "noise" emitted by an advanced technological society, i.e, radio, television, and other signals, could be picked up on earth should the financing be provided for the proper equipment. [28]

Unfortunately, as usual, general unanimity did not necessarily follow one man's "unity." The New York *Post* reported: "William Markovitz of

Marquette University, Milwaukee, said the principles of celestial mechanics, Newtonian gravitational, and Einstein [sic] relativity equations are all violated by the claims that space ships have entered our·atmosphere, even landing and taking off." [29]

Responding to a question posed by Dr. J. Allen Hynek, "Why should extra-terrestrial visitors try to communicate with us? We would observe but wouldn't try to communicate with a new species of kangaroo in Australia," [30] Markovitz thumps his chest of dogma and sounds the flattoned clarion of anthropocentricity: "Intelligent human beings are not in the class of kangaroos. A more appropriate case is that of Columbus. When he landed in the new world he did communicate with the natives." It is really depressing that within thirty-one words, of which one in three is an article, a preposition, or a conjunction, such self-importance can accommodate so many errors of reasoning. The fact remains that to extraterrestrials we may not be recognizably intelligent, and besides, are not intelligent human beings *in* the class of kangaroos? It seems probable that the physicist would claim he was not dividing mankind and contending that the dull would be kangarooish and the bright would not. All that aside, however, human beings *are* in the class of kangaroos; both are mammals, and Mammalia is a *class.* Perhaps he intended to say "order" or "family" or "genus." If he had, he might have reflected a little less dimly on a magazine called *Science,* in which his remarks first appeared. The foolishness of the remaining score of words seems hardly worth analyzing, let alone the remainder of his remarks.

Yet such scientific and unprejudiced perceptions were not solely the province of the pedagogue. The laity indulged in similar predispositions.

Snippy was not in his usual place on the evening of September 7. Two days later, Harry King, brother of Mrs. Berle Lewis, who had owned the three-year-old gelding, discovered the carcass on the Colorado desert a few miles from its home. "No flesh remained on the head, neck and shoulders [wrote George Nobbe]. The hide was pulled back to expose the skull. The vital organs were gone, no fluid remained in the brain cavity and spinal column, and all the blood had been drained from the animal's body." [31]

Mr. and Mrs. Lewis and Mr. King reexamined the area on the eleventh and found "what appeared to be 15 circular exhaust marks covering an area of about 100 by 50 yards. At one spot, near a chico bush that had been squashed to within ten inches of the ground, they discovered six identical holes, each 2 inches wide and 4 inches deep." [32]

"I don't believe in flying saucers. I believe the horse was killed by lightning. . . . I didn't go out to investigate," [33] explained Alamosa

County Sheriff Ben Phillips, adding that there had been Flying Saucer reports from the area in which Snippy had died for half a decade.

September 16 found Mrs. Lewis at the mystery site once again. On this occasion, she allegedly discovered a small fleshy blob, with some horsehair on it, clinging to a shrub. When she broke the skin, green ooze seeped over her fingers and burned her hand. It required a number of washings and an hour before the irritation subsided.

After the death of the horse became public, half the nearby residents recalled seeing UFOs during the preceding year. Each had his or her own story to tell.

On October 9, one month after Snippy was found, a pathologist from Denver performed what autopsy could be managed on the carcass and ascertained that the animal had not been struck by lightning and was lacking all the natural fluids of the body. Later, Dr. Robert O. Adams, of Colorado State University, a veterinarian, said Snippy had succumbed to a disease and had had his throat slit by a strong-stomached Samaritan.

Those who don't think much of the Flying Saucer saga nodded knowingly; others dismissed the unimaginative diagnosis and went on believing.[34]

Throughout the year, sightings continued all over the world, but once again the pattern of diminishing arrivals was becoming apparent. Dramatic reports especially were on the decline. However, they had not ceased.

In England, on the very early morning of October 25, Constable Clifford Waycott and Roger Willey pursued a cross-shaped luminescent UFO over a ten-mile stretch at speeds of up to ninety miles an hour. Then the light vanished. The British Minister of Defence, Denis Healy, was queried about the matter in the House of Commons. Tory Peter Mills asked, "What are your plans to deal with a possible recurrence of this flying object?" It was the opposition member's contention that it was up to the Labour Minister "to help clear up this business as to whether or not we are looking at our equipment, or machines from another country, or, indeed, another planet."[35]

Other areas of the Commonwealth were being heard from as well. Canada, for example.

A 35 mm. transparency, taken by prospector Warren Smith in Calgary, Alberta, was examined by a photographic analysis center in Rockcliffe, Ottawa. It had already been classified as an "unretouched" picture of an object estimated to be nearly fifty feet across and a dozen feet thick. RCAF Squadron leader E. B. Chase has evaluated it as "the best one yet."[36]

A twenty-yard UFO was reported over Shag Harbour, Nova Scotia, flying "faster than any plane." [37] A sighting recorded over Falcon Lake, Manitoba, was investigated by the Canadian Department of National Defence, but Minister Leo-Alphonse Joseph Cadieux stated: "It is not the intent of the Department of National Defence to make public comments on the alleged sighting.[38]

However, British Columbia was the major center of UFO activity in 1967, with twenty-three sightings reported to the Royal Canadian Mounted Police before the first of August, in contrast to seven for the previous year. One of the better sightings was monitored by Brian Gratton, his wife Pat, Shawn Broe, and several other employees and guests on his dude ranch in the Cariboo area. Gratton reported:

> They had red and green blinking lights and shifted, bobbed, and weaved in the sky. I saw one of them veer off toward Green Lake and the front of it looked like some kind of space craft. It was saucer-shaped. Some nights you could hear a drone or hum like a high tension wire. The sound woke my mother out of her sleep two miles away. The cattle were restless and even the dogs on the ranch were acting up.[39]

The Canadian Defence Minister, like his counterpart across the North Atlantic, was called upon in relation to Flying Saucers—but in a rather different context. He unveiled an invitational UFO landing pad in St. Paul, Alberta; one had already been established at Port McNeill, British Columbia. Yet these are hardly to be compared with the gesture of the Canadian government made in 1954, when, in a hush-hush, top-secret scheme, it designed a one-thousand-square-mile restricted zone as a stipulated landing location for UFOs, over which no aircraft was permitted to fly without specific and special permission. The Ottawan hope was that aliens would contact the Defence Research Board Experimental Station at Suffield, Alberta, and they would be assured of a safe-conduct touchdown on their own earthport. Unfortunately, the extraterrestrials apparently were unaware of the preparations, or, perhaps, quite reasonably, had their doubts about trusting human beings.[40]

Two of the most inexplicable occurrences recorded in the 1967 Canadian archives included the episodes involving Pierre Charbonneau and Steve Michalak.

On August 23, Captain Charbonneau, commanding a Viscount for Air Canada, on Halifax-to-Boston flight, observed a series of flashing white lights. Halifax radar confirmed the presence of objects at fifty thousand feet. Despite their being located in an area of the sky subject to an eighty-knot jet stream, the phenomena remained for more than two days.

Steve Michalak was a fifty-year-old Winnipeg industrial mechanic who asserted he had suffered severe chest burns from emanations spewing out of holes in a "glaring red" saucer. "I don't just believe it's from another planet," he concluded. "I know it." [41] After two of his men had looked into the incident, Condon remarked, "There is no doubt the man was burned by something. Our inquiry was indecisive." [42]

The general attitude of Canadian scientists was a little less rigid than that of their American colleagues. Denying that the National Research Council intended to establish a UFO investigation, Dr. Richard Rettie, the director of its Space Research Facilities Branch, said:

I am perfectly prepared to believe that there are societies elsewhere in the universe which are at least as well advanced technologically as we are. I am willing to believe that such a society might wish to get in touch with us if they knew we existed. I am also prepared to believe that such a society might wish to study our behavior, much as man studies an ant hill. I am not, however, prepared to believe that such a society would behave in such an illogical fashion as to fool around in flying saucers and to approach people in woods with friendly offers to help us do wonderful things, while ignoring the easily recognizable structure of our society. They would damn well have the ability to approach us in an unmistakable fashion. Reports of such activities can, I am certain, be dismissed as a prank, as charlatanism, as sensation seeking or, unfortunately, as temporary or permanent mental unbalance. [43]

Yet, Dr. R. C. Tennyson, assistant professor at the University of Toronto's Institute for Aerospace Studies, took the position that "anything is possible. It's really just a matter of more scientific inquiry to determine if it's a natural or extraterrestrial phenomenon. I think it's time that scientists took a serious look at UFOs. *Right now we are all novices in the field.*" [44] (Emphasis added.)

And, going even further, Dr. G. H. Patterson, director of the University of Toronto's Institute for Aerospace Studies, announced in September the inception of an investigation into the enigma of Unidentified Flying Objects. [45]

World scientific opinion seemed to be inclining that way. Less than three months later, Prof. Feliks Zigel, of the Moscow Aviation Institute, called for a "joint effort of all the scientists of the world" [46] to solve the mystery of aerial unknowns.

A UFO organization which boasted the membership of the astronomer and mathematician had collected more than two hundred reports before Zigel made his public statement. An example of one was offered by the scientist:

"A luminous orange-colored crescent flying with its bend forward, it's surface is only a little duller than that of the moon." [47] Reportedly, it was such a UFO which had been observed over the Ukraine during the previous September.

The professor said that astronomers had deduced the diameter of the crescent to be between five and six hundred yards and its speed at over three miles a second.

Zigel stated that the possibility that the phenomena might be craft of extraterrestrial origin "merits serious consideration." [48]

The year concluded with a continuation of the seeming rise in Soviet interest in ufology. A report reached the West that Maj. Gen. Porfiry A. Stolyarov was establishing a systematic study of Unidentified Flying Objects, somewhat similar to NICAP. In a brief mention of the officer and his proposal, *The New York Times* pointedly noted that he was "reported to be ill" [49] without further elaboration but needing no additional suggestiveness.

Nonetheless, one could hardly avoid imagining a discussion between the chief of state and the head of the military, in either Washington or Moscow:

"Sir, aliens are on the outskirts of the city."

"True, but it's all right. They are *our* aliens."

Chapter 17

THE LAST GODS GOING HOME

The day of Flying Saucers was descending, the twilight of the gods was nearing fast. Sightings of UFOs now networked the world. Even "unknowns," just in this country and conceded as such by the Air Force, were numbered high in three figures. But additional reports merely raised statistical totals, not excitement. The luminaries were flown or swiftly fading: Dan Fry and his Americanese-speaking saucer voice; Truman Bethurum and his girl friend, Aura, from the planet Clarion; Menger the Saturnian and his Venusian wife; the delightful Orfeo Angelucci, the Hans Christian Andersen of the twenty-first century; the four Georges—Adamski, Van Tassel, King, and Williamson—and their gullibles' travels; George Marlo and his space ship for-celebrities-only; Gloria Lee and her telepathic Jovians; Buck Nelson and his 385-pound dog (extremely shaggy); Dan Martin and the Mercurians; Gerald Herd's invasion of the bees; Gabriel Green, innovator of interplanetary politics; Bender, Barker, Luchesi, and Roberts and the Three Men in Black; and, perhaps by far the most unbelievable, the wrong-way Corrigans of saucerdom—Otis T. Carr, who invented the OTC-X1 Circular Foil Craft to fly to the moon, and Norman E. Colton, whom many believe to be the inventor of Otis T. Carr. The tales or hoaxes were simply not of the quality that made the Age of Flying Saucers. However, of undimmed interest and mystery were the ubiquitous Unidentified Flying Objects.

In Umeå, Sweden, three pilots and a control tower recounted seeing a ball of emerald light, on the night of January 31, 1968, and another airline employee reported an object descending from about a thousand-yard altitude, at less than two hundred miles an hour, which pulsed, changed from green to red to violet, and then seemed "to explode near the ground." [1]

While in Los Angeles the possibility of moon microbes was being discussed, by Dr. Jack Green, in a speech before a branch of the American Institute of Aeronautics and Astronautics, Russian columnist V. Lyustiberg, of the Moskovski Komsomolets, wrote that Flying Saucers were a capitalistic aeropsychological opiate to hallucinate the oppressed. [2]

"When it becomes necessary to distract the reader from tough problems," he wrote, "Western leaders have three ready sensations which never fail: flying saucers, the Loch Ness monster, and the abominable snowman."[3]

The new open-mindedness of Dr. Hynek continued to evidence itself. On the morning of March 11, the New York radio station WINS broadcast that the Air Force consultant was seeking persons who saw and remembered some portion of the 1897 sighting complex.[4]

Another ultimately identifiable potential UFO was introduced about this time in the form of the German-designed and -built hovercraft called the Flying Disk. Eleven feet across, the fiberglass paraboat had a listed speed of thirty miles an hour and a cost of $2,900.[5]

The excitement regarding signals from outer space—of such regularity and rhythm as to suggest to many scientists an indication of the existence of super civilizations—which had been fired in late 1968, dimmed in the winter. Called "pulsars," they seemed less and less likely to have an artificial origin.[6]

Yet as this promise of other planetarians faded, enthusiasm for UFOs increased in the Soviet Union, where more and more sightings were being reported. A NICAP-like organization was formed, the Unidentified Flying Object Section of the All-Union Cosmonautics Committee, under the direction of Dr. Feliz Zigel, assistant professor of astronomy at the Moscow Aviation Institute, and General Porfiry Stolyarov. The organization assumed a definitely receptive attitude toward extraterrestrialism.[7]

For the most part, attention of ufologists was directed toward the activities of Dr. Edward U. Condon and his University of Colorado project. The investigation, which had been scheduled to expire on February 1, 1968, had been extended until the end of June. Unfortunately, the Air Force–sponsored investigation had not proved satisfactory to many persons, including those originally supporting it. On April 30, 1968, the physicist had announced completion of the field studies, saying the final report of the project would be delivered to the National Academy of Sciences, in the autumn.[8] However, John Fuller's article "Flying Saucer Fiasco," which appeared in May, caused a considerable stir among the majority of persons interested in a legitimate investigation of Unidentified Flying Objects. If the objective of the Air Force-financed study had been to satisfy the public that an unbiased evaluation was under way, Fuller's article had to be regarded as devastating.

Notwithstanding the fact that 80 percent of the orignal staff were not physical scientists but psychologists and that Robert J. Low, who was to coordinate operations, had taken his master's degree in business administration, a degree of optimism prevailed among students of ufology, although Low's comment that the investigation "comes pretty close to the criteria of nonacceptability" [9] as a venture for the University of Colorado did not heighten enthusiasm. Early on in the game, however, such verbal indiscretions were to cause many more problems. The Elmira, New York, *Star-Gazette* carried a story, which was quoted, in part, by Fuller:

> Unidentified flying objects "are not the business of the Air Force," . . . Dr. Edward U. Condon said here Wednesday night. . . . "It is my inclination right now to recommend that the Government get out of this business. My attitude right now is that there's nothing to it . . . but I'm not supposed to reach a conclusion for another year. . . ." [10]

Considering that the statement was made on January 25, by which date Condon had investigated no cases personally, nor had any substantive evaluation been made (since, after all, the project was only three months old), the attitude was something less than scientific. Still, it may well have reflected not merely an intellectually prejudiced attitude but also an emotional one, for, according to Fuller: "Condon himself was heard to say that he wished the project could give the money back [to the Air Force]." [11] However, it is most likely that Fuller's allusion to an interoffice memorandum written by Robert J. Low did more damage to the image of the group than anything preceding its own official report. Referring to the August 9, 1966, message, headed "Some Thoughts on the UFO Project," which had been composed prior to the completion of contractual arrangements for the investigation, Fuller quotes Low as having written:

> Our study would be conducted almost exclusively by nonbelievers who, although they couldn't possibly *prove* a negative result, could and probably would add an impressive body of evidence that there is no reality to the observations. The trick would be, I think, to describe the project so that, to the public, it would appear a totally objective study but, to the scientific community, would present the image of a group of nonbelievers trying their best to be objective, but having an almost zero expectation of finding a saucer. One way to do this would be to stress investigation, not of the physical phenomena, but rather of the people and groups who report seeing UFO's. If the emphasis were put here, rather than on examination of the old question of the physical reality of the saucer, I think the scientific community would quickly get the message. . . . I'm inclined to feel at this early stage that, if we set up the thing right and take pains to get the proper people involved and have success in presenting the image we want to present to the scientific community, we could carry the job off to our benefit. . . . [12]

Now, May of 1968 had arrived, the investigation of the project was completed, and a report of the results, presumably to be first given to the

National Academy of Sciences in September, was in preparation. Yet, regardless of what it ultimately concluded about UFOs, the group's image had been seriously impaired by its own actions. Impaired to such a degree that it seemed likely to share the same fate—albeit, within a more restricted circle of interest—as the Warren Commission Report. For if, less than five years after its issuance, the conclusions of the latter were severely doubted by more than two thirds of the American public, there was every reason to believe that the Condon Committee Report had a reasonable chance of achieving a similarly dubious status.

The entire climate may well have been what have prompted Rep. L. Mendel Rivers and his House Committee on Space and Astronautics to reverse their decision of more than two years earlier and agree to a symposium on the subject of Unidentified Flying Objects. Six highly qualified witnesses testified: Dr. J. Allen Hynek, of the Dearborn Observatory, Northwestern University, astronomer and Air Force consultant; Dr. Carl Sagan, of Cornell University, astronomer formerly with Harvard University; Dr. Robert L. Hall, of the University of Illinois, sociologist; Dr. James A. Harder, of the University of California, engineer; Dr. Robert M. L. Baker, senior scientist, Computer Sciences Corporation; and Dr. James E. McDonald.

David R. Saunders writes:

> The testimony emerging brought together considerable weighty persuasion that the UFO problem needed far more attention than that which the Condon Committee or the Air Force was willing or able to give. . . .[13]
> The group as a whole agreed flatly that UFOs were worthy of serious investigation. They agreed in general that they thought the objects were more than optical illusions or psychological aberrations. . . . They recommended further study, beyond that of the Condon Committee. . . .[14]
> Dr. Hynek recommended the development of a technique for studying reports with scientific respectability. . . .[15]

Dr. McDonald went on to quote Vice Admiral R. H. Hillonkoeter, former CIA director, who eight years ago had said: "It is imperative that we learn where UFOs come from, and what their purpose is."[16]

The testimony of Dr. McDonald and his colleagues before the House Committee on July 29 was published as the greater portion of John Fuller's latest contribution to the field of ufology.[17] Considering the stature of the men whose opinions were recorded at that Congressional conclave, the publication of their fascinating analyses and speculations can hardly be ignored by the serious student of the subject.

The *outré* aspects of the subculture of saucerology were many, and a number of these reflected facets even more incredible than the centerpiece itself. None was more bizarre than the attempts of some peripheral figures to incorporate into the Age of Flying Saucers elements of the American assassination pattern which flourished in the 1960's. Stories of UFOs being seen over Dallas during November, 1963, and therefore of the possibility that extraterrestrials were responsible for the death of John F. Kennedy ricocheted about, although they were rarely to see print. The discovery that Sirhan B. Sirhan read Blavatsky, and other occult material, did little to diminish these claims, although the material is only very obliquely related to the literature of saucerology.

Spring of 1968 brought certain such interlacing attempts to print when a Larry Klein, writing in *Saucer News*, listed a number of persons—from Chou En-lai and Raul Castro through John Lennon and Otto Preminger to Adam Clayton Powell and Robert Welch—as "fallen angels" who operate in the cause of Satan. A confusing, even confounding, state of affairs until one comes to realize that "Robert McNamara [former Secretary of Defense and present president of the World Bank] is a captain of a Flying Saucer. He is a fallen angel in the murdered body of Robert McNamara. This murder took place in 1959." [18]

However, to return to the assassination aspect, we also find the author stating:

"History will bear out that James [sic] Garrison, the New Orleans prosecutor, is a strong angel from God, and that the John F. Kennedy murder is of a spiritual and supernatural meaning and consequence." [19]

Without question, the strangest of all Flying Saucer–assassination connections arose in a totally unrelated manner. In December of 1968,[20] Jim Garrison summoned to New Orleans for questioning before the grand jury Fred L. Crisman, of Tacoma, Washington, who had figured so prominently in the 1947 Maury Island mystery, which was partially investigated by Kenneth Arnold.[21] Having made his appearance, Crisman left New Orleans and was not mentioned again by the district attorney's office, as of mid-1970.

Another minor connection between the two fields is found in the person of the Rev. Raymond Broshears, who had once roomed with David W. Ferrie, one of the deceased alleged conspirators (the other being Lee Harvey Oswald) accused, with Clay L. Shaw, by Garrison, of conspiring to assassinate John F. Kennedy. The minister—he also identifies himself as a "gifted Oracle, lecturer, publisher" [22] —stated "that Mr. [Lyndon] Johnson who was responsible, directly or indirectly, for the assassination of President Kennedy should be put to death." [23] The pastor of the Church of God of Holy Orthodox Christian[24] wrote an article on the death of the Kennedy brothers for an essentially saucer newspaper in the summer of 1968.[25]

The New York Times gave major coverage to a considerable Argentinian flap which began in May and was still flourishing more than two months later.[26] The Buenos Aires periodical *La Razón* told of a young couple losing consciousness in their automobile, only to awaken five thousand miles away on the outskirts of Mexico City. Although the story was not validated, legions were positive that one of only two possible solutions could explain it: extraterrestrials or the Central Intelligence Agency.

Copilot Humberto Raul Guardabassi, flying an Argentine airline craft over the Strait of Magellan, sighted a UFO:

> It was 9:15 P.M., visibility was unlimited and the Patagonian evening was beautiful. Here appeared a gigantic disk about 13 kilometers [about 8 miles] from us, of a bluish color. Below, in the center of its belly, the color changed to red shading to yellow, such as might be produced by combustion.[27]

Ariel Ciro Rieti, president of Argentina's Observation Committee of Unidentified Flying Objects, announced his invention of a saucer detector. Maria Elodia Letzel told of meeting an alien, and, according to the *Times,* a government official stated: "I have no doubt that flying saucers have arrived here. I worry about what they're up to. I can't understand why they've picked Argentina." [28]

The impact of the age appeared to have no limits. In Cleveland, on July 24, black nationalist Fred Ahmed Evans was jailed as a suspect in an investigation of a riot that took ten lives. Mr. Evans attributed his earlier prediction of race conflict on his knowledge of astrology—but this interest, he said, originated when he sighted a Flying Saucer.[29]

The Final Report of the Scientific Study of Unidentified Flying Objects, "conducted by the University of Colorado under contract to the United States Air Force," [30] was released to the public on January 8, 1969.

The Condon committee derived, first, from the Scientific Advisory Panel on Unidentified Flying Objects, of January 14–18, 1953, commonly called the Robertson Panel. This was comprised of Prof. P. H. Robertson of the California Institute of Technology, who chaired the sessions, Prof. Samuel A. Goudsmit, physicist, and Prof. Thorton Page, astronomer. The general conclusion of this group was that there was no evidence suggesting "that these phenomena constitute a direct physical threat to national security." [31] or indicating "a need for the revision of current scientific concepts." [32] Perhaps the most interesting passage is the one citing the Air Force adviser's apprehension that some "skillful hostile propaganda" might turn the UFOs into a "distrust of duly constituted authority." [33]

A dozen years later, Gen. E. B. LeBailly, head of the Office of Information of the Secretary of the Air Force, suggested to the military director of the Air Force Scientific Advisory Board that, since the Air Force's Project Blue Book had, as of June 30, 1965, investigated 9,265 reports, of which "663 cannot be explained," further examination might be warranted. A portion of his letter of September 18, 1965 said:

> To date, the Air Force has found no evidence that any of the UFO reports reflect a threat to our national security. However, many of the reports that cannot be explained have come from intelligent and well qualified individuals whose integrity cannot be doubted. In addition the reports received officially by the Air Force include only a fraction of the spectacular reports which are publicized by many private UFO organizations.
>
> Accordingly, it is requested that a working scientific panel composed of both physical and social scientists be organized to review Project Blue Book—its resources, methods and findings—and to advise the Air Force as to any improvements that should be made in the program to carry out the Air Force's assigned responsibility.

General LeBailly's communication, at least in part, resulted in the establishment of the Ad Hoc Committee to Review Project Blue Book which is usually identified, after its chairman, as the O'Brien Committee. Section IV of the Condon Report is titled "Case Studies," and constitutes approximately one quarter of the document. Three orders of material are examined: (a) ten cases predating the project; (b) thirty-five cases investigated in the field by the project; (c) the remainder, thirteen in number, being evaluations of photographs.

For the first group, the following conclusions were reached (the numbers corresponding to the case numbers specified in the report):

1. Insufficient data, no firm conclusion.[34]

2. ". . . the probability that at least one genuine UFO was involved appears to be fairly high." [35]

3. Identified.[36]

4. Insufficient data, no firm conclusion.[37]

5. Insufficient data, no firm conclusion.[38]

6. Of several sightings some were attributed to Jupiter, but one, of three women and a young girl reporting a close observation of a UFO, elicited a "no explanation is attempted" comment.[39]

7. An Air Force pilot, whose "reputation is irreproachable," [40] is strongly inferred to have faked two photographs of a red Flying Saucer.[41]

8. Lacking supporting testimony in a single-witness observation, a sighting was "neither verified nor refuted," [42] and "the report is unexplained." [43]

9. "The evidence is not sufficient to justify any definite conclusion." [44]

10. A nuclear physicist's powers of observation and evaluation regarding a light source, in poor weather, is severely questioned, and the case remains unresolved.[45]

Among conclusions drawn from cases investigated by the group were the following:

11. A UFO was observed air-to-air for approximately seven minutes, "pacing" the plane for two. The pilot, rejecting all other possibilities, said a satellite reentry was a "possible" explanation. The report decided it was a suitable one, attributing the phenomenon to a fragment of a satellite which had returned to earth more than half an hour earlier and a third of the circumference of the planet away.[46]

12. "The case remains interesting but unexplained." [47]

13. Regarding a multiple sighted UFO: "The case therefore must be regarded as unexplained. . . ." [48]

14. Of three sightings: in two instances "the evidence is less substantial, one case having low credibility and [the] other marginal strangeness"; however, in one case, "the evidence [was] strong for both its reality and its strangeness." [49]

15. Unresolved, since the observer, while thought to be "sincere and curious," was regarded as "scientifically unreliable." [50]

16. "The case is not fully clarified," but assumed to be an emotionally motivated misinterpretation of natural objects.[51]

17. "On the basis of available evidence, it is impossible to say whether or not the event reported is real." [52]

18. Conclusion: balloons.[53]

19. Condon, having dispatched an observer to an alleged projected landing of a Flying Saucer, as announced by a telepath-type contactee, was doubtlessly disappointed that the commander of the extraterrestrial craft canceled the arrival.[54] (This incident rather reflects the attitude that brought Dr. Condon to New York, in the summer of 1967, to attend a Flying Saucer convention.)

20. A persistent "beeping" sound and UFO sightings over a period of three weeks were deduced to have been caused by a (when discovered) dead, six-inch-long, saw-whet owl.[55]

21. "The case is therefore not satisfactorily explained." [56]

22. Not easily interpreted data and solitary testimony led to the conclusion that the case was unlikely to lead to constructive information.[57]

23. Probable plane.[58]

24. Probable hoax.[59]

25. Probable power-line flashes.[60]

26. Admitted hoax.[61]

27. Attempts to photograph UFOs with an all-sky camera over seven-

teen nights during a flap, resulting in nine thousand exposures, produced but two, probably explainable, unknowns.[62]

28. Probable planes.[63]

29. Probable flares.[64]

Section IV details the panel's evaluation of thirteen photographic cases, the majority of which are dismissed in one manner or another. The Great Falls, Montana, film (case 47)[65] is admittedly unresolved, but airplanes are suggested as a possibility; the Barra Da Tijuca, Brazil, photographs (case 48)[66] are described as informationally inadequate, but as dubious evidence; and the famous Trementon, Utah, film (case 49)[67] is said to show birds. The remaining cases, save one, are explained to the satisfaction of the investigator (William K. Hartmann), an astronomer. The exceptions are the McMinnville, Oregon, photographs, which have long been regarded as among the most persuasive ever offered in substantiation of the intelligently operated craft thesis. The report itself testified:[68]

Various McMinnville residents, including the bankers Wortman, offered to sign affidavits vouching unreservedly for the reputation and veracity of the witnesses. . . .

. . . various reputable individuals volunteered to attest to the witnesses' veracity. They appear to be sincere, though not highly educated or experienced observers. During the writer's [Hartmann's] interview with them, they were friendly and quite unconcerned about the sighting. Witness II was at work plowing his field and did not even get off his tractor. From interviews throughout this district one gained the impression that these were very industrious farm people, not given to unusual pranks.[69]

It was specifically ascertained that the negatives had not been retouched, and other photographic and optical trickery was rejected after photometric analysis. The Condon committee concluded:

This is one of the few UFO reports in which all factors investigated, geometric, psychological, and physical, appear to be consistent with the assertion than an extraordinary flying object, silvery, metallic, disk-shaped, tens of meters in diameter, and evidently artificial, flew within sight of two witnesses. It cannot be said that the evidence positively rules out a fabrication, although there are some physical factors such as the accuracy of certain photometric measures of the original negatives which argue against a fabrication.[70]

Dr. J. Allen Hynek, somewhat after the fashion of the O'Brien panel's advice, "strongly believes that the teams [investigating UFO reports] should have four or more members," says Condon's group.

He recommends giving each report what he calls the "FBI treatment," by which he means not only thorough interviewing of the persons who made the re-

port, but in addition an active quest in the neighborhood where the sighting occurred to try to discover additional witnesses. Against such thoroughness must
be balanced the consideration that the cost per case goes up proportionately to
the number of persons in a team, so that the larger the team, the fewer the cases
that can be studied." [71]

This is rationalization on the part of the official analysis. The absurdity
of the size of the pittance alloted for this investigation is ignored.

Notwithstanding the fact that their own series of conclusions to cases
described leave numerous incidents unresolved, the official summation
states:

Our general conclusion is that nothing has come from the study of UFOs in
the past 21 years that has added to scientific knowledge. Careful consideration of
the record as it is available to us leads us to conclude that further extensive study
of UFOs probably cannot be justified in the expectation that science will be advanced thereby.

It has been argued that this lack of contribution to science is due to the fact
that very little scientific effort has been put on the subject. We do not agree. We
feel that the reason that there has been very little scientific study of the subject is
that those scientists who are most directly concerned, astronomers, atmospheric
physicists, chemists, and psychologists, having had ample opportunity to look
into the matter, have individually decided that UFO phenomena do not offer a
fruitful field in which to look for major scientific discoveries. [72]

The Condon Report perhaps brought digression and time, for those
who really sponsored it. But since, if the phenomena are manifestations
of intelligently operated extraterrestrial craft, they may be expected to
continue for some time to come, even at so low a price as was paid, little
profit was gained.

The odds against UFOs being Flying Saucers are extraordinarily high,
but if it was possible to diminish the unbelievability factor, the Colorado
study managed to do it, better than the vast majority of receptive ufologists who preceded it.

The Age of Flying Saucers came to its official conclusion on December
17, 1969, when the entire Establishment, as represented by the administration of Richard M. Nixon, spoke to the subject for the final time
through its perennial apologist and propagandist, the United States Air
Force. On that date the Office of the Assistant Secretary of Defense
(Public Affairs) issued a press release, numbered 1077-69, which read:

AIR FORCE TO TERMINATE PROJECT "BLUE BOOK"

Secretary of the Air Force Robert C. Seamans, Jr., announced today the termination of Project Blue Book, the Air Force program for the investigation of unidentified flying objects (UFOs).

In a memorandum to Air Force Chief of Staff General John D. Ryan, Secretary Seamans stated that "the continuation of Project Blue Book cannot be justified either on the ground of national security or in the interest of science," and concluded that the project did not merit future expenditures of resources.

The decision to discontinue UFO investigations was based on an evaluation of a report prepared by the University of Colorado entitled *Scientific Study of Unidentified Flying Objects,* a review of the University of Colorado's report by the National Academy of Sciences, past UFO studies, and Air Force experience investigating UFO reports during the past two decades.

Under the direction of Dr. Edward U. Condon, the University of Colorado completed an 18-month contracted study of UFOs, and its report was released to the public in January, 1969. The report concluded that little if anything had come from the study of UFOs in the past twenty-one years that had added to scientific knowledge, and that further extensive study of UFO sightings was not justified in the expectation that science would be advanced.

A panel of the National Academy of Sciences made an independent assessment of the scope, methodology, and findings of the University of Colorado study. The panel concurred in the University of Colorado's recommendation that "no high priority in UFO investigations is warranted by data of the past two decades." It concluded by stating that "on the basis of present knowledge, the least likely explanation of UFOs is the hypothesis of extraterrestrial visitations by intelligent beings."

Past UFO studies include one conducted by a Scientific Advisory Panel on UFOs in January, 1953 (Robertson Panel), and a review of Project Blue Book by the Air Force Scientific Advisory Board Ad Hoc Committee, February-March, 1966 (Dr. Brian O'Brien, chairman). These studies concluded that no evidence had been found to show that any of the UFO reports reflect a threat to our national security.

As a result of investigating UFO reports since 1948, the conclusions of Project Blue Book are: (1) No UFO reported, investigated, and evaluated by the Air Force has ever given any indication of being a threat to our national security; (2) there has been no evidence submitted or discovered by the Air Force that sightings categorized as "unidentified" represent technological developments or principles beyond the range of present-day scientific knowledge; and (3) there has been no evidence that sightings categorized as "unidentified" are of extraterrestrial vehicles.

Project Blue Book records will be retired to the USAF Archives, Maxwell Air Force Base, Alabama. Requests for information will continue to be handled by the Secretary of the Air Force, Office of Information (SAFOI), Washington, D.C. 20330.

And there, for all practical purposes, the mystery of Unidentified Aeronautical Phenomena remains: unknown, uninvestigated, and unlikely to be. If it is ever to be raveled in a straight comprehensible line leading to the truth, it will probably be by accident, or by some lone Planck or Einstein, cogitating in the creative solitude of his genius.

The investigation of the phenomena scattered through our skies should be made with reason, not with mind-clogging predispositions and prejudices. Intelligent inquiry and accurate evaluation can be made only with reason and a rational perspective.

Now, in a few concluding thoughts about UFOs, it is suggested that we realize that the "unknown" is not necessarily a relative term, although it may be of temporary application. That is, it should not be assumed that an apparently inexplicable happening is something less than that. And, at least, the intelligent man must grant that, even if a mystery is ultimately soluble, with the knowledge and imagination mankind has recessed within one of its many minds, it may only be dispelled by some of its most hidden, least employed, or rarest intellectual faculties.

The American astronomer Simon Newcomb proved to his intellectual conviction that flying was impossible, and Edison decided against "inventing an air ship," preferring to devote his "time to objects which have some commercial value." He knew that "at least air ships would only be toys." J. W. Campbell conclusively established, in 1938, that it would require one million tons of takeoff weight to push a pound of payload on a lunar orbiting trip. The truth is that it requires less than one two-hundredth of that. The English astronomer Richard van der Riet Wooley clearly saw the concept of space travel as "utter bilge." That was in 1956.[73] So, for a moment, forget the "real" world in which you live. The society of telephones, radio, television, visaphones, tape recorders, boats that move above the water, not on it, rockets examining Venus, men flying at 25,000 miles an hour and landing on the moon . . . the world hardly any mind of two thousand years ago could conceive.

Speculate.

For centuries, we failed to discover the truth about the solar system because we believed it functioned around us. We have not really been dissuaded from that conviction. We still believe the solar system functions around us, and not only the solar system, but the galaxy and the universe itself. When we question the origin of Flying Saucers, we get one of three kinds of answer: (a) They come from outer space. They are interplanetary; they are interstellar; they are intergalactic. (b) They are conceived, constructed, and operated from Earth. (This answer is frequently politically oriented.) (c) They come from the inner earth.

However, I would like to point out that there are other fascinating improbabilities which are considerably more interesting and imaginative.

Some will be immediately obvious. Perhaps they don't come from "out there" or "over there" or "in there." Maybe they come from "back there" or from a time before ours. This is just as likely, it would seem, as their coming from the center of the earth, which defies all concepts we have about the physical nature of the planet on which we live. Or what if they come from the future?

What about parallel worlds? Maybe while you are sitting there, someone else is sitting there. We are learning very quickly that the dimensions described when most of us were in school are not necessarily the dimensions that control; they are only the dimensions we see. It may be that everywhere you walk, another being walks. Discard the spiritual interpretation; discard the mystical. Something real and concrete might be where you are. Ultimately, within the context of our ignorance, we really do not know if all the ancient laws are true. Perhaps two things can exist in the same place at the same time or in incalculable alternations.

And what of the 87th dimension or the 136th or the 219th? Why must we assume that the world in which we function sustains only us and only on our terms?

Then there is the possibility that UFOs are merely animals or another state of being, a protoplasmic phenomenon or a more advanced condition of existence of which we, an aspect of its evolution, have no comprehension. After considering some of the incredibly imaginative speculations of the zoologist Ivan Sanderson[74] along this line, I am certainly not prepared to reject totally his protoplasmic or amoebalike creatures floating in space. Why not animals whose life food is electric, magnetic, or etheric? Or could these strange phenomena be mental projections, projections of ultraspace, or parabeings outside our Earth? Why do they have to be things? Why do they have to be light? Why do they have to be energy? Why do they have to be anything found, even obliquely, in the lexicography of our imagination? There are so many possibilities. Why must people limit them to "out there" and "over there" and "down there" —the dullest available explanations.

How delightful if UFOs are coming to view us as once Irish folk went to see the wee people. Are we only elves sitting beneath a starry bush, in a galactic coppice. Maybe our great universe—"our" because too many would be affronted at the suggestion that it did not belong to us—has swirled this little galaxy into a position in the cosmos that it has never reached before. What if, over the last ten years, fifty years, five hundred years, what if since the sightings first began, the world we live in and the edge of the system in which we reside have been shifted across the endless ways of sky, leaving us, now, someplace where no living thing has ever been before—except that which was here.

May there be out there, flying around, where we invaded, perceptions in what we call saucers, saying: "Do you really believe that in that solar system over there, on that third planet from the sun, there can be intelligent life?" They might contest our answer. "Do you really believe that it is possible that globe is logically controlled and operated?" An ominous inquiry. How can one help but wonder if somewhere out in space, projecting, riding, or being what we call UFOs, one vast intelligence of life turns to another, saying: "Do you believe in flying worlds?"

Yet the problem of the UFOs is apart from the true concern of this work. They were there, all evidence suggests, before the earliest twig was taken up to scratch a straight line in the ground; they will be there, it seems as evident, until that moment of the accidental flash of insight. And actually it doesn't matter; it's part of something else.

In truth—

It is all over. The golden Age of Flying Saucers is gone. Only the UFOs are left. And this is like taking the heroes out of history and leaving catalogs of dates. The romance, albeit highly, perhaps entirely, falsified, has been edited out by reason, and only the statistics remain. A dull, diminished return for the hopes invested by hundreds of thousands of persons.

Do not be deceived by the sporadic spurts of UFO sightings nor by the belated discovery of the subject by a few writers, however deft. An Exeter, New Hampshire, report, which, seen in context, is of minor interest, a hardly heard echo of another day. The Lonnie Zamorra semicontact, in New Mexico, which was immeasurably more impressive, but says it all again. Even the much publicized Barney and Betty Hill contact claim is a drab substitute for the tales of Adamski, Angelucci, and Menger. And yet, the simple truth is that UFO sightings can't get any more concrete than they have without becoming Flying Saucer reports.

The Age of Flying Saucers could have begun any time shortly after the Second World War, and the same events would probably have followed. But the approximate date is important, because people became entranced by the concept of something in the skies, visitors to this planet who would do for us what we could not do for ourselves—namely, teach us to become civilized at a time when we were concluding a second horrendous global conflict, at a time when the great father images were dying or dead, at a time when the powers of the world, both good and evil, were falling. Roosevelt was gone, Hitler was gone, Mussolini was gone, Stalin and Chiang were soon to go, Hirohito was dethroned, and Winston Churchill deposed. All the titans, human and destroyed. However, even worse than that, once there had been somewhere left to hide when things got bad: a cave, a church, a forest, an island, or a mountain top. Now, the age of the *bomb*. And nowhere left to hide.

Was the result of this—not directly but as a correlation—Flying Saucers? For something else had happened, the third factor in the trinity of doom. In the phrase of some philosophers, "God died." The question then suggests itself: Did he recur, responding to the vacuum in the souls of men, as visitors from outer space? This came to pass at the end of what we hoped was the last of war, at the fall of great father images of towering stature, at the inception of the most horrible device ever conceived and created by the mind of man, at the apparent demise of the Deity, and at the inception of the need, the terrible need, for somebody to do for us what we could not do for ourselves, to teach us to be civilized.

The need arose, and for what may be the final time, Man reached without to find the strength within. In the future, unless he thrusts himself into a near-decimating devastation and must climb up from the intellectual oblivion of animalism once again, it will be difficult for the rational mind of Man to play half-wit to the dream dealers, even the one he houses in himself. That is why the Age of Flying Saucers is not merely mythic, but legendary—a tale told by romantics, full of hope and symbols, signifying fear.

UFOs may come, of course, proving to be vessels from the stars. Still, whether that ever happens or not really has nothing to do with the Age of Flying Saucers. If a UFO actually lands on the White House lawn one day, is patently a Flying Saucer, and spacial aliens disembark, establishing interplanetary relations, it will be an aspect of science and astropolitics—but it won't have anything to do with what has been discussed. It will happen, if ever, long after the dream ended.

We know why it ended. It was crushed in the vise of antidream, and science turned the screw. Man exploded upward into the mysterious vastness from whence the gods and the impossible had poured since time began. The final fruition of fable was being swept aside by adventures infinitely more exciting as man wheeled out about the earth, flashed around the far side of the moon, put hardware on the planets, flung capsules far beyond the sun. When heroes scale Olympus, immortals shrink into the endless emptiness of superfluity.

But why did it begin?

What was the need that brought into this period of science and enlightenment the last of myths—the Age of Flying Saucers? What made so large a portion of mankind throw open arms and hearts and hopes to welcome messianic visitors from outer space?

They were the first to know that man's own God was dead.

NOTES

CHAPTER 2

1. Kenneth Arnold and Ray Palmer, *The Coming of the Saucers* (Amherst, Wisconsin, privately printed, 1952).
2. Edward J. Ruppelt, *The Report on Unidentified Flying Objects* (Garden City, New York, Doubleday and Company, 1956), p. 16.
3. Los Angeles *Times* (June 26, 1947).
4. A term applied to aerial lights seen by combat pilots, especially over Europe, during World War II. While C. G. Jung's contention that it derived from the German *feu* may have some second- or third-level etymological foundation, the Allied flyers actually drew the phrase from the American comic strip "Smokey Stover," in which it was asserted that "where there's foo, there's fire."
5. Los Angeles *Daily News* (June 29, 1947).
6. Ruppelt, *op. cit.*, pp. 16–27.
7. Harold T. Wilkins, *Strange Mysteries of Time and Space* (New York, The Citadel Press, 1959).
8. The greatest concentration of unknown aerial objects reported in the United States prior to the modern Age of Flying Saucers, which began in 1947, spanned the period from autumn, 1896, to early summer, 1897, with the "flap" peaking during the month of April. Commencing with sighting reports in northern California, accounts from ever more easterly points followed, until finally a New York newspaper carried a detailed description of the (or a similar) object appearing over Yonkers on the night of April 30, 1897.
9. *The UFO Evidence*, Richard Hall, ed. (Washington, D.C., The National Investigations Committee on Aerial Phenomena, 1964), p. 129.
10. *Ibid.*, p. 157.
11. *Ibid.*, pp. 30, 129.
12. *Ibid.*, pp. 33, 129.
13. Lloyd Mallan, *The Official Guide to UFO's* (New York, Science and Mechanics Publishing Co., 1967), p. 17.
14. *The UFO Evidence*, p. 106; also Ruppelt, *op. cit.*, pp. 15–24.
15. Donald E. Keyhoe, "The Flying Saucers Are Real," *True* (January, 1950).
16. Ruppelt, *op. cit.*, p. 22.
17. *Ibid.*, p. 16.

CHAPTER 3

1. Edward J. Ruppelt, *The Report on Unidentified Flying Objects* (Garden City, New York, Doubleday and Company, 1956), p. 16.
2. *Ibid.*, pp. 31–32.
3. *Ibid.*, p. 32.
4. *Ibid.*
5. Donald H. Menzel and Lyle G. Boyd, *The World of Flying Saucers* (Garden City, New York, Doubleday and Company, 1963), p. 34.

6. Donald E. Keyhoe, *Flying Saucers from Outer Space* (New York, Henry Holt and Company, 1953), p. 32.

7. Ruppelt, *op. cit.*, p. 34.

8. *Ibid.*, p. 39.

9. Menzel and Boyd, *op. cit.*, p. 38.

10. Jacques Vallee, *Anatomy of a Phenomenon* (Chicago, Henry Regnery Company, 1965), p. 52.

11. Ruppelt, *op. cit.*, p. 37.

12. Coral E. Lorenzen, *Flying Saucers: The Startling Evidence of the Invasion from Outer Space* (originally titled *The Great Flying Saucer Hoax*) (New York, Signet Books, 1966), p. 23.

13. *The UFO Evidence*, Richard Hall, ed. (Washington, D.C., The National Investigations Committee on Aerial Phenomena, 1964), p. 106.

14. Keyhoe, *op. cit.*, p. 33.

15. *The UFO Evidence*, p. 130.

16. *Ibid.*

17. Ruppelt, *op. cit.*, p. 40.

18. Menzel and Boyd, *op. cit.*, pp. 108–109.

19. *Ibid.*, p. 111.

20. Ruppelt, *op. cit.*, p. 41.

21. *Ibid.*

22. *Ibid.*, p. 42.

23. Menzel and Boyd, *op. cit.*, pp. 80, 85.

24. Vallee, *op. cit.*, p. 55.

25. Keyhoe, *op. cit.*, p. 40.

26. *The UFO Evidence*, p. 84.

27. *Ibid.*, p. 23.

28. Ruppelt, *op. cit.*, pp. 50, 55.

29. Menzel and Boyd, *op. cit.*, pp. 93–94.

30. *The Saturday Evening Post* (May 16, 1953).

31. Ruppelt, *op. cit.*, p. 52.

32. *Ibid.*, p. 60.

33. *Ibid.*

34. *The UFO Evidence*, p. 130.

35. *Ibid.*, p. 53.

36. *True* (January, 1950).

37. *Ibid.*

38. Rudolf Lusar, *German Secret Weapons in the Second World War* (New York, Philosophical Library, 1959).

39. *Saucers*, Vol. 5, No. 1 (Spring, 1957), pp. 10–11.

40. Gerald Heard, *The Riddle of the Flying Saucers: Is Another World Watching?* (London, Carroll & Nicholson, 1950), p. 20.

41. *Atlantic City Press* quoted in *Saucer News* (December, 1955), p. 4.

42. *Flying Saucers* (*Look*, with United Press International and Cowles Publications, Inc., 1967).

43. Ayn Rand, *Atlas Shrugged* (New York, Random House, 1957).

CHAPTER 4

1. *The Australian Flying Saucer Magazine* (May, 1953, quoted in *Saucers*, September, 1954, pp. 4–5).

2. *Saucers* (September, 1954), p. 6.

3. *Nexus* (August, 1954), p. 7.
4. Richard Wilson, *Look* (February 27, 1951).
5. Edward J. Ruppelt, *The Report on Unidentified Flying Saucers* (Garden City, New York, Doubleday and Company, 1956).
6. *Ibid.*, pp. 102–103.
7. *Ibid.*, pp. 96–97.
8. Donald H. Menzel and Lyle G. Boyd, *The World of Flying Saucers* (Garden City, New York, Doubleday and Company, 1963), p. 127.
9. Ruppelt, *op. cit.* (1960 edition), p. 276.
10. Menzel and Boyd, *op. cit.*, p. 127.
11. *Ibid.*
12. James W. Moseley, *Nexus* (November, 1954), pp. 5–8.
13. Lloyd Mallan, *The Official Guide to UFO's* (New York, Science and Mechanics Publishing Co., 1967), p. 37.
14. *The UFO Evidence*, Richard Hall, ed. (Washington, D.C., The National Investigations Committee on Aerial Phenomena, 1964), p. 131.
15. *Ibid.;* also Ruppelt, *op. cit.*, pp. 111, 113.
16. *The UFO Evidence*, p. 84.
17. *Ibid.*, p. 113; also Ruppelt, *op. cit.*, pp. 112–113.
18. Ruppelt, *op. cit.*
19. *Ibid.*, p. 117.
20. *Ibid.*, p. 120.
21. *Ibid.*
22. *Ibid.*, p. 122.
23. *Ibid.*
24. *The UFO Evidence*, p. 107.
25. *Life* (April 7, 1952); also Ruppelt, *op. cit.*, pp. 132–133.
26. *Ibid.*
27. *The UFO Evidence*, p. 107; also Ruppelt, *op. cit.*, p. 132.
28. Ruppelt, *op. cit.*, p. 138.
29. *Time* (June 9, 1952).
30. Ruppelt, *op. cit.*
31. *Ibid.*, p. 118.
32. "Special Report No. 14," *Project Blue Book* (United States Air Force).
33. *The UFO Evidence;* also Ruppelt, *op. cit.*, p. 141.
34. Ruppelt, *op. cit.*
35. *Ibid.*, p. 157.
36. *Ibid.*
37. *The UFO Evidence*, pp. 38–39.
38. Nash & Fort. *True* (October, 1952).
39. *Ibid.*
40. Ruppelt, *op. cit.*, p. 158.
41. *Ibid.*, p. 164.
42. *Ibid.*
43. Mallan, *op. cit.*, pp. 48–49.
44. *Saucer News* (December, 1956).
45. Brad Steiger, *The Flying Saucer Menace* (New York, Universal Publishing and Distributing Corp., 1967), pp. 44–45.
46. John Keel, *True.*
47. Ruppelt, *op. cit.*, p. 187.
48. *Ibid.*, p. 189.

CHAPTER 5

1. Edward J. Ruppelt, *The Report on Unidentified Flying Objects* (Garden City, New York, Doubleday and Company, 1956), p. 210.
2. *Ibid.*, p. 211.
3. *Ibid.*, p. 212.
4. *Ibid.*, p. 223.
5. *The New York Times* (January 28, 1953).
6. *The Flying Saucers Are Real* and *Flying Saucers from Outer Space* (New York, Henry Holt and Company, 1950 and 1953).
7. Donald E. Keyhoe, *Flying Saucers from Outer Space* (New York, Henry Holt and Company, 1953).
8. Desmond Leslie and George Adamski, *Flying Saucers Have Landed* (London, Werner Laurie, 1953), p. 171.
9. Bob Grant, *Real*, Vol. 17, No. 3 (August, 1966), p. 11.
10. Desmond Leslie and George Adamski, *Flying Saucers Have Landed* (London, Werner Laurie, 1953).
11. Kenneth Arnold and Ray Palmer, *The Coming of the Saucers* (Amherst, Wisconsin, privately printed, 1952).
12. Leslie and Adamski, *op. cit.*, p. 172.
13. *Ibid.*, p. 173.
14. *Ibid.*, p. 188.
15. *Ibid.*, pp. 185–208.

CHAPTER 6

1. Albert K. Bender, *Space Review*, Vol. 2, No. 4 (October, 1953), p. 1.
2. Bridgeport *Sunday Herald*, undated clipping; reprinted in *Saucers* (March, 1954), p. 10.
3. *Saucer News*, Vol. 3, No. 2 (February/March, 1956), p. 4.
4. *Ibid.*, p. 5.
5. Albert K. Bender, *Flying Saucers and the Three Men in Black* (Clarksburg, West Virginia, Saucerian Books, 1963).
6. *Ibid.*
7. Lloyd Mallan, *The Official Guide to UFO's* (New York, Science and Mechanics Publishing Co.), pp. 44–52, 78–79.
8. James W. Moseley, *Saucer News* (April/May, 1958), pp. 10–13.
9. Not the Wilkins of *Flying Saucers on the Attack*.
10. *Flying Saucers* (June, 1957), p. 84.
11. Steven Tyler, *Pageant* (July, 1966), p. 46.
12. *Ettela'at* (Tehran, Iraq, October 15, 1954).
13. Truman Bethurum, *Aboard a Flying Saucer* (Los Angeles, DeVorss and Company, 1954).
14. *Ibid.*, pp. 32–33.
15. *Ibid.*, p. 34.
16. *Ibid.*, p. 36.
17. Unspecified quotes following the last citation are also drawn from *Aboard a Flying Saucer*.

CHAPTER 7

1. Daniel W. Fry, *The White Sands Incident* (Pasadena, California, Franklin Thomas, 1956).
2. *Ibid.,* p. 22.
3. *Ibid.,* p. 59.
4. New York, The Citadel Press, 1954.
5. Herman Oberth, "Flying Saucers Come from a Distant World" *American Weekly* (New York Journal American, October 24, 1954).
6. *Ibid.*
7. New Orleans *States-Item* (August 2, 1969).
8. Brad Steiger, *The Flying Saucer Menace* (New York, Universal Publishing and Distributing Company, 1967).
9. *Saucer News* (October/November, 1955).
10. Harold T. Wilkins, *Flying Saucers Uncensored* (New York, The Citadel Press, 1955).
11. Morris K. Jessup, *The Case for the UFO* (New York, The Citadel Press, 1955), pp. 17–18.
12. *Ibid.,* pp. 23, 26.
13. *Ibid.,* p. 27.
14. *Ibid.*
15. *Ibid.,* p. 28.
16. *Ibid.,* p. 33.
17. *Ibid.,* p. 34.
18. *Ibid.,* p. 37.
19. *Ibid.*
20. *Ibid.,* p. 39.
21. Fry, *op. cit.,* p. 40; also his *Step to the Stars* (Lakemont, Georgia, CSA Publishers, 1956).
22. Jessup, *op. cit.,* p. 40.
23. *Ibid.,* pp. 47–48.
24. *Ibid.,* p. 49.
25. Morris K. Jessup, *The UFO and the Bible* (New York, The Citadel Press, 1956).

CHAPTER 8

1. Aimé Michel, *The Truth about Flying Saucers,* trans. from *Lueur sur les Soucoupes Volantes* (New York, Criterion Books, 1956).
2. Morris K. Jessup, *The UFO and the Bible* (New York, The Citadel Press, 1956).
3. Earl Nelson, *There Is Life on Mars* (New York, The Citadel Press, 1956).
4. Frank Edwards, *Strangest of All* (New York, Citadel Press, 1956).
5. Rupert T. Gould, *Enigmas* (London, Philip Allan and Company, 1929).
6. Buck Nelson, *My Trip to Mars, the Moon and Venus* (Grand Rapids, Michigan, UFO-rum—Grand Rapids Flying Saucer Club, 1956).
7. James W. Moseley, *Saucer News* (June/July, 1956).
8. George W. Van Tassel, *The Council of the Seven Lights* (Los Angeles, DeVorss and Company, 1958), p. 81.
9. *Ibid.*
10. *Ibid.,* p. 83.
11. *Ibid.*
12. *Ibid.,* p. 15.
13. *Ibid.*
14. Long John Nebel, *The Way Out World* (Englewood Cliffs, New Jersey, Prentice-Hall, Inc., 1961), p. 50.

15. *Ibid.*
16. *Ibid.*
17. George W. Van Tassel, *Into This World and Out Again* (Los Angeles, DeVorss and Company).
18. Howard Menger, *From Outer Space to You* (Clarksburg, West Virginia, Saucerian Books, 1959), p. 24.
19. *Ibid.*, pp. 26–27.
20. *Ibid.*, p. 31.
21. *Ibid.*, p. 33.
22. *Ibid.*, p. 36.
23. *Ibid.*, pp. 51–52.
24. *Ibid.*, p. 74.

CHAPTER 9

1. Howard Menger, *From Outer Space to You* (Clarksburg, West Virginia, Saucerian Books, 1959), p. 91.
2. *Ibid.*, p. 92.
3. *Ibid.*, pp. 99–100.
4. *Ibid.*, p. 121.
5. *Ibid.*, p. 126.
6. Long John Nebel, *The Way Out World* (Englewood Cliffs, New Jersey, Prentice Hall, Inc., 1961), p. 64.
7. Steven Tyler, *Pageant* (July, 1966).
8. Donald E. Keyhoe, *Flying Saucers: Top Secret* (New York, G. P. Putnam's Sons, 1960), pp. 108–109.
9. *Ibid.*, p. 113.
10. *The UFO Evidence,* Richard Hall, ed. (Washington, D.C., The National Investigations Committee on Aerial Phenomena, 1964), p. 168.
11. *Flying Saucers* (February, 1965).
12. Keyhoe, *op. cit.*, p. 115.
13. *Ibid.*
14. Donald H. Menzel and Lyle G. Boyd, *The World of Flying Saucers* (Garden City, New York, Doubleday and Company, 1963), p. 176.
15. Keyhoe, *op. cit.*, pp. 128–129.
16. *Flying Saucers* (February, 1960).
17. *Ibid.* (October, 1959).
18. *Ibid.* (May, 1958).
19. *Ibid.* (July, 1959).
20. *Saucer News* (June, 1963).
21. *Ibid.*
22. *Ibid.* (September, 1962).
23. *Ibid.* (June, 1963).

CHAPTER 10

1. *Flying Saucers* (February, 1961, pp. 27–58), reprinted from *APRO* (Aerial Phenomena Research Organization) *Bulletin.*
2. Joao Martins, *O Cruzeiro* (Rio de Janeiro, Brazil, March 8, 1958).

3. *Ibid.*
4. *O Jornal* (Rio de Janeiro, Brazil, February 22, 1958). *Diario No Noite* (São Paulo, Brazil, February 22, 1958).
5. *O Globo* (Rio de Janeiro, Brazil, February 27, 1958).
6. *O Jornal* (February 26, 1958).
7. *O Globo* (February 27, 1958).
8. *United Press* (February 24, 1958). For other material on the Brazilian sighting, see *Diario do Congresso Nacional* (Brazilian Government Printing Office, February 27, 1958); *O Cruzeiro* (May 3 and June 7, 1958); *Correio de Manha* (February 23 and 25, and April 17, 1958); *O Jornal* (April 17, 1958); *O Globo* (February 21, 24, and 28, 1958); *Jornal do Brazil* (Rio de Janeiro, Brazil, April 17, 1958); *Ultima Hora* (Rio de Janeiro, Brazil, February 21, 22, and 23, 1958); *Folha da Tarde* (Rio de Janeiro, Brazil, February 25, 1958); *Diario Carioca* (Rio de Janeiro, Brazil, February 23, 1958); *O Estados de São Paulo* (São Paulo, Brazil, February 23 and 25, 1958).
9. Donald E. Keyhoe, *Flying Saucers: Top Secret* (New York, G. P. Putnam's Sons, 1960), pp. 158–159.
10. *Ibid.,* p. 163.
11. *Ibid.,* pp. 164–165.
12. C. G. Jung, *Flying Saucers: A Modern Myth of Things Seen in the Skies* (New York, Harcourt, Brace and Company, 1959).
13. Zurich, Rascher Cie. AG., 1958.
14. Orfeo Angelucci, *The Secret of the Saucers* (Amherst, Wisconsin, Amherst Press, 1955).
15. Fred Hoyle, *The Black Cloud* (London, William Heinemann, Ltd., 1957).
16. John Wyndham, *The Midwich Cuckoos* (London, Michael Joseph, Ltd., 1957).

CHAPTER 11

1. *Flying Saucers* (July, 1959), pp. 14–19; reprinted from Detroit, Michigan, *Times* (circa late February, 1958).
2. Donald E. Keyhoe, *Flying Saucers: Top Secret* (New York, G. P. Putnam's Sons, 1960), p. 30.
3. *Ibid.,* p. 31.
4. New York *Herald Tribune* (February 25, 1959).
5. Keyhoe, *op. cit.,* p. 32.
6. *Ibid.*
7. *Flying Saucers* (July, 1959), p. 17.
8. Keyhoe, *op. cit.,* p. 34.
9. *Saucer News,* Vol. 6, No. 2 (February/March, 1959), pp. 10–14.
10. Edward J. Ruppelt, *The Report on Unidentified Flying Objects* (Garden City, New York, Doubleday and Company, Inc., 1956), p. 157.
11. Keyhoe, *op. cit.,* p. 33.
12. Richard Gehman, *True* (January, 1961).
13. *Ibid.*
14. Long John Nebel, *The Way Out World* (Englewood Cliffs, New Jersey, Prentice-Hall, 1961), p. 74.
15. See *ibid.,* pp. 73–81, for more on the Oklahoma episode.
16. Orfeo Angelucci, *The Secret of the Saucers* (Amherst, Wisconsin, Amherst Press, 1955).
17. The foregoing quotations are from Angelucci's *Son of the Sun* (Los Angeles, DeVorss & Company, 1959), which is recommended for the full story of Adam.

CHAPTER 12

1. Ray Palmer, *Flying Saucers* (December, 1959), p. 8.
2. *Ibid.*, p. 9.
3. *Ibid.*
4. *Ibid.*, p. 10.
5. *Ibid.*, pp. 10–13.
6. *Ibid.*, p. 16.
7. *Ibid.*, pp. 19–21.
8. *Flying Saucers* (May, 1962).
9. Long John Nebel, *The Way Out World* (Englewood Cliffs, New Jersey, Prentice-Hall, Inc., 1961), p. 68.
10. *Ibid.*
11. *Ibid.*, pp. 68–69.
12. Frank Edwards, Jackie Gleason, and Gray Barker on *The Long John Nebel Show* (February 5, 1960).
13. Nebel, *op. cit.*, p. 54.
14. *The Long John Nebel Show* (February 19, 1960); also see Nebel, *op. cit.*, pp. 54–56.
15. Author's files, courtesy of Long John Nebel.
16. *Saucer News*, Vol. 7, No. 2 (June, 1960), p. 16.
17. Edward J. Ruppelt, *The Report on Unidentified Flying Objects* (Garden City, New York, Doubleday & Company, Inc., 1956).
18. Lawrence J. Tacker, *Flying Saucers and the U.S. Air Force* (Princeton, New Jersey, D. Van Nostrand Company, Inc., 1960), p. 31.
19. *Ibid.*, p. 15.
20. Ruppelt, *op. cit.*, p. 20.
21. Tacker, *op. cit.*, p. 20.
22. Donald H. Menzel and Lyle G. Boyd, *The World of Flying Saucers* (Garden City, New York, Doubleday & Company, Inc., 1963), pp. 108–109.
23. *Ibid.*
24. Tacker, *op. cit.*, p. 22.
25. *Ibid.*, p. 33.
26. *Ibid.*
27. Ruppelt, *op. cit.*, p. 59.
28. *Ibid.*, p. 225.
29. *Flying Saucers* (July, 1961), pp. 15–16; reprinted from *Australian Flying Saucer Review*.
30. George D. Fawcett, *Flying Saucers* (September, 1961), p. 53.
31. *Flying Saucers* (September, 1961), p. 57.
32. *Ibid.*, p. 49.
33. *Ibid.*, p. 49.
34. *Ibid.*, p. 50.
35. *Ibid.*
36. *Ibid.*, p. 57.
37. *Ibid.*
38. Richard Ogden, *Saucer News*, pp. 11–12.
39. *Ibid.*
40. *Ibid.*
41. *Ibid.*
42. Lloyd Mallan, *The Official Guide to UFO's* (New York, Science and Mechanics Publishing Co., 1967), p. 14.
43. *Ibid.*, p. 15.
44. *Ibid.*
45. Dan Martin, *The Watcher* (Clarksburg, West Virginia, Saucerian Publications, 1961), p. 2.

46. *Ibid.*, p. 3.
47. *Ibid.*
48. *Ibid.*, p. 6.
49. *Ibid.*, p. 7.
50. *The Book of Enoch*, same being apocryphal, but not of *The Apocrypha*; Ecclesiasticus, of *The Apocrypha*. II:14.
51. Martin, *op. cit.*, p. 7.
52. *Ibid.*, p. 8.
53. *Ibid.*, p. 15.

CHAPTER 13

1. Donald E. Keyhoe, *The True Report on Flying Saucers*, No. 1 (New York, Fawcett Publications, Inc., 1967).
2. *Saucer News*, Vol. 8, No. 1 (March, 1961), p. 13.
3. Roberto Pinotti, *Flying Saucers* (January, 1966), p. 54.
4. Daniel W. Fry, *Step to the Stars* (Lakemont, Georgia, CSA Publishers, 1956).
5. Frank Carter, *Flying Saucers*, pp. 10–16, 66–74.
6. *Saucer News*, Vol. 8, No. 1 (March, 1961), p. 14.
7. Alex Sanders, *Flying Saucers* (May, 1962), p. 33; reprinted from *Star Weekly Magazine* (July, 1961), article by Mark Gayn.
8. *Ibid.*, pp. 35–36.
9. *Ibid.*, pp. 36–37.
10. New York, Citadel Press, Inc., 1957.
11. Lloyd Mallan, *The Official Guide to UFO's* (New York, Science and Mechanics Publishing Co., 1967), p. 12.
12. Brinsley Le Poer Trench, *Flying Saucers* (January, 1963), p. 21.
13. Gray Barker, *Book of Saucers* (Clarksburg, West Virginia, Saucerian Books, 1965), pp. 51–52.
14. Clarksburg, West Virginia, Saucerian Books, 1959.
15. (New York, Channel 9, WOR-TV).
16. *Life* (March 9, 1962).
17. *Flying Saucers*, No. 2 (New York, Dell Publishing Company, Inc., 1967), pp. 22–23.
18. *La Domenica del Corriere* (Italy, October 28, 1962).
19. Ralph Rankow, *Flying Saucers*, p. 18.
20. *Ibid.*
21. *La Settimana Incom Illustrata* (Italy, December 23, 1962).
22. Roberto Pinotti, *Flying Saucers* (January, 1966), p. 59.
23. *Ibid.*, pp. 59–60.
24. *Saucer News*, p. 11.
25. *Ibid.*
26. Jacques Vallee, *Anatomy of a Phenomenon* (Chicago, Henry Regnery Company, 1965), pp. 160–161.
27. *Saucer News*, p. 12.
28. *Ibid.*
29. *Ibid.*, pp. 12–13.
30. *Ibid.*, p. 13.
31. *Correio de Manha* (Rio de Janeiro, Brazil, August 26, 1962).
32. *Ibid.*

CHAPTER 14

1. *The UFO Evidence,* Richard Hall, ed. (Washington, D.C., The National Investigations Committee on Aerial Phenomena, 1964), p. 140.

2. *Flying Saucers* (June, 1964), p. 56.

3. Modesto, California, *Bee* (February 28, 1963).

4. *Flying Saucers, loc. cit.;* also *The UFO Evidence, loc. cit.*

5. *Flying Saucers, loc. cit.*

6. *Ibid.*

7. *Ibid.*

8. *Saucer News* (September, 1963), p. 18.

9. *Flying Saucers, loc. cit.*

10. *Ibid.*

11. Gordon H. Evans, *Flying Saucers* (August, 1964), pp. 9-10.

12. *Ibid.,* p. 9.

13. *Ibid.,* p. 10.

14. *Flight International* (England, August 15, 1963).

15. (August 15, 1963).

16. Racine, Wisconsin, *Journal Times* (August 5, 1963); also *Flying Saucers* (June, 1964), p. 58.

17. *The UFO Evidence,* p. 141.

18. *Flying Saucers* (September, 1963), pp. 63-64.

19. *Ibid.* (January, 1966), pp. 50-51.

20. Lloyd Mallan, *The Official Guide to UFO's* (New York, Science and Mechanics Publishing Co., 1967), p. 9; Painesville, Ohio, *Telegraph* (May 9, 1964); *Saucer News* (September, 1964), p. 9.

21. Mallan, *op. cit.*

22. Mallan, *op. cit.,* p. 10; Coral Lorenzen, *Fate* (August, 1964), pp. 27-38; The National Investigations Committee on Aerial Phenomena *Special Bulletin* (June 8, 1964).

23. Charles Richards, *United Press International* (April 26, 1964).

24. Mallan, *op. cit.,* p. 10.

25. Mallan, *op. cit.*

26. Frank Edwards, *Flying Saucers—Serious Business* (New York: Lyle Stuart, 1966), p. 247.

27. Several, among scores, of sources for the Lonnie Zamora (Socorro, New Mexico) incident: Painesville, Ohio, *Telegraph;* The National Investigations Committee on Aerial Phenomena *Special Bulletin; Fate; Saucer News* (September, 1964); *Flying Saucers* (April, 1965); Frank Edwards, *op. cit.;* Mallan, *op. cit.*

28. *Saucer News* (September, 1964), p. 9.

29. *Ibid.,* p. 8.

30. *Ibid.*

31. Albuquerque *Journal* (April 28, 1964).

32. Coral Lorenzen, *Fate* (August, 1964).

33. Los Angeles *Herald Examiner* (April 28, 1964).

34. Los Angeles *Times* (April 28, 1964); *Saucer News,* p. 9.

35. Los Angeles *Herald Examiner* (April 28, 1964); Albuquerque *Tribune* (April 28, 1964); Lorenzen, *op. cit.,* pp. 41-42; *Saucer News,* p. 10.

36. Lorenzen, *op. cit.,* p. 42.

37. Albuquerque *Journal* (April 29, 1964).

38. Albuquerque *Tribune* (April 29, 1964).

39. *Ibid.*

40. *Ibid.*

41. *Ibid.*

42. *Saucer News* (December, 1964), pp. 19-20.

43. New York *Journal American* (September 11, 1964).

44. Mallan, *op. cit.,* pp. 50-51.

45. George D. Fawcett, *Flying Saucers* (March, 1966), pp. 58–60; *ibid.* (October, 1966), p. 30.

46. *Flying Saucers* (January, 1966), pp. 28–38.

47. *Ibid.*

48. Richmond, Virginia, *Times-Dispatch* (January 15, 17, 1964); also *Flying Saucers* (January, 1966).

49. *Ibid.*

50. *Ibid.*

51. John A. Keel, *Flying Saucers: UFO Reports* (New York, Dell Publishing Company, Inc., 1967), pp. 58–60.

52. Edwards, *op. cit.*, p. 282.

53. *Ibid.*, p. 302.

54. Alameda, California, *Times-Star* (August 10, 1965); reprinted in Edwards, *op. cit.*

55. Brad Steiger, *Flying Saucer Menace* (New York, Universal Publishing and Distributing Corporation, 1967), p. 45.

56. London *Daily Express* (August 27, 1965); also Kazakhstan, U.S.S.R., *Pravda* (September, 1965), reprinted in Edwards. *op. cit.*

57. John G. Fuller, *Incident in Exeter* (New York, G. P. Putnam's Sons, 1966).

58. *Ibid.*, p. 13.

59. *Ibid.*

60. *Ibid.*, p. 14.

61. *Ibid.*, p. 73.

62. *Ibid.*

63. *Ibid.*

64. Mallan, *op. cit.*, p. 23.

65. Fuller, *op. cit.*; Edwards, *op. cit.*, pp. 297–300; Mallan, *op. cit.*, p. 23; Steiger, *op. cit.*, p. 46; *Saucer News* (December, 1965), p. 15, and (March, 1966), p. 21; *The True Report on Flying Saucers*, No. 1 (New York, Fawcett Publications, Inc., 1967), pp. 26–28; *et. al.*

66. Freeport, Texas, *Brazo-Sport Facts* (September 6, 9, 1965); *Saucer News* (March, 1966), p. 28; Edwards, *op. cit.*, pp. 295–297; *The True Report on Flying Saucers*, p. 93.

67. *Saucer News* (March, 1966), p. 24.

68. *Ibid.*, p. 26.

69. Edwards, *op. cit.*, p. 259.

70. *Ibid.*, p. 261.

71. John J. Robinson, *Saucer News* (March, 1966), pp. 4–8; Edwards, *op. cit.*, pp. 255–270; Fuller, *op. cit.*, pp. 230–238.

72. *Flying Saucers* (October, 1966), p. 39; reprinted from *The Cosmic Brotherhood International Weekly* (Yokohama, Japan).

73. *Ibid.*

74. San Diego, California, *Union* (October 1, 1965).

75. *Saucer News* (March, 1965), p. 24.

76. St. Paul, Minnesota, *Pioneer Press* (October 25, 1965) and Minneapolis *Star* (October 25, 1965).

CHAPTER 15

1. Brad Steiger, *Flying Saucer Menace* (New York, Universal Publishing and Distributing Corporation, 1967), pp. 22–26.

2. *Ibid.*

3. *Ibid.*

4. Steiger, *op. cit.*

5. Lloyd Mallan, *The Official Guide to UFO's* (New York, Science and Mechanics Publishing Co., 1967), p. 49.

6. Steiger, *op cit.*, pp. 25–26.
7. Mallan, *op. cit.*, pp. 64–65.
8. *Ibid.*
9. Donald E. Keyhoe, *True* (January, 1966), pp. 35–36.
10. *The New York Times* (March 22, 1966).
11. *Ibid.*
12. *Ibid.*
13. *Ibid.* (March 23, 1966).
14. *Ibid.*
15. *Saucer News* (June, 1966), p. 24.
16. Re March Michigan sightings also see: La Crosse, Wisconsin, *Tribune* (March 14, 1966); Detroit *News* (March 14, 21, 22, 1966); Battle Creek, Michigan, *Engineer and News* (March 17 and 21, 1966); Marshall, Michigan, *Evening Chronicle,* (March 21, 1966); Kalamazoo, Michigan, *Gazette* (March 22, 1966); Indianapolis, Indiana, *Star* (March 22, 1966); South Haven, Michigan, *Daily Tribune* (March 22, 1966); New York *Daily News* (March 24, 25, 1966); New York *Herald Tribune* (March 23, 1966); New York *World-Telegram* (March 25, 1966); New York *Journal-American* (March 26, 27, 1966); United Press International (various dates) *Saga* (June, 1967), pp. 22–25 and 70–76; *Flying Saucers* (June, 1967), pp. 9–11.
17. *The New York Times* (March 27, 1966).
18. Steiger, *op. cit.*, pp. 29–30.
19. *Saucer News.* (Spring, 1967), p. 26.
20. John Fuller, *The Interrupted Journey* (New York, The Dial Press, 1966).
21. Boston *Traveler* (October 25, 26, 1965); Gloucester, Massachusetts, Daily *Times* (October 27, 1965); Manchester, New Hampshire, *Union Leader* (October 26, 1965).
22. Fuller, *op. cit.*, p. 6.
23. *Ibid.*
24. *Flying Saucers* (October, 1966), p. 30.
25. (September 18, 1966).
26. *Saucer News* (Spring, 1967), p. 12.
27. *Ibid.*
28. James E. MacDonald, *The Problem of the Unidentified Flying Object* (Privately printed summary of the remarks, 1967).
29. *Ibid.*
30. *The New York Times* (October 21, 1966).
31. *Ibid.*
32. *Saucer News* (Spring, 1967), pp. 32–33.
33. Spokane, Washington, *Review* (November 18, 1966).
34. Vancouver, Canada, *Sun* (July 22, 1966).
35. Malvern, Arkansas, *Daily Record* (August 23, 1966).
36. London *Flying Saucer Review* (March/April, 1967), pp. 6–7.
37. Greenville, Mississippi, *Delta Democrat Times* (September 2, 1966).
38. *Flying Saucer Review, loc. cit.*
39. Wheeling, West Virginia, *Intelligencer* (November 17, 1966); Martins Ferry, Ohio, *Times-Leader* (November 19, 1966); *Saucer News* (Spring, 1967), p. 36.
40. *Saucer News* (Spring, 1967), p. 36.
41. *Ibid.*
42. Theodore Flournoy, *Des Indes à la planète Mars: Etude sur un cas de somnambulisme avec glossolalie* (Geneva, Switzerland, Eggimain, 1900).
43. Gray Barker, *They Knew Too Much About Flying Saucers.* (New York, A Tower Book, 1967), p. 10.
44. *Ibid.*, p. 12.
45. *Ibid.*, p. 17.
46. *Saucer News* (Spring, 1967), p. 36.
47. Barker, *op. cit.*, p. 18.
48. *Saucer News* (Spring, 1967); Steiger, *op.cit.*, p. 44.

49. Jim and Coral Lorenzen, *UFOs over the Americas* (New York, New American Library, 1968), pp. 122–147.

50. *Ibid.*

51. J. Allen Hynek, "Are Flying Saucers Real?" *Saturday Evening Post* (December 17, 1966), pp. 17–21.

52. *Flying Saucer Review*, p. 30.

53. New York *World Journal Tribune* (September 21, 1966); Burlington, New York, *Free Press* (September 24, 1966); Boston *Globe* (October 24 and 26, 1966); Hynek, *loc. cit.*; *Saucer News* (Winter, 1966–67), p. 12.

54. *Saucer News* (Spring, 1967), p. 15.

55. *Ibid.*

56. Herman Oberth, *By Rocket to Interplanetary Space* (Germany, 1923).

57. Huntsville, Alabama, *Times* (February 1, 1967), reprinted in Steiger, *op. cit.*, p. 30.

58. *Ibid.*

CHAPTER 16

1. For this, and other magazines mentioned, see Appendix IV.

2. (February 4, 1967), pp. 70–73.

3. *Flying Saucers: UFO Reports, No. 2* (New York, Dell Publishing Company, 1967), pp. 14–15.

4. *Ibid.*, p. 15.

5. *Saucer News* (Summer, 1967), p. 22.

6. Orlando, Florida, *Sentinel* (February 3, 1967); London *Sunday Telegraph* (February 5, 1967); Newark, New Jersey, *Star-Ledger* (January 29, 1967); *Flying Saucer Review*, London (March/April, 1967), p. 10.

7. New York *World Journal Tribune* (March 31, 1967).

8. Arizona *Daily Wildcat* (April 6, 1967).

9. Author's copy of the transcript of the address, courtesy of Dr. McDonald.

10. *The New York Times* (April 24, 1967).

11. New York *World Journal Tribune* (April 23, 1967).

12. Eric Wright, *National Enquirer* (September 10, 1967).

13. *Ibid.*

14. *Ibid.*

15. *Ibid.*

16. *Ibid.*

17. New York *World Journal Tribune* (April 12, 1967).

18. *Bulletin of Atomic Sciences* (June, 1967), pp. 43–44.

19. Donald E. Keyhoe, *Flying Saucers: Top Secret* (New York, G. P. Putnam's Sons, 1960), p. 30.

20. *Ibid.*, p. 31.

21. *UFO Evidence*, Richard Hall, ed. (Washington, D. C., The National Committee on Aerial Phenomena, 1964), pp. 173–177.

22. *The New York Times* (June 11, 1967).

23. *Ibid.*, June 18, 1967.

24. Newcastle, England, *Journal* (August 11 and 18, 1967); *Orbit*, Vol. 8, No. 2.

25. *Orbit*, Vol. 8, No. 2.

26. *The New York Times* (September 5, 1967).

27. *Ibid*; also Boston *Record American* (September 5, 1967); Toronto *Daily Star* (October 6, 1967).

28. Ross Yockey, New Orleans *States-Item* (September 22, 1967).

29. *Science* (September, 1967); New York *Post* (October 9, 1967).

30. *Ibid.*

31. New York *Sunday News* (October 22, 1967); the New York *Post* (October 9, 1967).
32. New York *Sunday News* (October 22, 1967).
33. *Ibid.*
34. New York *Post* (October 22, 1967).
35. London *Daily Express* (October 25, 1967); London *Daily Sketch* (October 26, 1967).
36. Calgary *Albertian* (October 14, 1967); Ottawa *Citizen* (October 21, 1967); *Saucer News* (Winter, 1967/1968), p. 16.
37. Toronto *Daily Star* (October 12, 1967); Toronto *Telegram* (September 18, 1967).
38. Toronto *Daily Star* (November 7, 1967).
39. Jon Ruddy, "Look There's a Flying Saucer" *Maclean's,* Toronto (November, 1967), p. 35.
40. *Ibid.,* pp. 93–94.
41. *Ibid.,* p. 93.
42. *Ibid.*
43. *Ibid.,* p. 36.
44. *Ibid.,* p. 92.
45. *Ibid.,* p. 36.
46. Henry Kamm, *The New York Times* (December 10, 1967).
47. *Ibid.*
48. *Ibid.*; also *Smena,* U.S.S.R. (April, 1967).
49. *The New York Times* (December 10, 1967).

CHAPTER 17

1. New York *Daily News* (February 1, 1968).
2. New Orleans *States-Item* (February 14, 1968).
3. *The New York Times* (February 18, 1968).
4. See Chapter 2, footnote 8.
5. *The New York Times* (February 18, 1968).
6. *The New York Times* (March 10, 29; April 4, 12, 14; May 21, 1968); New York *Post* (March 11, 1968); *Time* (March 15, 1968); *Life* (May 3, 1968).
7. *Soviet Life* (February, 1968); *Smena,* U.S.S.R. (September, 1968).
8. *The New York Times* (May 1, 1969).
9. John Fuller, *Look* (May 14, 1968), p. 58.
10. *Ibid.*
11. *Ibid.*
12. *Ibid.*
13. David R. Saunders and R. Roger Harkins, *UFOs? Yes!* (New York, The New American Library, 1968), p. 13.
14. *Ibid.,* p. 14.
15. *Ibid.*
16. *Ibid.,* p. 15.
17. John Fuller, *Aliens in the Skies* (New York, G. P. Putnam's Sons, 1969).
18. *Saucer News* (Summer, 1968), p. 8.
19. *Ibid.*
20. *The New York Times.*
21. See Chapter 2.
22. Santa Fe, New Mexico, *The Luminator* (June/July, 1968), p. 8.
23. New York *Free Press* (August 15, 1968), report of Los Angeles interview by Stan Borman; see Paris Flammonde, *The Kennedy Conspiracy* (New York, Meredith Press, 1969), pp. 39–40.
24. See Flammonde, *op. cit.,* pp. 37–40, on *outré* religious sects.
25. *The Luminator,* p. 4.

26. *The New York Times* (July 14, 1968).
27. *Ibid.*
28. *Ibid.*
29. *The New York Times* (July 25, 1968).
30. *Scientific Study of Unidentified Flying Objects,* Edward U. Condon, director (New York, *Bantam Books,* 1969).
31. *Ibid.,* p. 918.
32. *Ibid.*
33. *Ibid.*
34. *Scientific Study of Unidentified Flying Objects,* p. 248.
35. *Ibid.,* p. 256.
36. *Ibid.,* p. 257.
37. *Ibid.,* p. 260.
38. *Ibid.,* p. 266.
39. *Ibid.,* p. 270.
40. *Ibid.,* p. 270.
41. *Ibid.,* p. 273.
42. *Ibid.,* p. 274.
43. *Ibid.,* p. 273.
44. *Ibid.,* p. 277.
45. *Ibid.,* p. 280.
46. *Ibid.,* pp. 281–282.
47. *Ibid.,* p. 285.
48. *Ibid.,* p. 286.
49. *Ibid.,* p. 290.
50. *Ibid.,* p. 291.
51. *Ibid.,* p. 295.
52. *Ibid.,* p. 300.
53. *Ibid.,* p. 305.
54. *Ibid.,* p. 306.
55. *Ibid.,* p. 310.
56. *Ibid.,* p. 316.
57. *Ibid.,* pp. 323–324.
58. *Ibid.,* p. 326.
59. *Ibid.,* p. 329.
60. *Ibid.,* p. 331.
61. *Ibid.,* p. 332.
62. *Ibid.,* pp. 333–334.
63. *Ibid.,* p. 339.
64. *Ibid.,* p. 341.
65. *Ibid.,* pp. 407–415.
66. *Ibid.,* pp. 415–418.
67. *Ibid.,* pp. 418–426.
68. *Ibid.,* pp. 396–407.
69. *Ibid.,* p. 399.
70. *Ibid.,* p. 407.
71. *Ibid.,* p. 17.
72. *Ibid.,* p. 1.
73. Roscoe Drummund, New York *Herald Tribune* (April 6, 1966).
74. Ivan Sanderson, *Uninvited Visitors* (New York, Cowles Education Corporation, 1967); also see Vincent Gaddis, *True,* "Are Flying Saucers Really Creatures That Live in Outer Space?" (August, 1967).

OUTLINE HISTORY OF
THE UNITED STATES AIR FORCE AND
UNIDENTIFIED FLYING OBJECTS

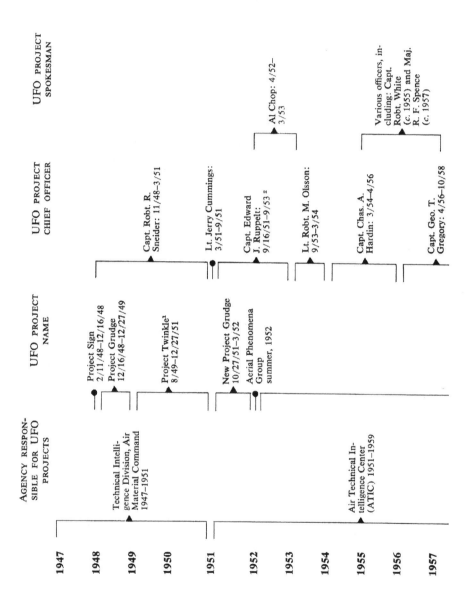

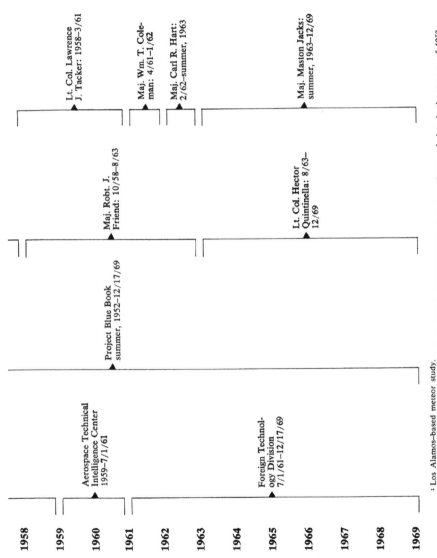

1958 1959 1960 1961 1962 1963 1964 1965 1966 1967 1968 1969

Aerospace Technical Intelligence Center 1959–7/1/61

Foreign Technology Division 7/1/61–12/17/69

Project Blue Book summer, 1952–12/17/69

Maj. Robt. J. Friend: 10/58–8/63

Lt. Col. Hector Quintinella: 8/63–12/69

Lt. Col. Lawrence J. Tacker: 1958–3/61

Maj. Wm. T. Coleman: 4/61–1/62

Maj. Carl R. Hart: 2/62–summer, 1963

Maj. Maston Jacks: summer, 1963–12/69

[1] Los Alamos-based meteor study.
[2] Lt. Robt. M. Olsson substituted for Capt. Edw. J. Ruppelt during his two-month tour of duty in the summer of 1953.

MAJOR UNITED STATES AIR FORCE PANELS, REGULATIONS, REPORTS, AND RELEASES

September 23, 1947   Lt. Gen. N. F. Twining letter to Brig. Gen. George Schulgen recommending the establishment of a security classified Air Force group to investigate Unidentified Flying Objects.

December 30, 1947   Maj. Gen. L. C. Craigie letter to commanding general at Wright-Patterson Air Force Base directing that a "retricted" classification, 2-A priority group, code-named Project Sign, be established under the Air Material Command.

December 13, 1948   Dr. James E. Lipp, Rand Corporation, letter to Brig. Gen. Donald Putt speculating on the possibility of extraterrestrial visitations.

February, 1949   George E. Valley (Massachusetts Institute of Technology), Scientific Advisory Board, U. S. Air Force, evaluation of Project Sign data, Report No. F-TR-2274-IA, Appendix C, recommending continuation and implementation of investigation of Unidentified Flying Objects.

August, 1949   The Project Grudge Report No. 102 AC 49/15-100, classified "Secret," recommending that the operation be "reduced in scope."

December 27, 1949   U. S. Air Force Press Release No. 629-49, disestablishing Project Grudge.

December 27, 1951   Final report of Project Twinkle, established to photograph Unidentified Flying Objects, revealing the program to have had little success.

April 3, 1952   Air Force press release announcing that investigation and analysis of Unidentified Flying Objects had not been discontinued.

April 29, 1952   Air Force Regulation No. 200-5, directing official attitude toward Unidentified Flying Objects and proper processing of reports of same.

May 8, 1952   Secretary for Air Thomas K. Finletter's press statement saying the Air Force would continue studying Unidentified Flying Objects.

July 29, 1952   Maj. Gen. John Samford's press statements attempting to explain the Air Force interpretation of Unidentified Flying Objects, in general, and the Washington "flap" of July, 1952, in particular.

August 1, 1952   The Project Grudge Report No. 102 AC 49/15-100 declassified.

January 14–18, 1953   The meeting of the Scientific Advisory Panel on Unidentified Flying Objects, also known as the Robertson Panel, after the chairman H. P. Robertson, which, in effect, recommended the pacifying of the American people with regard to the excitement caused by Unidentified Flying Objects.

August 26, 1953   Air Force No. 200-2, an updated policy statement on the official attitude toward Unidentified Flying Objects and the proper processing of reports of same.

November 2, 1953   Air Force Regulation No. 200-2A. Amended version of Air Force Regulation No. 200-2. Several other minor changes were introduced to the basic regulation at subsequent times, until it was superseded by Air Force Regulation No. 80-17.

May 5, 1955   Project Blue Book Special Report No. 14 (Project No. 10073) released to the press.

September 28, 1965   Maj. Gen. E. B. LeBailly's letter to the military director, Scientific Advisory Board, recommending a scientific panel be established to evaluate the situation and suggest further policy.

February 3, 1966   The U. S. Air Force Scientific Advisory Board Ad Hoc Committee to Review Project Blue Book, chaired by Dr. Brian O'Brien, met.

March, 1966   The U. S. Air Force Scientific Advisory Board Ad Hoc Committee to Review Project Blue Book submitted a report recommending a broad, in-depth study be accorded the subject of Unidentified Flying Objects.

August 31, 1966   Col. Ivan C. Atkinson, deputy director of the Air Force Office of Scientific Research, approached the University of Colorado (after several other universities had declined the offer) to conduct an investigation of Unidentified Flying Objects, under the auspices and with the financial support of the U. S. Air Force.

September 19, 1966   Air Force Regulation No. 80-17, generally similar in intent to its predecessor, superseded Air Force Regulation No. 200-2 and its various amendments.

October 7, 1966   Public announcement of the establishment of the Scientific Study of Unidentified Flying Objects.

November 1, 1966   The Scientific Study of Unidentified Flying Objects, under the direction of Edward U. Condon, commenced at the University of Colorado.

November 8, 1966   Air Force Regulation No. 80-17A. Amending above.

October 26, 1967   Air Force Regulation No. 80-17(C1). Amending above.

January 31, 1968   Proposed date for concluding the program of the Scientific Study of Unidentified Flying Objects.

September 30, 1968   Air Force Regulation No. 80-17(C2). Amending above.

October 31, 1968   The final report of the Scientific Study of Unidentified Flying Objects was submitted.

January 8, 1969   The final report of the Scientific Study of Unidentified Flying Objects released to public.

December 17, 1969   The United States Air Force news release No. 1077-69 announced the termination of Project Blue Book and the retirement of its records to the USAF Archives, Maxwell Air Force Base, Alabama, thus concluding all official investigation, evaluation, and recognition of phenomena previously classified as Unidentified Flying Objects.

A HISTORY AND DIRECTORY
OF UNIDENTIFIED FLYING OBJECT
AND FLYING SAUCER ORGANIZATIONS

The following cites all of the major Flying Saucer and Unidentified Flying Object organizations in the United States and many of the secondary ones. A number of other minor formations, ones whose main or sole purpose is the publication of a journal of some description, are noted in the subsequent appendix under the heading of the periodical they sponsor. Principal foreign organizations are also included here.

UNITED STATES
(MAJOR)

1. *Aerial Phenomena Research Organization, The,* 3910 East Kleindale Rd., Tucson, Ariz. 85716. Founded in January, 1952, by its present directors, Mr. and Mrs. L. J. (Coral and Jim) Lorenzen. Still functioning in 1970. Accepts extraterrestrial origin of UFOs, including possibility of interplanetarian contact. Has representatives in various countries. Open membership. Publication: *The A.P.R.O. Bulletin.*

2. *Aetherius Society, The,* 674 Crenshaw Blvd., Los Angeles, Calif. 90000. Founded in London during the midfifties by its present chairman, George King, who later transferred the operation to southern California (November, 1960). Still functioning in 1970. Propounds extraterrestrial origin of UFOs and publishes Mr. King's—designated by the space people as "the voice of interplanetary parliament"—psychic communications with aliens as well as with major spiritual figures of Christianity. Has representatives in various countries. Open membership. Publication: *Cosmic Voice; Aetherius Society Newsletter.*

3. *Amalgamated Flying Saucer Clubs of America,* 2004 North Hoover St., Los Angeles, Calif. 90027. Founded in January, 1959, by its present president, Gabriel Green. Still functioning in 1970. Supports

extraterrestrial origin of UFOs, accepting reports of contacts between humans and aliens. Has representatives in various foreign countries. Open membership. Publication: *Flying Saucers International.*

4. *College of Universal Wisdom, The,* P.O. Box 458, Yucca Valley, Calif. 92284. Founded in 1958 by its present president, George Van Tassel, it is the "scientific research branch" of the Ministry of Universal Wisdom, Inc. Still functioning in 1970. Propounds extraterrestrial origin of UFOs, emphasizing contacts beween humans and alien visitors. Activities mostly confined to the United States. Accepts contributing "associates," but has no regular membership. Holds annual conventions in fall. Publication: *Proceedings.*

5. *International Flying Saucer Bureau,* Bridgeport, Conn. Founded in 1952 by Albert K. Bender. Published *Space Review.* Dissolved October, 1953.

6. *National Investigations Committee on Aerial Phenomena,* 1536 Connecticut Ave., N.W., Washington, D.C. 20000. Founded in 1956 by Townsend Brown and shortly thereafter reorganized into its permanent form by its retired director, Maj. Donald E. Keyhoe. Still functioning in 1970. For several years Richard Hall served as acting director, and following his departure from the committee, certain duties were assumed by assistant director Gordon I. R. Lore, Jr. Accepts extraterrestrial origin of UFOs, but for years completely rejected contactee cases; now, although still highly skeptical, the attitude has modified very slightly. The organization's investigations are international in scope. Open membership. Publication: *The UFO Investigator.*

7. *Saucer and Unexplained Celestial Events Research Society,* P.O. Box 163, Fort Lee, N.J. 07024. Founded in 1954 by James W. Moseley, it subsequently devolved into the publishing apparatus for *Saucer News,* its journal. The society's name, function, and periodical were bought by Gray Barker in 1968. New address for *Saucer News:* Saucerian Books, Clarksburg, W. Va. Accepts all possibilities re UFOs: earthian, inner-earthian, extra-earthian, mystical, as well as contactees. Subscriptions, but no regular membership.

8. *Understanding, Inc.,* P.O. Box 206, Merlin, Oreg. 97532. Founded in midfifties by present director, Daniel W. Fry. Propounds extraterrestrial origin of UFOs and supports reports of contacts between humans and aliens. Open membership. Publication: *Understanding.*

UNITED STATES
(MINOR)

9. *Aerial Phenomena Investigations and Research Center, The,* 636 West Cambourne, Ferndale, Mich. 48220. Founded in 1968 by Kevin J. Collins. Publication: *The UFO Phenomenon.*

10. *Aerial Phenomena Investigations Committee, The,* P.O. Box 87, Rugby Sta., Brooklyn, N.Y. 11203. Founded in February, 1959, by Eugene R. Steinberg. Publication: *UFO Reporter.* Magazine absorbed by *Saucer News,* and group dissolved in 1965.

11. *American UFO Committee, The,* 2875 Sequoyah Dr., N.W., Atlanta, Ga. 30300. Founded by Ricky Hilberg. Publication: *UFO Sighter.*

12. *Borderland Sciences Research Associates,* 1103 Bobolink Dr., Vista, Calif. 92083. Founded by Meade Layne (d. summer, 1961). Subsequent director: Riley Crabb. Supports etheric origin of UFOs. Publication: *Round Robin.*

13. *Christian Zion Advocate, The,* P.O. Box 48, Neah Bay, Wash. 98357. Functioned under a variety of designations since 1953. Publication: *The Humanitarian.*

14. *Civil Commission of Aerial Phenomena.* Dissolved about 1960.

15. *Civilian Flying Saucer Investigations Bureau,* 6101 Sturgeon Creek Pkwy., Midland, Mich. 48640. Founded in 1963. Publication: *CFSIB Newsletter.*

16. *Civilian Research, Interplanetary Flying Objects* (Ohio). Supported extraterrestrial origin of UFOs, probably extrasystemic. Publication: *Orbit.* Organization dissolved and publication of periodical suspended.

17. *Civilian Saucer Intelligence* (New York). Founded on February 16, 1954, by Eliot Rockmore. Dissolved in late 1950's.

18. *Cleveland Aerial Phenomena Investigations Club,* 3132 W. 142nd St., Cleveland, Ohio 44111. Founded June, 1964.

19. *Decatur UFO Group* (Illinois). Founded in 1957. Dissolved.

20. *Extraterrestrial Phenomena Investigating Committee,* P.O. Box 622, Schenectady, N.Y. 12300. Founded in 1967 by Jennifer Stevens. Bulletin: *UFO Sky Watch.*

21. *Florida U.F.O. Study Group,* P.O. Box 1355, De Land, Fla. 32720. Founded on April 21, 1968, by George D. Fawcett. Still functioning mid-1969.

22. *Flying Saucer International,* P.O. Box 34, Preuss Sta., Los Angeles, Calif. 90000. Founded by Max Miller. Operated from 1953 to 1960. Publication: *Saucers.* Dissolved.

23. *Flying Saucer Investigating Committee,* P.O. Drawer G, Akron, Ohio 44305. Founded autumn, 1961, by Americo E. Candusso. Publication: *FSIC Bulletin.*

24. *Flying Saucer News Club of America,* 364 West 45th St., New York, N.Y. 10036. Publication: *Flying Saucer News.*

25. *Foundation for Philosophic Advancement, The.* Publication: *Alternate Horizons Newsletter.* Still functioning in 1968.

26. *Grand Rapids Flying Saucer Club.* (Michigan). Founded in 1951. Supported extraterrestrial origin for UFOs, accepted contactee stories. Publication: *Uforum.* Organization dissolved and publication of periodical suspended, probably prior to 1960.

27. *Houston UFO Bureau,* 3302 Askew, Houston, Tex. 77017. Founded summer, 1964, by Gary Kitpatrick. Publication: *UFO Mystery.*

28. *Interplanetary Foundation.* See *Planetary Space Center, The.*

29. *Interplanetary Intelligence of Unidentified Flying Objects,* 3005 Eubanks St., Oklahoma City, Okla. 73100. Founder and director: William F. Riefer. Publication: *Interplanetary Intelligence Report.*

30. *Long Beach Interplanetary Research Group,* 1227 East Second St., Long Beach, Calif. 90802. Founded in 1957 by A. Rowe, secretary. Publication: *Understanding* (not to be confused with Daniel W. Fry's organization and journal of similar and same names).

31. *Morse Fellowship, The,* P.O. Box 370, Littleton, Colo. 80120. Informal group established by Louise Morse in early 1950's; incorporated in 1960; still functioning in 1969. The organization is essentially spiritual/mystical. Publication: *Through the Portals.*

32. *National Investigations Commission on Aerial Phenomena,* 5108 South Findlay St., Seattle, Wash. 98118. Although sometimes designated NICAP, it is not to be confused with the Washington, D.C., organization

bearing a similar name. This group has used several names since its founding in January, 1955. It supports the extraterrestrial origin of UFOs. Publication: *NICAP Reporter*.

33. *New England UFO Study Group*, 20 Buckingham Rd., Norwood, Mass. 02062. Founded autumn, 1959, assumed above name in 1964. George D. Fawcett, director.

34. *North Jersey UFO Group*. Founded in 1954 by Lee R. Munsick. Publication: *UFO Newsletter*. Organization dissolved and publication of periodical suspended.

35. *Pennsylvania and New Jersey Two-State Study Group*. Founded in 1965 by George D. Fawcett.

36. *Philadelphia Investigations Committee of Aerial Phenomena*. 6100 Belden St., Philadelphia, Penn. 19149. Founded summer, 1964.

37. *Planetary Space Center, The*, 24720 Carlyle St., Dearborn, Mich. 48124. Founded in 1954 by Laura Mundo. Publication: *Interplanetary News*. Organization dissolved and publication of periodical suspended.

38. *School of Thought*, P.O. Box 257, June Lake, Calif. 93529. Founded in February, 1960, by Sister Hope Troxell. Spiritual/mystical orientation. Publication: *Cosmic Frontiers*. Still functioning in May, 1969.

39. *Solar Cross Foundation, The*, 5132 Lincoln Ave., Los Angeles, Calif. 90042. Founded summer, 1957. Robert Short, director. Publication: *Inter-Galaxy News*.

40. *Solar Light Center*, Rt. 2, Box 572-J, Central Point, Oreg. 97501. Founded midsixties. Publication: *Starcraft*.

41. *Solar Space Foundation*, P.O. Box 622, Joshua Tree, Calif. 92252. Founded in 1957; still functioning in 1968. Publication: *Solar Space-Letter*.

42. *Tucson Science Club*, 5350 East Fort Lowell, Tucson, Ariz. 85716.

43. *UFO Research Committee, The*, 3521 S.W. 104th St., Seattle, Wash. 98100. Founded in 1968. Publication: *The U.F.O.R.C. Journal*.

44. *UFO Research Organization*, 739 75th Ave. N., St. Petersburg, Fla. 33702. Founded autumn, 1964, by E. R. Sabo. Publication: *UFO Researcher*.

45. *Universal Research Society of America,* 118 Oberreich St., La Porte, Ind. 46350. Founded summer, 1965, by Charles A. Maney.

46. *Universarian Foundation, Inc.,* 3620 S.E. 84th St., Portland, Oreg. 97200. Founded in early 1960's by Zebrun Walace Carlsleigh.

GREAT BRITAIN

47. *Aetherius Society, The.* See United States (Major).

48. *British Flying Saucer Society.* See *British U.F.O. Research Organization.*

49. *British U.F.O. Research Organization,* 3 Devonish Rd., Weeke, Winchester, Hampshire. Founded in September, 1962, absorbing the *London U.F.O. Research Organization,* established in 1959, the *British Flying Saucer Bureau,* established in 1952 as an English branch of Albert K. Bender's (United States) *International Flying Saucer Bureau,* and a half-dozen other groups. Its present member societies include:
—British Flying Saucer Society (Bristol)
—Cambridge University Group for the Investigation of U.F.O.s (Cambridge)
—Direct Investigation Group on Aerial Phenomena (Stockport, Cheshire)
—Fleet Street U.F.O. Study Group (London)
—Halifax Branch, British U.F.O. Research Organization
—Imperial College of U.F.O. Research Group
—Isle of Wight U.F.O. Investigation Society
—Leeds University U.F.O. Group (Leeds, Yorkshire)
—Merseyside U.F.O. Research Group (Lancashire)
—Northern Ireland Branch, British U.F.O. Research Organization
—Scottish U.F.O. Research Society (Edinburgh)
—Slough U.F.O. Group (Buckinghamshire)
—South Lincolnshire U.F.O. Study Group
—Stratford-on-Avon U.F.O. Group (Warwickshire)
—Surrey Investigation Group on Aerial Phenomena
—Tyneside U.F.O. Society (Northumberland)
Still functioning in June, 1969. Open membership. Publication: *BUFORA Journal.* The society hereafter: B.U.F.O.R.A.

50. *Cambridge University Group for the Investigation of U.F.O.s.* See B.U.F.O.R.A.

51. *Contact,* 43 Walton Bridge Rd., Shepperton, Middlesex.

52. *Direct Investigation Group on Aerial Phenomena.* See B.U.F.O.R.A.

53. *Fleet Street U.F.O. Study Group.* See B.U.F.O.R.A.

54. *Halifax Branch, British U.F.O. Research Organization.* See B.U.F.O.R.A.

55. *Imperial College of U.F.O. Research Group.* See B.U.F.O.R.A.

56. *Isle of Wight U.F.O. Investigation Society.* See B.U.F.O.R.A.

57. *Leeds University U.F.O. Group.* See B.U.F.O.R.A.

58. *Merseyside U.F.O. Research Group.* See B.U.F.O.R.A.

59. *Northern Ireland Branch, British U.F.O. Research Organization.* See B.U.F.O.R.A.

60. *Scottish U.F.O. Research Society.* See B.U.F.O.R.A.

61. *Slough U.F.O. Group.* See B.U.F.O.R.A.

62. *South Lincolnshire U.F.O. Study Group.* See B.U.F.O.R.A.

63. *Stratford-on-Avon U.F.O. Group.* See B.U.F.O.R.A.

64. *Surrey Investigation Group on Aerial Phenomena.* See B.U.F.O.R.A.

65. *Tyneside U.F.O. Society,* 41 Deanham Gardens, Fenham, Newcastle upon Tyne. Founded in early 1960's. Publication: *Orbit* (issuance now suspended). See B.U.F.O.R.A.

ADDITIONAL COUNTRIES

66. Belgium: *Belgian Interplanetary Study Circle,* Maasfortbaan 187, Lier, Antwerp.

67. Japan: *Cosmic Brotherhood Association,* Naka, P.O. Box 12, Yokohama.

68. The Netherlands: *Netherlands Study Group for Ufology,* G.P.O. Box 1524, Amsterdam.

69. New Zealand: *Civilian Saucer Investigation,* P.O. Box 72, Onehunga, S.E. 5, Auckland.

For information regarding groups elsewhere, contact magazines in the field, published in the country of interest, or one of the major organizations in the United States.

A HISTORY AND DIRECTORY OF UNIDENTIFIED FLYING OBJECT AND FLYING SAUCER PERIODICALS

The following is an extremely comprehensive list of publications in the Unidentified Flying Object and Flying Saucer fields, ranging from quasi-scientific through contactee and mystical journals. Such organs, in most instances, even where not noted, may have suspended publication; however, all have at least an historical significance. A half dozen of the major publications, including all of the longest published still being issued, are noted with asterisks (*). These are among the most respected and informative of periodicals in this field, especially to the uninitiated, and tend to cover the complete range of reportage from simple sightings to alien reports.

1. *A.P.R.O. Bulletin, The* (The Aerial Phenomena Research Organization), 3910 East Kleindale Rd., Tucson, Ariz. 85716. Issued 1952 to present. Coral Lorenzen, ed.*

2. *Australian Flying Saucer Review,* P.O. Box 32, Toorack, Melbourne, Victoria, Australia. First issue: December, 1959. Peter E. Norris, ed.*

3. *Awareness* (Journal of the International Sky Scouts; later changed to *Contact*), 43 Walton Bridge Rd., Shepperton, Middlesex, England. Jimmy Goddard, ed.

4. *Brothers* (Cosmic Brotherhood Association journal), Naka, P.O. Box 12, Yokohama, Japan. First issue: Winter/Spring, 1962. Dr. Yoshiyuki Tange, ed.

5. *BUFORA Journal* (British U.F.O. Research Organization, which absorbed earlier London U.F.O. Research Organization, founded 1959), 3 Devonish Rd., Weeke, Winchester, Hampshire, England. First issue (combined): midsixties. J. Cleary-Baker, ed.*

6. *CFSIB Newsletter* (Civilian Flying Saucer Investigations Bureau), 6101 Sturgeon Creek Pkwy., Midland, Mich. 48640.

7. *Clypeus,* Casella Postale 604, Torino-Centro, Italy. Gianni Settimo, ed. (Italian language).

8. *Controversial Phenomena Bulletin.* Issued January, 1964, to 1968. Later became *Probe.* Armand A. Laprade, ed.

9. *Cosmic Voice* (The Aetherius Society journal). This publication originated in England in mid-to-late 1950's and moved to the United States with the organization founder, George King, in the early 1960's. George King, ed.

10. *Flying Saucer Digest,* P.O. Box 9811, Cleveland, Ohio 44100. First issue: Winter, 1967. Allan J. Manak, ed.

11. *Flying Saucer News* (Flying Saucer News Club of America), 346 West 45th St., New York, N.Y. 10036. James Rigberg, ed.

12. *Flying Saucer News, The* (Cosmic Brotherhood Association journal), Naka, P.O. Box 12, Yokohama, Japan. First issue: early 1960's. Shinapachi Hagiwara, ed. (Japanese language).

13. *Flying Saucer Review,* 21 Cecil Court, Charing Cross Rd., London, W.C.2, England. Charles Bowen, ed. First issue: January, 1955. Founded by Waveney Girvan (d. October 22, 1964); Derrick Dempster, ed.*

14. *Flying Saucers* (Official Quarterly Journal of the Civilian Saucer Investigation), P.O. Box 72, Onehunga, S.E. 5, Auckland, New Zealand. First issue: 1953. Harold H. Fulton, ed.

15. *Flying Saucers,* Amherst, Wis. Issued 1957 to present. Ray Palmer, ed.*

16. *Flying Saucers Comics,* 730 Third Ave., New York, N.Y. 10017. Dell Publishing Company, Inc. First issue: April, 1967.

17. *Flying Saucers International* (Amalgamated Flying Saucer Clubs of America), 2004 North Hoover St., Los Angeles, Calif. 90027. Issued early 1960's to present. Gabriel Green, ed.*

18. *FSIC Bulletin, The* (Flying Saucer Investigating Committee), P.O. Drawer G, Akron, Ohio 44305. Americo E. Candusso, ed.

19. *Het Interplanetair Nieuwsbulletin* (Belgian Interplanetary Study Circle Journal), Maasfortbaan 187, LIER, Antwerp, Belgium. First issue: mid-sixties.

20. *Humanitarian, The* (The Christian Zion Advocate), P.O. Box 48, Neah Bay, Washington 98357.

21. *Informationen der Gesellschaft fur Interplanetarik,* Wien, 19, Pyrkerg, 21 Austria. First issue: early 1960's (German language).

22. *Inter-Galaxy News* (The Solar Cross Foundation), 5132 Lincoln Ave., Los Angeles, Calif. 90042. James Jordan, ed.

23. *International Paranormal Bulletin, The* (Netherlands Study Group for Ufology), G.P.O. Box 1524, Amsterdam, Holland. First issue: early sixties. A. F. van Wieringen, ed.

24. *Interplanetary Intelligence Report* (Interplanetary Intelligence of Unidentified Flying Objects), 3005 Eubanks St., Oklahoma City, Okla. 73100. H. C. Hewes, ed.

25. *Interplanetary News* (The Planetary Space Center; formerly Interplanetary Foundation), 24720 Carlyle St., Dearborn, Mich. 48124. Laura Mundo (Marxer), ed. (Suspended publication.)

26. *Little Listening Post* (The Little Listening Post), 4811 Illinois Ave., N.W., Washington, D.C. 20000. Issued 1954 to 1965.

27. *Luminator, The* (newspaper), P.O. Box 1804, Santa Fe, N.M. 87501.

28. *NICAP Reporter* (National Investigations Commission on Aerial Phenomena), 5108 S. Findlay St., Seattle, Wash. 98118. Robert J. Gribble, ed.

29. *NZSSR* (New Zealand Scientific Space Research newsletter), P.O. Box 21007, Henderson, Auckland, New Zealand. First issue: late 1950's. Fred and Phillis Dickeson, eds.

30. *Orbit* (Civilian Research, Interplanetary Flying Objects). Ohio publication issued from 1954 to 1957. Leonard Stringfield, ed.

31. *Orbit* (Journal of the Tyneside U.F.O. Society), 41 Deanham Gardens, Fenham, Newcastle upon Tyne, England. First issue: early 1960's. J. Leslie Otley, ed. (Suspended publication.)

32. *Probe.* See *Controversial Phenomena Bulletin.*

33. *Proceedings* (The College of Universal Wisdom), P.O. Box 458, Yucca Valley, Calif. 92284. First issued in the late 1950's, continuing to present. George Van Tassel, ed.

34. *Round Robin* (Borderland Sciences Research Associates), 1103 Bobolink Dr., Vista, Calif. 92083. Riley Crabb, ed.

35. *Saucerian (Bulletin), The,* Clarksburg, W. Va. Issued September, 1953, to spring. 1963, when purchased by *Saucer News.* Gray Barker, ed.

36. *Saucer News* (Saucer and Unexplained Celestial Events Research Society), Clarksburg, W. Va. James W. Moseley, ed., until 1968, after which Gray Barker, ed.*

37. *Saucers* (Flying Saucer International), 1420 S. Ridgeley Dr., Los Angeles, Calif. 90000. Issued 1953 to 1960. Max Miller, ed.

38. *Saucer Scoop,* 6464 34th Ave. N., St. Petersburg, Fla. 33700. First issue: mid-1960's. Joan Whritenour, ed.

39. *Saucers, Space & Science,* 17 Shetland St., Willowdale, Ont., Canada. First issue: early 1960's. Gene Duplantier, ed.

40. *Searchlight* (Interplanetary News Service), 3 Courtland St., New Brunswick, N.J. 08902. Issued mid-1960's to present. Timothy Green Beckley, ed.

41. *Sociedade Brasileira de Estudos Sôbre Discos Voadores,* Rua Sen. Pedro Velho, 50 ap. 201 (Cosme Velho), Rio de Janeiro, Brazil. First issue: late 1950's. W. Buhler, ed.

42. *Solar Space-Letter* (Solar Space Foundation), P.O. Box 622, Joshua Tree, Calif. 92252. Issued 1957 to 1968 or later. President of the Solar Presidium on Saturn, ed.

43. *S.P.A.C.E.,* 267 Alhambra Circle, Coral Gables, Fla. 33134. Issued 1956 to 1962. Norbert F. Gariety, ed.

44. *Spacecraft News,* Clarksburg, W. Va. An interim publication of Gray Barker's, mid-1960's, between the sale of his *The Saucerian Bulletin* to *Saucer News* and his subsequent purchase of *Saucer News.* (Suspended publication.)

45. *Spacelink,* 15 Freshwater Court, Crawford Street, London, W.1., England. Lionel Beer, publisher (Fred Smith, former publisher: 1964–1967; first issue under new publisher: early 1968). Edgar Hatvany, ed.

46. *Space Review* (International Flying Saucer Bureau), Bridgeport, Conn. Issued 1952 to October, 1953. Albert K. Bender, ed.

47. *Space Review,* 2 Station Rd., Frimley, near Aldershot, Hampshire, England. S. R. Stebbing, ed.

48. *S. P. Newsletter,* P.O. Box 2431, Fullerton, Calif. 92633. Issued 1962 to 1968 or later. C. A. Honey, ed.

49. *Starcraft* (Solar Light Center), Rt. 2, Box 572-J, Central Point, Oreg. 97501. Issued mid-1960's to present. Marianne Francis, ed.

50. *Through the Portals* (Morse Fellowship), P.O. Box 72, Alamogordo, Tex. 88310. Louise Morse, ed.

51. *UFO Chile,* Casilla 13202, Santiago, Chile. First issue: 1967 (Spanish language).

52. *UFO Critical Bulletin,* 1916 Seventeenth St., N.W., Washington, D.C. 20000. Issued circa 1960. Richard Hall, ed.

53. *U.F.O.I.C.* (UFO Investigation Committee newsletter), P.O. Box E170, St. James, Sydney, Australia. First issued mid-1960's.

54. *UFO Investigator, The* (National Investigations Committee on Aerial Phenomena), 1536 Connecticut Ave., N.W., Washington, D.C. 20000. Issued 1956 to present.*

55. *Ufology Bulletin* (affiliated with Ventura UFO study group). Twenty-four issues published. (Suspended publication.)

56. *UFO Magazine* (affiliated with The American UFO Committee), 3403 W. 119 St., Cleveland, Ohio 44111. Ricky Hilberg, ed.

57. *UFO Nachrichten,* 62 Wiesbaden-Schierstein, Milanstr. 5 (fr. wörthster.) Germany. Karl L. Veit, ed. (German language).

58. *UFO Newsletter* (North Jersey UFO Group). Thirteen issues published between 1954 and 1960. Lee R. Munsick, ed.

59. *UFO Phenomenon, The* (Official Publication of the Aerial Phenomena Investigations and Research Center), 636 West Cambourne, Ferndale, Mich. 48220. First issued October/September, 1968. Kevin J. Collins, ed.

60. *U.F.O.R.C. Journal, The* (The UFO Research Committee), 3521 S.W. 104th St., Seattle, Wash. 98100. First issue: 1968.

61. *UFO Reporter* (Aerial Phenomena Investigations Committee), P.O. Box 87, Rugby Sta., Brooklyn, N.Y. 11203. Eugene R. Steinberg, ed., until publication purchased by *Saucer News,* 1965.

62. *UFO Researcher* (UFO Research Organization), 739 75th Ave. N., St. Petersburg, Fla. 33702. E. R. Sabo, ed.

63. *Uforum* (Grand Rapids Flying Saucer Club). Michigan publication first issued in early 1950's. (Suspended publication.)

64. *UFO Sighter* (American UFO Committee), 2875 Sequoyah Dr., N.W., Atlanta, Ga. 30300. Ricky Hilberg, ed.

65. *UFO Sky Watch* (Extraterrestrial Phenomena Investigating Committee journal), P.O. Box 622, Schenectady, N.Y. First issue: 1967. Jennifer Stevens, ed.

66. *Understanding* (Long Beach Interplanetary Research Group), 1227 E. Second St., Long Beach, Calif. 90802. Not to be confused with Daniel W. Fry's publication and organization. A. Rowe, ed.

67. *Understanding* (official publication of Understanding, Inc.), P.O. Box 206, Merlin, Oreg. 97532. First issue: mid-1950's. Daniel W. Fry, ed.

68. *Uranus* (Markham House Press, Ltd.), 31 Kings Rd., London S.W.3, England. David Wrightman, ed.

69. *Voice of Universarius, The* (Universarian Foundation, Inc.), 3620 S.E. 84th St., Portland, Oreg. 97200. First issued early 1960's. Zebrun Walace Carlsleigh, ed.

A HISTORY AND DIRECTORY OF UNIDENTIFIED FLYING OBJECT AND FLYING SAUCER MOTION PICTURES AND TELEVISION PROGRAMS

The fullest information obtainable regarding each production is included. Unfortunately, in most instances the motion-picture companies have offered little or no cooperation on this very difficult research (virtually nothing has been written or even cataloged in this field, with the one exception noted below), but where at least the year of release was ascertainable, although perhaps almost nothing else, the film is included in the chronology. Other productions, only the names of which have emerged in the research, are noted at the conclusion of the more detailed data.

Additionally, mention must be made of the assistance of noted motion-picture critic Carlos Clarens and his outstanding book *An Illustrated History of the Horror Film* (New York: Capricorn Books, 1967), without which the comprehensiveness of the following would have been impossible.

MOTION PICTURES

1936—*Flash Gordon* (Thirteen-chapter serial). Universal Pictures (USA). Director: Frederick Stephani. Screenplay: Frederick Stephani, George Plympton, Basil Dickey, Ella O'Neill, from comic strip by Alex Raymond. Photography: Jerry Ash, Richard Fryer. Players: Larry "Buster" Crabbe, Jean Rogers, Priscilla Lawson, Charles Middleton. The best films of this kind ever made.

1938—*Mars Attacks the World*. Universal Pictures (USA). Feature-length film based on Alex Raymond's *Flash Gordon* comic strip.

1945—*D-Day on Mars*. Players: Roy Barcroft. Martians prepare to attack Earth.

1950—*The Flying Saucers.* Colonial Productions, Inc. (USA). Distributed by Film Classics. Producer and writer: Mikel Conrad. Players: Mikel Conrad, Pat Garrison, Virginia Hewett.

1951—*The Day the Earth Stood Still.* 20th Century-Fox (USA). Director: Robert Wise. Screenplay: Edmund H. North. Photography: Leo Tover. Players: Michael Rennie, Patricia Neal, Hugh Marlowe, Sam Jaffe, and Billy Gray. A messianic figure arrives in a Flying Saucer with a great robot. His philosophy of goodness is rejected, and he departs. Special effects excellent.

1951—*The Man from Planet X.* United Artists–Wisberg–Pollexfan (USA). Director: Edgar Ulmer. Screenplay: A. Wisberg and J. Pollexfan. Photography: John L. Russell. Players: Robert Clarke, Margaret Field. Alien with large head and inscrutable face lands in Scotland, planning to prepare Earth for invasion by mesmerizing local inhabitants.

1951—*The Thing.* RKO Radio (USA). Producer: Howard Hawks. Director: Christian Nyby. Screenplay: Charles Lederer, from *Who Goes There?* by John W. Campbell, Jr. Photography: Russel Harlan. Player: James Arness (in the title role).

1952—*Red Planet Mars.* United Artists–Veiller–Hyde (USA). Director: Harry Horner. Screenplay: John L. Balderston. Photography: Joseph Biroc. Players: Peter Graves, Andrea King, Herbert Berghof. A poor threat-to-the-world film with chauvinistic, even political right-wing, overtones.

1953—*Cat Women of the Moon.* Astor Picture (USA). Producers: A. Zimbalist and Jack Rubin.

1953—*Invaders from Mars.* National Pictures Corp. (USA). Color. Director: William Cameron. Screenplay: Robert Blake. Photography: John Seitz. Players: Helena Carter, Arthur Franz, Leif Erickson, Hillary Brooke. Aliens treat women and children gently.

1953—*Island in the Sky.* Wayne Fellows Production. Released by Warner Bros. (USA). From a novel by Ernest Garu.

1953—*It Came from Outer Space.* Universal Pictures (USA). Three-dimensional. Director: Jack Arnold. Screenplay: Harry Essex, from story by Ray Bradbury. Photography: Clifford Stine.

Players: Richard Carlson, Barbara Rush. Extraterrestrials from doomed planet land in fireball craft to spearhead invasion. They abduct and/or simulate humans, introducing them into society (as in *The Invasion of the Body Snatchers*).

1953—*Phantom from Space.* Planet Film Plays, Inc. Released by United Artists (USA). Director: W. Lee Wilder. Screenplay: Bill Raynor and Myles Wilder. Photography: William Clothier. Players: Ted Cooper, Noreen Nash. A very inferior 1930's-serial–type film, featuring a comic-book–costumed alien.

1953—*The War of the Worlds.* Paramount (USA). Producer: George Pal. Director: Byron Haskin. Screenplay: Barre Lyndon, from the novel by H. G. Wells. Photography: George Barnes (Technicolor). Players: Gene Barry, Ann Robinson, Henry Brandon, Les Tremayne, Bob Cornthwaite, Sandro Giglio, Lewis Martin, Jack Kruschen, Bill Phipps. Probably the best of the extraterrestrials-as-hostile films, as opposed to the beneficent aspect of *The Day the Earth Stood Still.* Special effects very good and generally superior.

1954—*Killers from Space.* RKO Radio (USA). Director: W. Lee Wilder. Screenplay: Bill Raynor. Photography: William Clothier. Players: Peter Graves, Barbara Bestar. Bug-eyed monsters just looking for a home. As they are hostile, the human hero blows them up.

1955—*This Island Earth.* Universal Pictures (USA). Color. Director: Joseph Newman. Screenplay: Franklin Coen, Edward O'Callaghan. Photography: Clifford Stine. Players: Jeff Morrow, Faith Domergue, Rex Reason. Inhabitants of doomed planet plan to colonize Earth, but one key alien turns human and mankind is saved.

1956—*The Earth versus the Flying Saucers.* Columbia (USA).

1956—*Forbidden Planet.* Metro-Goldwyn-Mayer (USA). Color. Director: Fred McLeod. Screenplay: Cyril Hume. Photography: George J. Folsey. Players: Walter Pidgeon, Anne Francis, Leslie Nielsen, Warren Stevens, Jack Kelly, James Drury. Not a Flying Saucer film, but related in that its theme incorporates an ancient, extinct superrace of extraterrestrials on another world.

1956—*The Invasion of the Body Snatchers.* Allied Artists (USA). Director: Don Siegel. Screenplay: Daniel Mainwaring, from original story by Jack Finney. Photography: Ellsworth Fredericks. Players: Kevin McCarthy, Dana Winter, Carolyn Jones, King Donovan. Pods from outer space bloom into replicas of human beings, whom they replace. The best of all non-machine-invasion films.

1956—*Unidentified Flying Objects.* Greene-Rouse Productions. Released by United Artists (USA). Director: Winston Jones. Screenplay: Francis Martin. Photography: Howard A. Anderson, Ed Fitzgerald, Burt Spievogel. Documentary.

1957—*Invasion of the Saucer Men.* Malibu Productions. Released by American International (USA). Producer and director: James H. Nicolson and Robert J. Gurney. Screenplay: Paul Fairman.

1957—*The Monolith Monsters.* Universal Pictures (USA). Director: John Sherwood. Screenplay: Norman Jolley, Robert M. Fresco, from a story by Jack Arnold and Robert M. Fresco. Photography: Ellis W. Carter. Players: Grant Williams, Lola Albright, Les Tremayne.

1957—*Twenty Million Miles to Earth.* Columbia Pictures (USA). Director: Nathan Juran. Screenplay: Charlott Knight, Ray Harryhausen. Photography: Irving Lippman, Carlos Ventimiglia. Players: William Hopper, Joan Taylor. Although not a Flying Saucer film, it deals with extraterrestrialism, and the special effects are excellent.

1957—*The Twenty-seventh Day.* Columbia Pictures (USA). Director: William Asher. Screenplay: John Mantley. Photography: Henry Freulich. Players: Gene Barry, Valerie French, George Voskovec. A messianic messenger from beyond.

1958—*The Blob.* Paramount Pictures (USA). Color. Director: Irvin S. Yeaworth, Jr. Screenplay: Theodore Simonson and Kate Phillips. Photography: Thomas Spalding. Players: Steve McQueen, Aneta Corseaut.

1958—*I Married a Monster from Outer Space.* Director: Gene Fowlie. Players: Tom Tryon, Gloria Talbot. A bridegroom and his friends are abducted and simulated, as in *It Came from Outer Space.*

1958—*It! The Terror from Beyond Space.* Vogue Pictures, Inc. (USA). Producer: Robert E. Kent. Screenplay: Jerome Bixley.

1958—*The Lost Missile.* United Artists (USA). Players: Robert Loggia, Larry Kerr, Ellen Parker. Extraterrestrial missile or spaceship threatens earth but is destroyed.

1958—*The Space Children.* Paramount Pictures (USA). Director: Jack Arnold. Screenplay: Bernard C. Schoenfeld. Photography: Ernest Laslo. Players: Michael Ray, Adam Williams, Peggy Weber.

1958—*Space Master X7.* 20th Century-Fox (USA). Regal Scope Production. Producer: Edward Glasser. Screenplay: George W. Yatse and Daniel Mainwaring.

1958—*Warning from Space* (Japan). Player: Bantaro Maike.

1958—*The War of the Satellites.* Allied Artists (USA). Director: Roger Corman. Screenplay: Lawrence Louis Goldman. Photography: Floyd Crosby. Players: Dick Miller, Susan Cabot, Richard Devon.

1959—*Angry Red Planet.* Player: Nora Hayden. Heroic earthman on Mars.

1959—*Invisible Invaders.* Premium Pictures. Released by United Artists (USA). Screenplay: Samuel Newman.

1959—*The Mysterians.* RKO Teleradio Pictures, Inc. Originally *Chikyu Boeigun.* Toho Film Company, Ltd. (Japan). Director: Inoshiro Honda. Screenplay: Takeshi Kimura, from story by Jojiro Okami. Photography: Hajime Koizumi. Players: Kenji Sahara, Yumi Shirakawa. Alien invasion à la *The War of the Worlds.*

1959—*Plan 9 for Outer Space.* Distributing Corporation of America.

1960—*Assignment Outer Space.*

1960—*The Village of the Damned.* Metro-Goldwyn-Mayer (England). Director: Wolf Rilla. Screenplay: Sterling Silliphant, from *The Midwich Cuckoos* by John Wyndham. Photography: Geoffrey Faithfull. Players: George Sanders, Barbara Shelly, Lawrence Naismith. Mysteriously the women of a village are impregnated by alien essences, and they produce a clan of gestalt-linked children, who are, by human standards, ruthless. An excellent nonmachine-invasion film, matched in this genre only by *The Invasion of the Body Snatchers.*

1961—*Journey to the Seventh Planet.* American-International (USA/Sweden). Producer and director: Sidney Pink. Players: John Agar, Greta Thyssen. Not a Flying Saucer film, but featuring alien life in the form of a telepathic-hypnotic-cycloptic brain which projects phantasmal loreleis to spacemen from Earth. It is set on Uranus.

1961—*Planets against Us.* Player: Michael Lemoine. Confederation of planets plans attack on Earth.

1962—*Invasion of the Star Creatures.* American International Pictures.

1963—*The Day Mars Invaded the Earth.* 20th Century-Fox/API (USA). Director: Maury Dexter. Screenplay: Harry Spaulding. Players: Kent Taylor, Marie Windsor. Very similar to *The Invasion of the Body Snatchers,* but not quite so polished.

1963—*Invaders from Space.* Shintoho Company, Ltd. (Japan). Director: Teruo Ishii. Starman from the Emerald Planet does good works on Earth.

1963—*The Unearthly Stranger.* Anglo-Amalgamated (England). Director: John Kirsh. Screenplay: Rex Carlton. Photography: Reg Wyler. Players: John Neville, Gabriella Licudi. A female extraterrestrial is touched by humanism.

1964—*Attack from Space.*

1964—*The Invaders.* Ken Dixon.

1964—*Mutiny in Outer Space.* Player: Susannah York. Alien fungus invades space station.

1965—*The Planet of the Vampires.* American International Films (Italy). Fulvio Lucisano. An outright out-of-this-world horror film.

1966—*D-Day on Mars.* Director: Spencer Bennett. Photography: Bud Thacker. Player: Ray Bancroft.

1966—*X from Outer Space.* American International Films (Japan). Player: Toshiya Wazaki. Radioactive dinosaur-sized chicken visits earth and is defeated by scientists, astronauts, and astronautettes.

Date unknown—*Invasion of the Neptune Men.* Walter Manley Enterprises. Toei Company, Ltd. (Japan). Producer: Hiroshi Okawa. Director: Koji Ota. Features a caped ultrahero who prevails against robotic invaders.

TELEVISION PROGRAMS

A number of television programs, especially those designed for younger children, have touched upon the theme of exterrestrialism, frequently in cartoon form. Among the most important of such productions directed mostly toward adult audiences have been the following:

(Series)

Star Trek. Players: William Shatner and Leonard Nimoy.
Lost in Space. Player: June Lockhart.
The Invaders. Player: Roy Thinnes.

(Series frequently featuring programs of this genre)

Outer Limits
Twilight Zone. Created by Rod Serling.

BIBLIOGRAPHY

Adamski, George, *Questions and Answers by the Royal Order of Tibet*. Laguna Beach, Calif.: The Royal Order of Tibet, 1936 (paperback).
——, *Inside the Space Ships*. New York: Abelard-Schuman, Ltd., 1955.
——, with Leslie, Desmond, *Flying Saucers Have Landed*. London: Werner Laurie, 1953.
Adler, Bill (ed.), *Letters to the Air Force on UFOs*. New York: Dell Publishing Company, 1967 (paperback).
Allen, W. Gordon, *Spacecraft from Beyond the Three Dimensions*. New York: Exposition Press, 1959.
Allingham, Cedric, *Flying Saucers from Mars*. London: F. Muller, 1954. New York: British Book Center, 1955.
Angelucci, Orfeo, *Nature of Infinite Entities*. Amherst, Wisc.: Amherst Press, no date.
——, *The Secret of the Saucers*. Amherst, Wisc.: Amherst Press, 1955.
——, *Concrete Evidence*. Phoenix, Ariz.: Franky G. Miller, 1958.
——, *Son of the Sun*. Los Angeles: DeVorss and Company, 1959.
Arnold, Kenneth, and Palmer, Ray, *The Coming of the Saucers*. Amherst, Wisc.: privately published, 1952 (paperback).
Barker, Gray, *They Knew Too Much About Flying Saucers*. Hyde Park, N. Y.: University Books, 1956.
——, *The Bender Mystery Confirmed*. Clarksburg, W. Va.: Saucerian Books, 1962.
——, *The Strange Case of Dr. M. K. Jessup*. Clarksburg, W. Va.: Saucerian Books, 1963.
——, *Book of Adamski*. Clarksburg, W. Va.: Saucerian Books, 1965 (paperback).
——, *Book of Saucers*. Clarksburg, W. Va.: Saucerian Books, 1965.
Beckley, Timothy Green, *The Shaver Mystery and the Inner Earth*. Clarksburg, W. Va.: Saucerian Books, 1967 (paperback).
——, *Book of Space Brothers*. Clarksburg, W. Va.: Saucerian Books, 1968.

Bernard, Raymond, *The Hollow Earth*. Mokelumne, Calif.: Health Research Company, 1963.

Bethurum, Truman, *Aboard a Flying Saucer*. Los Angeles: DeVorss and Company, 1954.

————, *Voice of the Planet Clarion*. Privately published. No other publication data.

————, *Facing Reality*. Privately published. No other publication data.

Brasington, Virginia, *Flying Saucers in the Bible*. Clarksburg, W. Va.: Saucerian Books, 1963.

Chase, Frank Martin, *Document 96*. Clarksburg, W. Va.: Saucerian Books, 1968.

Condon, Edward U., *Scientific Study of Unidentified Flying Objects* (Condon Report). New York: Bantam Books, 1969.

Constance, Arthur, *The Inexplicable Sky*. New York: Citadel Press, 1956.

Cox, Donald, and Stoiko, Michael, *Spacepower: What It Means to You*. New York: Winston, 1958.

Cramp, Leonard G., *Space, Gravity, and the Flying Saucers*. London: Werner Laurie, 1954. New York: British Book Center, 1956.

David, Jay, *The Flying Saucer Reader*. New York: New American Library, Inc., 1967.

Davidson, Leon, *Flying Saucers: An Analysis of the Air Force Project Blue Book Special Report No. 14*. White Plains, N. Y.: privately published, 1956 (paperback).

Dean, John W., *Flying Saucers and the Scriptures*. New York: Vantage Press, 1964.

Edwards, Frank, *Stranger than Science*. New York: Lyle Stuart, 1959.

————, *Strange People*. New York: Lyle Stuart, 1962.

————, *Flying Saucers: Serious Business*. New York: Lyle Stuart, 1966.

————, *Flying Saucers: Here and Now*. New York: Lyle Stuart, 1967.

Elkins, D. T., *Extraterrestrial Communication*. Clarksburg, W. Va.: Saucerian Books, 1963.

Faria, Jose Escobar, *Discos Voadores* (contatos com sêres de outros planêtas). São Paulo, Brazil: Ediçoes Melhoramentos, 1961.

Fort, Charles, *The Book of the Damned*. New York: Boni and Liveright, 1919.

————, *New Lands*. New York: Boni and Liveright, 1923.

————, *Lo!* New York: Claude Kendell, 1932.

————, *Wild Talents*. New York: Claude Kendell, 1932.

————, *The Books of Charles Fort*. New York: Henry Holt and Company, 1941.

Fry, Daniel W., *Steps to the Stars*. Lakemont, Ga.: CSA Publishers, 1956 (paperback).

————, *The White Sands Incident*. Privately published, 1956 (paperback).

————, *To Men of Earth*. Published in combined edition with *The White Sands Incident*. Merlin, Oreg.: Understanding, Inc., 1964.

Fuller, John, *Incident in Exeter*. New York: G. P. Putnam's Sons, 1966.
———, *The Interrupted Journey*. New York: Dial Press, 1966.
———, *Aliens in the Sky*. New York: G. P. Putnam's Sons, 1969.
Gibbons, Gavin, *The Coming of the Space Ships*. London: Neville Spearman, 1956.
———, *They Rode in Space Ships*. London: Neville Spearman, 1957.
Girvan, Waveney, *Flying Saucers and Common Sense*. London: F. Muller, 1955.
Gonzáles Ganteaume, Horacio, *Platillos voladores sobre Venezuela*. Caracas: privately published, 1961.
Gould, Rupert Thomas, *Enigmas*. London: P. Allan & Company, Ltd., 1929.
Hall, Richard (ed.), *UFO Evidence*. Washington, D.C.: NICAP, 1964 (paperback).
Heard, Gerald, *The Riddle of the Flying Saucers: Is Another World Watching?* London: Caroll and Nicholson, 1950.
Herrman, Joachim, *Das falsche Weltbild, Astronomie und Aberglaube*. Stuttgart, Germany: Gesellschaft der Naturfreunde, 1962.
James, Trevor, *They Live in the Sky*. Los Angeles: New Age Publishing Company, 1958.
Jessup, Morris K., *The Case for the UFO*. New York: Citadel Press, 1955.
———, *The UFO Annual*. New York: Citadel Press, 1956.
———, *The Expanding Case for the UFO*. New York: Citadel Press, 1957.
———, *UFO and the Bible*. New York: Citadel Press, 1957.
Jung, Carl G., *Flying Saucers: A Modern Myth of Things Seen in the Skies*. New York: Harcourt, Brace & World, Inc., 1959.
Keyhoe, Donald E., *The Flying Saucers Are Real*. New York: Fawcett Publications, 1950.
———, *Flying Saucers from Outer Space*. New York: Henry Holt and Co., 1953.
———, *The Flying Saucer Conspiracy*. New York: Henry Holt and Co., 1955.
———, *Flying Saucers: Top Secret*. New York: G. P. Putnam's Sons, 1960.
Klass, Philip, *UFOs—Identified*. New York: Random House, 1968.
Kraspedon, Dino. *My Contact with Flying Saucers*. London: Neville Spearman, 1959 (translated from the Portuguese by J. B. Wood).
Lee, Gloria (Byrd), *Why Are We Here*. Los Angeles: DeVorss and Co., 1959.
———, *The Changing Condition of the World*. Los Angeles: DeVorss and Co., 1962.
Le Poer Trench, Brinsley, *The Flying Saucer Review's World Roundup of UFO Sightings*. New York: Citadel Press, 1958.
———, *The Sky People*. London: Neville Spearman, 1960. Clarksburg, W. Va.: Saucerian Books, 1961.

Loftin, Robert, *Identified Flying Saucers*. New York: David McKay Co., 1968.

London, Jack, *Before Adam*. New York: The Macmillan Company, 1907.

Lorenzen, Coral E., *The Great Flying Saucer Hoax* (later *Flying Saucers: The Startling Evidence of the Invasion from Outer Space*). New York: New American Library, Inc., 1962.

———— and Jim, *UFOs over America*. New York: New American Library, Inc., 1968.

Lusar, Rudolph, *German Weapons and Secret Weapons of World War II and Their Development*. New York: Philosophical Library, 1959.

Manas, John H., *Flying Saucers and Space Men*. New York: Pythagorean Society, 1962.

Maney, Charles Albert, with Hall, Richard, *The Challenge of Unidentified Flying Objects*. Washington: privately printed, 1961.

Martin, Dan, *The Watcher*. Clarksburg, W. Va.: Saucerian Books, 1962.

Menger, Connie (Marla Baxter), *Song of Saturn*. Clarksburg, W. Va.: Saucerian Books, 1968 (paperback).

Menger, Howard, *From Outer Space to You*. Clarksburg, W. Va.: Saucerian Books, 1959.

Menzel, Donald H., and Boyd, Lyle G., *The World of Flying Saucers*. Garden City, N. Y.: Doubleday & Company, Inc., 1963.

Michel, Aimé, *Lueurs sur les soucoupes volantes*. Paris: Mame, 1954. In United States, *The Truth about Flying Saucers*. New York: Criterion Books, 1956.

————, *Mystérieux Objets célestes*. Paris: Arthaud, 1958. In United States, *Flying Saucers and the Straight Line Mystery*. New York: Criterion Books, 1958 (translated from the French by the Civilian Saucer Intelligence of New York).

Miller, Max, *Flying Saucers: Fact or Fiction*. Los Angeles: Trend Books, 1957.

Miller, R. De Witt, *Forgotten Mysteries*. New York: Citadel Press, 1956.

Mitchell, Helen and Betty, *We Met the Space People*. Clarksburg, W. Va.: Saturnian Books, 1966 (paperback).

Mosley, James W., *Book of Saucer News*. Clarksburg, W. Va.: Saucerian Books, 1967 (paperback).

Mundo, Laura, *The Father's Plan and the Flying Saucers*. Detroit: The Planetary Space Center, 1963.

————, *Flying Saucers and the Father's Plan*. Clarksburg, W. Va.: Saucerian Books, 1963.

Nebel, Long John, *The Way Out World*. Englewood Cliffs, N. J.: Prentice-Hall, Inc., 1961.

————, with Teller, Sanford M., *The Psychic World Around Us*. New York: Hawthorn Books. Inc., 1969.

Nelson, Buck, *My Trip to Mars, the Moon, and Venus*. Grand Rapids, Mich.: Grand Rapids Flying Saucer Club, 1956 (paperback).

Nelson, Earl, *There Is Life on Mars*. New York: Citadel Press, 1956.

Norkin, Israel, *Saucer Diary*. New York: Pageant Press, Inc., 1956.

Owens, Ted, *How to Contact Space People*. Clarksburg, W. Va.: Saucerian Books, 1969.

Philip, Brother (Williamson, George H.), *The Brotherhood of the Seven Rays*. Clarksburg, W. Va.: Saucerian Books, 1960 (U. S. edition of *The Secret of the Andes*, published in England by Neville Spearman, London).

Plantier, Jean, *La Propulsion des soucoupes volantes par action directe sur l'atome*. Tours: Mame, 1955.

Reeve, Bryant and Helen, *Flying Saucer Pilgrimage*. Amherst, Wisc.: Amherst Press, 1957.

Richardson, Cyril George, *Venus Speaks*. London: Regency Press, 1954.

Robb, Stewart, *Prophecies on World Events by Nostradamus*. New York: Oracle Press, 1961.

Roerich, Nicholas, *Altai-Himalaya*. New York: F. A. Stokes Co., 1929.

Ruppelt, Edward J., *The Report on Unidentified Flying Objects*. Garden City, N. Y.: Doubleday & Co., Inc., 1956.

Sanderson, Ivan T., *Uninvited Visitors*. New York: Cowles Education Corp., 1967.

Saunders, David R., and Harkins, R. Roger, *UFOs? Yes!* New York: New American Library, 1968.

Schopfer, Siegfried, *Fliegende Untertassen—ja oder nein?* Stuttgart-Weil der Stadt: W. Hädecke, 1955.

Scully, Frank, *Behind the Flying Saucers*. New York: Henry Holt and Co., Inc., 1950.

Sherwood, John C., *Flying Saucers Are Watching You*. Clarksburg, W. Va.: Saucerian Books, 1967 (paperback).

Sievers, Edgar, *Flying saucers über Südafrika*. Pretoria, South Africa: Sagittarius-Verlag, 1955.

Space Review. Booklet reprint of entire file of *Space Review,* the publication edited and published by the International Flying Saucer Bureau, Bridgeport, Conn., from October, 1952, through October, 1953, inclusive. Clarksburg, W. Va.: Saucerian Books, 1962.

Stanton, L. Jerome, *Flying Saucers: Hoax or Reality?* New York: Belmont Productions, 1966 (paperback).

Steiner, Rudolph, *Cosmic Memory*. Englewood, N. J.: Rudolph Steiner Publications, Inc., 1959.

Stranges, Dr. Frank, *Flying Saucerama*. New York: Vanguard Press, 1959.

Stringfield, Leonard H., *Inside Saucer Post 3-0 Blue*. Cincinnati, Ohio: Civilian Research, Interplanetary Flying Objects, 1957.

Stuart, John, *UFO Warning*. Clarksburg, W. Va.: Saucerian Books, 1967.

Telano, Rolf, *The Flying Saucers*. Clarksburg, W. Va.: Saucerian Books, 1962.

Unger, Georg. *Flying Saucers*. East Grimstead, Sussex, England: New Knowledge Books, 1958.

Valee, Jacques, *Anatomy of a Phenomenon*. Chicago: Henry Regnery Company, 1965.

————— and Janine, *Challenge to Science*. Chicago: Henry Regnery Company, 1966.

Van Tassel, George, *I Rode a Flying Saucer*. Los Angeles: DeVorss and Co., 1952.

—————, *Into This World and Out Again*. Los Angeles: DeVorss and Co., 1957.

—————, *The Council of the Seven Lights*. Los Angeles: DeVorss and Co., 1958.

Webb, Wells Allen, *Mars, The New Frontier*. Farren Publications, 1957.

Wilkins, Harold Tom, *Flying Saucers from the Moon*. London: P. Owen, 1954.

—————, *Flying Saucers on the Attack*. New York: Citadel Press, 1954.

—————, *Flying Saucers Uncensored*. New York: Citadel Press, 1957.

—————, *Strange Mysteries of Time and Space*. New York: Citadel Press, 1959.

Williamson, George Hunt, *Other Tongues, Other Flesh*. Amherst, Wisc.: Amherst Press, 1953.

—————, *Road in the Sky*. London: Neville Spearman, 1959.

—————, *Secret Place of the Lion*. Amherst, Wisc.: Amherst Press, 1959.

—————, with Bailey, Alfred C., *The Saucers Speak*. Los Angeles: New Age Publishing Company, 1954.

—————, with McCoy, John, *UFOs Confidential*. Los Angeles: Essene Press, 1958.

INDEX

ROBERT F. KENNEDY
NEW YORK

United States Senate

WASHINGTON, D.C.

May 9, 1968

Mr. Gray Barker
Publisher, Saucer News
Box 2228
Clarksburg, West Virginia 26301

Dear Readers:

As you may know, I am a card carrying member of
the Amalgamated Flying Saucers Association. Therefore,
like many other people in our country I am interested
in the phenomenon of flying saucers.

It is a fascinating subject that has initiated
both scientific fiction fantasies and serious scientific
research.

I watch with great interest all reports of unidentified flying objects, and I hope that some day we will
know more about this intriguing subject.

Dr. Harlow Shapley, the prominent astronomer,
has stated that there is a probability that there is other
life in the universe.

I favor more research regarding this matter, and
I hope that once and for all we can determine the true facts
about flying saucers. Your magazine can stimulate much
of the investigation and inquiry into this phenomenon
through the publication of news and discussion material.
This can be of great help in paving the way to a knowledge of one of the fascinating subjects of our contemporary world.

Sincerely,

Robert F. Kennedy

Top: George Adamski, to many the "father of contactees," among other less worldly achievements, was granted an audience with the Queen of the Netherlands so that he might relate to Her Majesty his incredible encounters with Venusians, Martians, and Saturnians. (*Sam Vandivert*)

Right: George Van Tassel, among the most prominent of the contactees, is regarded by the informed as the founder of the successful Flying Saucer convention. (*Sam Vandivert*)

Orfeo Angelucci is counted among the few major contactees. His extraordinary tales of his adventures are widely recognized as the most beautiful and effectively allegorical of all Age of Flying Saucer legends. (*Sam Vandivert*)

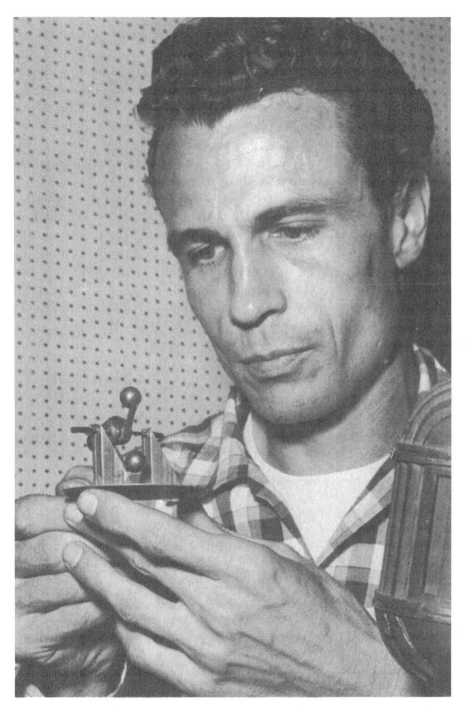

Howard Menger, here seen holding his "free energy motor," is numbered among the six premier contactees and is usually accepted as the most important one to arise from East Coast saucerology. (*Sam Vandivert*)

Right: George King, of England, who may be conceded first rank among non-American contactees in the United States, is remarkable for his psychic contacts with major historical figures of Christianity's spiritual hierarchy and for his position as "the voice of interplanetary parliament." (*David Field*)

Bottom: Daniel W. Fry, one of the half-dozen contactees of primary importance, while employed as a technician at White Sands, New Mexico, was swept to New York and back within an hour by a remotely controlled scout-type Flying Saucer. (*Courtesy of Daniel W. Fry*)

Left: Truman Bethurum is among the best-known of the second tier of contactees. His stimulating experiences have included a meeting with a lovely female captain of a space "scow" from the astronomically-yet-to-be-discovered planet Clarion. (*Courtesy of Truman Bethurum*)

Bottom: Dr. Frank Stranges, a secondary contactee in the historical context but prominent in recent years, asserts he made contact with the extra-earthian Thor while within the military nerve center of the United States, the Pentagon. (*Courtesy of Dr. Frank Stranges*)

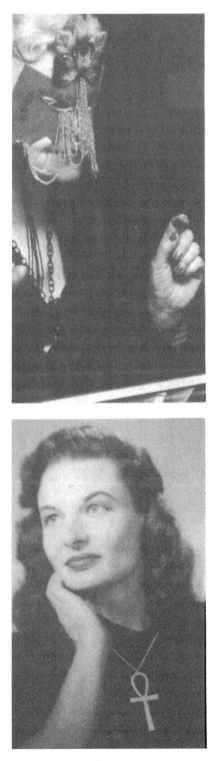

Left: Pauline Peavy is among the most intriguing of the subcultural personalities related to the Age of Flying Saucers. She is a medium who is in touch with "the Elders," the overspirits of the cosmos who rule all. (*Sam Vandivert*)

Opposite: Otis T. Carr (left), Long John Nebel, and a model of the OTC-X1 Circular Foil (Space) Craft, the ultimate version of which was expected to travel to the moon in five and a half hours and, since it would then be downhill, return in somewhat less time. (*Sam Vandivert*)

Left: Gloria Lee (Byrd) maintained psychic contact with Jovians (Jupitarians) until her death and then, it was claimed, returned in spirit-form through other mediums. (*Courtesy of Gray Barker*)

Norman E. Colton and the working prototype of the OTC-X1 Circular Foil (Space) Craft, immediately prior to its planned launching in Oklahoma City. The one-man brain-trust of this incredible countdown is shown addressing the press, as a few technicians watch. (*Sam Vandivert*)

Kenneth Arnold, whose original UFO sighting resulted in the modern coining of the phrase "Flying Saucer," shaking hands with, and receiving the congratulations and support of, former President Dwight D. Eisenhower, on winning the Republican nomination for lieutenant governor of Idaho in 1962. On the left are his running mate, Governor Robert E. Smylie (glasses), and Mrs. Smylie. (*Courtesy of Ray Palmer*)

Top left: Major Donald E. Keyhoe, director of the widely respected UFO investigation group, the National Investigations Committee on Aerial Phenomena, as he appeared, while being "silenced," on a television program analyzing Flying Saucers. (*August C. Roberts*)

Top right: James W. Moseley, the founder of *Saucer News,* one of the three or four best and oldest Flying Saucer publications, was also its editor until 1969, when responsibility for the continuation of the magazine was assumed by Gray Barker. (*Sam Vandivert*)

Coral and Jim Lorenzen, among the foremost and longest-established investigators of Flying Saucers in this country, head the oldest organization and periodical functioning without interruption in this field. The Aerial Phenomena Research Organization has operated for more than a decade and a half. (*Courtesy of the Aerial Phenomena Research Organization*)

Left to right: August C. Roberts, well-known ufological photographer, Dominic Lucchesi, investigator, and Gray Barker, author, publisher, and now editor of *Saucer News.* Each member of this trio can date his role in the field of Flying Saucers back almost twenty years. (*Sam Vandivert*)

Bottom left: Frank Scully, one of the earliest recorders of the Age of Flying Saucers, published his first book on the subject in 1950. He may be best remembered for his contribution to the "little men" aspect of the collective lore. (*Courtesy of Gray Barker*)

Bottom right: Gabriel Green, California saucerologist who heads the Amalgamated Flying Saucer Clubs of America, once ran for the Presidency of the United States on a "space ticket." (*Courtesy of Gabriel Green*)

Left: Olavo T. Fontes, Brazilian physician, became the most recognized (excepting certain British and French figures) of all foreign investigators. He served the Aerial Phenomena Research Organization in his country. (*Courtesy of the Aerial Phenomena Research Organization*)

Bottom left: Dr. Edward U. Condon was director of the U.S. Air Force–sponsored University of Colorado project to investigate UFOs, an operation that bred more controversy than it buried. (*August C. Roberts*)

Bottom right: Dr. J. Allen Hynek has long been the best-known, and often the only, scientific adviser consulted by the United States Air Force. After almost two decades as the establishment's most effective "debunker," the astronomer began to have severe doubts about his own skepticism. (*Courtesy of Dr. J. Allen Hynek*)

In recent years Project Blue Book has been headed by Lt. Col. Hector Quintanilla, Jr. (seated); Lt. Carmon L. Marano (standing center), S/Sgt. Harold T. Jones (standing left), and Miss Marilyn H. Stancombe constituted his staff at the time this photograph was taken. (*U.S. Air Force photo*)

Dr. Donald H. Menzel has been for many years the most vocal and vehement scientific critic of serious UFO study. The astronomer recently told the author that he grants absolutely no possibility that the various phenomena seen have anything other than the most natural and comprehensible explanations. (*Courtesy of Dr. Donald H. Menzel*)

Second of two photographs of an alleged UFO, assertedly taken on night of August 8, 1965, at Beaver, Pennsylvania, by high-school student James Lucci (*Courtesy of the National Investigations Committee on Aerial Phenomena*)

First of three photographs of an alleged UFO, reportedly sighted on afternoon of August 3, 1965, above road, near Santa Ana, California, by Orange County highway inspector Rex Heflin (*Courtesy of the National Investigations Committee on Aerial Phenomena*)

Two alleged Flying Saucers photographed by well-known contactee Daniel W.
Fry (*Daniel W. Fry*)

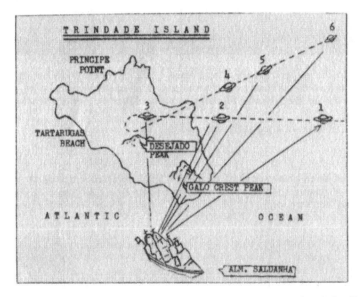

Almirante Saldanha was anchored close to the point near the Galo Crest
Peak, and photographer Barauna was at the stern. The UFO was first seen
over the sea, coming toward the island. The first photo was taken at position
1, with the object flying at low speed. Photo 2 was shot when the object was
behind the Gale Crest. Photo 3 was taken a few seconds after the turn made
by the UFO near Desejado Peak. Photos 4 and 5 failed to register the UFO,
which was then flying at high speed. The last picture, the sixth, was taken
when the object was moving away close to the horizon line. It disappeared a
few seconds later. (*Copyright © 1960 by the* A.P.R.O. Bulletin. *Courtesy
of the Aerial Phenomena Research Organization*)

Opposite top: First of the Trindade Island UFO photographs (*Copyright ©
1960 by the* A.P.R.O. Bulletin. *Courtesy of the Aerial Phenomena Research
Organization*)
Opposite center left: Second of the Trindade Island UFO photographs

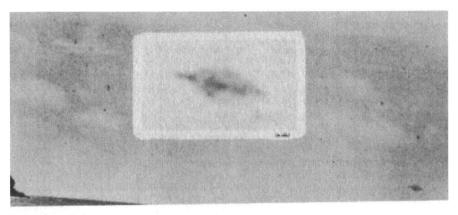

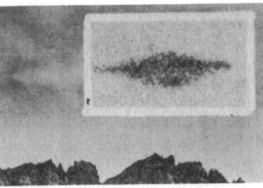

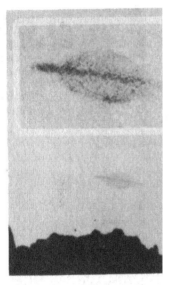

Right: Third of the Trindade Island UFO photographs (*Copyright © 1960 by the* A.P.R.O. Bulletin. *Courtesy of the Aerial Phenomena Research Organization*)

Bottom: Sixth of the Trindade Island UFO photographs (*Copyright © 1960 by the* A.P.R.O. Bulletin. *Courtesy of the Aerial Phenomena Research Organization*)

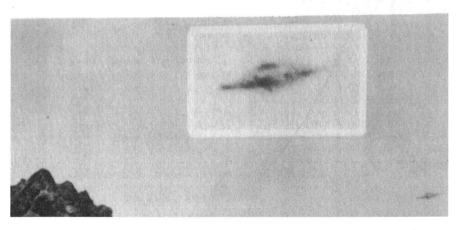

The AVROCAR Mark II VTOL aircraft, built by A. V. Roe, Limited, of Canada, was constructed for the U.S. Army, which designated it VZ-9V. It was often called the Flying Saucer. This experiment was a failure and discarded. (*Courtesy of the U.S. Army Transportation School, Fort Eustis, Virginia, Department of the Army*)

A fifteen-foot-diameter balloon-launched space device used in Walker Air Force Base, New Mexico, test, which caused many UFO reports in the area in 1966 and 1967 (*Copyright © 1968 by the Columbus (Ohio)* Dispatch. *Courtesy of Paul Massa and the Columbus* Dispatch)

Space children, born of alienly impregnated earth women, in Metro-Goldwyn-Mayer's *The Village of the Damned*, based on the late John Wyndham's "The Midwich Cuckoos" (*Courtesy of Metro-Goldwyn-Mayer*)

68746181R00178

Made in the USA
Lexington, KY
18 October 2017